Nisei Naysayer

ASIAN AMERICA

A series edited by Gordon H. Chang

The increasing size and diversity of the Asian American population, its growing significance in American society and culture, and the expanded appreciation, both popular and scholarly, of the importance of Asian Americans in the country's present and past—all these developments have converged to stimulate wide interest in scholarly work on topics related to the Asian American experience. The general recognition of the pivotal role that race and ethnicity have played in American life, and in relations between the United States and other countries, has also fostered the heightened attention.

Although Asian Americans were a subject of serious inquiry in the late nineteenth and early twentieth centuries, they were subsequently ignored by the mainstream scholarly community for several decades. In recent years, however, this neglect has ended, with an increasing number of writers examining a good many aspects of Asian American life and culture. Moreover, many students of American society are recognizing that the study of issues related to Asian America speak to, and may be essential for, many current discussions on the part of the informed public and various scholarly communities.

The Stanford series on Asian America seeks to address these interests. The series will include works from the humanities and social sciences, including history, anthropology, political science, American studies, law, literary criticism, sociology, and interdisciplinary and policy studies.

A full list of titles in the Asian America series can be found online at www.sup.org/asianamerica

Nisei Naysayer

THE MEMOIR OF MILITANT
JAPANESE AMERICAN
JOURNALIST JIMMIE OMURA

James Matsumoto Omura
Edited by Arthur A. Hansen

STANFORD UNIVERSITY PRESS
STANFORD, CALIFORNIA

Stanford University Press
Stanford, California

Grateful acknowledgment is made to the Nichi Bei Foundation and
the Japanese American National Library for generously supporting the
publication of this volume.

Printed in the United States of America on acid-free, archival-quality paper

Library of Congress Cataloging-in-Publication Data

Names: Omura, James Matsumoto, 1912–1994, author. | Hansen, Arthur A.,
    editor, writer of introduction.
Title: Nisei naysayer : the memoir of militant Japanese American journalist
    Jimmie Omura / James Matsumoto Omura ; edited by Arthur A. Hansen.
Description: Stanford, California : Stanford University Press, 2018. |
    Series: Asian America | Includes bibliographical references and index.
Identifiers: LCCN 2017057765 (print) | LCCN 2018020518 (ebook) | ISBN
    9781503606128 (electronic) | ISBN 9781503604957 | ISBN
    9781503604957 (cloth : alk. paper) | ISBN 9781503606111 (pbk. : alk.
    paper)
Subjects: LCSH: Omura, James Matsumoto, 1912-1994. | Japanese American
    journalists—United States—Biography. | Journalists—United
    States—Biography. | Japanese Americans—Evacuation and relocation,
    1942-1945.
Classification: LCC PN4874.O66 (ebook) | LCC PN4874.O66 A3 2018 (print) | DDC
    070.92 [B] —dc23
LC record available at https://lccn.loc.gov/2017057765

Typeset by Classic Typography in 11/14 Adobe Garamond

Cover photo: "Jimmie Omura as editor of San Francisco's *New World
Daily News*, 1934-35." Omura Papers, Green Library, Stanford University

Cover design: Rob Ehle

To my wife, Karen, my two sons, Gregg and Wayne, and my grandsons, Brian and Travis,

and

To those Americans of Japanese ancestry whose constitutional and human rights were unjustly sacrificed during World War II on the altar of national security

—James Matsumoto Omura

To Debra Gold Hansen, my beloved wife and esteemed colleague, and in fond memory of my parents, Haakon and Anna, and my brother, Roy,

and

To those Japanese Americans who, like James Omura, resisted oppression before, during, and after World War II

—Arthur A. Hansen

To refuse to run with the herd is generally harder than it looks. To break with the most powerful among that herd requires unusual depth of character and clarity of mind. But it is a path we should all strive for if we are to preserve the right to think, speak, and act independently, heeding the dictates not of the state or fashionable thought but of our own consciences. In most places and most of the time, liberty is not a product of military action. Rather, it is something alive that grows or diminishes every day, in how we think and communicate, how we treat each other in our public discourse, in what we value and reward as a society, and how we do that.

—THOMAS E. RICKS, *CHURCHILL AND ORWELL: THE FIGHT FOR FREEDOM*

Contents

Editor's Note

ARTHUR A. HANSEN

Because James Omura's 1994 death deprived him of having his autobiographical manuscript critically reviewed by peers or professionally copyedited, some significant changes were made prior to publication. First, its working title, "Shattered Lives," was changed so as to better represent it as a memoir rather than a standard historical study. Second, two of its chapters—one on the history of Japan and the other on Japanese American resisters of conscience within the U.S. Army—were pruned to enhance the work's unity and cohesion. Third, all chapter subtitles were stripped to achieve a narrative flow harmonious with a life-review document, while new chapter titles were provided. Fourth, the author's prologue was truncated so as to render it more germane and proportionate to its purpose. Fifth, redundant material in the manuscript, most of which resulted from unintended computer glitches, was expunged. Sixth and finally, when possible the author's absent footnote references were editorially generated and his incomplete ones fleshed out.

Apart from minor changes in word choice, sentence structure, and the length of selected quoted passages, James Omura's manuscript has been faithfully reproduced. All such alterations were transacted "silently," both to avoid being a distraction to readers and for aesthetic reasons. In no cases have the names of people and places provided by the author been changed for the sake of anonymity.

Since the memoir of James Omura deviates from the standard genre with respect to its utilizing ample bibliographical and discursive notes, it was necessary to devise a means of clearly distinguishing these notes from my own editorial notes. Accordingly, the memoirist's notes (supplemented where necessary by me) appear as footnotes using Roman numerals, while my more detailed, contextual notes are indicated by Arabic numerals and collected as notes at the end of the volume. Within the memoir proper, all insertions by James Omura are enclosed in parentheses, while all bracketed insertions are mine.

To avoid possible confusion by readers over the use of Japanese American generational terms, their respective meanings are as follows: *Issei*, immigrant generation, denied, until 1952, U.S. citizenship; *Nisei*, U.S.-born citizens, children of Issei; *Kibei*, Nisei educated in Japan; *Sansei*, third-generation Japanese Americans; *Yonsei*, fourth-generation Japanese Americans. As for the term *Nikkei*, it is employed generically to designate all Americans of Japanese ancestry.

Contributors

Frank Chin (b. 1940), a fourth-generation Chinese American, was born in Berkeley, California, raised in San Francisco and Oakland, and graduated in 1965 from the University of California, Santa Barbara. He is a widely acclaimed writer of plays, novels, short fiction, and essays, who has won three American Book Awards. An Asian American theater pioneer, Chin founded the Asian American Theater Workshop and was the first Asian American to have a play produced on a major New York stage. Two of his coedited anthologies, *Aiiieeeee!* (1974) and *The Big Aiiieeeee!* (1991), also established him as a forerunner in the development of Asian American literature. For the second work, Chin contributed an essay, "Come All Ye Asian American Writers of the Real and the Fake," which celebrated the valiant World War II roles of journalist James Omura and the Heart Mountain Relocation Center's Fair Play Committee in mobilizing—against the U.S. government and the Japanese American Citizens League—the sole organized draft resistance movement in the ten War Relocation Authority-administered imprisonment camps for Japanese Americans. Later, Chin's classic oral history-driven documentary novel, *Born in the USA* (2002), detailed and dramatized this same inspiring message of bold resistance to oppressive power. The Frank Chin Papers are housed in the California Ethnic and Multicultural Archives of the Special Collections Department of the University of California, Santa Barbara, Library.

PREFACE: "A UNIQUELY GENUINE PERSON"

Yosh Kuromiya (b. 1923), a second-generation Japanese American born and raised in the San Gabriel Valley of southern California, had his Pasadena Junior College education aborted when he and his family, along with other West Coast Americans of Japanese descent, were summarily evicted from their homes and communities and unjustly imprisoned in American-style concentration camps. After detention at Pomona Assembly Center in Los Angeles County, Kuromiya was incarcerated at Wyoming's Heart Mountain Relocation Center. In early 1944 the twenty-one-year-old Kuromiya joined the camp's Fair Play Committee (FPC), an inmate organization protesting on civil rights grounds the U.S. government's military draft of American citizens of Japanese ancestry. As one of sixty-three FPC members refusing preinduction physical examinations, Kuromiya was arrested, tried at a Cheyenne federal court in Wyoming's largest mass trial, and sentenced to three years imprisonment at Washington's McNeil Island Federal Penitentiary. In late 1947 President Harry S. Truman granted full pardons to Kuromiya and all other draft resisters. In the postwar period, Kuromiya graduated from California Polytechnic State University, Pomona, and then compiled a highly successful landscape architect career. From the early 1980s onward, he has championed the wartime dissent and historical legacy of the Heart Mountain Fair Play Committee, the World War II Japanese American draft resisters, and James Omura.

INTRODUCTION: JAMES OMURA AND THE
REDRESSING OF JAPANESE AMERICAN HISTORY

Arthur A. Hansen (b. 1938), a third-generation American of Irish-Norwegian descent, was born in Hoboken, New Jersey, and came of age in Santa Barbara, California. He earned all of his academic degrees at the University of California, Santa Barbara, and is now a professor emeritus of History and Asian American Studies at California State University, Fullerton (CSUF). During his CSUF tenure he was the founding director of both the Center for Oral and Public History and its Japanese American Oral History Project. Between 1991 and 1995 he edited for publication the six-volume *Japanese American World War II Evacuation Oral History Project*. In 2007 the Association for Asian American Studies presented him its Distinguished Lifetime Achievement Award. Most of his scholarly writings, including those on James Omura, have focused upon the resistance Japanese

Americans mounted against their community's World War II oppression by the U.S. government and the Japanese American Citizens League leadership. Formerly the senior historian at the Japanese American National Museum, Hansen is currently serving this Los Angeles-based institution as a historical consultant. In 2018 the University Press of Colorado will publish an anthology of his writings titled *Barbed Voices: Oral History, Resistance, and the World War II Japanese American Social Disaster.*

MEMOIR: NISEI NAYSAYER

James Matsumoto Omura (1912–1994), a second-generation Japanese American, was born on Bainbridge Island, Washington, and graduated in 1932 from Seattle's Broadway High School. Between 1933 and 1936 Omura edited the English-language sections of three Japanese vernacular newspapers in Los Angeles and San Francisco. In 1938–42, Omura was employed by San Francisco floral enterprises; after 1940 he was also the editor-publisher of *Current Life*, the magazine of arts, letters, and public affairs he founded to enlighten and activate American-born Japanese. It was in this capacity that on February 23, 1942, he testified at the San Francisco hearings of the Tolan Committee and registered the sole voice of protest to the U.S. government's projected forced mass eviction and incarceration of the West Coast's Japanese American population. Electing to "voluntarily" resettle out of the coastal defense zone into the unrestricted interior city of Denver rather than submitting to involuntary imprisonment, Omura established a free placement bureau there to facilitate employment opportunities for the swelling number of other Japanese-ancestry resettlers. After contributing articles to the English sections of Denver's two Japanese vernacular papers, the *Colorado Times* and the *Rocky Shimpo*, in early 1944 Omura accepted the latter's editorship. His brief tenure in this role led to his militant endorsement of the organized and Constitution-based draft resistance movement spearheaded by the Heart Mountain Relocation Center's Fair Play Committee (FPC). It also resulted in the U.S. government forcing Omura to resign his position and, in late 1944, trying him in a federal court with FPC leaders on conspiracy to aid and abet violation of the Selective Service Act of 1940. Although exonerated, Omura was demonized for his dissidence by Denver's Japanese American community, forcing him to abandon journalism and to pursue instead a postwar career of distinction as a landscape contractor. In 1981 he testified at the Seattle hearings of the Commission on Wartime Relocation and Internment of Civilians and thereafter devoted the remainder of his life to sustaining the agenda of the National Council for Japanese American Redress, defending both the patriotic valor and civil propriety of the World War II draft resisters—and his support for them—from persistent defamations by the Japanese American Citizens League (JACL), and writing his anti-JACL-themed memoir. The repository for the James Omura Papers is the Green Library at Stanford University.

AFTERWORD: "WHO WRITES HISTORY?"

Frank Abe (b. 1951), a third-generation Japanese American born in Cleveland and raised in northern California's Santa Clara Valley, is a University of California, Santa Cruz, graduate. He featured James Omura in *Conscience and the Constitution* (2000), his PBS film on the largest organized resistance to the World War II incarceration of Japanese Americans, and writes about Omura and the Heart Mountain draft resisters on his blog at Resisters.com. He was a founding member of the Asian American Journalists Association in Seattle, and Frank Chin's Asian American Theater Workshop in San Francisco. As an actor he appeared as a Japanese American Citizens League leader in the 1976 NBC-TV movie *Farewell to Manzanar*. With Chin he helped to create the first two "Days of Remembrance" in 1978–79 to publicly dramatize the campaign for redress. Abe reported for KIRO Newsradio in Seattle and served as communications director for two King County (Washington) executives and the King County Council. He is currently collaborating with the Wing Luke Asian Museum in Seattle on a graphic novel dramatizing the resistance to wartime incarceration, including that of James Omura.

Foreword

"Let Us Now Praise Famous Men"

FRANK CHIN

James Omura is famous for going before a congressional committee in 1942 and asking, "Has the Gestapo come to America? Have we not risen in righteous anger at Hitler's mistreatment of the Jews? Then, is it not incongruous that citizen Americans of Japanese descent should be similarly mistreated and persecuted?"

Omura was talking about the Japanese American Citizens League (JACL). James Matsumoto Omura was born in 1912 on Bainbridge Island in the state of Washington. He carved himself out a career as a journalist writing for, then editing, then owning and publishing English-language Japanese American newspapers and magazines from Seattle to Los Angeles.

He had a special interest in Nisei arts and ideas, and encouraged Nisei intellectuals to essay their thoughts on the being, meaning, and future of Japanese in America, and Japanese Americans. His magazine *Current Life* was distinguished by the quality and variety of the writing. *Current Life* won the admiration and support of Pulitzer Prize-winning author William Saroyan. Virtually all the prewar Nisei poets and writers and thinkers, including Toshio Mori, Ferris Takahashi, Hisaye Yamamoto, and Toyo Suyemoto, were nurtured in *Current Life* and other publications Omura edited.

It was as the publisher and editor of *Current Life* that James Omura appeared before a congressional committee studying the necessity of concentration camps for the Nikkei, to repudiate the leadership of Mike Masaoka

This item originally appeared in the *Rafu Shimpo* on June 25, 1994, to commemorate the recent death of James Matsumoto Omura (1912–1994). Reprinted by permission from the Los Angeles News Publishing Company, d.b.a. *THE RAFU SHIMPO*.

and his Japanese American Citizens League. He said the JACL was being appointed the leaders and representatives of Japanese America without having consulted, sought, or obtained the approval of the 120,000 Japanese Americans concerned. He called the JACL "Quislings."

Before this same committee the leaders of the JACL declared that 25 percent of the Nisei were disloyal and only with JACL's help could the government separate the wolves from the sheep. "How could they have ever been mistaken for a civil rights organization?" Jimmie often wondered aloud.

When the Japanese attacked Pearl Harbor and brought America into World War II, the JACL's betrayal of Japanese America to White racist demagoguery was already a fait accompli. The JACL had invented and asked for a loyalty oath to distinguish between the good and evil Japanese Americans, and it had fingered thousands of Issei and Kibei-Nisei as potential saboteurs and joined the local police and the FBI in their arrests.

And after asking for concentration camps in which persons of Japanese ancestry would have their behavior modified, be "Americanized," and—following the JACL's fifteen pages of recommendations—be turned into "Better Americans for a Greater America," they intimidated the Nikkei into entering the camps without protest or resistance by lying to them about a nonexistent U.S. Army "contingency plan" to use force to imprison all 120,000 persons of Japanese ancestry on the West Coast within twenty-four hours.

The U.S. Army had 174,000 men in uniform in December 1941 with 488 machine guns and forty rickety tanks from World War I. Even if they wanted to, the army had neither the manpower nor the arms and vehicles needed to accomplish Masaoka's "contingency plan."

All this Jimmie Omura summed up in a phrase that has become famous, if not credited: "The JACL sold Japanese America down the river." Since then, many Nisei have said, "The JACL sold Japanese America down the river," but not too loudly, for the camps gave Japanese America to the JACL to run as its own police state.

The latest summation of the JACL betrayal is known as "The Lim Report." From the first hints of incarceration, Omura sought to resist any racially selective orders on constitutional grounds and assert the Nisei rights as U.S. citizens in the courts. The JACL declared all test cases to be seditious, traitorous, and un-American because they brought bad publicity to the Nisei. Omura appealed to the Nisei for money to hire a lawyer and pursue a test case, but because of the JACL police state no one dared to respond. Jimmie's attempt at going for a redress of constitutional grievance fizzled. Still, Jimmie didn't take the hint.

Omura wanted to keep writing. He didn't feel he'd be free to write if he were evicted and incarcerated, so he "voluntarily evacuated" to Colorado and eventually, in two years, became editor of the English-language section of the Denver *Rocky Shimpo*.

Omura's editorials on the right and wrong way for Nisei to resist the draft inspired the Issei and the Nisei alike, especially at Wyoming's Heart Mountain camp, where unlike the resistance at the other nine camps administered by the War Relocation Authority, there was leadership and organization. At the other camps, Nisei were individually calling the government's bluff. If the government takes away their citizenship rights, they're no longer citizens. And if the government really thinks they're Japanese, then the government can't draft them, but must send them back to Japan.

The strategy was to embarrass the government into saying it'd made a mistake: the Nisei were obviously U.S. citizens; restore the Nisei to their precamp condition, *then* draft them, everybody's happy, on with the war. Jimmie thought this strategy for restoring the constitutional rights of Nisei was wrongheaded, to say the least.

Omura had already been fingered by the FBI thanks to the JACL's Minoru Yasui. Yasui went out of his way to personally promise Jimmie, to his face, "[I will] see you behind bars." Knowing the JACL and the FBI were ready to pounce, Omura chose his words carefully when he editorialized on Nisei draft resisters. These are the words that got him arrested:

> Those who are resisting the draft are too few, too unorganized and basically unsound in their viewpoints.
>
> Expatriation is not the answer to our eventual redemption of democratic and constitutional rights. Unorganized draft resistance is not the proper method to pursue our grievances.
>
> We do not dispute the fact that such rights have been largely stripped and taken from us. We further agree that the government should restore a large part of those rights before asking us to contribute our lives to the welfare of the nation—to sacrifice our lives on the field of battle.
>
> But ours should not be an act of rashness or haste. There is no reason why we should not petition for a redress of grievances, but there is every reason why we should resist the draft in the way it is being done now.

The Heart Mountain Fair Play Committee refused to respond to the draft until their "citizenship status" was "clarified" in the courts. Their strategy was to use the draft to test the constitutionality of the exclusion and detention of American citizens of Japanese ancestry. If the exclusion and detention were legal, then the Nisei were no longer citizens. If they were not legal then the government could not draft the Nisei until all their rights and properties were restored and the wrongs redressed.

Eighty-eight Nisei men at Heart Mountain resisted the draft and were convicted in Cheyenne's federal court and imprisoned in Leavenworth, Kansas, and McNeil, Washington, federal prisons. They were among the 262 draft resisters pardoned on Christmas Eve 1947 by President Harry S. Truman.

James Omura was tried with seven leaders of the Heart Mountain Fair Play Committee as a coconspirator, in a conspiracy to cause violations of the Selective Service. He wrote letters appealing to the people he had published in his various newspapers and *Current Life* for help with the expenses of his defense. He didn't receive a dime in the mail. Not only did the cream of Nisei poets and writers not send any money; they didn't send any letters. He was acquitted but by JACL design, financially ruined and ostracized from the society controlled by the JACL police state.

From this moment on, James Omura would be thought of as dead. His career in Nisei journalism was over. The leaders of the Fair Play Committee, Kiyoshi Okamoto, Paul Nakadate, Frank Emi, Minoru Tamesa, Isamu Horino, Ben Wakaye, and the Issei Zen man, Guntaro Kubota, had their convictions reversed in appeals court.

Before the Fair Play Committee trials, the JACL openly threatened the draft resisters and James Omura with social ostracism in the pages of the JACL weekly *Pacific Citizen*. The JACL's Joe Grant Masaoka and Minoru Yasui proudly worked as shills for the FBI to try and intimidate and threaten the resisters into giving up their cause, and turn fink on them.

After the trials the JACL made good on its threat. Last year [1993], Jimmie told us: "When I was acquitted, I felt I was vindicated. Vindicated as a person. Vindicated in my profession. I returned to Denver and tried to obtain work. I was hounded from one job after another. It took me three months to finally find a job. Actually I eventually went into landscape contracting. Because there I felt that I couldn't be molested or harassed by people who were against me."

His ostracism from the Japanese American community was so complete that even his admirers, including Michi Weglyn, who quotes and writes about him in her book *Years of Infamy*, and the draft resisters themselves, thought the James Omura who dared repudiate the JACL was dead.

No, he was actually living in Denver. To the Japanese Americans there he might have been better off dead. He said the ostracism was not physical or violent. He wasn't attacked in the streets or beat up. "Most of all it was one of these subtle sort of things. You could feel it. You could feel the tenseness. I was in a bowling league and I could feel the tenseness. It got so bad that I couldn't bowl any longer. It was no fun, I can tell you that."

The Bernstein Commission hearings on redress in the early 1980s brought Jimmie back into Nisei history from the dead. When redress activist Henry Miyatake approached me at the hearings in Seattle and told me there was a Jimmie Omura who wanted to meet me, I was dumbfounded.

Could this be *the* James Omura who said the JACL sold Japanese America down the river? He was. He wanted to meet me because of what I said about the JACL betrayal before the commission. And Lawson Inada and Shawn Wong and I wanted to meet him. That first meeting we sat with Jimmie Omura in a pizza parlor and felt we had found a long-lost uncle.

He had inspired the Heart Mountain draft resisters to make their stand in 1944, and through the 1980s he inspired the resisters to come out of the shadows of their social ostracism, tell their stories, and reclaim the history they had made. It was something to see.

Men who had never spoken of their resistance jail terms appeared in broad daylight to meet James Omura. And Jimmie found himself living like an old uncle. Frank Emi was pleased to have Jimmie stay at his house in San Gabriel. Mits Koshiyama and Dave Kawamoto were gushing all over having Jimmie stay at their homes in San Jose. Yosh Kuromiya in Los Angeles. Jimmie was on the road again, writing and working on a book about Japanese America, the JACL, the camps, the resisters, and himself—the storyteller, nitpicker, gossip, and old crank of the Japanese American family. Jimmie was a necessary old man. I think he even spent a night in my house.

Jimmie was at work on his book when he was struck with a heart attack and died, in Denver, at 6:35 a.m., June 20, 1994. He had lived to see the resisters he championed begin to be restored to the community. After forty years of silence and obscurity, Jimmie began to be rediscovered and his work recognized by Asian America. The Asian American Journalists Association honored him. The National Coalition for Redress/Reparations honored him. But Japanese America, Asian America, never knew Jimmie well enough.

Preface

"A Uniquely Genuine Person"

YOSH KUROMIYA

James Matsumoto Omura was everything the Japanese American Citizens League (JACL) was not. It is difficult to define one without the other.

Like two opposing astrological signs, they held in common the relevance of any particular issue because they were inextricably locked on to a common axis, yet held conflicting perceptions and ideologies on dealing with the issue because they approached the subject with a set of opposing survival dynamics.

The JACL, pragmatically, felt the future of Japanese Americans lay in their convincing America of their worthiness and credibility through good deeds, eventually attaining the social acceptance of the broader American public and thereby political empowerment. In short, "the end justifies the means." They proceeded to draw an exceedingly wide swath as to the moral and ethical limits of those means.

James Omura, on the other hand, saw the "end and means" as two phases of a single aspiration. The worthiness of any goal was part and parcel of the moral integrity of the process by which the goal was achieved. In terms of the Nisei (second-generation Japanese Americans) during the World War II crisis: to believe in the primacy of our citizenship, and therefore our loyalty, as a foregone conclusion, and not something to be earned or proven. Innocent until proven guilty. To be what we already are. His commitments were based on these precepts.

As events evolved, the pragmatic JACL approach seemed to prevail. Yet the visionary ideals of James Omura, a few of his contemporaries, and many more in the growing new generation of Asian American intellectuals and "realists" expressed doubts of the "model minority" myths. There was hope!

My initial awareness of James M. Omura was in 1942 (precamp) after his famous query on February 23 at the San Francisco hearings of the Tolan Committee—"Has the Gestapo come to America?"—as the national JACL continued its witch hunt against the Issei (immigrant-generation Japanese Americans, ineligible for U.S. citizenship) and Kibei (Nisei educated in Japan) as potential enemy spies. This transpired over three months after President Franklin Roosevelt was presented with the Munson Report findings of no immediate threat of espionage by the Japanese population either on the West Coast or in Hawai'i. The JACL declared James Omura as "Public Enemy Number One" and proceeded to destroy him in the eyes of the Japanese American community.

During the 1944 Nisei draft controversy at Wyoming's Heart Mountain incarceration camp, Omura supported the constitutional basis of the draft through his editorials in the English section of the *Rocky Shimpo*, an ethnic vernacular newspaper in Denver. However, he also warned of legal entanglements, especially in the lower courts, where constitutional veracity held little weight.

Later that same year, Omura was indicted as a coconspirator counseling draft evasion along with seven leaders of the Heart Mountain Fair Play Committee (FPC). Omura had never set foot in Heart Mountain, nor had he met any of the FPC leaders. He had obviously been set up by the JACL. Omura was cleared of all charges, but court costs had virtually wiped out all his savings. Further, he lost his *Rocky Shimpo* editorship and was blackballed at other publishing firms under the influence of the JACL. The Denver-area Japanese American community had turned its back on Omura financially, socially, and in employment out of fear of JACL reprisals.

In 1981 James Omura reemerged as a witness in the Seattle session of the Commission on Wartime Relocation and Internment of Civilians (CWRIC). He had virtually disappeared since his JACL-inspired censure and abandonment by the Denver-area Japanese American community. Frank Chin, a Chinese American playwright, became aware of the Heart Mountain draft resistance and the FPC, and having met James Omura in Seattle after his CWRIC testimony, proceeded to reunite him with the few surviving Heart Mountain draft resisters he could locate, including me, along with FPC leader Frank Emi.

When Jimmie Omura had speaking engagements or other business in the Los Angeles area, he often stayed in Frank Emi's home. On one occasion Frank also had a speaking engagement, in San Jose, so he asked my wife, Irene, and me to take Jimmie in. It was on very short notice and within fifteen minutes Emi and Omura appeared at our front door. We quickly cleared space in our spare bedroom, hoping it would suffice. Jimmie spent most of the day quietly in the room, reading or writing, so I was careful not to disturb him. When necessary for his research, I would drive him to the Los Angeles Public Library or to other sources of information. I was very comfortable in his presence and felt honored that he referred to us as his "home away from home." However, once when he popped up unannounced, we did suggest to him that he allow a couple of days warning of his arrival. Fortunately, we didn't have prior commitments on that particular occasion, but he could have been locked out of his "home away from home" for the entire day.

I detected in Jimmie a rare quality of sincerity and honesty that I seldom encountered in my then seventy years of existence on earth. I was, of course, familiar with the conventional "face-saving" rituals we were all conditioned to accept as sincerity and honesty, but with Jimmie it was a deeper, more frightful commitment that often seemed to put his very survival at risk.

Omura's decision to place the telling of his life story in the capable hands of Dr. Arthur Hansen was no accident either. Although it would take years for him to review and order the awesome volume of notes and narratives thrust upon him, thanks to his dedication, James Matsumoto Omura's style of sincerity and honesty will be forever preserved.

Introduction

James Omura and the Redressing of Japanese American History

ARTHUR A. HANSEN

James Matsumoto Omura (1912–94) was the foremost editorial voice raised against the U.S. government's World War II exclusion and incarceration of Japanese Americans. He was also the chief spokesperson decrying the Japanese American Citizens League's (JACL's) collaborative role in this shameful development. The lone Nikkei journalist to editorialize against the JACL-endorsed federal policy of drafting imprisoned Japanese American citizens into the military, Omura was the first Nikkei to seek governmental redress and reparations for wartime violations of civil liberties and human rights. The heroic role he played in redeeming the tarnished repute and self-esteem of the Japanese American community has been grossly underrecognized and generally unheralded by Nikkei and non-Nikkei Americans alike. Without question, James Omura deserves to be accorded a place of honor in U.S. history commensurate with that already consecrated for resisters Gordon Hirabayashi, Minoru Yasui, Fred Korematsu, and Mitsuye Endo.[1]

In 2003 I authored a chapter for an anthology that honored the distinguished historian Roger Daniels's career-long contribution to Asian American history. I titled this piece "Return to the Wars: Jimmie Omura's 1947 Crusade against the Japanese American Citizens League."[2] Assuredly, it had been Omura's animus toward the JACL that fueled the "wars" to which, in mid-May 1947, he was "returning" as the newly reappointed English-section editor of Denver, Colorado's *Rocky Shimpo* vernacular newspaper.[3] After all, only three years previously, due in great measure to the behind-the-scenes machinations of JACL's national and regional leadership, Omura

was flushed out of his initial four-month tenure, in early 1944, as the
Rocky Shimpo's English-section editor by the U.S. government and subsequently—along with the seven leaders of the Fair Play Committee (FPC) at
Wyoming's Heart Mountain Relocation Center[4]—indicted, arrested, jailed,
and forced to stand trial in a Cheyenne, Wyoming, federal court for unlaw-
ful conspiracy to counsel, aid, and abet violations of the military draft. Even
though Omura, unlike the FPC leadership, was acquitted of this charge, his
legal vindication did not prevent the Denver-area JACL power brokers from
mobilizing an extralegal vendetta against him within the Nikkei community. Indeed, they so effectively harassed and demonized Omura as to make
it virtually impossible for him to gain sustainable employment or to revel
in the rewards of a viable social and cultural life, and these deprivations in
turn hastened his 1947 divorce from his Nisei wife, Fumiko "Caryl" Omura
(née Okuma).[5]

As discerning readers of *Nisei Naysayer* will discover, Omura discloses
within his memoir's pages all of the above information save for what transpired during his May–December 1947 editorial stint with the *Rocky Shimpo*.
However, by thus curtailing his autobiographical account with his being
"down and out" in Denver at the end of World War II, Omura inadver-
tently bolsters the conventional historical narrative stamped on his life by
his contemporary critics and latter-day chroniclers that his militant 1934–44
opposition to the JACL leadership of the Japanese American community
and the U.S. government's wartime treatment of Japanese Americans was
brought to a halt before the end of World War II. While poetically accurate,
this perception violates historical veracity, since within the short interval
of Omura's 1947 *Rocky Shimpo* tenure, he used his editorial position to a
greater degree than at any time previously as a bully pulpit to criticize his
nation's government, institutions, and practices, and far more often and
pointedly to wage war against the JACL. As Omura promised his readers in
his opening editorial column of May 16, 1947, "Nisei America: Know the
Facts," he would pursue "a progressive type of journalism [to] freely criticize
wherever occasion demands." He also issued a warning to the JACL leadership: "Those who have disagreed with us in the past and have been unpar-
donably guilty of working nefariously in the shadows may evince certain
misgivings with our return to the Nisei journalistic wars. They have cause
to feel uneasy."

Omura's bite more than matched his bark. His special brand of "lib-
eralism" pervaded his columns: he praised the Committee for Industrial

Organizations, urged Nisei to join unions, and called for the abolition of race-, sex-, and creed-based restrictions in union constitutions;[6] he lauded advances toward interracial progress and advocated legislation against racial discrimination;[7] and he simultaneously disparaged the dangers to democracy of both communism and its magnification as a threat by the House Un-American Activities Committee.[8]

Then too about one-fifth of Omura's some 120 editorial columns criticized the JACL. On May 27 he castigated its leaders for having been "autocratic and arrogant" and contended that "we need something beside the JACL." Then on June 26 he explained that the JACL did not deserve criticism for failing to "avert the Evacuation" but, rather, for its "dereliction of duty to defend with all its might the civil rights of the then discredited Nisei racial minority." Omura's July 23 editorial was more personal and pointed: "The JACL lended its helping hand to the government in a vain effort to railroad this editor to Leavenworth." In his August 2 column Omura blasted the "selfish and arrogant" JACL leadership for denying "the right of any Nisei to hold views contrary to its own."

As for the JACL's chief spokesperson, Mike Masaoka, his attitude, according to Omura's August 19 column, had been "narrow, arrogant, [and] overbearing." The other high-level JACL officials, added Omura on August 26, "cannot properly deny that they have engaged and are still engaging in invidious reprisals against the few who courageously assail the leadership of the organization." In the very next day's column, he charged that the JACL hierarchy had seen in the war "a golden opportunity to promote the organization to a position of influence."

Even at a time when, as Omura put it in his September 8 column, the JACL was "engaged in a worthwhile campaign to rectify certain injustices," he nonetheless felt that "the organization's activities in Washington are merely patterns in the design to achieve authoritarian control of Nisei society." On September 10, Omura berated JACL bigwigs for "impotency," "inferiority," and a lack of "forthright leadership." Insofar as Omura had a good word for the JACL, it pertained to its stand on communism: "The Japanese American Citizens League follows the best procedure in refusing even to wink at Communism."[9]

On December 4 a small item in the *Rocky Shimpo* announced that Omura had tendered his resignation and asked to be relieved of his duties as of December 15. Certainly personal finances figured heavily in Omura's decision. So also did fatigue. Throughout much of his editorship, Omura had operated the Omura Landscape Service, and this double duty exacted its price. As he had commented in an adversarial open letter to Togo Tanaka, a national JACL leader and a Chicago-based columnist for the English-language section of the *Colorado Times*,[10] Denver's competitor Japanese American community newspaper, such a schedule had reduced his sleep at night to four or five hours.[11] This revelation prompted a left-wing JACLer, Joe Oyama of New York, to write Omura a note: "Take the advice of an old hand, Mr. Omura. You can't do two things at one time. Otherwise, you do both badly. My advice to improve your paper is to quit and devote full time to your 'going business.'"[12] The December 4 *Rocky Shimpo* announcement by Omura signaled that he had decided to heed Oyama's sardonic recommendation about quitting his paper to enhance his budding career as a landscape architect, but surely *not* so as to "improve" the *Rocky Shimpo*. Indeed, only the prior day that paper reported Omura being named a recipient of a national rose-culture award and cited his membership in the American Rose Society, the American Horticultural Society, the National Garden Institute, and the Colorado Forestry and Horticultural Association.

Before officially abdicating his position as the *Rocky Shimpo*'s editor, Omura fired a volley of parting shots, aimed first at the JACL and then at the *Colorado Times* and its most opinionated columnist, Minoru Yasui, a staunch JACL advocate and Omura's arch-nemesis. On December 3 Omura dedicated his editorial to the possible role that liberals in the JACL could play to reform the organization. Such liberals, he claimed, had frequently solicited him to join the organization and assist in this process. But he had declined on the grounds that if the leadership had rejected his advice from outside the JACL's ranks, it was absurd to think that it would listen to him as a member. Still, the liberal element in the JACL represented the best hope for reforming the organization. Institutional salvation could only come about, though, if the leadership recanted its wartime performance and revised its current campaign in Congress so that the legislation sought would materially help a majority of the Nisei and not merely a chosen few.

Having dealt with the liberals in the JACL, Omura then turned in his December 9 editorial to the "fanatics" within the organization. He charged that such individuals, who pervaded the league's top leadership, presented the view that the JACL was engaged in a high calling and could therefore demand unqualified allegiance from other Nisei. But the JACL's numerically small membership (six thousand out of a total Nisei population of eighty-five thousand "eligible" Nisei, including thirty thousand Nisei war veterans) proved that such fanaticism lacked popular appeal. Because the fanatical leaders, whom Omura saw as being both intelligent and unbalanced in their organizational devotion, had made (and continued to make) so many personal sacrifices to promote the JACL, they were virtually immune to and even resented constructive criticism. In the long run, concluded Omura, the liberals in the JACL would have to reform the organization before the fanatics destroyed it.

In his editorial assessment of the state of "Denver Nisei Leadership" for the December 12 issue of the *Rocky Shimpo*, Omura drew a damaging comparison between his newspaper's approach to this state of affairs and that of the *Colorado Times*. Whereas the rival Denver vernacular deplored

FIGURE 1. Jimmie Omura, "Liberty Calling" program on KLZ radio, Denver, Colorado, October 12, 1947. In the first of two broadcasts on "Japanese Americans' problems in Denver," the *Rocky Shimpo* editor stressed discrimination faced by Nikkei in employment, education, and housing. In contrast, the second broadcast's featured speaker, *Colorado Times* publisher Fred Kaihara, maintained that discrimination in no way hampered Denver's Japanese American community. Omura Papers, Green Library, Stanford University.

the inadequacy of the city's Nisei leadership, it nonetheless defended it and shielded it from the *Rocky Shimpo*'s criticism. This craven policy by the *Colorado Times* was anathema to Omura, who had operated the *Rocky Shimpo* on the premise that what should be courted was truth and democratic progress, not public favor. "Ours," exulted Omura, "is the journalism of the Bennetts, the Danas, the Goulds—the men who built American journalism and lifted it from the Milquetoast, fawning journalism of personal editors." Because of the *Rocky Shimpo*'s forthrightness, it got vilified by a paper like the *Colorado Times*, for which firmness and fairness were lower priorities than flattering the community and gaining its goodwill. "This situation," accused Omura, "is accentuated by our violent enemies, such as the Yasuis, who inaccurately report statements we make before public groups and clothe them in language to incite resentment and aggravate ill feelings." A particularly "vicious example" was Yasui's attempt to attribute to Omura the "patently false and absolutely untrue" allusion that none of the Nisei leaders in Denver are any good at all. "We have labeled this statement," explained Omura, "a lie. Mr. Yasui has threatened to sue us unless we retract. We have refused to retract. The next move is Mr. Yasui's."

Omura's editorial swan song, titled "Not without Regret," appeared in the *Rocky Shimpo*'s December 15 edition. He regretted that his plan to put the newspaper on a sound financial footing had never been implemented. He regretted, too, his stepping down from his post on the basis of sheer "nostalgia," for he was among those people "who live, breathe and virtually eat journalism." He was sorry, practically speaking, that his exit was prompted by the declining fortunes of the Nisei vernaculars in Denver (compared to the boom wartime years), owing to the escalating competition posed by their revitalized West Coast counterparts. Furthermore, he was doleful that at this late juncture the English-language sections of the vernaculars, in spite of having an important role to play, were still a "financial flop" and a "crummy adjunct" to the Japanese-language sections. He regretted, finally, that the new approach to policy he had introduced in the *Rocky Shimpo*—cosmopolitanism, principled candor, and progressive democratic reform—had not yet been adopted by other Nisei vernaculars. "The current policies of Nisei newspapers," mourned Omura, "cater to the provincialism of the Nisei and make no effort whatsoever to guide its readers to a broader and more liberal outlook. It is a policy that looks backward and fails to keep pace with the individual intellectuality of the Nisei."

Predictably, in the December 18 issue of the *Colorado Times*, Yasui responded to Omura's sweeping indictment of him and his newspaper. He dealt with the last of these matters first. The *Colorado Times* did not fancy itself as being in the same "grandiose and pretentious" tradition of journalism as Omura claimed for his paper. But the *Colorado Times* also had not, as charged by Omura, catered to public favor. It believed in factual and objective reporting of the news. Its interest in reporting national and international news was circumscribed by the seeming insignificance of such news to Nisei. Rather, the paper tried to cover news on topics of interest to local Nisei residents, such as discrimination (though never in a "carping" or crusading manner). It also sought to encourage Nisei and put their activities in "the best possible light in order to advance the interests of the Nisei in our community and in our nation."

As for Omura's barbs against him, Yasui expressed amazement that the *Rocky Shimpo* editor had named him as a "violent enemy." Yasui had considered suing Omura but now felt this action pointless, given his resignation.[13] It is enough, declared Yasui, that "a disturbing factor in Denver journalism is now gone," and he apologized to the *Colorado Times'* readership for having subjected them to his quarrels with Omura and the *Rocky Shimpo*. But if Min Yasui was silent about Jimmie Omura in the *Colorado Times* for the rest of 1947, he was hardly through with him.

On December 29 Yasui's *Colorado Times* column revisited the very issue most responsible for the bad blood between him and Omura—wartime Nisei draft resistance. What provoked Yasui's editorial was President Harry Truman's Christmas granting of amnesty (the restoration of full political and civil rights) to virtually all of the approximately 315 Japanese Americans convicted of violating the Selective Service Act. While never mentioning the name of Jimmie Omura or the Heart Mountain FPC and localizing his concern to the thirty-one pardoned draft resisters from Colorado (mostly former Amache, or Granada, concentration camp inmates), he did implicate the first two parties in his comments. Broadly, Yasui was charitable toward those who had resisted the draft so as "to register a legal protest against evacuation." He emphasized the extenuating circumstances leading to their actions and expressed the belief that the pardons had been "unnecessarily long-delayed." At bottom, however, Yasui's commentary represented a critique of the FPC, Omura, and the Nisei draft resisters. "As a protest against evacuation," pronounced Yasui, "many Nisei listened to the 'latrine gossip' that circulated in camps, and decided that they would refuse to answer the draft call." These Nisei, "ill-advisedly, contended that they ought not to be called upon to fulfill their obligations as a citizen until their rights as a citizen were fully restored." Fortunately, the stigma produced for Japanese America by these "draft evaders" was more than offset by the overwhelming number of Nisei who chose to serve their country in the army and sometimes ended up wounded or worse. Yasui then delivered his peroration on Nisei wartime patriotism:

> We hope and believe that this will be the last of the Nisei draft evasion cases.
>
> At a time when other Nisei boys were slugging against the enemy, reports of draft violation hit the morale of our Nisei GI's. On the home front, refusal to serve was construed by the public as out-right disloyalty. But now, almost two years later, we believe that this is the end of that sad and shameful story.
>
> A moral that we can safely draw, now that it seems to be completely over and done with, it seems to us, is that as citizens and as human beings, we must first fulfill our obligations to the nation and society before we can legally or socially expect that our complete rights will be granted to us. Let us hope that we, as Nisei, have learned this lesson.

Thus, by the closing of 1947 the dust had cleared sufficiently so that a reasonably astute observer could make sense out of the state of Japanese American affairs in Denver. Omura's retreat to private pursuits removed a formidable if progressive counterweight in the JACL's hegemonic control of public life in Japanese Denver. The existence in Colorado's capital city of a large and active JACL chapter, along with a favorable press (both the *Colorado Times*, thanks to Min Yasui and Togo Tanaka, and the mainstream *Denver Post*, courtesy of Bill Hosokawa) to promote its agenda and social gospel, ensured that the JACL would prevail. This prevalence extended, as the moral of Yasui's editorial in the *Colorado Times* on December 29, 1947, well testified, to how the immediate Japanese American past would be configured within (and even outside of) Denver's Nikkei community.

According to the JACL's worldview, the basic lesson Nikkei needed to learn from their World War II history, as dramatized by their 1944 response to the draft, was that unlike other Americans, they were largely bereft of human and civil rights and needed to fulfill their national obligations, particularly military service, before these withheld rights would be granted to them. The lesson's subtext was that the JACL's wartime policy of "constructive cooperation" with the U.S. government was prudent, practical, and patriotic, while those who had advocated or practiced resistance on constitutional grounds (that is, Omura, the FPC, and Nisei draft resisters) were misguided, mischievous, or treasonable. The real heroes of Japanese American wartime history, in the eyes of JACL leaders, were those valiant Nisei who carried out their duty by answering the call to enlist voluntarily or allowed themselves to be drafted into the army so that they could "go for broke" for their country. In contrast, dissidents like Jimmie Omura were simply tilting at windmills.

This same JACL-shaped historical narrative was disseminated throughout Japanese America by the organization's newspaper, the *Pacific Citizen* (*PC*). One of its two principal interpretive voices was Denver-based columnist Bill Hosokawa, the other being its editor, Larry Tajiri, who moved to Denver and was employed by the *Denver Post* after the *PC*'s transfer in 1952 from its wartime home in Salt Lake City, Utah, to Los Angeles. The *PC* was the unofficial voice of early postwar Japanese America. Because Mike Masaoka was a veritable one-man gang lobbying Congress for the JACL-crafted program covering Japanese American rights and benefits, he amplified the *PC*'s version of Japanese American history within a strategic national center. During wartime Masaoka had strongly supported Nisei military service, viewing it as the best way of "proving" their loyalty. The all-Nisei 442nd Regimental Combat Team's first volunteer, Masaoka had served as a public relations officer and in that capacity was a very effective pitchman for the JACL's rendition of Japanese American history.

As for Jimmie Omura, for over three decades following his December 1947 resignation from the *Rocky Shimpo* editorship, he disappeared from Japanese American society and was erased from Japanese American history. He remained a Denver resident but lived apart from the Nikkei community. In 1951 Omura remarried another Nisei woman, Karen Haruko Omura (née Motoishi), and together they raised their two boys, Gregg and Wayne. Until illness in the late 1970s forced him into retirement, Omura operated a successful landscaping business and achieved prominence as an executive officer in state and national professional landscaping associations.

FIGURE 2. Jim Omura, Omura Landscaping, Denver, Colorado, in the 1950s. After resigning the *Rocky Shimpo* editorship in 1947, Omura devoted himself to building a successful landscaping business. In addition to working on private homes and developments, he also tackled civic projects in the greater Denver area. Omura Papers, Green Library, Stanford University.

The postwar JACL played a key role in expunging Jimmie Omura's name and memory from Japanese American history and consciousness. While he prospered in landscaping, the JACL thrived as an organization. Its expanding membership encompassed the Nisei elite, and outside of Japanese America it was viewed as that community's representative. This situation crystalized as early as 1948, as can be seen through one of JACL advocate Togo Tanaka's *Colorado Times* columns reprinted in the *Pacific Citizen* on September 25 that year.

Although Tanaka began his column pointing out how Japanese Americans had been transformed from a despised into an accepted, even respected American minority group, his primary motivation for writing it was to rejoice over the reversed estates of JACLers and anti-JACL resisters since camp

days. Then, "pressure boys" within such morally defiled places as the War
Relocation Authority (WRA) detention centers had intimidated and se-
duced the Nikkei majority into believing that JACL leaders were informers
who had sold out their ethnic community for self-advancement and needed
to be punished with beatings and banishment. Having accomplished this
objective, resistance "messiahs" were themselves removed from the camps as
"troublemakers" and confined to high-security isolation and segregation penal facilities administered by the WRA. According to Tanaka, each of these
charismatic resistance leaders, such as Harry Ueno at the Manzanar camp
in California (where Tanaka and his family were incarcerated in 1942), had
been transformed into "a martyr to his glowing cause." However, opined

FIGURE 3. In the 1960s, Jim Omura not only was an active member and officer in
the Associated Landscape Contractors of Colorado, serving two terms as its president,
but also enacted the same roles within the Associated Landscape Contractors of
America (ALCA). Here he is shown at the 1967 annual ALCA meeting in Dallas,
Texas, discharging his vice-presidential duties. Omura Papers, Green Library, Stanford
University.

Tanaka, posterity would not vindicate them. In fact, just three years after the war it was apparent to him that these individuals had not "contributed anything more than zero to securing the present position of Japanese Americans in U.S. life." After puncturing the historical pretensions of camp resisters, Tanaka turned his pen to obliterating them, via Ueno (the central figure in the so-called Manzanar Riot of December 6, 1942), from the collective memory of Japanese and mainstream America: "This ex-fruit-stand clerk has disappeared into the obscurity and oblivion from which he reared his sallow head, and no one seems to care very much if at all. Thus, the story endeth."[14]

While JACL spokespersons Minoru Yasui and Togo Tanaka were not literally conspiring to oust resisters from the Japanese American World War II story and to refigure the JACL's role in it, they effectively worked in tandem toward those very ends. Whereas Tanaka was exorcising those who had resisted the dismantling of the Nikkei community's traditional cultural arrangements by the alliance between the U.S. government, the WRA, and the JACL, Yasui was extirpating those who had resisted that same alliance's compromising of Nisei citizenship rights.

Neither Yasui nor Tanaka presumed to write books about Japanese American history and its defining World War II experience. However, another prominent JACL leader, Bill Hosokawa (who founded and edited the inmate newspaper at the Heart Mountain detention center in Wyoming), did tackle this task by authoring or coauthoring four interrelated publications: *Nisei* (1969),[15] *East to America* (1980),[16] *JACL in Quest of Justice* (1982),[17] and *They Call Me Moses Masaoka* (1987).[18]

Setting aside these books' overall quality, what is instructive here is Hosokawa's erasure of resisters from the Japanese American wartime story. Nowhere appears the name of Jimmie Omura. This could hardly have been simply an oversight. Both Hosokawa and Omura had been born and raised in the Seattle, Washington, area, figured significantly in the 1942 Tolan Committee hearings, were associated with Heart Mountain political developments, and resettled in wartime Denver and remained living and working there in the postwar period. Hosokawa does mention draft resisters in the last three of his above-noted books but only perfunctorily and as a foil, variously, to discredit the purported revisionism of historians (like Roger Daniels),[19] to glorify the compassionate efforts of JACLers (like Minoru Yasui and Joe Grant Masaoka) to "save" the resisters,[20] and to highlight their meager number and lack of heroic merit relative to Nisei soldiers.[21] As for

Harry Ueno and other militant anti-JACL resisters in WRA camps, Hosokawa was also silent, with the single exception of a reference in *Nisei* to Joe
Kurihara, "perhaps the chief agitator in Manzanar."[22]

Between publication of Hosokawa's *Nisei* in 1969 and his *East to America*
in 1980, American society and culture, including the Nikkei community,
underwent a tumultuous upheaval. As the mounting protests against the
Vietnam War, racism, and sexism evinced, passivity and obedience to authority and tradition had ceased being admired. Historians were drawn
to outspoken individuals and activist groups who had stood up for social
justice and enlarged democratic rights. Moreover, they used this tradition
of dissent to promote contemporary developments and personalities. Con-
versely, they subjected the past's sacred cows—whether individuals, institutions, movements, or events—to rigorous and skeptical scrutiny and, if
necessary, strong criticism, and this legacy, too, was put into the service of
present-day politics.

This state of affairs vis-à-vis Japanese American history was evident in
seminal books by Roger Daniels and Michi Nishiura Weglyn. As Moses
Richlin's foreword to Daniels's *Concentration Camps USA* (1971)[23] noted,
"[He] has given special attention to the resistance and protest of the evacuees, an aspect neglected or glossed over by others."[24] Daniels's acknowledgments discreetly intimated his break with the JACL interpretation: "The late
Joe Grant Masaoka . . . would not have agreed with some of my strictures
about the Japanese American power structure, but would, I am sure, have
defended my right to make them."[25] Devoting considerable space to the
Heart Mountain draft resistance movement and Omura's correlated role,
Daniels contrasted his perspective with that of the JACL-WRA.

> This account of the "loyal" Japanese American resistance . . . calls into
> question the stereotype of the Japanese American victim of oppression
> during World War II who met his fate with stoic resignation and responded
> only with superpatriotism. . . . The JACL-WRA view has dominated the
> writing of the evacuation's postwar history, thereby nicely illustrating E. H.
> Carr's dictum that history is written by the winners. . . . [But] there are those
> who will find more heroism in resistance than in patient resignation.[26]

Community historian Michi Nishiura Weglyn used similarly bald terminology in her title and text for *Years of Infamy* (1976).[27] That book's dust
jacket featured the Manzanar camp's controversial plaque blaming "hysteria, racism, and economic exploitation" for the ten WRA "concentration

camps." As Raymond Okamura's review stated, Weglyn wrote "from the perspective of an outraged victim." She relied heavily on primary sources and "discarded preconceptions," such as benevolent administrative-inmate cooperation, and invested her data with experiential meaning. Her selection of opening photographs coupled "WRA brutality" and the Nikkei response of "defiance and resistance" to such oppressive actions.[28] Weglyn was mute about the draft resistance movement at Heart Mountain, but for one chapter's epigraph she summoned Omura's Tolan Committee testimony: "Has the Gestapo come to America? Have we not risen in righteous anger at Hitler's mistreatment of the Jews? Then, is it not incongruous that citizen Americans of Japanese descent should be similarly mistreated and persecuted?"[29] Moreover, Weglyn provided copious, empathetic coverage of camp resisters in all of the WRA camps (including the Moab and Leupp isolation centers for "troublemakers" and the Tule Lake Segregation Center for "disloyals").[30] Even her dedication—"To Wayne M. Collins, who did more to correct a democracy's mistake than any other person"—conveyed the book's resistance motif. A civil rights lawyer and social crusader, Collins had been instrumental to the closing of the notorious Tule Lake stockade,[31] and also spent many postwar years restoring citizenship rights for nearly five thousand Tuleans who had renounced them.

Omura was oblivious to this new resistance historiography. But as an early-1980s retiree, when his public identity as Jimmie Omura was increasingly supplanted by James Omura, he reflected on his journalistic past, including his crusade against the JACL leadership. Plagued by an acute cardiac condition, Omura decided to write his memoirs and emphasize the wartime era. Perhaps, in so doing, he could vindicate the Japanese American community and himself for the damage the U.S. government and the JACL had inflicted on both.

His decision coincided with the Nikkei community's campaign to achieve redress and reparations for its wartime mistreatment. Aware that the congressional Commission on Wartime Relocation and Internment of Civilians (CWRIC) had scheduled 1981 hearings within ten U.S. cities, Omura resolved to testify at those being held at his birthplace of Seattle.[32]

During his preretirement days, Omura did not ordinarily maintain a day-by-day diary. However, in the crucial interval roughly spanning his CWRIC testimony on Wednesday, September 9, 1981, in Seattle, and his death on Monday, June 20, 1994, in Denver, Omura faithfully compiled a rather meticulous daily journal logging his activities, thoughts, and feelings. The availability of this longitudinal record not only permits his memoir's readers to obtain helpful information bearing on its intellectual and social construction, but also, and of greater moment, affords access to still another consequential period in Omura's life beyond the memoir's restricted chronological domain, wherein he mounted a relentless war of words against the U.S. government and the JACL for their egregious World War II disregard of civil and human rights.

In what follows in this introduction to Omura's memoir, I will draw strategically upon entries from what I have termed the memoirist's "Redress Diary" (supplemented by other relevant source material) to illuminate how the act of representing his life history to posterity simultaneously provided Omura with a propitious opportunity to redress the wartime wrongs that had been suffered by him, personally, his racial-ethnic community, collectively, and the American ideal and practice of constitutional democracy, globally.

By focusing on this tripartite mission within Omura's Redress Diary, I have remained largely silent or cursory about such topics as family and personal relations, financial concerns, political and social affiliations, leisure-time activities, and behavioral idiosyncrasies. Although these concerns are abundantly represented within Omura's diary, I have elected to leave them for contemplation and interpretation by future biographers.

Before turning to the contents proper of James Omura's Redress Diary, perhaps a few words are in order about diaries as a literary genre, followed by some thoughts about how the diary Omura maintained between 1981 and 1994 correlates with diary-keeping conventions.

The term "diary" is derived from the Latin word *dies*, which means "days" and suggests a daily activity, something done day to day. Although classified within the genre of "life writing" or "self-discussion," a diary differs from other forms within this category, such as autobiography, biography, memoir, correspondence, and travel literature, by being more immediate and intimate. The most common type of this genre form is a personal diary, wherein the diarist typically includes her experiences, thoughts, and feelings and often comments as well on current events outside of her direct experience. Generally speaking, a diary is for the diarist's own use and not meant to be read by anyone else. Accordingly, while entries in the diary are customarily meticulously dated, simple mechanics such as proper spelling of names and places are accorded less attention. The reasons governing why a person keeps a diary, however, are exceedingly variable, as are the values and uses that a given diarist assigns to his diary's contents.

In comparing Omura's diary to this template for the genre, it does not deviate noticeably in too many particulars. His diary is a carefully dated daily record of his experiences, thoughts, and feelings that also permits a consideration of contemporary events occurring outside of his personal frame of reference. It is assuredly the case, too, that Omura's entries include a fair number of mistakes in spelling and grammar. Still, internal and external evidence combine to make it clear that his entries commonly represent rewrites of earlier scribbled drafts. This practice likely reprised the procedure he had acquired and honed to exactness as a journalist. This is true as well in regard to Omura's penchant for embellishing his entries with precise and nuanced depictions of people, locations, and situations. Moreover, consistent with the fieldwork notes generated by workaday journalists, the entries made by Omura in his diary contain within them the tangible promise of being transmuted into public representation.

This brings us to the mutable qualities of diaries noted above that account for their idiosyncratic character: the diarist's rationale for even sustaining a diary and the worthiness and benefits he imputes to its contents. In Omura's case, his rationale was manifold. For one thing, he wanted to monitor his health, which when he began his diary in 1981 was precarious to the point of being life-threatening. For another thing, he wanted to better discipline his mind and more efficiently manage his discretionary time, both of which traits had become derailed somewhat after retirement by a surfeit of televised sports viewing. Also, he desired to regain his former power and fluidity as an expository prose writer. While Omura had written hundreds of articles, essays, op-ed pieces, and the like over his journalistic career, he had never written a book-length manuscript. He at least tacitly realized that if he was to now do so at age sixty-nine, he would have to be health conscious, focused, exercise self-restraint, and write on a very regular and fairly rigorous basis. A diary was certainly not a panacea, but keeping one did have the potential to return dividends for Omura's intended enterprise.

The value and worthiness Omura believed his projected book possessed was to help dramatically revise the standard narrative of the Japanese

American World War II story, as both an American and a Japanese American event of major historical and contemporary significance. What he was far less sure of when he launched his book project was whether there were a sufficient number of others who shared his belief—particularly Japanese American community members and serious-minded inquirers into the World War II Nikkei experience of whatever racial and ethnic descent or intellectual and political persuasion. It did not take long, however, before his voluminous face-to-face interactions, telephone conversations, and postal exchanges made him acutely conscious that the story he had to tell was widely viewed, most especially by progressive Japanese Americans of all generations, as a spirited vehicle for gaining appropriate redemption.

Perhaps Michi Nishiura Weglyn said it best when she wrote to Omura in mid-1987: "Walter [Weglyn] and I can hardly wait for the publication of your opus. Do stay well and energetic for the sake of our history, for the sake of the shamed, whose self-esteem must be restored."[33] Increasingly, Omura logged expressions of lofty sentiment like this one into his diary. Doing so, along with reading over such testimonials repeatedly and sharing them selectively with entrusted members of his support community, produced the collateral value of certifying Omura's confidence in what he was doing and of strengthening his determination to complete the job before it was too late to do so. Having finished a draft of his diary only a few days before his death, Omura bequeathed the charge of assessing his memoir's worth (as well as that of his Redress Diary) to posterity.

Among the numerous compliments extended to Omura during the final year of his life, 1994, only a solitary one surfaces in his Redress Diary. In late January, Alex Kajitani of the Nikkei Club at the University of Colorado, Boulder, wrote to Omura to thank him for his presentation to his campus organization, and then added respectfully, "Your achievements and aspirations are an extremely important part of the Japanese American experience."[34]

That Omura chose to insert this undergraduate's salute to him into his Redress Diary discloses the distinctive nature of the private-cum-public record that he so devotedly compiled throughout the last thirteen years of his life. Consistent with most garden-variety diarists, Omura enfolded his daily experiences, ideas, and sentiments within his diary. More often, though, his entries corresponded with those logged by special-interest diarists, people dedicated to variable passions (e.g., travel, research, health, family, business, gardening, sports, scholarship, or politics). In the case of Omura, his particular special interest, the palpable core of his diary, was clearly *redress*—for himself, his racial-ethnic community, and his country's governmental polity of constitutional democracy. Accordingly, since Kajitani's formulation conjoined Omura's "aspirations" as well as his "achievements" with the "Japanese American experience," it quite likely struck a responsive redress chord within him.

Personal redress for Omura functioned at multiple levels. Most basically, it embraced identity. For much of his coming-of-age interlude, even his very name had been problematic. In spite of his birth appellation as Utaka Matsumoto, he had become confused as a youth by overhearing Pacific Northwest Issei friends and business associates of his *yoshi* (adopted) father (Tsurumatsu Matsumoto) address him as "Omura-san."[35] Although by 1931 Utaka would assume the name James Matsumoto Omura, as a late-1920s Alaskan cannery worker and Pocatello, Idaho, junior high school pupil he sported a miscellany of monikers: James Matsumoto, James Royal, Jimmy Royal, Jimmie Matsumoto,[36] Jimmie Hollingworth Royal,[37] Jimmie Idaho, James Hollingworth Royal, J. Hollingworth Royal, and J. H. Royal.[38] With the dawning of the 1930s, however, he settled permanently on "Jimmie" for his diminutive name, and then in 1943 legally switched his formal name to James Matsumoto Omura. Without dwelling on this jumbled identity in his diary, Omura does succeed in redressing it (that is, putting it to rest) by implicitly yet unequivocally representing himself as James Matsumoto Omura the diarist and Jimmie Omura the journalist.

An identity-related topic that Omura overtly scrutinizes to an extensive degree in his Redress Diary is that of family. In pre-diary years this primary institution had been far more abstract and shadowy than corporeal for him. For one thing, there was his father's nebulous parental origins. Then at age six Omura "lost" his mother (Harue Higashi Matsumoto) and his three younger siblings (two girls, Hanako and Taeko, and a boy, Chikara). When Omura's mother contracted a mysterious disease upon her fourth son's birth, it was decided to have her, plus the two girls and Chikara, go live with family members in Japan, and for Omura and his two older brothers, Yoshito and Kazushi (Casey), to remain with their father on Bainbridge Island. A few years later, eleven-year-old Yoshito was banished permanently by his father from the island because of a juvenile prank he perpetrated against a Caucasian farmer.[39] Also, upon reaching thirteen, Jimmie himself left home to work at a Ketchikan, Alaska, cannery. Thereafter, Omura's contact with his father was sporadic, with Yoshito practically nil, and with Casey largely episodic, being performed mostly through postal communication until terminated altogether in middle age. For the remainder of his life, Omura never again saw (or even corresponded by mail with) his mother, while the early death of Chikara foreclosed any possible future relationship with him.

Omura's difficult and time-consuming efforts between 1981 and 1994 to remedy, or redress, his "orphaned" status is registered intensely in his diary's pages. Therein we witness his resourcefulness, as one who had never set foot in Japan and knew so little Japanese, in ferreting out leads to his two sisters' whereabouts in Japan so as to make contact with them, to flesh out their past and present lives, and to forge a filial bond, however fragile, between them and him. Further, within Omura's late 1990 diary entries, we experience Omura solicitously "reuniting" in Seattle with his recently deceased, tubercular brother Casey, the sibling to whom he had been most connected emotionally and intellectually.[40] Omura now paid fraternal homage to Casey by settling his modest estate, exchanging remembrances of him with his surviving friends, and arranging for his ashes to be interred in the family sepulcher at the Nagasaki village of Katsusa, Japan. Lastly, in this same vein, we behold Omura's sojourning north from Seattle to Monroe, Washington, to convey news of Casey's death to Matsue Ohmura, the widow of Omura's oldest brother, Yoshito Ohmura, and their children, and in so doing to complete the circle of family redress.

Less poignant perhaps but certainly more powerful than the above varieties of personal redress embedded in Omura's diary was his quest for vocational reclamation as a journalist. It will be recalled that upon resigning his *Rocky Shimpo* editorship in mid-December 1947 to launch a horticultural career, he had regretted this decision because he counted himself among those people "who live, breathe and virtually eat journalism." Far more than a workaday journalist, Omura was a crusading, conscience-driven one, a member of the press who passionately committed himself to reform causes, especially when they involved matters of civil liberties, historical veracity, legal propriety, or personal and institutional rectitude.

For three postwar decades Omura had placed his perfervid vocational identity on hold while achieving professional and financial success as a landscape contractor.[41] But after testifying at the 1981 CWRIC hearings in Seattle and being encouraged by kindred progressive spirits (mostly within but also outside the Japanese American community) to use his pen, as in the distant past, to proclaim truth to oppressive power, Omura increasingly assumed the posture of a reborn journalist fired by the aim of redemption.

In some ways, performing such a role was harder than it had been for him during the World War II era. After all, he had now to contend with both a perilous health condition and writing skills that had become seriously eroded through abject neglect. Additionally, he was woefully out of touch with the general and scholarly literature being published in Asian American and Japanese American studies as well as community developments covered within Nikkei vernacular newspapers and Asian American periodicals.[42]

However, other forces were now at work that tipped the balance in his favor. Whereas before, he had been largely bereft of significant others with whom to share his perspective, he now was gaining a cadre of valued cohorts who empathized with his intents, respected his critical assessments, and applauded his signal contributions to a common cause of historical revision, community revitalization, and social justice. If in the past he had been castigated and even condemned as a pariah, he was now more often celebrated as a courageous patriot. Welcomed back to the pages of the Asian American/Japanese American press by a largely post-Nisei generation of steadily more intrepid editors, Omura not only reclaimed his standing as a journalist, but also garnered acclaim from his peers, as quintessentially exemplified by the lifetime achievement award the Asian American Journalists Association bestowed upon him in 1989. For Omura, this action, as reverberated in his diary, most definitely represented a formidable species of vocational redress.

As a plenitude of entries in his diary punctuate, Omura's long and profound alienation from affective membership within the Japanese American community was significantly reduced, if never altogether reversed, during the final thirteen years of his life. Simultaneously, he selectively reconnected with former Nikkei friends and associates and nurtured new relationships with still other compatible Nikkei. This development occurred not merely in the West Coast areas of Los Angeles, San Francisco, and Seattle, but within the midwestern region of Chicago as well, and even within his uneasily adopted province of Denver. Because so many of these people aided and comforted him and were his coparticipants in reinterpreting American and Japanese American life, Omura largely ceased feeling himself to be the proverbial "odd man out." Without extinguishing his singularity as a Nikkei resister, he was enfolded into the comparatively secure ranks of a community of resisters, the majority of whose affiliates were similarly forthright reformist Americans of Japanese ancestry. Membership in such a mostly caring and transparent community blunted the sharp pangs of Omura's estrangement and allowed him to concentrate his time and energy on redressing the wrongs that the security-obsessed U.S. government, in conjunction with the accommodating and opportunistic JACL leadership, had wreaked on his racial-ethnic community.

Omura's preoccupation with redressing the damage suffered by the Japanese American community pervades his diary entries. Whether he is discussing his review of books, such as Bill Hosokawa's *JACL in Quest of Justice* and Mike Masaoka's *They Call Me Moses Masaoka*; his assessment of an exhibition script, like the Smithsonian Institution's "A More Perfect Union"; his evaluation of a commissioned institutional inquiry, as with Deborah Lim's *The Lim Report*; or his reaction to a public commemoration, for example the erection of an honorific statue of Minoru Yasui in Denver's Sakura Square, the Nikkei community redress theme is always paramount.

What ties the above items together is Omura's overarching disdain for how the JACL's self-serving hegemonic version of Japanese American history sacrificed inconvenient truth on the altar of pragmatic invention. Using words as his weapon, Omura ripped away the authority of JACL spokespersons. Thus, in his review of the Hosokawa volume, which he first encountered in a Los Angeles hospital bed in 1982, Omura acidly inveighs, "There are errors in interpretation and misleading premises predicated either on lack of information or altered to suit the author's purpose." Likewise, Omura launches his Masaoka autobiography review essay, which was emphatically rebuffed by a legion of periodicals, with this merciless reproach: "History indeed is infinitely the poorer and literature thereby greatly diminished by publication of this fabricated account of the historic Japanese American episode of World War II."

While Omura's denunciation of Masaoka's "dramatic story of a Japanese American devoted to the welfare of his people in this country and in the land of his ancestry"[43] and the JACL story by Hosokawa (who also coauthored the Masaoka memoir) was exacerbated by mutual animosity, his reaction to these works transcended the provincial realm of personal relations. What outraged Omura (and his support community) was what such purportedly "historical" literature screened or cagily finessed—that the JACL, the nominal leaders of Japanese America, had collaborated with the U.S. government in the eviction and detention of their own racial-ethnic population. It also galled Omura and his "ilk" that the JACL leadership had so zealously embraced their collaboration as an action undertaken "willingly," "gladly," "cheerfully," and "happily." Such words of "gutless servility," as deemed by Omura, cut deeply into the sensibility of Nikkei and forever remained "a constant reminder of our humiliation [as a people] . . . deceived into being pied-pipered into concentration camps."[44] It was why he, as opposed to Masaoka and Hosokawa, never regarded monetary redress as something "cheapening" Nikkei but instead chose to champion the high-stakes brand of judicial redress pursued by the William Hohri-led National Council for Japanese American Redress. It was also why Omura scorned the JACL's expurgated version of the *Lim Report* as "another JACL hoax,"[45] and toiled so diligently to both sanction and refine Deborah Lim's unvarnished, highly critical inquiry into the JACL's controversial wartime conduct.

As for the Smithsonian exhibition and the Yasui statue, Omura's concern with them, as rendered in relatable diary entries, was prompted chiefly by matters of a constitutional nature.[46] Opened to the public on October 1, 1987, the exhibition "A More Perfect Union" for the bicentennial of the Constitution was fittingly subtitled "Japanese Americans and the U.S. Constitution." Nonetheless, the subject focus of this exhibition, to be curated by Tom Crouch, was confounded at its 1981 conception. This was because it was expected to be a conversion of an earlier exhibition that the Go for Broke veteran's organization had mounted at San Francisco's Presidio Army Museum on the heroic World War II exploits of the 442nd Regimental Combat Team.

In the spring of 1986, when Japanese American activists were expressing discontent that the Smithsonian's advisory committee was dominated by Nikkei and non-Nikkei veterans, one of the committee's few nonveteran members who shared the activists' concerns, Aiko Herzig Yoshinaga, distributed copies of the exhibit script to selected activists, including Omura, and requested them to send the committee feedback as to how the emphasis on the military experience might be best counterbalanced. Omura honored this request and in the following year provided Crouch with a detailed constructive critique of the script. Remonstrating that the script bordered on being propaganda, he took particular exception to its contention that "the

JACL had traditionally fought for the rights of Japanese Americans" and its avowal that the JACL had no other choice in 1942 but to cooperate with the government in the mass exclusion and incarceration of Japanese Americans. Omura also reminded Crouch that the JACL had opposed test cases challenging the constitutionality of wartime actions against Japanese Americans. Moreover, he compared this behavior against that of the Heart Mountain Fair Play draft resisters, who "demonstrated their dedication and fidelity to the fundamental principles enunciated in our sacred Constitution," and the twenty-one court-martialed Japanese American military resisters who "questioned confinement [by the U.S. government] of their family members in concentration camps while requiring them to submit to their supreme sacrifice in the field of battle."[47] Surely, concluded Omura, in a script so weighted with military achievements, room should be provided for stories like these and others that squared more directly with the exhibit's explicit constitutional theme. This situation for him was a glaring shortcoming that required redress.[48]

With respect to the Yasui statue proposed for installation in Denver's Sakura Square, Omura's discontent with such an action also revolved around constitutional matters. Yasui spent nine months in solitary confinement within Portland, Oregon's Multnomah Jail after having challenged unsuccessfully in the courts the constitutionality of his arrest for violating the dusk-to-dawn curfew that General John DeWitt, in the wake of Executive Order 9066 on February 19, 1942, had imposed upon Americans of Japanese ancestry living within designated military borders. His Supreme Court test case also earned for Yasui, a JACL member, the enmity of that organization's leadership, which not only resented such actions but also labeled Yasui a self-styled martyr and called into question his loyalty as a U.S. citizen.

Upon Yasui's release from jail, he was remanded to the Minidoka Relocation Center in Idaho, where he enjoyed the reputation as a champion of civil rights. Then, in early 1944, following the government's reactivation of the military draft for Nisei, Yasui became an ardent defender of this policy, telling Nisei in an open letter that they should "welcome" the draft and not try to evade this responsibility of citizenship. He also circulated a petition that committed Nisei to serve in the military in return for restoration of certain designated citizenship rights, though this restoration was tendered as a request rather than demanded as a precondition. "We feel," stated the petition, "that the cheerful and willing assumption of our obligations as American citizens reciprocally calls for the unequivocal restoration of our full citizenship rights."[49]

Shortly after having made this overture of reconciliation to the JACL, Yasui left Minidoka and, after a brief stay in Chicago, resettled in Denver, where he solidified his institutional allegiance. Omura believed that Yasui also developed a close working relationship in Denver with the offices of the WRA, the federal marshal, and the FBI. In the early spring of 1944 Yasui became angered by Omura's *Rocky Shimpo* series of incisive editorials that supported not only the Heart Mountain Fair Play Committee's doubting of the legality and decency of imposing the draft on imprisoned Nisei, but also its correlated intention to prepare a test case to determine this action's constitutionality. Yasui principally blamed Omura's editorials for the fact that a growing number of draft-age Heart Mountain Nisei had chosen not to report for their draft physicals and thus were confined in county jails throughout Wyoming to await their impending federal court trial in Cheyenne for draft evasion. This led an aggravated Yasui to pay a mid-April visit to Omura's newspaper office. On that occasion, as recalled by Omura four decades later, "Min Yasui said to me, 'I'm going to see you go to prison one way or another.'"[50]

In rapid succession thereafter, two related developments ensued: the *Rocky Shimpo*'s federal alien property custodian threatened to close the paper down if Omura was not at once removed as editor, leaving him no other choice but to resign, which he did on April 18; and Yasui, along with fellow JACLer Joe Grant Masaoka, in April and May, conducted interviews with Nisei "draft delinquents" at the Cheyenne County Jail. It was the U.S. attorney for the District of Wyoming, Carl Sackett, who approved the Yasui-Masaoka duo's request to undertake their mission. As the person who had drafted an indictment that a grand jury returned, sealed, on May 10, 1944, charging seven FPC leaders and Omura with "conspiring to counsel, aid, and abet" draft-age Heart Mountain men to evade conscription, Sackett hoped that he might secure "intelligence" to assist him in the successful prosecution of this case. Although the desired result did not materialize, the conduct of the interviews by Yasui and Masaoka and the report they sent to the WRA, JACL, and very possibly the U.S. attorney and the FBI left little doubt that "Joe Masaoka and Min Yasui of the JACL had lent a helping hand not just in fighting the spread of draft resistance in the internment camps, but also in jailing the resisters, their leaders, and a newspaperman who had dared to criticize their organization."[51]

Mulling over all this in his diary in 1990, only four years after the National JACL Committee on Redress's chair had been none other than Minoru Yasui, apparently hardened Omura's conviction that Yasui was decidedly not a Nikkei civil rights hero meriting a memorial statue in Sakura Square.

This perfervid belief also no doubt deepened Omura's resolve, and that of many of his allied community of resisters, that Japanese Americans warranted redress from the JACL for the damage that its leadership had irresponsibly inflicted upon them through its wartime decisions and actions. It was this sentiment, of course, that constituted the driving force for the construction by James Omura of both his Redress Diary[52] and the memoir, *Nisei Naysayer*, that you are about to read.

Nisei Naysayer

THE MEMOIR OF MILITANT
JAPANESE AMERICAN
JOURNALIST JIMMIE OMURA

James Matsumoto Omura

Prologue

What is it that they say about third sons? This is the story of a third son of an immigrant family of six children, stricken early in life by tragedy that tore it apart. He came from a peculiar separatist-style society, felt the lash of economic discrimination in childhood, and was constantly reminded of his limitations springing out of his racial heritage. His struggles will take the reader to the far north, even beyond the Aleutian Islands chain; to the parched Great Plains of North Dakota; a boxcar jaunt across the United States; the migrant trails of California; and his uncertain career in journalism on the Nisei vernacular press. Most Asian American readers will more likely be interested in his editorial bout with the Japanese American Citizens League (JACL), of which he is noted as its leading critic. He won the sobriquet "editorialist" for his World War II editorials denouncing the internal policies of his government under the administration of President Franklin D. Roosevelt and was credited by the U.S. War Department as "the single most influential voice in Japanese American camp resistance." Target of the U.S. Justice Department, he was brought to trial in Cheyenne, Wyoming, and acquitted by a federal court jury on November 1, 1944. The verdict appeared to be a vindication of his editorial goal, but not among his own ethnic community in Denver, Colorado. The harassment and vindictiveness of his own people drove him into seclusion from Asian America for over thirty years, and he emerged only in the fall of 1981 when recognized at his appearance at the Seattle, Washington, hearing of the Commission on Wartime Relocation and Internment of Civilians mandated by the Congress of the United States.

In the twilight of his life, he has won recognition in a variety of *Who's Who* volumes published in the United States, England, and other nations, but he never expected any similar recognition among his ethnic contemporaries. In 1992, marking the fiftieth anniversary of Executive Order 9066, the grassroots National Coalition for Redress/Reparations, Northern California Division, honored him at a candle-lighting ceremony in San Francisco, California, in the company of such prominent stalwarts of civil liberties as Wayne Millard Collins, Ernest Besig, and Walt and Millie Woodward of Bainbridge Island, Washington, and the American Friends Service Committee. It was his second recognition from the Asian American community. Earlier, in 1989, he was named the recipient of the first Lifetime Achievement Award of the Asian American Journalists Association. In the long reach of history, more lasting is his place in the chronicles of the time in such works as *Americans Betrayed*, by Morton Grodzins; *To Serve the Devil*, by Paul Jacobs and Saul Landau; *Years of Infamy*, by Michi Nishiura Weglyn; *The Big Aiiieeeee!* by Frank Chin and others; *Keeper of Concentration Camps*, by Richard Drinnon; *Concentration Camps USA*, by Roger Daniels; and *Heart Mountain*, by Douglas Nelson.

Countless literary works have appeared dealing with the historic Japanese American World War II episode. Early chroniclers depended upon the propaganda claims of the War Relocation Authority/JACL consortium, while some later writers have buttressed this ideology by repeating the JACL propaganda foisted upon its nondiscriminative public. The word "betrayal" was first heard on February 23, 1942, at the San Francisco hearings of the Tolan Congressional Committee. The most rabid present-day accuser is the playwright-writer Frank Chin. Is Japanese America existing in a faked history? One can hardly argue against Chin. It is this writer who claims the JACL had written its leading critic out of Japanese American history. The Bill Hosokawa books, commissioned by the JACL, make no mention of its leading nemesis. "If false fact takes root," declared Goethe in 1833, "if it is generally assumed, if it becomes a kind of credo admitting no doubt or scrutiny—that is the real evil, one which has endured through the centuries." This book which you will read shall attempt to correct, not all, but a small measure of that cockeyed history to which Japanese America has been exposed.

ONE

Bainbridge Island Beginnings, 1912–1923

Katsusa is an expanding city in modern Japan, but in the embryo years of the Meiji Restoration[1] it was a typical farming and fishing village on the southwestern tip of the historic Shimabara Peninsula. It is here in this Japanese municipality, which I may never see except in my imagination,[2] that my familial roots are planted and where the family sepulcher holds the remains of my parents, two brothers, and a sister.

This memoir begins somewhere in the prefecture of Nagasaki with a male child's birth, on July 3, 1871. The child was promised in adoption to Katsusa's headmaster. His wife, Saiyo, had favored him with daughters but no son to carry on the family name. That this adopted boy, or *yoshi*, came from a family of equal or higher status was unquestioned, for in the exceedingly class-conscious social order of the period, it was beneath any Japanese family's dignity to lower itself in the pecking order.

The headmaster's surname was Matsumoto. Saiyo also came from a long-established Matsumoto clan in the region. The Matsumotos named their adopted infant Tsurumatsu. In 1882 the headmaster passed away when Tsurumatsu was eleven years old. His dissatisfaction with his adopted home life surfaced shortly after the funeral when Tsurumatsu proclaimed that he was going to Nagasaki to seek work.

There is no record of Tsurumatsu's five-year sojourn in the ancient port city of Nagasaki. Furthermore, my father was never talkative about his past personal life. By the beginning of the 1920s, our family had moved to a beachfront bungalow on Eagle Harbor, near the Winslow ferry dock on Bainbridge Island, off the coast of Seattle, Washington. In a rare personal reminiscence, he explained to two of his sons, Kazushi and I, that he had scouted the vessels docked at Nagasaki and was aware that an American ship was preparing to sail on the morning tide. He then recounted his departure for America and the purpose of his decision.

> It was a very dark night. I waited until very late that night and then crept aboard quietly up the gangway and hid on deck. The ship was well out on the high seas when I was discovered by a deckhand. He took me to the captain. The captain was most understanding and assigned me as a "Captain's Boy."[3] I came to America as a stowaway on an American ship. I was sixteen years old. I would have to go into the army the next year. I didn't want to go into the military!

In common with peasant youths throughout the realm, Tsurumatsu had a strong dislike for military service. For six and two-third centuries of the shogunate, Japan had been served by professional samurai warriors. In 1873 the Meiji Restoration's Compulsory Military Conscription Ordinance went into effect. With the shogunate's abolishment in 1868, a citizen army replaced the prevailing institution of professional soldiers. Opposition came chiefly from the three hundred thousand-strong samurai class and the rural peasantry. In 1877 thirteen thousand samurai, led by the disenchanted Saigo Takamori of Satsuma, clashed with a Meiji force of sixty thousand at Kumamoto in the greatest rebellion of the early Meiji years. The samurai were defeated and Saigo committed suicide. The incident is known as the Seinen War. It was followed in 1879 by the Peasants' Uprising,[4] which was quickly doused. Although this development did not result in the subjugation of the peasantry, many peasant youths went abroad—particularly to the frontier west of the United States—to evade military service.[5] Tsurumatsu was among this group's vanguard.

The details of Tsurumatsu's journey to America are unfamiliar, except that the American ship called at the Hawaiian port of Honolulu. He reached mainland America through the port of San Francisco, the West Coast's only available port of that period. Tsurumatsu remembered Pacific Street and the wild goings-on in the Barbary Coast, but San Francisco was not a stop for long. At the time of his arrival, a restaurateur named Charles Tokujiro Sasaki was gathering a group of twenty-four Japanese for the purpose of opening an eatery in Seattle. Tsurumatsu joined the Sasaki troupe, and in that year, after Sasaki had opened the Lemon Cafe on the waterfront boulevard of Western Avenue, Tsurumatsu served a stint there as fry cook.

Seattle was simply a small village on the western shores of Washington Territory. Its 1880 U.S. Census count stood at 3,533. No transcontinental railroads linked the town, while the first steamship service to the Pacific Northwest was inaugurated in 1881 by the Kobe (Japan) to Vancouver (British Columbia) line. But Seattle was on the verge of phenomenal growth. By 1890 its population had increased to 43,825. In the year before Tsurumatsu's arrival, the immigrant Japanese in the Puget Sound areas were almost all fugitives of cargo boats. The number residing in Japantown was nine, and even with the addition of Sasaki and his twenty-four helpers the number was less than forty. The total number of immigrant Japanese in the entire United States in 1887 was recorded at 1,352, half of whom were students.[i] Thus, history is the poorer for the sparseness of information available about Tsurumatsu's first nineteen-year sojourn in the Pacific Northwest that preceded the Gentlemen's Agreement of 1907.[6]

Upon his arrival in the United States Tsurumatsu acquired the name "Omura" and was widely known by that name. Within the white community, his given name became Anglicized to "Tommy." Even though Tommy maintained his legal surname, during my youth on Bainbridge Island I never heard my father addressed other than by the Omura surname. It is my belief that Omura might well have been his birth family name prior to his adoption.

Only days before the 1942 military eviction of Japanese from Bainbridge Island, my eldest brother, Yoshito, legally changed his name to Ohmura, spelling his name with an *h* in accordance with its correct pronunciation. "Everyone called your father Omura-san," a transplanted Bainbridge Islander in the Colorado city of Denver declared to me in 1988. I permanently assumed the Omura surname in 1931 and became quite well known as Jimmie Omura because of my occupation as writer and editor of various vernacular newspapers in California.[ii] Two days before his eightieth birthday,

---

i Inazo Nitobe, *The Intercourse between the United States and Japan: A Historical Sketch* (Baltimore: Johns Hopkins Press, 1891), 167–68.

ii The legalization of Omura as my surname was effected in 1943 when I became concerned over the witch-hunting activities of the Japanese American Citizens League (JACL). My concern was not misplaced. Within two months, the U.S. attorney undertook a wide-ranging investigation of my past, owing to a JACL-filed complaint. [Ed. See petition of Utaka Matsumoto and Fumiko Okuma for change of names to James Matsumoto Omura and Caryl Fumiko Omura, filed as Civil Action No. A 37923 in District Court City & County of Denver, Colo., Div. 3, September 9, 1943, in James M. Omura Papers, Green Library, Stanford University.]

my second older brother, Kazushi (aka "Casey") died in Seattle.[7] Thereafter, a legal paper came to light among his documents addressed to our father and dated January 13, 1915. The document referred to Tommy O'Muir, the surname being an Anglicized corruption.[8]

My father had minimal education and none in English when he came to the United States. His later facility in English indicates his having attended some type of classroom while he lived in Seattle. The most likely possibility is a trade school such as Edison High School.[9] Tommy was a jack-of-all-trades but his principal occupation was that of a builder and carpenter. He could build a house from scratch and outfit it with electrical components and plumbing. He possessed other skills, such as in oceanography and engineering and his ability to decipher architectural drawings. He owned a two-sleeper launch that he used for navigating around the Puget Sound on work assignments and for fishing expeditions. He is known to have traversed the Strait of Juan de Fuca and down the Pacific coastline of Washington as far south as at least Grays Harbor.

No information has been found to indicate when and how Tommy arrived on Bainbridge Island. The weather on the island is very similar to conditions at Katsusa, with the exception of the monsoons, and it is probable that familiarity with the climate and panorama drew him to the island. Bainbridge Island's earliest immigrant Japanese residents used the portal of Port Blakely, but although my father was no stranger to Port Blakely or its shifting millworkers, his name does not appear in the Port Blakely Mill Company records. A journeyman butcher when he went to Winslow,[10] he practiced that profession for at least three years after his 1907 marriage and his subsequent employment as a foreman at the Hall Brothers Winslow Marine Shipbuilding and Drydock Company.[11]

Twelve miles long and four miles wide, Bainbridge Island lies eight nautical miles due west of the port of Seattle. Winslow, bordering Eagle Harbor, is the island's principal community. Now primarily a bedroom community for commuters of the Queen City, the island also serves as a summer home for wealthy entrepreneurs and corporation executives, and as a tourist haven. Much of the island is canopied with trees, both deciduous and evergreen. Bainbridge Island also experiences a great deal of rainfall as it is adjacent to the rain forests of the Olympic Mountains. Winslow lies in the heart of perhaps the nation's most aesthetic and tasteful panoramic wonderland, where the pristine nature of the Puget Sound Basin has been preserved from helter-skelter building. The view is breathtaking, with the majestic, snow-covered Mount Rainier rising sentinel-like behind the city of Seattle, the rambling range of the Olympics to the west, and in the distant north the hulking mound of Mount Baker near the Canadian border visible on clear days. Moreover, Bainbridge is economically the most significant of the many islands dotting the Puget Sound waterway.

The first white men seen on the island were Lieutenant Charles Wilkes (1798–1877) and members of his 1841 expedition, which was commissioned by the Congress of the United States to learn more about the disputed Oregon Territory. The Lewis and Clark Expedition had surveyed the land portion and Wilkes was dispatched to seek aquatic information. Flora and fauna were ordered to be collected wherever Wilkes made land, and it was for that purpose that he anchored his ship on the southernmost harbor of the island. He named the site Port Blakely and the second harbor, three miles north, Eagle Harbor. The island was named Bainbridge in honor of a naval hero of the War of 1812, Captain William Bainbridge (1774–1833). It is not difficult to understand Wilkes's rationale in conferring the name Eagle Harbor, because of the large number of eagles that inhabited the harbor.[12]

In 1854 a British naval expedition, headed by the explorer Captain George Vancouver (1757–98), arrived in the same Port Blakely Harbor at which Wilkes had made his original stop. Accompanied by an armed tender, Vancouver anchored his sloop in the shadows of Restoration Point[13] at the mouth of the harbor. There he found the island populated by a Salish native tribe called the Suquamish. Mistaking their hunting huts as villages, he demonstrated disdain for their dwellings. Chief of the southern tribe was Sealth and the northern chief was Kitsap, a leader of the warrior tribe. Sealth was intimidated by the British show of arms and chose to cooperate. Kitsap wanted to fight. Under tribal law, autonomy for the decision rested with Chief Sealth because of Captain Vancouver's site of landing on the island. Chief Sealth signed the unjust Treaty of Point Elliott,[14] which turned over the island to the British. The island had served as a homeland for the Salish tribe for as long as five thousand years. Under the treaty negotiated by Vancouver, the native people were compelled to begin an exodus to a site on the eastern Cascades. The gunboat intimidation of Captain Vancouver was a mere echo of Commodore Matthew C. Perry's subjugation of Tokugawa Japan, almost in the same year.[15] Although Port Blakely became a key logging center, loggers and homesteaders had already penetrated this wooded island around Madison Bay prior to Vancouver's arrival.

In speaking of Bainbridge Island, it would be impossible not to mention Port Blakely. Even though Port Blakely was long past its glory days when I was born, it remained the principal subject of conversations. The first Japanese on the island were recorded by the Kitsap County Census of 1883[16] as two cargo boat escapees discovered at the Port Blakely Mill Company. Around the turn of the century, a Japanese village was established on the harbor's south side across from the mill. It became the island's only self-contained community of minority people. Within its perimeter were a dance hall, theater, silent movie house, and a plethora of commercial establishments, including an ice cream parlor, a poolroom, a barbershop, a jeweler, a watch-repair shop, a laundry, a grocery, a hardware shop, and a community bathhouse, or *furoya*.

The Bainbridge Japanese village, at its peak, hosted upwards of eight hundred immigrant Japanese. The majority of them used Port Blakely as a stepping stone to greater economic prospects in California and the vast inland empire to the east, and for work in the Pacific Northwest. The mill itself employed three hundred Japanese at any given time, and most of these worked just long enough to build a nest egg for more lucrative prospects.

Port Blakely's economic importance got a shot in the arm in 1863 when a retired British naval captain named William Renton (1818–91) relocated his sawmill to the harbor from Port Orchard on the Olympic Peninsula, where huge cargo boats were finding difficulty in maneuverability. Renton had first established his sawmill at Alki Point in what was later to become West Seattle. He was compelled to move because of the high wind factor.

William Renton was born in the sawmill town of Acadie in what is now known as Nova Scotia. Members of his family were confirmed believers in the sixteenth-century British ideology of the dominance of white people over their darker-skinned counterparts.

The dominant groups on Bainbridge Island were people of British, Scandinavian, and Euro-American nationalities. Thus, Renton's devotion to Anglophilism led to the perpetuation of the Elizabethan ideology, which in 1944 was well delineated by the then-prominent U.S. historians Charles and Mary Beard.

> England had been torn by religious controversies and the intrigues of
> Europe that resulted in constant warfare when high-spirited Queen

Elizabeth [I] rose to power in 1558. Much versed in the secular learning of the Renaissance, she was determined that her dominion would be Protestant under the Church of England. She sponsored the concept of exploitations of competing powers, acquisition of possessions and primacy in business dealings. Thus was born the Elizabethan Age of arrogance and elitism.[iii]

Although William Renton appears not to have been actively involved in racist matters, he nevertheless instituted the concept of racial enclaves in housing and the policy of segregated workplaces in his mill. This had a chilling effect on the attitudes of the white settlers toward nonwhites on the island. The native Suquamish were relegated furthest from the mill on Restoration Point, and the twenty-five native Hawaiians were next. The Chinese, the earliest of Asians to arrive, gained a primary site in the north flatland, which had to be circumnavigated by the favored white workers who resided in the highland. The later-arriving Japanese were given the south shore as a site.

Direct racial agitation appears not to have surfaced during the Renton stewardship, which ended in 1891 with his death. Between 1893 and 1903, when the Port Blakely Mill Company was managed by Renton's nephews, John and James Campbell, its payroll records began carrying the pejorative "Jap." The lowest on the employee totem pole were the Japanese, except for the East Indies recruits. This racist attitude, which had begun in the Campbell regime, worsened and intensified and actually turned hostile in 1903 under the mill's third and last management. Subheadings in the payroll books for the period 1905–7 were divided into "WHITE, JAP and TOTAL." Other nonwhites were listed under the "WHITE" heading.

Management's callous attitude toward the Japanese was apparent in fatal accident matters. Andrew Mason Prouty has reported the management of Skinner and Eddy as saying, "Serves him damn well right!" in the fatal accident of a Japanese immigrant worker.[iv] Nor did other injured immigrant Japanese workers receive even the common courtesy of being listed by name on the company books. They were in fact designated by numbers, such as "Jap #1054, Jap #1117, etc."

The institution of segregation started by William Renton in 1863 infused the island population with an aura of race prejudice somewhat similar to the treatment accorded Negroes in the South. Further reinforcement was drawn

iii Charles A. Beard and Mary R. Beard, *The Beards' Basic History of the United States* (Garden City, NJ: Doubleday, Doran, 1944), 4–5.
iv Andrew Mason Prouty, "Logging with Steam in the Pacific Northwest: The Men, the Camps, and the Accidents, 1885–1918" (master's thesis, University of Washington, 1973), [n.p.].

from the "Yellow Peril" incidents propagated in California by racist bigots and disseminated through literature. Anglo children reacted to the opinions of their elders and engaged in stoning incidents. Stoning of the Japanese was a favorite pastime of white children in the nearby streets of Seattle.

Reflecting on his school days experience in Port Blakely, a former Japanese student observed, "When I went to school, the white students threw stones, saying 'Here comes a Jap again.'"[v] An eyewitness reports that women domestics were also stoned.[vi] The tempo of hostilities against people of Japanese origin increased with the sense of fear generated by Japan's stunning victory in the Russo-Japanese War of 1904–5. White supremacy had suffered a fatal setback and reprisals were heaped on Japanese millworkers.

By 1895 the Port Blakely mill had reached its peak of production and proudly proclaimed itself to the lumbering industry as the "biggest sawmill in the world." Island lumber was being shipped around the Pacific Rim, as far south as the southern tip of Chile, the islands of the South Seas, Australia, and the Orient. When rail transportation became available, mill products were also shipped to Colorado and Kansas.

The Port Blakely millworks was hit by its second disastrous fire in 1907. It was rebuilt in smaller increments. By then, large commercial-sized trees were near exhaustion and operation was on the decline. It ceased operation in 1924 and the logging era on Bainbridge Island came to an end. Workers made an exodus to other regions. Port Blakely's economic importance dwindled and today it is a quiet little suburban town.

Winslow came to the fore as an economic force after the deterioration of Port Blakely when an immigrant Japanese farmer named Shinichi Moritani successfully experimented with strawberry culture out at the Point, where Eagle Harbor doglegs to the right. The discovery gave birth to a new economy on Bainbridge Island. Six agricultural sites were hewed out the following year by the immigrant Japanese on the logged-off, littered land just north of the town at Winslow Heights. Stumps, large stones, and a myriad of underbrush and noncommercial trees were dynamited and removed with horsepower and human sinew. The land was leased from the Newly Land Company at very economical rates because of its primitive state. The berry

---

v As quoted in Kazuo Ito, *Issei: A History of Japanese Immigrants in North America* (Seattle: Japanese Community Service, 1973), 635–36.

vi Sam Nakao, interviewed by Stefan Akio Tanaka, July 14, 1975, as cited in Stefan Akio Tanaka, "The Nikkei on Bainbridge Island, 1883–1942: A Study of Migration and Community Development" (master's thesis, University of Washington, 1977), 95.

plants took a liking to the slightly acidic and sandy soil and thrived. The production that came from this strawberry culture replaced the fading lumber industry as the chief economic factor on the island.[vii]

The year 1907 is remembered as a crisis year for the immigrant Japanese. Rumors ran rampant throughout the Far West about a Chinese-type exclusion[17] against the Japanese. Immigrants by the thousands flocked to Far West port cities, bombarding ships for passage back to their homeland to secure spouses. My father by this time had become a journeyman butcher at Winslow Meat Shop. He wrote to his adopted mother, Saiyo, with a request to arrange a *baishakunin*, or go-between, marriage, a common practice in Japanese culture. Saiyo selected an uncommon twenty-two-year-old maiden in Nagasaki, the elder daughter of a milk processor. Her name was Harue and she was slender and taller in stature than most Japanese women. The couple was married in Katsusa on October 15, 1907. Tommy was thirteen years her senior and about six inches shorter in height. Harue was demure, learned, quiet, and even-tempered. They spent almost a year in their homeland and Tommy brought his bride to America in the fall of 1908. They made their home in Winslow, where Tommy continued his work at the Winslow meat market. The Root-Takahira negotiation, commonly known as the Gentlemen's Agreement, was signed in 1908 and it capped the panic of the immigrant Japanese. The terms restricted the immigration of Japanese laborers and produced the phenomenon known as the "Picture Bride Era."[18]

I was born the third son of Tommy Tsurumatsu and Harue Matsumoto. My given name was Utaka but the white community called me "Shola." By the time of my birth, my father was a foreman at the Winslow Shipbuilding and Drydock Company. My birth occurred on November 27, 1912,[19] in the doctor's combination office and residence, the first of our family to be attended by a licensed physician and the first to be born outside the home. In an era of doctor shortage in the Far West, that was something of a distinction and was due to the prominence and popularity of my father in the community. The doctor noted the time of birth exactly at 10 p.m. It was reported later that a furious storm raged outside and rain pelted down in "bucketfuls." Teased in my youth as a storm child, it was direly predicted that I would find rough sledding in the road of life. I have no doubt about the storm and deluge for late November being the start of the elemental

---

vii See Tanaka, "Nikkei on Bainbridge Island," 103–7.

fury that roils out of the turbulent North Pacific and hammers the homes of the Puget Sound Basin. Although at the time of the storm-child characterization I responded to the archaic caricature as an old wives' tale, I am less certain in my declining years, having weathered a difficult and somewhat exasperating experience in life.

In looking down the road of life I have traveled and all the tribulations that I have encountered, the happiest moments of my life were the six years of the childhood I spent in the big house on the bluff and the freedom we enjoyed as children wandering the expansiveness of ten fenced acres. Even though they were carefree days, this period was more memorable for it was the only time that our family was all together.

The house on the bluff was a large, two-story frame. The kitchen ran the length of the house and beneath it was a quarter-basement-type cellar. It had a spacious living room, around which was a master bedroom, plus two others. The only modern amenity lacking was a telephone, which was compensated for by a courier service three times weekly. Mother fired up the wood fireplace but the house was heated and never cold. My two brothers and I spent most of our indoor hours upstairs where we had our beds and study desks. When Father had visitors, which was often, the kitchen was his personal province.

The chief features of the ten-acre site were a huge, towering hay barn and an orchard of about forty fruit trees. Most of the trees were apples of two varieties, Gravenstein and McIntosh. In addition, it included a pair of plum, pear, and Royal Ann cherries, and a lone sour cherry tree. Mainly the area was sown in alfalfa and timothy, which was allowed to go fallow. Mint and herbs grew behind the big house and Mother established a small vegetable garden on the upper slope of the bluff. The house looked out on the inland crescent of Eagle Harbor. Located on the backwater harbor site, it was an isolated location. The closest house was to the west across a deep gulch that formed our boundary line. The only other house was a small bungalow at the head of our outlet road, a quarter of a mile away. To the north and the east were barbwire-fenced pasture lands. The harbor was to the south.

Despite the isolated nature of the site, I never felt lonely. I had no outside children to play with but I did have two older brothers and, as time passed, two younger sisters and a baby brother. Our favorite spot was down by the boathouse. I never understood that attraction, for none of us took to the water (even though we had no fear of it). The boathouse itself contained only a rowboat. Father had his launch anchored forty feet inside the harbor to account for the change of tides.

The boathouse was the scene of a near tragedy. It was an Indian Summer noontime in late October. I was not quite four years old. Mother called us for lunch. I lifted my right foot to enter the kitchen, the stoop being a little high for my small limbs. Then a strange thing happened and froze my foot in midair. A feeling overcame me of something like doom pervading the household. The house was strangely quiet and the thought came to me that it was like a tomb. I sat down beside my brother Kazushi but couldn't shake off a feeling of disaster. I remember staring into the spacious living room and noticing all the windows and doors were open for airing the house. I noticed, too, the white curtains being ruffled by a gentle breeze. I looked at my brother but he appeared unconcerned. Mother was cutting vegetables on the far north counter, presumably preparing them for the evening meal. I was troubled and looked again into the living room, at Mother, and thought of calling my brother's attention to this strange feeling that possessed me, but gave up when I saw that he was digging into his roast beef sandwich voraciously. It was when I hastened to catch up that the spell broke.

We went back to our play down by the boathouse. I was in the lead, and two-thirds of the way down I suddenly spied our sister lying face up in the harbor waters.

"Look!" I said, pointing, "Hanako's drowned."

"Watch her!" my brother said sharply. "I'll go and get Mother."

It seemed a long time before Mother and my brother came and I felt I couldn't just stand and watch. Hanako lay so still in the water that I was convinced she had drowned. The wavelets splashed against her left cheek and a trickle seeped into her lower nostril. I thought of trying to lift her out of the water but a wee voice inside me cautioned: "What if I should try and fail. Would I be doing greater damage?" My sister was a large girl and I was not yet four.

Then Mother came. She picked up a seven-foot piece of lumber on the bank and used it to pole Hanako to the bank. Then with one scoop, she lifted her out, turned, and immediately started up the bluff path. We trailed uncertainly behind and I thought Mother was taking our sister to the house. But Mother went right past the kitchen door and up the back pathway. By this time, we had fallen a good twenty feet behind her. When we were five feet from the double aluminum gate that opened to the outlet road, Mother tossed a command over her left shoulder.

"Stay there!" she said.

We reached the gate and watched. I marveled at Mother, never changing her grip, never slackening her pace carrying Hanako up the outlet road. She was headed to a bungalow at the top of that road. It was a quarter of a mile from the harbor to the bungalow. I saw the screen door open, a brief conversation, then Mother entered. We stayed at that aluminum gate until gloom drove us indoors, where we continued our vigil in the kitchen, facing the door and watching the electric clock above.

It was almost six-thirty when the door flung open. The moment Mother saw us waiting, she flashed a broad smile.

"Hanako will be all right!" she announced.

"I came home to give you your dinner. I'm going back to bring your sister home. We'll return at nine o'clock."

She left while we were eating. Nine o'clock came and went. When the clock reached ten, I began to worry. Then, at eleven, I was certain that something was wrong, a relapse of some sort. It was agonizing waiting with a multitude of doubts. Then the door flew open at 11:25. Mother flashed her smile.

"Hanako is right behind me," she said.

The door was left wide open. The night was pitch-black. One minute passed, two, three, four, and then Hanako made her appearance. She entered the house with a sheepish grin on her face. We were relieved. The hour was late and way past our bedtime. We slept the sleep of the unconcerned. Hanako had never before ventured down by the harbor. Thereafter, none of our sisters ever left the bluff.

Mother was not known to speak ill of anyone. So it was a rare occasion when she mentioned the landlord. "I don't like him," she said. She described him as a short person with a handlebar moustache and pointed whiskers. His eyebrows were bushy and his eyes piercing. He was bent over and walked with the aid of a cane.

"He is an *oni*, a devil,"[20] Mother said. "He is not a good man," she continued. "His eyes are fierce and they glare into you. I don't like him; I'm afraid of him."

Mother called the landlord "Mr. Cougar," but it was probably more correctly Mr. Krueger. Cougar was all right with us because we could identify it with the jungle animal. We had never seen a live *oni* and we were intrigued to get a peek at one. We romped through the tall, dry grass with Rover to the western fence to look across the gulch at the shrub-covered cottage of the landlord. He seemed not to be about and we headed back. On our way back, I chanced to step on a board hidden by the tall alfalfa grass. I looked down and was horrified to see a nail protruding through my right foot.

"Kazushi, come here," I yelled. "I stepped on a nail."

"I'll get Mother," he said, taking a quick look.

Mother knelt down and ordered me to lift my foot. Then, with one yank, she pulled the board free. The nail had gone through the flesh part of my foot and it had not bled. The wound was bathed in a solution and bandaged heavily. "Don't walk on it," she cautioned. The healing was quick but the incident brought an end to my barefoot days. It reminded me of John Green-leaf Whittier (1807–92), the nineteenth-century American poet. "From my heart I give thee joy, I was once a barefoot boy!"[21]

On hot summer afternoons, Mother would gather us on the veranda where we would sip cool drinks, flavored with mint, and relax like pluto-crats from the heat of the day. The gulls would be playing over the harbor water and the bald eagles climbing high into the golden firmament. Once, an eagle flushed from the adjacent field, clutching in his claws a frightened young hare. My eyes met with that of the young rabbit and a wish came over me that I could rush to its rescue. Eagles were common over the har-bor, and one afternoon one flew across the harbor, dangling a large, listless snake at least six feet long.

Father was so busy that we seldom saw him around the house. He was not only a foreman at the shipyard; because of his facility in English he also functioned as a liaison between the white community and the immigrant Japanese of the island. Whenever he was home in the evenings and week-ends, he would usually be lured away by visitors of both races. The paternal situation deteriorated to such an extent that he gradually became a figure-head rather than a real father. It was our custom to gather for a light snack before bedtime. Mother usually regaled us with some happenings of the day or entertained us with a brief anecdote. One particular night, she was strangely silent, sitting beside me with a teacup cradled in her two hands and her elbows on the table. I felt discomfited by her silence, and the worry that was in my mind poured forth.

"Why doesn't Father stay home at nights?" I asked.

"Your father is a big man," Mother replied. "He's a foreman at the ship-yard. He is a very busy man. People ask for his help, both white people and our people. He is a very busy man."

One late afternoon, Mother hurried us through dinner and shooed us into the spacious parlor, explaining that Father was having VIP visitors. She stirred up the fire in the fireplace, laid down a mat by the stairwell, and dropped two large, fluffy, decorative cushions on the floor. With a Japanese paperback in hand, she sat down with her back to the stairwell. We clustered around her. My attention was more on what was happening in the closed kitchen than on Mother's translation. The clump of hobnailed boots came clearly, and hearty greetings announced the arrivals. Then, everything was quiet. After a while, a thin voice was raised in song, interspersed with hearty comments and genial laughter.

"What are they doing?" I asked.

"Your father and his friends are getting drunk," Mother replied.

"Who are they?" I inquired.

"The mayor, the town bookkeeper, the doctor, the sheriff . . . " and her voice trailed off.

It was the next evening when this event impacted on my mind. Loud voices trickled upstairs from the kitchen. "Wonder what's happening," I said to my brother Kazushi. "Guess I'll go down to see." I found Mother sitting quietly on a straight-back chair in the middle of the kitchen. Near the cellar steps was a tall Anglo man and he was talking across the room to another man sitting on the open stoop. Upon my entering, the tall Anglo moved across to his companion and continued the conversation in lowered tones. I knelt down beside my mother's right knee.

"You kids stay out of the way," the tall Anglo warned just as he plunged down into the cellar. It was then that I became aware of Kazushi, who had followed me and was kneeling at Mother's left knee.

"Who are these men?" I asked.

"Sheriff's men," Mother responded.

"What do they want?" I continued.

"They're looking for your father's still," Mother declared.

The sheriff's men eventually departed empty-handed. What rankled inside me was the sheriff participating in the drinking bout the night before and then raiding our household. I didn't think this was according to Hoyle.

His daughter was in the same class at Winslow Public School, and I was leery about her presence and avoided her proximity.

With Father tied up in his private affairs, Mother became the central focus of our childhood lives. She was our source of entertainment and information. We were fascinated with the stories she told, the folklore of ancient Japan, some of which she would ad lib and others take from Japanese paperbacks and interpret for our benefit in English. She kept us enthralled with "Momotarō,"[22] "Kitsune,"[23] the story of the forty-seven *ronin*,[24] and many others. It was through these translations that I gathered some words and phrases of the Japanese idiom. These I called "street talk" of the common folks. I probably understood more than what I spoke, for unless used frequently, it becomes difficult to articulate any language.

One evening in 1917, Mother transfixed us with an *obake*,[25] or ghost thriller. It was about a pretty Japanese woman who entered a roadhouse and transformed herself into a ferocious tiger. Then, as a tiger, she would pounce on passersby and tear them apart. When the deed was done, she would assume her human self and depart from the roadhouse none the wiser. This *obake* story was merely a prelude to the "Weeping Willow Tree" that stood at the southeast corner of our ten-acre plot.

"That tree is haunted!" Mother declared.

"When the moon is full, a ghost climbs down from the tree and walks around the yard."[26]

I was so intrigued about the Weeping Willow Tree that the next morning after breakfast I went alone to the edge of the bluff and made a searching scrutiny of the tree. The drooping nature of the branches reminded me about the "Western Witch" Mother had also told us about, with scraggly, unkempt hair. In the bright sunlight, it otherwise looked innocent enough. I noticed that the roots of the willow tree stretched into the harbor waters and a good portion of it was exposed.

The harbor path ran right beside the Weeping Willow Tree, and it was the route the courier used to bring messages for Father. The courier was a slender man of small stature with a genial sort of personality. He always gripped an unlighted corncob pipe between his teeth. He favored a Scottish-style cap. He would customarily hail us with a cheery greeting as he passed. Then, on his return, he would fill his corncob pipe, light it, and puff leisurely away on it while he watched our play for twenty minutes or so. His eyes would have a friendly glint and an amused smile crinkled his face. We would take the opportunity of his presence to chat with him of things in general.

"Find a rubber!" my brother Kazushi shouted out suddenly.

"I see one," I answered, pointing toward the outer bulkhead, having spotted what appeared like a deflated balloon bobbing in the waters.

"No, no!" the courier said sharply. "Don't touch it; it's dirty. Don't ever touch it."

The sharpness of the courier's tone drained all the fun in my system. I felt like I had committed a mortal sin. I was so embarrassed and felt ashamed. I wanted to deflect the sting by changing the subject.

"Is that tree haunted?" I asked, nodding toward the Weeping Willow Tree. The courier turned and after a long scrutiny finally replied, "Yes, that tree is haunted!"

His voice was grave and his speech was solemn. Then he launched into an extraordinary tale. He said an incident happened a very long time ago when the community was called Madrone. There was a bad man, he said. He committed an unforgivable sin out at the Point, so named because Eagle Harbor doglegs to the right down to the Weeping Willow Tree before making a sweeping inland crescent back toward its mouth. Actually, the courier stated the crime, but time has erased it from my memory.

"The whole town of Madrone chased this man," the courier continued. "They caught up with him in the field above." He nodded his head in the direction of the shortcut path. "Someone had the foresight to bring along a rope. They dragged the man down to that tree and strung him up. Ever since, that tree has been haunted!"

The courier had confirmed what Mother had said.

Bainbridge Island, where I was born in 1912, was far from a racial utopia. Discrimination and race intolerance were strongly rooted in the predominantly Scandinavian, British, and old-line Yankee-stock island residents. By the time of my birth, much of the hostility and antagonism toward people of Japanese descent had gone underground and the two races existed in a peculiar separation-style society with minimal contacts, and hardly any social communications and fraternization took place. Tolerance was thinly veiled, surface deep, and intolerance was always ready to erupt given a reasonable excuse.

I had no outside playmates in childhood, and I did endure jeers and name-calling from afar. On a summer morning in 1917, for example, I was down on the beach skipping pebbles on the harbor surface with my brothers when our play was interrupted.

"Skibbees, skibbees, skibbees,"[27] came the jeers.

The tormentors were a Mutt and Jeff combo, and the insult was being shouted from the docks of the new strawberry cannery. Then the pair disappeared. It was the first time I had heard the expression but knew it was meant derogatorily by the sound of the boys' voices. Just as I was beginning to think the two boys had gone away, they returned. They were armed with stones that they threw in our direction between more shouts of "skibbees, skibbees, skibbees."[viii] My two brothers responded in kind, adding choice words of their own. The stones all fell far short of their targets as the distance was more than three hundred feet.

Ten days later an encore occurred. The tide was up and we were playing as usual around the floating boathouse. This time the offending duo came armed with a slingshot and a catapult sling similar to the type with which David slew the giant Philistine, Goliath.[28] The pebbles began to fall twenty feet from us and we began a slow retreat up the slope. Two-thirds of the way up, I felt a gentle tap on my forehead. The ground was searched by my brother Kazushi and he concluded that it was a fragment that had chipped off in flight and sailed. After a council of war, we considered arming ourselves likewise but gave up the notion because of the possibility of injury. As events turned out, the tormentors did not return again.

The atmosphere in our home was as American as it could be. It would have been hard to find any evidence of Orientalism in our home, except for a glass cabinet in the southeast corner of the parlor displaying costumed miniature dolls. These were taken out each year to observe Boy's and Girl's Days.[29] The language of our household was English. We did not jabber in Japanese, largely because we didn't know it and had no opportunity to apply it even if we did. Our household was different from other immigrant households in another respect. Very seldom were angry words uttered inside our

---

viii Though the insults sounded like "skibbees," the tormentors may well have been shouting "skivvies." In a book written by a JACL propagandist, it is claimed that no such word as "skibbees" exists in either English or Japanese. With due apology to this worthy, it should be pointed out that there are words and slang signifying the same type of perversion in both languages. The most probable is the British slang "skivvy," which was used to denigrate female servants, largely scullery maids and indentured servants, in old English Manor days. In Japanese, the word *sukebei* means lascivious, lewd, and lecherous.

home. Mother deserves a great deal of credit for maintaining a principled household, and because of our respect and affection for her we avoided causing her any displeasure.

This does not mean that we were perfect little angels. We did incur two incidents outside. When we refused to allow our sisters to participate on the swing, they appealed to their mother.

"You must all play together nicely," she rebuked us in her quiet, firm manner. "You don't have anyone else to play with."

Another incident was much more severe. We got involved in an argument and our arms were flailing in the air. Father was home doing his bookwork.

"I can't do my bookwork," he complained, "with all that noise. You boys will have to quiet down."

He then caught sight of Kazushi. He was leaning across Rover's doghouse and blood was oozing from his nose. I didn't have the faintest idea how that had happened, but it had been an accident.

"Who's responsible for that!" Father demanded. He was now angry.

No one answered.

"Unless the guilty one is pointed out, I'll pick one of you," he threatened.

Still no answer.

"Yoshito, go to the woodshed!" he ordered. Yoshito obeyed. "I don't want you boys fighting," he said as he followed Yoshito.

The woodshed meant a barber strop on one's behind. The strop was hung on a post. The yelps and cries of Yoshito soon rent the air. The discipline had a strong effect on me. I was braced against the swing's A-frame and winced with each yelp of my brother. We had not been fighting and I could not comprehend the justice of this punishment. I understood Kazushi's reticence, for in that period an unspoken taboo on squealing prevailed. This punishment had a lasting psychological effect on me and led to my gradual withdrawal from my father.

Our family had its share of childhood diseases. My brothers came down with the chickenpox and smallpox and all of my siblings wound up with measles. I escaped all of that but often had high fever and the common cold. One afternoon I came up from the boathouse to find Dr. Shepard[30] tacking a large white sign on the kitchen door.

"What's that?" I asked.

"Quarantine!" the doctor said.

"What does it say?" I inquired.

"This sign means no one can enter and you folks can't get out," he said.

Dr. Shepard also attended to Mother when she came down with child-birth disease. The doctor and the courier were the only white persons with whom I had any degree of communication during my childhood.

Mother took us outside of our boundary only twice: to a valley in Port Blakely to harvest shiitake, or large, meaty, black and dark brown mushrooms favored in Japanese cooking; and to Manitou Beach to dig for clams. Otherwise, the lack of land transportation inhibited our going anywhere on the island. Each time, a Ford touring sedan was furnished by an Issei man, dapperly dressed in black bow tie and tails. He would stand stiffly beside the car while we did what we did. He was not talkative and scarcely uttered a word to anyone. He was a small-statured man and wore spectacles. I thought he was a very odd person.

We were not aware that riding in the Ford touring sedan was a special treat at the time. It was one of the early vehicles that came off the assembly line at River Rouge in Michigan. It was the creation of Henry Ford to manufacture automobiles at a cost affordable to middle-class clientele. The Model T and Model A vehicles were soon to become a familiar sight on the landscape of America. We were on the beginning edge of that revolutionary change, yet unaware of it.

The two outings served as an opportunity for us to explore the environs beyond our home. Facing us was a ridge lined with trees, which caught our fancy more than the valley floor. I climbed it with my brother Kazushi and came upon a very lush, upright-foliage plant unknown to us. Mother was called and she identified them as edible dandelion plants. She gathered an armload, remarking, "They will be very delicious." Then, as she turned to go, she spied a plant we thought was a bloomed-out weed. "This is *fuki*, butterbur," she exclaimed. Despite the fact that it was overmatured she pinched a couple of young stalks from the heart of the plant.

My brother and I went on along the ridge of trees. The ridge itself dropped sharply to the channel below. Underneath the trees were many young globe-type white mushrooms popularly seen at chain stores throughout the nation. We followed the ridge to its western end and were surprised to find a wide expanse of sandy beaches. Port Orchard Channel, which bisected Rich Passage, was at low tide while Rich Passage seemed to be at full tide.

When we returned home, my thoughts were fixed on the edible dandelions. An hour later, I went to the kitchen to watch and wait. I watched

Mother lift the cover, stir the contents, and recover it. After an hour of waiting, my patience wore out.

"Mother, why must you cook it so long?" I asked.

"It's bitter *nigai*," she answered. "The bitterness must be cooked out."

The dandelions, for which I waited so eagerly, were served for lunch the next day. They had been fried with pieces of ham and seasoned and, as Mother had predicted, were truly delicious. I didn't care much for the *fuki*.

The trip to Manitou was an experience. There were little geysers gushing all along the sandy beaches upon our arrival. I raced my brother down to begin the harvesting. The geysers stopped when we approached. We could see the neck and dug furiously, but each time the neck receded a little more. The pace of the digging wore me out.

"I give up!" I yelled. "We'd have to dig to China for them."

Unknown to us at the time, these clams were the fabulous geoduck, pronounced "gooey duck," the gourmet delight of post–World War II America. They are noted for their extremely long necks and are found only in a few selected spots in the Pacific Northwest. Actually, Mother had come to harvest the shallower butter clams that we collected. The water inside the shells was very salty.

I was introduced into the Baptist religion when I was four years old, but I was not aware of it. In my young life I was very susceptible to flu. Mother had isolated me in a downstairs room and I had battled high fever all night long. I licked the fever in the late morning hours but was exhausted from the long struggle. I heard the door open and close and Mother's voice penetrated my consciousness.

"Utaka, there is someone here who wants to meet you." I followed Mother's voice with my eyes. I saw her standing a few feet from the door with a smile lighting her face.

"This is Miss Rumsey,"[31] she said, motioning to her left.

I shifted my gaze, and looking down on me was an Anglo woman with a broad, homely face. There was an expansive grin on her face. Over her head she wore a wide-brimmed brown hat, and in fact everything she wore was brown. The one exception was a gray pouch that hung by straps from her shoulders.

"I have something here for you," she said and fished out from the pouch a narrow, oblong book.

She held the book close to my eyes and flipped the pages as she briefly explained the allegories of the pictures. They represented Jesus, the Garden of Gethsemane, the hideaway of Ali Baba and the Forty Thieves, and Aladdin and his magic lamp. Then she noticed my tired eyes.

"You can read this after you've rested," she said. "I'll leave it with you as well as some other literature."

I devoured the literature that she left because of my insatiable appetite for reading and knowledge. One of the reading materials she left was a magazine called *Apostolic Faith*.[32] I liked the stories in it, the stories about the apostles, but more than that I was fascinated by pictures of Shetland ponies in the advertisements. The ponies were so cute. We had all that expanse of acreage and it seemed to be made to order for a Shetland pony. I promised myself that someday I would own a Shetland pony. Like many other young fantasies, that was not to be. Miss Rumsey came again the following year and left more literature and a small Bible. I was laid up again with the fever but more on the mend.

In January of 1919, I entered Winslow Public School.[33] Mother, despite her illness, still would prepare our meals and see us off to school. It was a cold, dismal morning after a torrential rain the night before. As I set out, she shouted out:

"Watch out for your younger brother. Wait for him after school. I want you boys to come home all together."

Winslow Public School was a towering structure. That first morning was so cold that breath came out in white steam. The kids were trying to keep warm by playing tag, skipping ropes, and playing hopscotch. The few Nisei students who were present were mere spectators, standing around with smiles and watching. It soon became apparent that we were simply being tolerated, for there was no communication with the Nisei in the classrooms or on the playgrounds. No socialization or fraternization. Nisei students were just at the school to learn, and as soon as school let out they scurried home. The situation appalled me and it griped me that my older brothers had not briefed me on what to expect.

The condition that prevailed in education was a reflection of the condition in the wider community. As I have already indicated, what existed at that time was a separatist society where the two races lived side by side with limited interactions. Name-calling was mothballed and was no longer popular. Outside of that "skibbees" incident, I was never subjected to any type of pejoratives. The word "Japan" never crossed the linguistic bounds. This did not hide the presence of intolerance, which lurked just below the surface. This separation-style society has been described by one historical researcher, Stefan Akio Tanaka, as "that of mutual toleration."[34] In actual fact, this perception was an illusion. The cultural society took extreme measures to hide Nisei transgressions against the white people from the public eye. The habit of the collaborationist policy had been acquired very early by the immigrant Japanese in the United States to counter prejudices of racial and economic discrimination. The more aggressive of Nisei children were punished within this sphere without distinction as to the precociousness of the transgressor or the seriousness of the transgression. It was simply a case of "no-no" to displease the white folks. The transgressors were summarily banished from their homes and the island. Thus the immigrant society attempted to maintain a public image that would be approved by the whites.

This method was also intended to exercise discipline within the cultural society. The problem with this system was its indiscriminate practice. Punishments were meted out unilaterally and lacked any sense of true justice. It amounted to a societal conspiracy for the infliction of indignities upon one of its own members and in that respect constituted a manifest injustice. The establishment of a separatist society on Bainbridge Island arose after an immigrant Japanese, Shinichi Moritani, founded an agricultural industry, strawberry culture, in 1908 to replace the dying logging industry at Port Blakely. Then, in 1917, a strawberry cannery was established on what is now the end of Weaver Road, which provided employment for two hundred workers—all white folks.[35] In appreciation for this contribution to the economy of the island, a surface tolerance of the Japanese was implemented. "There were no problems, everyone just kept to themselves," long-time residents of Bainbridge Island Ernest and Violet Lundgren told Stefan Akio Tanaka in an oral history interview recorded on May 25, 1976.[36]

Spring arrived early in 1919. By mid-February, the sun beamed down strong and the weather warmed up. Father had enrolled us in the Japanese Language School at the Japanese Hall, a five-minute hike from the Winslow Public School.[37] The heat waves danced in the sunny afternoon and I yearned to be out there. I wasn't much for learning Japanese and lasted only five days. In later years I would regret not having learned Japanese, for many opportunities were afforded where it would have been beneficial.

It was the first week of March that a blond boy came out from the school with a bat and ball.

"You fellows get out in the field," he said. "I'm going to hit some flies."

The crowd, basking in the sun, dispersed, most going to the left. The sort of student ostracism toward the Nisei that existed kept me rooted where I was. Just before he was to toss the ball up to hit, his eyes met mine.

"You, too!" he said.

I moved to the right where only eight fellows had gone. The blond boy hit to the left for some time and I noticed that no one was catching the ball. It was popping out of their hands. I had not even played catch before and I wondered at this. Then he began hitting to the right, and to my surprise I found no difficulty in catching the ball. In fact, a couple of other fellows did likewise. The following week, we had a choose-up. The blond boy selected me on the sixteenth pick. When two others declined to serve as catcher, he turned to me and said, "You're the catcher."

I made quite a stir as a baseball player and that reputation had unexpected dividends. White folks became more friendly and cordial and associations increased. This situation was not only at the school but also in the community, where I was known as "Shola" or Tommy's Boy. In 1923 the Winslow town team asked me to function as a substitute catcher. I was ten years old. That paved the way for my selection on the Winslow Public School team without even a tryout. Thereafter, I enjoyed a good reputation in the community as a ballplayer. That reputation had broken a lot of white ostracism.

We had just finished breakfast one Saturday morning in April 1919 when Father asked us to go to the green knoll in front and wait for him. It took him twice the "twenty minutes" to make his appearance.

"Your mother is very sick," he informed us. "The disease is incurable. I am taking your mother and the younger children to *Nihon*.[38] You boys have a choice. You can come with us if you wish."

We chewed on that. I really had no wish to go. *Nihon* was a foreign country. It was very far away. I liked the knowledge I was learning at school and I had just begun to play baseball and enjoying it no end. Then Father said something which made up our minds.

"If you come with us you can never come back," he said.

"I want to stay here," I responded immediately. Both of my brothers echoed my sentiment.

"In that case," Father said, "I will have to find a guardian for you boys. We have plenty of time—two months. We won't be going until school is out."

At the end of May, Father bundled the family onto the Winslow ferry. We went up on the top deck for a better view of the Sound, and Father joined us after settling Mother and the others in the lounge. Upon docking in Seattle, the four of us were the first to get off. We were halfway up the steep ramp when told to "Stay there!" A black touring sedan pulled up at the head of the ramp and Father went up alone to meet it. Mother and our sisters began the climb and I waited expectantly for a departing word from them. But they proceeded up with no sign of recognition. Father helped them into the touring car and it immediately headed south down Western Avenue.

I was mortified. Our family was being split up and we might never see any of them again. I thought it was thoughtless and insensitive of Father not to allow a moment of final farewell. It bothered me deeply. A second black touring sedan pulled up and we were motioned to finish our climb. This car went to the left and toward the hills. It pulled up beside a sloping lawn with the house well up toward the summit. We were expected because a man sitting on the porch got up and started down to greet us. Father went up to meet the man at a terrace break, where they stopped to confer. We watched. The man had a hard face and an ugly knife scar marred his left cheek. I didn't like the man's appearance.

"That man is your guardian," Father told us when he returned. "Do what he tells you. I want you to be good boys. Remember, I will be coming back in September. I promise you."

Then he was gone. The guardian motioned us to follow him.

"Let's climb that opposite hill and watch the ship sail out," I said.

We climbed the hill and sat upon its summit. The full expanse of Elliott Bay and Puget Sound beyond that lay before us. The ferryboats were steaming to the far shores and fishermen were out in force in launches and rowboats. Speedboats raced across the bay and tugs plied busily about. Just entering from the north was a giant cargo boat guided by a trio of tugboats. But there was no sign of a steamer heading out.

"I'm going to run away," Yoshito declared twenty-five minutes later. He wasn't much for patience, and headed north. We were so intent on watching for the steamer, we didn't notice the guardian creeping up on us.

"There were three of you, where's the third one," he startled our concentration.

"He said he was running away," I volunteered.

"That's dangerous," he said. "The cars go real fast in the city. He could be run over. Which way did he go?"

"He went that way," Kazushi said, pointing toward the north.

I lay down on my stomach and calculated the speed of the cars far below on the Rainier Valley[39] floor. I paced the cars with my head.

"I don't think they're going very fast," I declared.

"You can't tell from here," Kazushi said.

"We're pretty far up. It may seem they aren't going very fast from here."

The guardian was back in two hours, empty-handed, but he said he had alerted the police and they would find Yoshito. Just at dusk, a car with two large detectives pulled up. Yoshito, who hadn't been visible at first, slid out of the backseat. At sight of our brother, we rushed down to join him. We arrived just as a detective was reporting to the guardian at the terrace break.

"We found him on Twelfth Avenue," he said. "He was window-shopping. He was headed toward the waterfront. He was just sauntering casually."

It was almost dark by now and we followed the guardian to the house. Twenty feet from the porch, Yoshito said out loud, "I'm going to run away again." No one said a word.

The next morning at breakfast, the guardian informed us: "We will be going to your home on Bainbridge this afternoon. I have some business to take care of first." The information compelled us to stick around the house until midafternoon, when we departed.

The breakup of our family was a tragedy, both for those who remained in America and for the children taken to Japan. Mother had gone to her sister's place in Nagasaki and the children were left in the care of grandmother Saiyo at Katsusa. Father received periodic letters but the contents were never divulged to his sons. An example of this happened at the beachfront bungalow. I watched our post-office box for literature and specialty items I had ordered. When a letter showed up from Japan, I handed it to Father, waiting expectantly for news. "I guess they're asking for more money," he said. He began reading the letter and stopped. "This is written in *hiragana*,[40] I will have to get it translated." He went off with the letter and was gone three days. When he returned, he never mentioned anything. He always followed the same routine whenever a letter arrived, and sometimes he would be gone for five days. Actually, his adopted mother, Saiyo, kept him in the dark about the children, but it's difficult to believe that when the infant

Chikara died in a cholera epidemic in 1920,[41] he wasn't informed. By nature, Father was reticent and uncommunicative.

While Mother was in command of our childhood, we grew up in a principled fashion. But after the return of Father, we missed the restraining hand of Mother. This was displayed first in Yoshito, who demonstrated great independence, such as Father's, by going off unannounced and sometimes not returning home at night. As his independence increased, I had the feeling that he would someday get into trouble. One example of this was his invitation to me to accompany him to see a baseball game. "Let's go and watch a baseball game," he said. This was in the spring of 1920 and an invitation I could not ignore. We took the outlet road, climbed Johnson Hill Road, now Wyatt Way, and at its summit he said: "Stay there. I'll go see what's happening." He went forward twenty feet and when he returned said, "I guess there's no game today." I was skeptical of my brother's assumption and went forward to the exact spot to find out for myself. From this vantage point, no baseball diamond was in view at all. When I turned back, I found Yoshito heading for a little white box beside the front gate. From this box, he pulled out a quart of milk.

"What are you doing?" I asked.

"It's all right," he said. "I've done this before."

"It's stealing!" I protested.

He took the bottle and nonchalantly sat down under a spreading madrone tree on the corner. The white picket fence along the road was sheltered by a line of lilac bushes. The large, white-painted house stood two hundred feet back on a rise. Yoshito began to drink from the bottle.

"Let's go. We'll be caught," I urged.

"Aw, pipe down," he replied. "Here, take a sip." I was too agitated to enjoy the sip.

"Let's go, let's go," I insisted.

He finished the bottle and put the empty back in the white box. I was relieved when we headed down Johnson Hill Road. I swore to myself that I would never again go anywhere with my oldest brother.

It was shortly after this incident that I was in back of the residence one early afternoon when I noticed a movement at the top of Cannery Road, now known as Weaver Road. Shrubs lined the west side of the deep gulch, except for a third of the distance toward the grove of trees. I had no notion of anyone heading to our yard but out of curiosity followed the movement. When the open space was reached, I could clearly see it was a young white boy. As I watched, he dipped into the gulch and after some time clambered up on our side of the gulch. He cleared the four-foot wooden palings and came toward me through the golden wave of alfalfa.

"My name is Chris," he said. "I came over to play."

Chris was a handsome Caucasian boy of my stature. He had clear blue eyes, blondish hair, and a genial attitude. He came every Saturday afternoon after that. One day I found him on the apron of the bluff, looking intently toward the grove of trees.

"What do you see?" I asked.

"I was thinking," he said slowly at the end of a long pause, "why don't we ask the strawberry cannery for a summer job."

"That's a capital idea," I exclaimed.

We met at the junction of Johnson Hill Road and Cannery Road at ten next Saturday morning and walked to the cannery office. No one was about, although the door was wide open. No one answered our shouted inquiries. We retreated to the dock to ponder our next move. The telephone began to ring. It rang loud and incessantly. Finally, into the office rushed a slender young man. The conversation was extremely long, but the man could see us because of the large French windows that looked out on the docks. When finished, he came out on the dock.

"What are you fellows doing here?" he asked.

"We thought you might have summer jobs for us," Chris answered.

"Wait a minute," the man said. He went back into the office and held a fairly long conversation.

"Okay," he said to Chris. "Be here at eight Monday morning if you want to go to work."

"What about me?" I asked, feeling ignored.

"You can get a job on the farm," he replied. "There's plenty of jobs there. They need lots of pickers."

There was no mistaking this economic discrimination. I didn't know anything about farm work but could sense that he was lumping all Japanese people as agricultural workers of the type considered unfit for white men. I thought this denial at the cannery was unjust because the cannery depended on the production of the strawberry-growers. It was my first job application, but I knew more would follow. Chris and I walked up Cannery Road in total silence. When we parted at the junction, I felt I was saying farewell to a budding friendship. I did not see Chris again, but part of that was due to an event that followed.

That event occurred, I distinctly remember, on the third Saturday of July 1920.[42] It was as hot as a blister. "Let's play 'It' in the hay barn," Yoshito proposed. I had avoided the towering barn, repelled by its grim appearance and the black-painted sides. To my surprise, the hay barn had no east wall and the bright sunlight streamed into the interior. Bales of hay were stacked haphazardly throughout. I wound up being "It" for the longest time until I caught my oldest brother and beat him to the base. Twenty minutes later, Yoshito proclaimed: "I'm tired of this game. I'm going out." We came out of our hiding places and returned to the house.

Around four-thirty, I went down to the kitchen for a drink of water. People were running by the window, and with my interest peaked I opened the kitchen door and stopped the next passerby.

"What's going on?" I asked.

"Your barn's on fire," he said. I looked toward the back.

"You can't see it from there," he added. "You'll have to step out six feet."

He was right. A big pall of black smoke was rising high in the sky. Below it was a smaller puff of white smoke forming. The fire could be seen for miles around and people of the community were converging to contain it. In pioneer times, volunteers gathered to fight any natural disaster. Even though the distance from the harbor to the fire was too great, a water brigade was mounted. It lacked personnel and each man had to cover twenty feet in the vain effort. At nine o'clock, darkness had fallen. The same person who had alerted my attention stopped to report.

"We're going home," he said. "I think the fire's out. You don't have a barn anymore. We're leaving about eight men to watch for sparks and to make sure it won't flare up again."

I had no idea how the fire had started. I never played with matches and had never seen brother Kazushi with a match either. The probability was that Yoshito had dropped a matchbook. Ultimately, the hot sun could have ignited it. Like most matters, the subject never came up for discussion.

I found Father having a late dinner the next evening and said, "The barn burned down." His demeanor did not change and I had the distinct impression that he had already heard about it. "I'll go see the landlord next Saturday," he said quietly. Then on that Saturday morning, he said, "I'm going to see the landlord." That was ten in the morning and he returned at two-thirty. I had waited anxiously.

"How did it go?" I asked.

"Not good," he responded.

Two weeks later, he stated, "Be ready to move next Saturday morning." The tide was in and Father was able to bring his launch beside the floating boathouse. We helped in the loading. Yoshito remained behind to watch the house. When we turned the Point, I could see three piers extending into the harbor. The furthermost east was the Winslow ferry dock; next to it was the Standard Oil dock, and the closest was a private pier. Father stopped the launch at the private pier. Situated at the head of the dock and against a high bank was a bungalow, on the stoop of which sprawled a stout-appearing man. He watched us intently with nary a word.

Our destination was a two-story house, flush against the west roadside end of the corner lot at what is now the intersection of Madison Avenue and Parfit Street. We had to cart our belongings across an empty lot. The house had an interesting sunken living room, partially walled to form a hallway to a rear kitchen. The yard was quite large. I was left behind to guard the house. It took three trips to complete our move.

This site was only catty-corner to the Loverich's grocery store.[43] One night, Father hosted a poker party and stacked his winnings—all cartwheels[44]—on the hallway bureau shelf. We had to pass it regularly to take our meals. On the fourth day, the temptation overcame me and I slipped a cartwheel from the stack. Twenty cents was blown on a double-decker cone and some candies. It was not until then that I was overcome with guilt. When I found the back window of the storage shed was unclasped, I decided to hide there to avoid Father's wrath. I attended school regularly and sustained myself with luncheon meats and bread. Eighty cents ran out after a week and I decided to pilfer the neighbor's Royal Anne cherries. The moment I climbed up on a tree, the neighbor's little white dog set up a racket. The tree was forty feet from the porch, the lower portion of it being boarded. The dog's frantic barking surprised me.

Mr. Frank, our neighbor, calmed the dog the first time, but when it increased its frantic barking upon his turning the porch light off, he released the dog from its chain and followed it with a flashlight. The dog shot unerringly to the tree on which I was frozen. The dog jumped and barked around its trunk.

"Who's there?" Mr. Frank demanded.

He flashed his lamp beam on my face. Then, in a softer and kindlier tone, he said, "Climb down, son." When I hit the ground, he said, "You don't have to steal our cherries. If you want cherries, just knock on the kitchen door and ask for them. You can have all the cherries you want. Now, go home, son."

I wasn't a stranger to the Franks. I had played with their children. Mrs. Frank frequently had me in for lunch. I knew Mr. Frank only by sight. He was the engineer on the Winslow ferry.

The failed raid on the Franks' cherry tree made it imperative to confide in my brother Kazushi. He had taken over household chores after Father's return and handled the cooking. He was to slip me a large dish of dinner "on the QT."[45] This arrangement worked well for several nights but on the tenth night I was alerted by a loud commotion outside. I peeked out and saw my two brothers descending on the storage shed, demanding that I come out. In the glow cast by the open kitchen door, I saw Father standing and watching. I fought like a tiger but was overwhelmed and subdued. By that time, Father had slipped out the front door and it would be several weeks before I would see him again. The stack of cartwheels had disappeared.

"Father caught me preparing your plate," Kazushi explained. "He wanted to know what it was for. I had to tell him where you were." No one seemed to know about the pilfered cartwheel. I wrote about this incident in the 1960s to Kazushi and he called me "a thief." It was a reaction I had not expected. I never regarded myself as a thief. I wondered what he would call our father who confiscated my summer-long earnings in the strawberry fields. Oh, he gave me five dollars and the two-pound bag of peanuts and eight candy bars I shared with Kazushi.[46]

We moved again during the Easter week of 1921 to the "Beachfront Bungalow." It was to prove the most eventful, the most calamitous, and the most portentous period of my young adult life. Father had two families to support, and even though this was the beginning of the postwar prosperity called the Roaring Twenties, our family fortune took a tailspin. It was made worse by an accidental shooting that strained his pocketbook. But it was this phase of my childhood that was to shape my conscience and mold the idealism to which I would adhere in future life.

It was at the Beachfront Bungalow that I developed a broader perspective of rural Winslow and the environs of Bainbridge Island. It brought me into contact with community people and stripped away the cloistered solitude of childhood. People of Japanese extraction from elsewhere in the Pacific Northwest came looking for "Omura-san." The key issue in 1921 was the proposed Anti-Alien Land Act in the State Legislature at Olympia.[47] The berry-growers of the island were very much wrought up about the measure. Across the Sound in Seattle, the Japanese Association had assembled and funded a Nisei citizen group to fight the racist land act. The group was called the Seattle Progressive Citizens League. The effort failed and the measure became law in 1922. The defeat forced the group into hibernation until revived in 1928 by a blind newspaper publisher named James Yoshinori Sakamoto.[48]

I hung around to listen to the Issei who came to consult with my father. Until Father returned, these Issei would sit around and hold a gabfest. Beside the land issue, they expressed strongest opposition to the Industrial Workers of the World.[49] The IWW maintained cells in the state of Washington and hit the headlines at Everett, Washington. When a Seattle contingent arrived to provide moral support for striking lumber workers, an army of local authorities confronted them. In the melee that followed, a policeman was killed. The Seattle group disclaimed liability on a claim of being unarmed. The public sided with the IWW in this instance. Bainbridge Island Issei, who had worked hard to establish themselves, had little truck for the strikers, spelling out their name as "I Won't Work!" The Industrial Workers of the World were characterized as "Reds" by these Issei. It was in this light that I acquired my distaste for and antipathy toward communism.

Not long after our move to the Beachfront Bungalow, an altercation developed between my older brothers while Father was entertaining a visitor in the kitchen. "Be quiet!" Father shouted. Fearing the consequences, I tried to break up the argument. Kazushi was beyond mollifying. He transferred his hostility to me and I could not calm him down. He drove me to the top of my bed, from where I clawed at him. His head was bent forward when Father entered with a piece of stove wood in his hand. To my horror, he struck Kazushi on his head. I heard the conk of contact. Kazushi stopped instantly. I was appalled at Father, for Kazushi was the glue that kept us together. He cooked, sewed, mended clothes, and did all the household chores once done by Mother. Didn't all of that count?

The incident so shook me up that I moved out of the house to prevent future repetition. There was a captain's quarters,[50] in excellent condition, preserved from a discarded ship twenty feet from the main house, which I thereafter occupied. It had a kitchenette and a spacious bedroom with a clothes closet and bookshelves. My meals were taken at the main house but otherwise time was spent in this captain's quarters.

Two white boys came down to play with Yoshito a few days after school let out for the summer. I joined them but after two hours they decided to go see a white-run farm. I pleaded to go along but was told: "You're too young. You better stay here. The farm is pretty far away." That evening I was informed by Kazushi: "Yoshito is in jail! He was caught raiding a white farmer's vegetable farm. Father went to see what could be done."

The next morning, I was aroused by the sound of loud voices. I dressed hurriedly and opened the door just as a small man, toting a rifle, came up.

"Here's one!" he shouted.

"What do you mean?" I asked.

"You're one of the fellows who raided my vegetable garden," he declared.

"How could that be?" I asked. "I've been here all day." Then a large man, also toting a rifle, came up and asked, "You got him?"

"Maybe not," the smaller man replied.

They went off together. Yoshito did not come home. I surmised that Father had banished him. It was a method among immigrant circles to kowtow to the whites. Banishment also served as a disciplinary tool to keep children toeing the line. It was in this manner that the immigrant society maintained racial harmony. No consideration was given to the age of the miscreant or the seriousness of the transgression. Yoshito was eleven years old.

"Yoshito is working on the railroad in the Cascades. He is a water boy," I was informed by Kazushi four months afterward in the late fall. Yoshito had been in the seventh grade when he was banished. It didn't seem right to me to interrupt a child's education on a simple childhood prank. No one mentioned his two white companions who appeared to have eluded the farmer.

The first Easter, in 1922, Yoshito came home for a visit. He brought with him a trio of .30-30 rifles of which he appeared to be inordinately proud, polishing and sighting them constantly. He would brag how he could bring down a deer in the forest a hundred feet away. We became involved in an argument one morning and in a burst of anger I referred to him as "Rat Face" because of the sores on his face. That infuriated him.

"I'm going to get my gun," he shouted. "You better run." He leveled a rifle from the door of the main house. "You better run," he shouted. "I'll shoot!"

I really didn't believe he would shoot his own brother. I was at the edge of the dock platform, a distance of about forty-five feet, when I heard the crack of his gun. The next instant I slumped to the ground. There was no pain, no blood, but I was paralyzed. At that instant Kazushi rounded the embankment. He had heard the shot and saw me on the ground.

"What's going on here?" he asked in a loud voice."

"I'm shot!" I replied.

"I didn't shoot him, I didn't shoot him," I could hear Yoshito's anguished cries. "The bullet must have ricocheted. I didn't shoot him. I shot down by the boards by his foot. The bullet must have ricocheted; the bullet must have ricocheted."

"Can you get up?" Kazushi asked.

"No, I'm paralyzed," I said.

"I'll get Father," he stated.

Father came and asked the identical questions. "Lie still," he said. "I'll call the doctor." Father was a long time getting back from the Loverich grocery where he had gone. "They're trying to locate the doctor," he said.

It was two hours before Dr. Shepard showed up. The ground was turning cold as the sun slowly sank. I was getting chilled.

"Don't move. I'll have to call for a stretcher," he said.

It was another long wait, and when the stretcher finally came I was placed in the pilothouse bunk that, ironically, was the same bunk where the year before I had watched over an unconscious Nisei boy who was wounded in the head in a hunting accident. The Winslow ferry set off immediately when I was aboard. At the Seattle docks there was an ambulance waiting, and I was rushed in to the X-ray room and then wheeled into the north ward.

"The bullet is in deep," Dr. Shepard reported as he stopped by before returning to Winslow. "It is in a very critical area. It would be dangerous to operate immediately. You are too weak. You'll have to build up your strength. I'll come back and do the operation myself when you are ready."

It was five weeks before Dr. Shepard came back to do the surgery. "I'm going to administer a local," he said. "You'll be fully awake. When the local takes effect, you won't feel a thing. You can watch the operation."

He was right. I didn't feel a thing. But the operation hit a snag. "Oh, oh!" he said softly. "I'm going to have to probe. The bullet is deeper than I thought." It was the probing that caused some pain and discomfort.

"I've got it!" the doctor said triumphantly. He held the bullet in his forceps. The casing was shiny and unmarked. "Do you want to keep it as a souvenir?"

"No," I replied.

He dropped the bullet in a receptacle and it made a loud "clunk." "You were lucky," Dr. Shepard declared. "It went halfway through your rib. Had it gone through, it would have punctured your lungs. The bullet went in an upward trajectory."

Then Yoshito had been right. The bullet had indeed ricocheted. Three weeks later, the nurse advised me I was going home. She helped me with my rags. (Father considered clothes to be a luxury and ours were castoffs from the Salvation Army. Kazushi would cut, trim, and sew them to fit. I was compelled to wear wool knickerbockers long after they had gone out of style, and even in hot spring and summer weather, for lack of a suitable change.) I was weak, not having been out of bed in eight weeks, and nearly toppled over when asked to stand for putting on my socks and shoes. The nurse then had me sit on the edge of the bed. I had no feeling in my left chest. Father joined us halfway down the hall. When the wheelchair reached the front entrance, Father asked:

"Can't you walk?"

"No," I said.

"No, no, he mustn't!" the nurse cried out almost simultaneously.

Though it was the end of May and the sun was out, the wind that swept through the streets had a chill to it. I felt cold and I wondered about the nurse, who wore no wraps. The Yellow Cab took an awfully long time to arrive. At the ferry was Dr. Shepard.

"Come see me on July 10," he said. "You need to have the stitches taken out."

Recuperation was tedious and difficult. In the beginning it was necessary to use the walls of the woodshed for support to get between the captain's quarters and the main bungalow. Eventually I was able to go fifteen feet without support, and progressively more each time. The left chest was still paralyzed and it felt I had a big hole there. It was near the end of June when I managed to reach the corner of what is now Parfit Street and Madison Avenue and with the support of residential fences made it to the Congregational Church,[51] opposite the grounds of Winslow Public School. The destination was the Winslow Public Library,[52] but an open space of two hundred feet lay between. For forty-five minutes, I sat on the church steps and wondered whether I could make it. To my pleasant surprise, I covered the distance without incident. That gave me the confidence of making it to the doctor's office on July 10, it being another 150 feet catty-corner northwest.

Had I known the pain of removal, I would have been less optimistic. "It's healing well," Dr. Shepard said. I had not returned more than 130 feet when I collapsed by the side of the road. No one traveled the country road in the daytime in those days and I was left to my own devices. After a rest of forty-five minutes, I gritted my teeth and promised myself, "I'll make it back home even if I have to crawl." I did not have to crawl, though it was an exhausting ordeal. But I was sobered by the ordeal. Recuperation had to be begun all over again. By mid-August I had doubts about a recovery by the reopening of school. Then a miracle came in the third week when a floodgate seemed to have opened. I could feel the surge of strength in my left chest and recovery was rapid thereafter.

Father had gone to Port Townsend in September 1921 and Kazushi said he was building a large warehouse on the docks there. Port Townsend was on the Olympic Peninsula at the confluence of the Hood Canal and the Strait of Juan de Fuca. Father was home for three weeks during the seasonal holidays. This job was completed in May 1922 and almost immediately he went off to Seattle to build a private residence that took the rest of the summer.

That fall of 1922 my father went into the retail meat business. On my way to public school a shop seemed to have materialized out of thin air on the westernmost edge of the empty lot. Father purchased a long-body Dodge truck and converted it into a delivery wagon with compartments for meats kept from spoiling with dry ice. Kazushi, known as Casey at the school, was drilled in the meat trade and tended the store after school and Saturdays. He later quit school and tended the store full time. He was in the seventh grade at the time. Father seldom returned from his delivery route before nine o'clock. I had no particular interest in the business and only visited the shop two or three times.

I was aware that I had been taken out of Seattle General Hospital[53] too early but realized that was probably due to the financial pinch the hospitalization was causing. By the time I entered school in fall 1922, the meat shop had disappeared just as mysteriously as it had appeared. Casey made no mention of its demise. But both of my older brothers developed the same type of uncommunicative attitudes endemic in our father.

Not long after our moving into the Beachfront Bungalow, I acquired my nickname since white folks had a difficult time pronouncing my Japanese name. It happened rather unfavorably during a chase in an abandoned sawmill. The grocer, Mr. Loverich, stopped to watch and after twenty minutes halted me.

"I'm going to call you Shola," he declared.

"Do you know what that means?" Before I could answer, he continued: "That's Austrian. It means sole of a shoe. Your sole is flapping."[54]

True enough. The shoe was new with thick crepe soles. It was the only piece of apparel Father ever purchased. But the right crepe sole insisted on working loose. I had tied it with a strip of bed-sheet string and tacked it with staples, but nothing had worked. The nickname "Shola" spread like wildfire at school and in the community.

It was at this time that I immersed myself in reading and became particularly fascinated with early European history and the history of Asia Minor. The books came from the Winslow Public Library and it wouldn't take me long to devour eight to ten books at a throw. Father was extremely proud of Japan's conquest in the Russo-Japanese War, and I made it a point to search out accounts of that clash. But the events of an especially heroic nature left an indelible mark on my mind—the courageous soldiers of Sparta at Thermopylae; Roland and Oliver holding the pass so that their emperor, Charlemagne, could retreat and escape in safety with his retinue; Robin Hood and his Merry Men of Sherwood; the Knights of the Round Table; D'Artagnan and the Three Musketeers; the Dreyfus Affair; Jean Valjean; the magnificent political debates of William Gladstone and Benjamin Disraeli; and that redoubtable English valiant, Edward FitzGerald.[55] These readings and others were of great value in enhancing my education.

Our lives were lived no longer in relative solitude, and I developed a broader perspective of rural Winslow, including its main business settlement. Situated on the county road behind the Winslow Marine Shipbuilding Company, the town's commercial center was located a quarter of a mile from our home. Much of that distance was through a narrow forest pathway, which turned scary after dark. I remember being brought to a halt by an unexpected "Who" when walking home through the pathway one dark night. My heart jumped into my throat as I looked fearfully around. Then I spied an owl perched on a tree branch. The owl looked directly at me with what appeared to be an owlish grin. Then he repeated, "Who!" The experience was nerve-racking and thereafter I avoided the forest pathway on dark nights, taking the long way home by way of the county roads.

The forest pathway opened up on the Winslow Town baseball diamond, which was directly south of Erickson Avenue. It was at Erickson Avenue that the town business settlement began just along the north side of the county road. It started with the largest building, which was an apartment unit with rooms on the upper floor and the main floor taken up by a poolroom with a small space in front serving as a drugstore. Other businesses were a grocery store, a hardware store, a clothier, a stationery and novelty shop, a U.S. Post Office, a real estate office, and the town hall. It covered only two blocks and was split by a deep gulch. On the east side of the gulch was the barbershop, laundry, and bathhouse of the Nakatas. Other shops included a women's salon and Wyatt's Bakery. Across the street was the Winslow Meat Market. Beyond the vacant lot toward the east were greenhouses, a fuel depot, and Okamoto Brothers jitney service. The rural township of Winslow had little economic appeal beside the shipyard and the strawberry farms.

For my brother Casey and I there were few opportunities to earn spending money. The most productive method was to sell fish to the Issei farmers. Father would periodically go on fishing expeditions between jobs for a fortnight to three weeks and always return home with a harvest. Below his rear deck he constructed a funnel opening, and underneath the launch was a reservoir enclosed by heavy netting. The larger fish were kept alive and fresh in this sea emporium. These Father would allow us to take and sell to the farmers and keep the proceeds.

On our little red wagon, we would mount a galvanized washtub, fill it with seawater, and dump the live fish into it. Then with one of us pulling and the other pushing, we would cover our route. It was a long haul because the farms were far apart. We'd set out at ten in the morning and drag in just before midnight. As we knew nothing about pricing, it was left to the Issei farmers to pay whatever price they felt right. Overall, they seemed to be very generous and we'd return with seven to nine dollars, which we split.

Most of the money I earned in this manner went for subscriptions to various magazines such as *Collier's, Saturday Evening Post, Cosmopolitan, Redbook,* and *Police Gazette.* I was heavily into reading. The only other source of income was scrounging around the grandstand at the baseball diamond after a ball game. But this was not a dependable method of finding money since I was competing with other fellows in the hunt.

In June 1923, Father took me to Lummi Island opposite Bellingham Bay. We rode his launch with no incident. He had a summer-long repair job at the Fish Meal Plant operated by Mr. Kunimatsu,[56] a former acquaintance from Port Blakely. Lummi Island's main settlement was at Steven's Point, at its northern apex, and the Kunimatsu settlement was several miles south of it. Otherwise, the island around the promontory of the camp was rocky cliffs and the remainder was covered with evergreens.

The Kunimatsu settlement was reachable only by a private launch. It was a modest cluster of buildings, anchored by a longhouse consisting of a series of private rooms at each end and a kitchen and combination mess hall/recreation quarters. Behind the longhouse was the ever-present *furoya*. Surrounding the longhouse were several individual houses, in one of which a married couple resided.

The fertilizer plant was on the west side of the island. I was told it was a walk of forty-five minutes through a forested pathway. Having no curiosity about the structure, I was never to see it. Father's private launch also probably was holed up there. It was a dull summer for me and I speculated that Father had brought me along because of my gunshot wound and the long period of convalescence I had endured.

One event made a special impact upon me that Lummi Island summer. It was connected with the *furoya*. We decided on taking a bath one early afternoon, but I hesitated when I heard women's voices. The two Kunimatsu boys had gone in and the older son stuck his head out: "Come on, it's all right!" he said. Just as I attempted an entry, a woman screamed hysterically.

"*Chotto matte, chotto matte,*" she shouted. The words meant "Please wait, please wait!" She brushed by in her robe and I could hear her screaming even in the longhouse. In the bath, warming themselves, were a married couple. The woman tried to appear nonchalant, but I detected a glimmer of suspicion in her eyes. The Kunimatsu brothers appeared at ease, but I was discomfited inside. It was the only time in my life that I experienced mixed-sex bathing.

We ended our Lummi Island stay in early September. On our return to Bainbridge Island, Father stopped in treacherous Deception Pass to fish. We had no problem in getting a good catch. The fish took the bait as soon as we began to lower our lines. This type of fishing was not sporting but hard work without any rest. I had my eyes on the whirlpool forming toward the north entry and was relieved to hear Father say, "We better go. The riptides are beginning to stir." Deception Pass was noted as a deathtrap for the unwary.

In general, Bainbridge Island was a somnolent rural retreat and not a place for excitement. But on Halloween night 1923, things broke out of bounds. People were out for rowdiness. I joined a group headed out to Wing Point[57] to tear down a white picket fence. It fronted a big white house standing two hundred feet on a rise. The house was dark and appeared deserted as we approached. Seven feet from the target fence, lights suddenly blazed on and a strong spotlight flashed forth. A voice, amplified by a bullhorn, thundered out, "Anyone approaching the picket fence will get a round of buckshot." The farmer had been alerted and was waiting for us. We beat a retreat.

But the night was not done. At Erickson Road, we were informed of big doings at the Winslow Public School. It was said an outhouse had been lifted atop the towering structure, and a large crowd had gathered to watch the sheriff handle the matter. There were three sheriff's vehicles with lights flashing. The crowd was so large that I couldn't get close enough to see what was going on and decided to call it a night.

Religious teaching among the Japanese was in its infancy in the early 1920s, and the only church in Winslow was the Congregational Church at Madison and Winslow Way. I was invited by an Anglo boy to attend and arrived just as he was going up the front steps with his father. His father was a tall, slender, very personable sort of a man. He asked me to join them and then said to his son, "Why don't you invite him to your Pioneer Club meetings?" The Pioneer Club was similar to the Cub Scouts. It met that Friday evening in the basement of the church and planned a field outing to Seattle three weeks hence.

A dozen of us went on the field trip and we were housed in the loft of some church. That night a pillow fight broke loose and some of the elders came in to break it up. The pillow fight had moved about twenty feet to the east wall. I was standing on the end of my bed, holding a pillow in my hand. The man in a nightgown and wearing a nightcap, who seemed to be in command, demanded to know, "Who started this?" He turned and gave me a threatening look.

In the morning, we went to Woodland Park and then took in the Langendorf Bakery in the afternoon. It was there that I noticed the same aroma as when Father baked at home, which was not often. The bread came out in the same golden brown fashion and the other baked goods were similar in texture and essence. There was no doubt in my mind that Father was a master baker. Whenever he baked, the tantalizing aroma would filter through the house and lure us from upstairs to the kitchen. I really don't know what happened to the Pioneer Club. I knew of no further gatherings.

The breakup of our family resulted in tragic consequences for all of us. The hardships we endured at the Beachfront Bungalow in Winslow were nothing compared to the difficulties then transpiring in Katsusa. But I did not hear anything about it until the late 1980s while I was conducting research on my family roots for this manuscript. It involved the tracing of my two sisters in Japan and establishing a favorable communication with one of them, Hanako, who had become a stranger. Letters between us had to be translated because of my illiteracy in Japanese.

My infant brother, Chikara, as noted earlier, passed away in 1920. The life of our youngest sister, Taeko, was spared by Mr. Matsumoto, who cared for her and whose son later married the older of my younger sisters, Hanako.

Money sent by Father for the upkeep of our sisters never reached its intended purpose. The paternal grandmother, Saiyo, gave the money to her own youngest daughter because, as stated by her, "she was so poor." Saiyo died on October 30, 1933, and her youngest daughter, this aunt, took charge of the girls.[58] In 1987 Hanako wrote that her aunt was very mean and "made us to suffer." When she was studying under lamplight, Hanako was scolded and told to study by moonlight so as not to be so wasteful. She said her "awful aunt" forced her to go to the mountains and to the adjacent river after school to perform chores. When Hanako needed books to go to high school, she was told girls didn't need education.[59]

Another form of discipline the aunt used was to tie Taeko with ropes. When the aunt went out, Hanako would rescue her younger sister. When items were missing, meals would be withheld for days as punishment. It became common knowledge in the village. The elementary teacher got wind of it and shared her lunches with Hanako. When she was in the fifth grade, she became so miserable that she walked into the Ariake Sea with the intention of committing suicide. Fortunately, onlookers rescued her. When a *hakama* skirt[60] for formal wear Hanako had requested from Father arrived, it was taken away from her to be given to the aunt's own children. Hanako had nothing to wear except secondhand clothes, and both she and Taeko grew up as tomboys.

I was not aware of these situations. In early 1935, however, I did receive a telephone call from someone in Winslow informing me of a proposed sale of my sisters by an uncle into *geisha* life as entertainers. I was then editor of the *New World Daily* in San Francisco. The call prompted me to go to Seattle in the hopes of raising funds through my brothers. I was myself short of funds. Neither of my brothers was forthcoming. Casey had just landed a job with a woodcutting crew north of Seattle. He did provide me, though, with the whereabouts of our eldest brother. It was dusk when I reached the little town of National and found Yoshito standing at the entrance of a railroad car. He showed no pleasure in seeing me. He did not speak but listened to my pitch without comment. He showed no reaction and I sensed his antipathy.

In 1937 Casey returned to Seattle for treatment of an unknown disease, which was later diagnosed as tuberculosis but judged curable. He had received from our sisters a communication requesting money. He was able to elicit contributions from Yoshito and me. The money sent was invested in a grocery store. However, the Imperial Government prohibited further overseas letters as the situation in the Far East became more ominous. But prior to this prohibition, Father received information from the "awful aunt's" older sister of the pending sale of the sisters into prostitution. The same uncle, feeling freer since the "awful aunt" had passed on to her reward, was the projected seller.

Father left Winslow to abort the plan. Upon his arrival in Katsusa, he learned the truth of the treatment accorded his daughters. It so outraged him that he began the process of establishing a separate household. To attest to his intentions, he had removed a large portion of the *Koseki Touhon*,[61] the family register, from the record. In the meantime, he minded the store for Hanako. Before he could complete his project of a separate household, he passed away on May 20, 1938, while sleeping peacefully in his bed. Tommy Tsurumatsu Matsumoto, known in the Pacific Northwest as Omura, was laid to rest in the family crypt at Katsusa. He was sixty-seven. His wife, Harue, by her wish is buried there as well. Also in the crypt are the ashes of my youngest brother, Chikara, and youngest sister, Taeko, who died in February 1992 in Nagoya, and those of my second-oldest brother, Kazushi Matsumoto.

The cruel treatment of our sisters by members of the Monzaburo Matsumoto clan reveals that my father was adopted and not accepted as one who was born in the clan. Obviously, the clan Matsumoto did not regard the offspring of my father as true genealogical relations. Tsurumatsu had no intention of returning to his homeland, nor had his relations expected him to do so. But destiny ordained his presence in Katsusa, and so, as indicated, he died while tending to familial matters. Before his death, Father conveyed to his daughter Hanako his regret for being so stubborn that he drove his three sons from home and caused them such great hardships. I hold no malice toward my father, but it was nice to hear about his admission.

Hoping to improve her life, Hanako attended a Buddhist service and converted to the Nichiren Sect.[62] This conversion so disturbed a parishioner of her former religion that he pursued her with the intent to kill. She survived four attempts, and in 1988–89 wrote that the change in the faith gives her more peace and contentment. During the period she was being pursued by the fanatic devotee, the danger was transmitted through psychic vibrations to an Anglo psychic. She in turn made contact with our brother Casey, then confined in the tuberculosis sanatorium at Richland Highlands, north of Seattle.[63] "I believe your sister is in danger," she penciled on a postcard.[64]

"Your sister has been pushed about," she wrote in a second penciled note. "I see several changes and I feel she has not received the money. Moto Yoshioka is over in Japan right now. He is from Bainbridge Island. . . . He can look up your sister and help her into this country. I feel she is either in danger or very unhappy. . . . Best wishes and good luck."

This communication was found in the personal belongings of Casey in Seattle in December 1990 following his death.[65] No indication of what followed next could be found except that he responded to the seer's urgent communication.[66] Hanako was not brought to the United States and the danger in Japan passed.

The amazing correlation here is that this psychic in Seattle was right on the button with her prediction. The psychic's name was Gene Dennis. Being somewhat of a skeptic on mental telepathy, I marvel at the accuracy of Ms. Dennis. I learned of my sister's predicament in late 1987–88 and in December 1990 found a confirmation in Seattle. Could this be coincidence or is it more than that?

We were never told what disposition had been made of our dog, Rover, when our family split up. Nor did we know what happened to Father's private launch. In the seasonal holidays of 1924–25, we moved for the third time into the interior of the island. The place was known as the Johnson House and was three miles north in the area of Rolling Bay, a summer resort town. Father was not likely to move without sufficient reason, and I suspected it was the enmity of the grocer, Tom Loverich.

It happened one afternoon while waiting for the ferry. His youngest son and I were on the flatbed and the oldest Loverich boy was pacing back and forth near the truck. Ed made pretensions of leaping on his older brother and I playfully nudged him. Instead of jumping off as I expected, he fell flat on the dock, mashing his nose. He ran to the grocery and out came Mr. Loverich, who attempted to grab me. I moved from one side to the other, jumped off, and hightailed it home. "I don't want you ever on my trucks again," he shouted at me in wrathful anger.

The oldest son tried to calm his father by telling him that Ed was culpable, too, but to no avail. Mr. Loverich never forgave me. The two older sons would pick me up on their return from delivery but would always stop at the top of the hill, about a block away from the store, and let me off. "We better not let our dad see you riding the truck," I would be told. The ire of Mr. Loverich was such that I expected it would eventually reach Father when he traded at the store. I never patronized the grocery after the incident.

The Johnson House was reconstructed by my father but was incomplete when Mr. Johnson ran out of money. All it needed was some wallboard to cover two sides of a north room. Mr. Johnson, who operated a hauling business, also was unable to pay for labor. In lieu of it we were allowed to live in the house. The site was solitary, with the Johnsons living about 150 feet further north and nothing but forests all around. Behind the house was forty acres of woodland. It was back to isolation once again.

Father never displayed any great enthusiasm for education. Perhaps that was due to his quitting school when he was eleven years old in Katsusa. He always made a point not to be tardy at the beginning of a session but otherwise seemed indifferent to our progress. Thus, he had no consideration that we were now three-plus miles from the Winslow Public School. There was of course the school bus, which I rarely rode because of the atmosphere of coolness and uncomfortable silence. I preferred walking, which amounted to six and seven miles per trip. I walked it many times for well over a year, and although all island roads were hard-packed dirt, I never found it impassable to vehicles, as one historical researcher claimed.[67] The isolation of the island Japanese was due to the solitary nature of their lives. They were widely separated and sometimes hampered by their mode of travel. Conditions of the roads were never a factor.

During the decade of the 1920s, social affairs for Nisei children were sparse. The Japanese Association sponsored a picnic at the end of the school term in May. It was the time for gorging ourselves on ice cream, soda pop, and all sorts of goodies. And we would chortle with laughter at the antics of half-drunk Issei cavorting indecorously. There were three-legged races, blindfold races, and baseball. New Year's was a three-day holiday marked by rounds of visiting, drinking, and eating festive meals. The Issei saw ethnic movies at the Japanese Hall once a month and celebrated Tenchō-setsu, or Emperor's Birthday[68] with great gusto. Anyone would be hard-pressed to find a Nisei participating.

With the acute need for apparel, I put in a stint of picking strawberries. It was back-breaking work. We walked on our knees, and when I tried to get up I had to coax the knees and back to straighten up again. The hot summer sun made the work more difficult. I was a slow picker and could average only eight crates per day. At thirty-five cents a crate, that came to $2.80. But I was consoled that I was earning money. Issei growers never made direct payment to underage pickers, but instead paid their parents. I knew I was paid, although not how much. As noted earlier, when Father would return from Seattle with a two-pound bag of peanuts and eight bars of candies, I shared these items with my brother Casey. And Father would toss me a five-dollar bill. That constituted my summer earnings. I was disappointed with my take but said nothing, believing the remainder went to the upkeep of my sisters and infant brother. Our life on Bainbridge had been reduced to the barest minimum in spite of having looked forward to improved food and decent clothing.

Out in the fields in 1924, words buzzed of the Nagaishi boy picking thirty-two crates. His father ran the Main Fish Company in Seattle and was my father's fishing companion. They both had come from Nagasaki. One hot afternoon, this boy stopped by our place for a brief chat.

"How many did you pick today?" I asked.

"Only twenty-two," he said.

"Whew!" I exclaimed.

"You have to figure, I start at 4:30 in the morning when it's cool," he explained. "I've already put in a full day's work." It was 2:00 p.m. "I don't like to pick under the hot sun. Now, I'm on my way to the harbor for a swim."

I reflected on his achievement and wondered how many I could pick at full speed. The next day, I put myself to the test. Try as I could, the best I could do was thirteen crates. This same Nagaishi boy lost his life that winter in treacherous Deception Pass during an outing. His body was never recovered. Father spent a great deal of time in the fruitless hunt.

The following summer of 1925, a youngish grower named Mr. Ito offered four dollars per day to pick his field. He said frankly that his harvest was poor and not likely to be able to attract professional pickers. The offer was for both of us, Kazushi and me, but I took it as meaning apiece. This was Kazushi's first outside work and he was far faster than I. Once again, payment for our work was made to Father and we had no knowledge what it amounted to. We received the standard two-pound bag of peanuts, a dozen candy bars, and a ten-dollar bill apiece. The thing that bugged me most was my distaste of growing up as a berry worker or farmer. That seemed to be the only prospect on the island.

In September, before the opening of school, we made one more move, which was to the next cross street but about the same distance to the north as the Johnson House. Two doors north of us was the Keyes Place. Mr. Keyes operated the new Ford agency between the school and the business sector on Winslow Way. Our new site was a large farm consisting of a two-story residence, a large barn with the loft fixed up as living quarters for a handyman, a windmill, and an expansive back section ringed by high hills. Beyond the large barn, the place was neglected. I quartered myself in the barn loft, going to the main house only for my meals.

Pacific Northwest Coming of Age, 1923–1933

Troubled about our deteriorated fortune and seeing no satisfactory prospect ahead, I had been thinking for several years of leaving home. I had the feeling that the sort of life we were leading was strangling my ambition. I had no illusion of any green pasture beyond the horizon, but I was convinced life could not be any worse on the outside. I had taken note of cannery employment from talks of Father's friends, several of whom mentioned Kushi Contractor.[1]

On the day of my thirteenth birthday, I went in to Seattle in the hope of finding a job. The bell above the office door tinkled as I entered. I saw a portly man turn on a chair, look at me, and then stand up and put on his suit coat. He stood by the doorjamb and sized me up. I knew that I looked young and I hoped that would not work against me. I approached the counter and said, "I came to see about a cannery job."

The big man moved to the counter and I could hear pages being turned. "Yes, there's a job at Ketchikan,"[2] he said.

"Okay," I replied.

"It's for a six-month contract," he continued. "The pay is $350 on the contract."

"I'll take it," I declared.

"The ship sails on April 4th. You will have to be in this office the day before. It would be better if you could come in two days earlier," he stated.

"I'll be here," I promised.

I was exhilarated. The certainty of my leaving home now loomed ahead. With this decision reached, I confided in Casey, knowing that he would have to bear the brunt of Father's wrath. I tried to spare him that by urging that he do likewise.

"There's nothing here for you," I said.

"I have responsibilities," he answered.

But he agreed to keep my departure under wraps, an easy chore with Father's preoccupation with other matters.

I reported to Mr. Kushi two days before sailing, as promised.

"Bunks will be furnished at the cannery," he said. "You will need warm blankets, sheets, and a pillow."

"I have no money," I said.

"I can advance you twenty-five dollars," he offered. "You can shop for them on Second Avenue. There are lots of secondhand stores. You can get what you need real cheap. Everything will be new; you just pay less. You will also need a footlocker to hold your things. You can get it there also."

I followed Mr. Kushi's suggestions and made my purchases. The next morning in his office, Mr. Kushi added: "You might want to draw a script book, too. You can use it at the cannery. It's just like money." Each script book was for twenty dollars. It came in handy for purchasing fruits and pastries at the White Bunkhouse.

The boat we sailed on was the *S. S. Rogers*, a steady but lead-footed freighter consigned to Inland Passage service in preference to faster and modern vessels for the transpacific run. Our quarters were in the forward steerage. It was crowded with two-tiered steel bunks placed eighteen inches apart. I remained on deck to watch familiar sights fade into the distance until darkness fell. The steerage was filled with blue smoke and noisy with the strumming of banjoes and guitars and the incessant chatter of its passengers. The ship pulled in at Victoria, but when told it would sail in one hour, I did not want to chance being left behind.

The bunk below me was occupied by a man who put on a white uniform. On the second afternoon, he looked in on me. "I haven't seen you at any of the mess calls. What's the matter with you? Are you sick?" he asked.

"Yes," I replied.

Inspecting my face, he said: "You're seasick. I can fix that. Just follow me on deck. I'll fix it so you'll never be seasick again."

I followed the man up the deck. The ship was rolling and plunging in the high waves. A bitter wind swept the deck and cold sprays splattered aboard. The *S. S. Rogers* was taking the Outside Passage to Ketchikan.

The steward taught me to roll with the ship's motion and after that led me to the side of the ship, where we got drenched. The sick feeling had abated. "If you keep that up an hour, you'll be cured forever," he said, and left me to my own devices. I stood it as long as I could. We arrived in Ketchikan on the fifth day. I made six more trips to Alaska, the last one as far as the Bering Sea, and was never affected by seasickness again.

Ketchikan reveals a certain allure as a pioneer Alaskan city and therefore it came as a distinct disappointment when I saw it plastered against impervious cliffs and simply as a boardwalk town. It had only one long street crowded with establishments on both sides. Most of the shops sold novelties and served as tourist traps. It even had a drugstore Indian. To the south of

FIGURE 4. Between 1926 and 1936, Jimmie Omura was employed for seven seasons in various capacities within the Alaskan salmon cannery industry. This photograph captures him in April 1926 as a thirteen-year-old boy aboard the *S. S. Rogers* sailing from Seattle, Washington, to Ketchikan, Alaska, to report there for work at a salmon cannery. Later in his life, Omura coined the term "boys of summer" to describe the many Nisei youths who, like him, were seasonal cannery workers in Alaska. Omura Papers, Green Library, Stanford University.

town stood two tall totem poles, which leered down on the passersby and struck me as being gaudy. Ketchikan embraced a headland that fed into a densely forested valley of pines and spruces. It was said that a large Indian village was nestled among this evergreen wilderness. There was nothing of especial interest to attract my attention in Ketchikan.

Our quarters were in a large bunkhouse, and the Anglo engineers had a similar structure fifty feet south. The mess hall, the kitchen, and an office for the VIPs took the first floor; segregated quarters for Japanese and Filipino workers were upstairs. The contract crew numbered forty men, evenly divided by nationality.

When the first mess was called, I was the last to appear. I was looking around for seating when signaled to the VIP table. However, after the third week I went on night shift, so that privilege was of short duration. Except on Sunday mornings our menu was Japanese-style. On Sundays, we were treated with American-style breakfast: flapjacks, bacon or ham, eggs, plus coffee. But when salmon began running, it was fish, fish, fish—fried, baked, boiled, pattied, and what have you. With this lack of variety, the "schoolboys" were the most vociferous in their complaint.[3] "What, fish again!" The Issei, however, grumbled about the lack of green vegetables. I liked fish and was less provoked.

It took several weeks for the Anglo engineers to gear up the machinery, and this interval we spent in idleness. It rained ceaselessly day after day. When it did not rain, it snowed. Confined to the bunkhouse, the only entertainment was in watching gambling. It was one of the last seasons of professional gambling in the Alaska canneries. Workers who returned broke from cannery labor raised a public outcry against this practice of conducting professional gambling in canneries. Some were in hock to the contractor for years into the future. One Issei admitted that he was in hock for seven years. Gambling went on night and day. Saturday nights were set aside for gambling during the peak of the harvesting season.

I was young and inexperienced about worldly affairs and knew nothing about homosexuals. The subject was never heard of on Bainbridge Island. Ketchikan was different. A tall, youngish Issei man attempted to sodomize me. In my mortification, I transferred my quarters to the Filipino section. The would-be Issei sodomizer returned to Seattle three weeks later and I heaved a sigh of relief. My arrival at the Filipino section, however, aroused a great deal of interest. I couldn't understand the conversation, as it was carried on in the Tagalog language. Then a tall, husky Filipino looked in on me and asked if I had settled in. He had a forbidding expression. He just remained standing at the foot of my bunk and I wondered why. He was listening to the Tagalog talks. He then banged for attention and quiet settled down.

"You leave this boy alone," he said. "Anyone messing around with this boy will have to answer to me."

His statement gave me the gist of what was being talked about. This Filipino man had placed himself as a shield of protection over me. He was six feet tall, solidly conditioned, and well proportioned. His jet-black moustache, eyebrows, and sideburns, plus his darker complexion, gave his face a fierce appearance. His habits were more scholarly and studious than his companions'. There was no mistaking the respect others felt toward him. The chatter did not resume and he went back down the hall to his bunk. I later learned his name to be Julius Boros.[4] Once you got to know him, he was not as fierce as he seemed. Julius was a likeable fellow.

My work assignment at Ketchikan was night shift, tending the can-top machine. It was a boring job and kept me nodding away. The Anglo engineer was the only person I saw, but he never spoke to me. Engineers did not speak to Japanese workers. Any complaint they had was funneled to the white foreman, then to the superintendent, who relayed it to the Japanese foreman. The Japanese foreman discussed the matter with the individual involved. It was a cumbersome method. No complaint arose in my department. Later, when the packing season began, I tended the same machine, feeding back the can tops in reverse procedure.

I did not see the other operations until the tail end of my last day on the can-top machine. The last few cans were coming off the rotary sealing machine and being caught up by the retort crew. They were being stored on metal racks stacked on wooden skids. The racks then were placed in the retort, a long steel chamber, for cooking. When completed, the lye-wash crew placed the steel racks in a solution and brushed the cans with long-handled push-broom bristles. Restacked, they were trucked to the warehouse for cooling, labeling, and packing in cardboard cartons.

The schoolboys worked usually from June to mid-August. The contract crew returned to Seattle in early October. It was my first opportunity to see many Western movies, gorge myself on restaurant menus, and explore the environs of downtown Seattle. I hadn't prepared myself for it, but I ran smack into racial prejudice. Signs were posted in the windows of top-quality restaurants stating "WHITES ONLY," while in barbershops there were "NO JAPS WANTED" signs. Moviegoers of Japanese extraction were ushered to the balcony. At one leading downtown movie emporium, this practice continued even as late as the fall of 1931. It was not until my third visit to this theater that I was allowed on the main floor.

Seattle was one of the most racist cities on the Pacific Coast. Northwest-erners were predominantly of British and Scandinavian stock. Anti-Orien-talism was first manifested against the Chinese in 1882 at Tacoma, thirty-five miles south of Seattle. There townspeople, led by the Noble Order of the Knights of Labor,[5] tarred and feathered the Chinese and rode them out of the city. Then the Knights of Labor descended on Seattle and drove the Chinese to the docks for transport to San Francisco, though this action was halted by a court order in the eleventh hour. Many frightened Chinese elected to ship out. Demands were also made at Port Blakely on Bainbridge Island. It was only partially successful when William Renton agreed to dis-charge the Chinese millworkers but balked when it came to his Chinese domestics. The domination of the Knights of Labor was short-lived when discord in its national office led to dissolution on the local level. But anti-Orientalism was firmly entrenched in civic affairs.

Western-style restaurants operated by the Japanese came under attack from the American Legion, which attempted to blackball such establish-ments and set up picket lines to discourage patronage. The boycott failed to achieve the intended goals because the Japanese owners offered cleaner facilities and higher-quality meals at lower prices than their white competi-tors. These factors appealed to the workingmen. Pressures were also brought on suppliers not to service the Japanese restaurants. Similar attempts were made against Japanese laundries, cleaners, barbershops, and other entrepre-neurial efforts, but the Japanese continued to service and prosper. Attempts at setting up restrictive covenants and restrictions on the issuance of busi-ness licenses were also made to stifle the economic advance of the Japanese. People of Japanese descent were denied access to pools, tennis courts, and similar venues of entertainment.

With the ending of the Great War, antipathy against the Japanese grew when corporations and businesses refused to discharge the Japanese workers in deference to returning war veterans. Metropolitan newspapers led by the

Seattle Star,[6] the American Legion, labor unions, and white business entrepreneurs kept up an ongoing attack. The other two dailies, the *Seattle Times*[7] and the *Post-Intelligencer*,[8] though not as rabid as the *Star*, took up similar stances. These hostilities in Seattle toward the Japanese were reflected in the attitudes of people in the Puget Sound Basin.

Two weeks following the Ketchikan return, a Filipino compatriot proposed my being the "fifth man" on a wash-fish crew[9] at Anacortes, seventy miles up the Sound. Unlike Alaska canneries, the work was on a forty-eight-hour-week, eight-hour-day basis. Our work did not bring us into contact with other members of the workforce due to the unusually compartmentalized nature of the operation. People on the streets and in the city's shops were friendly and plain speaking. The work came to a halt at the end of November.

Phil Mendoza, a straw boss at Anacortes, came to see me at the U.S. Hotel in Seattle.[10] He had a job opportunity as a pantry man in distant Pocatello, Idaho, and stated his need for three hundred dollars. I was leery about loaning him such a large amount and informed him I'd sleep on it. He was back a few days later and stated that the staff—two black cooks and himself—would be leaving the King Street Station[11] on Friday, five days hence. I advised him of my doubts and he offered to take me along. Two days later, he came up with a diamond ring, which he said was appraised at $650, as security for the loan. I wanted to get out of Seattle, so I reasoned that if I held the diamond ring as security the deal might work out.

We left King Street Station that Friday morning. The train journey to Pocatello was long and boring. The black cooks kept to themselves and virtually ignored our presence. Idaho was miles on miles of flat sagebrush land. I was reminded of Zane Grey's novel, *The Wanderer of the Wasteland*. Our destination was the Hotel Bannock.[12] It proved to be the largest landmark hotel in this southeastern Idaho city. It was situated on the banks of the Bannock River.[13] We were led deep into a subterranean basement where the servants' quarters were located, and assigned to separate rooms.

Phil came into my room the first Saturday after work. He was dressed to kill. "I'm going to a dance," he announced. "I want to dazzle the ladies. Can you lend me the diamond ring?"

I was bothered by the request. It was the only tangible security I had for the three-hundred-dollar loan. He pleaded and pleaded and pleaded. I had grave misgivings but in the end succumbed to his entreaties.

The next morning my breakfast was brought down by one of the black cooks. I was surprised by that action as none of them had even spoken to me.

"Where's Phil?" I asked.

"He's gone," the man answered. "He was fired Saturday night and took off."

My heart sank. I had been hoodwinked out of three hundred dollars. What to do now? I would have to go out and find a job. I had been thinking about it ever since arriving. In midweek, the black cook said: "I talked to the driver who delivers vegetables to the hotel. His boss is Japanese. He will have his boss make the next delivery. Just sit tight!"

The following week I was called up to meet the Japanese truck gardener. He was a jolly, roly-poly Issei with a penchant for smiling. I thought he smiled too much. I noticed the sign on the truck read Okamura Gardens.[14] "I think I may be able to find a place for you," he said. "I'll have to speak to some people. I'll be back!"

He was back ten days later. He had come in a sedan instead of the truck. "Get your things," he said. "I've got a job for you. You're going to be a schoolboy for Mrs. Turner. Her husband is the county commissioner.[15] She's used to Japanese. She had a schoolboy from Japan who finished his studies and went back. You won't have any trouble."

Mrs. Turner was a small, short woman with a severe-appearing face. She showed no sense of congeniality. She was fond of citing frequently what a whiz the schoolboy from Japan had been. It felt like something of a reprimand for my apparent inadequacy. She did not take to my American ways and seemed merely to tolerate me.

I met Mr. Turner nine months later. He resided in Blackfoot, a town thirty-five miles north, where he was stationed. Mr. Turner was a large man and smelled of the stables. He had come to Pocatello to transact some county business. He looked respectable after taking a bath and changing to a suit. Ted Junior, their son, stayed with the mother. He was head of the Pocatello Abstract Company.[16] He had lost his left foot in a hunting accident and moved about on braces. He was a very sharp and pleasant person to be around. Mr. Turner took me to Blackfoot to see an Indian rodeo. It was mostly wild-looking Indian youths riding bareback with their long hair flying in the wind. It wasn't my idea of a rodeo and I didn't consider it a fun trip.

My stay in Pocatello lasted two years and a half and was highlighted by my achievement in baseball. I was a star third baseman on Franklin Junior

High's[17] baseball team but won greater distinction in American Legion baseball.[18] I was recruited by the Fourth District team; the entire team was named as the city's representative, the Pocatello Shoshones. Though held to a scoreless tie by District Two in the title-clinching game, District Four went undefeated. The fastball pitcher of District Two was the sole outsider to be named to the Shoshones. He was the only pitcher to keep the bats of District Four in check. I struck out three times, but on my final at bat I slammed out a triple, the lone extra base hit of the game.

The Shoshones defeated Caldwell, Idaho, in two straight games for the state American Legion title. The team then went on to the regional tournament at Livingston, Montana, where it lost 7 to 4 to the eventual tournament winner. I could not play in the state and regional games, unexpectedly being switched to the employ of Okamura Gardens. When I was a helper on the Okamura delivery wagon, I met five of my fellow teammates after their loss at the regional tournament and was pleased to hear them assert, "We could have won if you were there." That was high tribute! But it was not said without merit. At the time I was forced to quit, I had an improving .612 batting average. I led in triples and was second on the team in doubles. That represented a considerable loss for a tournament team.

Baseball was not the only sport in which I participated. In 1927 Franklin Junior High School won the district championship in football. I was a halfback on that team. I became a three-sport letterman by a fluke when the pole-vault pole of a competitor broke, which gave me a tie for first place in track and field competition. If the pole had not broken, I would have been second. Besides, I was inserted as just a proxy in this event.

But sports were not my only consideration. I read with interest and extensively concerning Big Bill Haywood[19] and the assassination of Idaho governor Steunenberg.[20] The *Idaho Statesman*[21] ran a series on the incident and on the IWW anarchist group. I also followed with keen interest the religious controversies involving the American orator Robert Ingersoll and the British philosopher Bertrand Russell.[22] I had first come across them while living at the Beachfront Bungalow in Winslow. They gave me my first glimpse of practical contrary opinion exhibited on the lecture platform and the perils of standing up for a principle. I would not be surprised if some of their indomitable spirit might have rubbed off on me in my later years.

But there was also a dark side to my Pocatello sojourn. The prominence I gained in sports drew the companionship of a boy named Gray. We went

Indian arrowhead hunting and would chat about vignettes of the times. He was insistent that I attend his Cub Scout meetings. I was not a member of the Latter-Day Saints church, which sponsored the Cub Scout pack, and at the time I was immersed in the philosophy of Mary Baker Eddy. I did finally consent. There were eighteen boys at the church. The scoutmaster was showing me how to tie knots and I noticed the others fading into an inner room. "Go see what they are doing?" he said to Gray. Gray went but did not come back. The scoutmaster went himself and shortly dismissed the group. Gray was silent on our walk to the Turner residence. He did not come around again. I saw him a couple of times from a distance at the school. I was disappointed that our friendship was terminated on such an insignificant factor as race.

On Saturday evenings I went downtown to window-shop, despite the fact that I lacked funds and had no means of refurbishing them. It was on one of those trips that I attended the much ballyhooed musical *Show Boat*. I also seem to remember hearing Paul Robeson sing in his deep bass tones "Ol' Man River." I don't remember any movies that I attended but I took a fancy to the legitimate theater.

The Native Americans poured into the city on Saturday afternoons and would take over the streets and street corners. It was always an ordeal to make one's way to downtown. Womenfolk would be wrapped in colorful Navajo blankets and cradling Indian children. The menfolk, looking fierce and untamed, milled about. Sometimes they deliberately blocked passages and never showed courtesy to yield. They would look at you with blank stares and mutter in guttural undertones. And ever present would be the unpleasant odor of the unwashed. I found the Native people always disturbing.

It was at the end of the spring 1928 school term that Mr. Okamura showed up unannounced. "Get your things; I'm taking you with me," he said. Mrs. Turner had conveniently absented herself at a neighbor's house. What probably bothered Mrs. Turner was my habit of spending all day at the ballpark, after the few chores had been cleared on Saturdays. I played for the school team, the American Legion team, and the town team. I think she'd rather that I spent my time studying. Nor was I the humble Japanese schoolboy. Mr. Okamura assigned me to an unlighted, unheated quarter above the cellar and I was told to work as a helper on the delivery truck. I was to be paid fifty cents per day. My quarters were shared with a dour, middle-aged eastern European. I thought he might be a Turk or an Armenian. He did not waste his words on me.

The lack of heat and light was not unbearable in the summer months. But when the snow in September covered the eastern Idaho landscape and the weather turned cold, conditions became critical. It seemed Mr. Okamura had tossed me in the cellar structure and forgotten all about me. The blankets for summer were insufficient in cold weather to keep me warm. I shivered under my covers while my companion would get up at 4:30 in the morning and pace and flap his arms for warmth. I loaded the truck until eleven at night and none of the Issei workers in the cellar bothered to speak to me. I could not study and realized that my grades were slipping.

Convinced that this situation could not go on, I walked the mile one Sunday morning to the Yamada Farm, the main competitor to Okamura, and confided my woes to Mrs. Yamada. I was informed that her husband and the foreman were out of state attending an agricultural conference. Mrs. Yamada listened quietly and then showed me an add-on room. It was unoccupied but electrically lit with a large wood stove in the center. I was assured that an ample store of firewood was available. She offered that room to me. Mrs. Yamada was a slender woman and mother of two young children. I moved in that afternoon. I did not attempt to collect my summer stipend and was only too happy to be leaving the Okamuras.

I saw the foreman only once when he returned with Mr. Yamada. He was a tall, husky man. He brushed by me and ignored me. He must have had a house nearby. On the other hand, Mr. Yamada was a small, wiry man and very friendly. Both Mr. Yamada and the foreman went to work regularly even though the foot-deep snow covered the fields. I wondered about it and was told by Mrs. Yamada that they were fixing the irrigation gates. I ran into Mr. Yamada while he was cleaning the rabbits he had shot. He said the rabbits had to be cured for ten days to kill the strong, wild odor that might be offensive to some people. When properly cured, rabbit meat is very tender and appetizing.

In the fall of 1928 we were required to attend a general school assembly and listen to Principal Carl Lathrop offer his state-of-the-school report. Toward the end of his talk, he announced the inauguration of a school newspaper. Then came the startling announcement: the editor of that publication was to be yours truly. I had not the foggiest notion of how to run a school paper. I had not even thought about being a writer. Moreover, Lathrop did not appoint an advisor. I was all alone.

I was still in the fog when the deadline approached. In self-defense, the account of the Lost Atlantis was inserted. I had been intrigued by this story and thought other students would also be interested. Ten days after its publication, I was called to the principal's office. Mr. Lathrop stood looking out the front window. No one else was in the room.

"Sit down," he said, "and shut the door."

I had no inkling what I had been called for. Mr. Lathrop kept looking out the window and did not speak for the longest moment. The silence put me ill at ease.

"Did you write that article?"

"No," I said.

"Who did? Where did you find it?" he asked.

"I took it out of a little pocket Blue Book I own," I replied.

"That's plagiarism!" he retorted. "You can't take an article someone else wrote and publish it."

There was a long silence and Mr. Lathrop went back to his window-gazing. I prepared myself for the worst.

"I want you to write the next story yourself," Mr. Lathrop said finally.

I was in no better position than before. What to do? I had read lots of Zane Grey stories about the West, and inspired by them to write about a proud stallion and its escapades with hunters, I set the stage in the Big Sky country of Montana. That would solve the plagiarism issue. Neither the imaginary stallion nor Montana could be faulted. The story was published in the spring edition, but I did not stick around for feedback.

In May 1929 a surprise offer came from my brother Casey. He was employed by the Long Bell Mill in Longview, Washington.[23] He said he was willing to defray my rail fare if I wished to return to the coast. He said a job awaited me at the mill also. I was eager to shake the dust of Pocatello, for economic prospects in Idaho were far from bright. I had fully expected to work for the Yamadas over the summer in repayment of their kindness, but I could not pass up this opportunity. Casey was already contracted to leave for Wrangell, Alaska, in six weeks and I could also go north, if I wished, after a month's stint.

Casey came out to Portland to meet me and we took the bus to the Longview sawmill. I was assigned to the skid chain on the night shift. Eventually, I was rotated to the No. 1 bin, which was right next to the saw and spilled out the largest pieces of lumber, 2 x 12s. The Japanese foreman usually lent a hand, but one night he was absent from work. Neighbors offered no help. There was no friendliness among the Issei crew. I was so angry that I swore I'd get away as soon as possible.

I got in contact with Mr. Kushi in Seattle and he arranged for my going to Hidden Inlet.[24] At the conclusion of the season, I was proclaimed a journeyman butcher and was told to apply thereafter for work in that capacity. Butcher was the highest status to which Oriental laborers could aspire in the canneries. It was rated as a semi-skilled trade in the industry. Among the Asian workers, butchers were VIPs.

The process begins with the catch. Salmons are kept in holding bins via conveyor belts. There is no refrigeration so salmons can't be held in the bins too long. That accounts for the long hours at the peak of the harvest. The fish are lined up by the feeder for the cutter. The rotary bar carries the salmon through the stationary knife, where the head is removed and the body then flipped on to the "Iron Chink"[25] table. The second butcher feeds it tail first into a huge rotating drum; the tail is gripped with pins. The drum carries the fish where its belly is slashed and innards removed and washed. Whatever remains is cleaned by the "wash fish" crew, which is made up in general by Alaska Natives. The conveyor belt carries the fish to the cutting machine, the packing machine, the can-top sealing machine, and finally to the retort stackers.

I returned to Seattle and was shipped to the railroad on the plains of North Dakota by the A. B. Contract Office. The destination was an "extra gang" holed up fifty miles east of Williston. Though I didn't know it until we began our move, the little community of Stanley was only a mile east. I was the sole recruit. The camp was on a siding in the middle of nowhere. The site was a vast, flat prairie that stretched interminably into the distance. The sun rose between twin buttes visible far on the eastern horizon. Dimly visible to the south were the vague outlines of a mountain range. The heat scorched the Great Plains, making sleep difficult until the cooling of the earth. I would sit beside the gang-car door and listen to the symphony of the myriad sounds of insect life that came alive after dark. Far to the south, the coyotes' howls would break the silence. Here one could feel the sounds and pulse of the awesome vastness of the great Dakota plains.

Six weeks later, the gang cars moved southeast of the Garrison Reservoir, which feeds the mighty Missouri, to the city of Underwood. Workers on the railroads went weeks and months without seeing any outside persons, especially womenfolk. Thus, when two carloads of prostitutes bore down on the gang cars at Underwood, the men broke out in catcalls, whistling, and hoots. Two dapperly dressed pimps chaperoned the prostitutes, who were said to have come fifty miles from Bismarck to the south. The women were dressed gaily and wore overly painted, hard faces. A single gang car up ahead was set aside for conjugation.

The second visit occurred at the Indian reservation village of Plentywood, nine miles from the Canadian border in northeastern Montana. One fellow in our gang car let out a war whoop at the sight of the prostitutes. At that moment, the Anglo timekeeper who was passing by stopped and looked up. His gaze locked with mine. He hesitated and then went on. On the third day, I was approached.

"I've got a whole boxcar to myself," he said. "Would you like to move in?"

"Is it heated?" I inquired.

"It's heated all the time," I was assured. "It's warm in the boxcar."

I was concerned about the heating because when the heat died down, it grew awfully cold. Talk was to the effect that the temperature would drop forty degrees below zero in northern Montana. I moved in but assumed an obligation to the timekeeper. Winter work is voluntary, although it was hard to scare up eight volunteers for a crew to straighten roadway rails. I felt compelled to answer each call. The foreman appeared to be a middle-aged Issei who kept his distance from the crew. His orders were given by pantomime from a hundred feet up the line.

I had purchased warm clothing at the J. C. Penney store in Plentywood. These consisted of felt insoles, a sheepskin vest, sheepskin gloves, heavy wool socks, and logger boots. My search at the first stop, the tiny hamlet of Antelope on the Big Beaver Indian Reservation[26] twenty miles from the Canadian province of Saskatchewan and ten miles from the Montana–North Dakota border, had been fruitless. The only bare spot on my body was my face, which could get mighty chilled even with the winter sun aloft. We started throwing off our heavier garments around ten o'clock, though I was forced to put them back on at three. But even this work broke the monotony.

The third and final winter quarter was at the town of Poplar, forty miles south of Plentywood and twenty-four miles east of Wolf Point, a major Montana city. We were now sixty miles from the Canadian border, where we remained until the spring thaw.

Throughout the cold winter months, the timekeeper made yeoman efforts to discourage my working on the railroad. "This is not the life for you," he would say. "If you keep working on the railroad, you'll wind up just like these other men. They are ignorant. They don't have any purpose in life. I've worked for the railroad for seventeen years. I've seen them go away, waste their earnings, and come back year after year. You should get away from this; do something else. You don't want to be like them."

In another conversation, the timekeeper confided: "I have a family and a young son. I want to help raise my son and be with my wife as a family. We have a nice little house. There's no future on the railroad. It's a poor life. I am quitting the railroad when the spring thaw comes. You should do what I intend to do; leave when the spring thaw comes."

I came to believe in the wisdom of the timekeeper's notion, and when spring rolled around I left for Seattle. It was when I reached J-Town[27] that I became aware of the great stock market crash of October 1929. Out in the solitude of the vast Dakota plains, no word concerning it had reached us. Nor were there newspapers at any of the winter quarters at which the gang cars stopped. J-Town had yet to be affected and life proceeded there as normal.

In Seattle I found employment as a helper for a drayage company but quit after coming close to stumbling down three flights of stairs. I had visions of my falling down those flights of stairs with the big steamer trunk tumbling after me and crushing me at the bottom. Unable to locate another job, I gave the *Courier* of Jimmie Sakamoto a try. As his wife, Misao, told me, they were not hiring. I was turning away when she asked me to wait. Mrs. Sakamoto went into a cubbyhole office and came out after a long wait. "Jimmie would like to speak to you," she said.

The office I entered was dark, small, and crowded. It was lit by a little night light. Before a desk, the figure of Sakamoto hunched over on his elbows. Above him to his left could be seen a typewriter, obviously on a flexible stand. Surprisingly, there was a second desk, beside which I sat down. Mr. Sakamoto neither stirred nor welcomed me and I simply waited for the great man to speak.

When he did speak, it was sudden, his voice hard, brittle, and overpowering. The words came out more like a pebbled growl. I was indignant and startled. "Why don't you go home?" he asked. "Your father was in here last week. We had a long talk. Your father is getting pretty old. He is almost in his eighties. He does not have many more years left. He is very lonely and you should go home and make his last years happy."

That all came out in a single blast. I had not known Father knew blind Sakamoto well enough to confide in him. Sakamoto's outburst aroused anger and resentment. His presumptions were intolerable. But his words set me to thinking. Then a few days later I chanced across an island acquaintance on a J-Town street. He conveyed a similar message. I listened and became more convinced that I probably should return home.

I asked this man to convey information to my father to meet me at the 2:30 p.m. ferry the following Friday afternoon at Winslow. He was there. We drove to the Johnson House, to which he had returned. To celebrate my return, he obtained a fresh-killed chicken and cooked it with rootstocks in soy sauce. It was all that he could afford. I called it Japanese goulash and I had eaten it many times.

The decision to go home brought an advantageous benefit. I closed my bank account just two days before the Oriental American Bank[28] closed its door. It was the first bank failure in J-Town and was the harbinger of difficult times ahead. The Great Depression worsened and it was beginning to take its toll in J-Town. Casey had left home in 1927 and was lending a hand to a family friend engaged in farming. I don't know that he ever went back home after his departure.

I continued my education at Bainbridge High School. The school lacked a student newspaper and I kept my reportorial efforts sharp by contributing to the community newspaper, the *Bainbridge Island Review*[29] of Port Blakely, and taking a course in journalism. The class was involved in a dual competition arrangement with a Montana journalism class. My offering, which was voted the best hands-down at Bainbridge High, also achieved top billing in Montana. It was probably due to this success that I was named a delegate to the State Student Leaders Conference, the first Nisei to win that designation.

The farewell speech to the delegates was given by a journalism professor at the University of Washington. The hall was a cylindrical-type structure with seats arranged perpendicularly. The podium was thirty feet below the assemblage. When the professor finished his keynote address, I addressed the podium.

"What would my chances be on the metropolitan dailies?" I asked.

"None!" he said laconically.

The professor's response tickled the audience. It prompted general laughter. I remained standing for further clarification.

"I didn't mean my answer to be humorous," the professor declared in a somewhat admonishing tone when the laughter subsided. "I was just stating a fact. Why don't you try Jimmie Sakamoto's *Courier*? He might have a spot for you."

His suggestion was out of the question. Rumor floated rampant that the paper was on the financial rocks. Besides, I had already tried. What I was hearing was that newspaper work in the Seattle area was not within the reach of the Nisei.

I was also enrolled in literature at Bainbridge. I state this because of a particular incident that occurred in class one afternoon. I was looking out the window during a recitation when the teacher, Miss Alice Howard, interrupted. "Some students think they are so good that they don't have to pay attention," she said. She then asked me for the answer. I was so upset by this public call-down that I gave the wrong answer on purpose. She then ordered me to stay after school.

"I knew the right answer," I said, as Miss Howard approached.

"I knew you knew the right answer," Miss Howard agreed. "What were you thinking?"

I had to think fast. I couldn't tell her she was covering old ground. I needed to grasp for a plausible answer.

"I was wondering what I would have for dinner," I blurted out. Of course, I was thinking of no such thing.

"Is that why you always study during the lunch hour?" she asked.

The fact was that we had no food with which to make lunch. It would be awkward to be among students having lunch with no lunch to eat. The stomach can get accustomed to go without eating.

I reached into my desk the next noon hour to get out a book and found an apple. If I refused the apple, I would offend Miss Howard. I realized her action came out of the goodness of her heart. It troubled me. Since I couldn't reject it, I ate the apple. It was followed by a thick piece of apple pie and an orange, a slice of cake, and sandwiches (topped by one made of roast beef). I did not know how to stop her.

Then Miss Howard said: "We were at dinner last night and the old librarian was there. I was talking about you and suddenly she cut in: 'That must have been the boy who used to check out books far beyond his age.' That must have been you!"

It was nice of Miss Gideon to remember me. She was a straitlaced librarian, tall and thin, favoring pince-nez glasses. She never smiled or spoke, just stamped the date. She had to stamp a lot of books for me because I checked out six to ten books at a throw.

I have no idea whether I would have remained at Bainbridge to complete my schooling. The Boys Club election on the final day, however, was a factor in my leaving. I was nominated for each position but lost by one vote. The results had a tendency to frustrate my prospects. I entered Broadway High School in Seattle[30] in the fall.

The early 1930s was a period of labor strife in the Pacific Northwest with the racketeering, strong-arm bossism of Dave Beck in Seattle[31] and with the rancorous John L. Lewis building his Congress for Industrial Organization (CIO) into a formidable threat to the American Federation of Labor (AFL).[32] Most accounts of the unionization of cannery workers tend to ignore the jurisdictional struggle by the upstart Filipino union in the fall of 1931. The Filipino group was prompted by two University of Washington Nisei students, Dyke Miyagawa and George Takigawa.[33] The movement blossomed after Issei workers had dispersed for winter work and schoolboys had returned to classes.[34] The Japanese cannery workers were kept in the dark as to any projected unionization.

The strength of the CIO cannery workers was the Filipino union, workers disenchanted with pay structures and living conditions resulting from the exploitation by labor contractors—in this case almost all of Japanese origin. Rallies were held but Japanese cannery workers did not participate in the dispute. Representing the labor contractors—Kushi, Nagamatsu, A. B., and others—was Clarence T. Arai, the first Nisei lawyer in the Pacific Northwest.[35] Arai personally circulated a petition, which would prove critical later, without proper orientation or attempt at defining consequences. Twenty-five names appeared on the petition, all of whom were unaware that signing the petition could lead to blacklisting.

My brother Casey and I signed the petition. Seattle metropolitan papers accused the upstart union as being infiltrated with communist radicals. The petition was submitted to the Seattle Central Labor Council.[36] The Filipino union won the right to represent the cannery workers in a jurisdictional battle within the AFL. The victory for the union was peculiar in that it only controlled hiring practices of Seattle-based cannery operators and did not encompass the total Alaskan salmon industry. Crews from Portland,

Oregon, and San Francisco could operate in nonunion status. The twenty-five signers of the labor contractors' petition were blacklisted, Arai being derelict in not obtaining amnesty from union reprisals. I was not apprised of the blacklist until the spring of 1932 when I applied for cannery work. None of the Japanese contractors would touch my case. I went to union headquarters downtown to plead my case. I was given a forty-five minute audience by George Takigawa. I pointed out a blacklist would jeopardize my graduation at Broadway High School, but he was unmoved. Nor would he consider the fact that I took no active part in opposing the union. He always came back to the fact that my name was on the petition.[37]

I went back to Mr. Kushi and appealed to him again. He informed me that a foreman from Portland would be coming to Seattle to recruit workers and he would recommend my name. On Mr. Kushi's recommendation, I was hired as a journeyman butcher at Union Bay, a cannery within the sphere of Ketchikan.[38] By this time, the Great Depression had eroded cannery wages, the common laborers receiving thirty-five dollars per month and journeyman butcher, the highest rated occupation, going at fifty-five dollars.

I obtained a schoolboy job with two retired teachers while attending Broadway. It was on Broadway and Pine streets. I received a visit one evening from an Issei woman, Mrs. Yamamoto of Beacon Hill. I knew Mrs. Yamamoto, who was accompanied by her eldest son.

"Franny goes out every night," she said. "I don't know where he goes. I don't want him to get into trouble. I want you to be with him wherever he goes. If I know he's with you, I won't worry!"

That was a tall order. I had been entrusted with a heavy responsibility. She had also conferred an extremely high honor. I was overwhelmed by the request. I knew her son from several seasons in the Alaska canneries. We had become close friends.[39] Mrs. Yamamoto operated a wholesale confectionary in J-Town. She was the mother of seven children, four boys and three girls. She was also one of two Issei women I had ever met whom I'd consider lovely with great charm.

The first schoolboy job lasted only to the seasonal holidays when the retired teachers moved to the country to be with a younger sister. I was fortunate to hook on with the Tibbals family in Queen Anne Hill. But a month later I came down with a severe flu. I was replaced by a former helper and moved upstairs to the guestroom. "You can stay with us as long as you want," Mrs. Tibbals told me. "But I won't be able to pay you the fifteen dollars per month." I required the stipend for carfare and lunch money.

I was sick a very long time, nearly two months. I couldn't be staying at the Tibbals with no work to do. Though very weak, I discussed my predicament with Miss Rumsey. Not long after, I was notified that space had been made for my staying at the Fujin Home, Japanese Women's Home.[40] Thereupon, I moved in. However, the long illness left its mark. I flunked my Spanish course and was compelled to retake the course in order to graduate. The teacher said I made B+ but because it was a retake, she was giving me a C. It was the only course I had ever flunked.

The racist climate at Broadway was not much different from that at Bainbridge. Strong antipathies existed toward Nisei students. Very little socialization and fraternization existed. Some teachers showed hostility. One was a red-haired typing teacher. I did well in a ten-minute typing test that counted 80 percent toward the course. She accused me of cheating in class and I was told to retake the test. I did better. The teacher offered no apology. I haven't figured out yet how one could cheat in a typing test.

Though this illustrates the extreme bias and insensitivity of this teacher toward Nisei students, there were others who came to my succor. The outstanding example was Miss Foote, a venerable history teacher, who encouraged me to try out for the debate team. The administration disqualified me due to age. In the meantime, I had entered an oratorical contest and Miss Foote prepared me for it. She arranged half a dozen "home room" practice sessions. It all came to naught when the contest was called off.

One spring afternoon while walking down the halls of Broadway, I was joined by a tall, slender Nisei girl who asked for my help to form a Japanese Students Club. I informed her that I disapproved of self-segregation, but was talked into meeting with the prospective advisor. "Many Japanese students have benefited from education at Broadway," Miss Thomle declared. "The purpose of the Japanese Students Club is to establish some sort of a memento to be given to the school in appreciation of the education obtained."

Couched in those terms, I was unable to refuse. I did the recruitment of the Nisei students and chaired the first five meetings. Entertainment was furnished by tiny-tot acrobats. Miss Thomle called for an election of officers. I was able to induce a large Buddhist delegation of thirteen and five brethrens of the Baptist Japanese Commons Club (JCC) to attend. This supplemented a dozen diehard regulars. I had no idea that the five JCC members had turned out to block my election. Their withholding their votes allowed the Buddhist group to outpoll the regulars by a single vote. No one said a word, but Miss Thomle was heard to snort.

I was never contacted the remainder of the spring term. I had become the forgotten man. On the last day of school, someone brushed in front of me as I was walking down the hall. Startled, I stopped. Miss Thomle, the advisor, had come to a halt several paces away.

"Jimmie, the fellows are holding a dance in the gym. You're welcome to join them if you wish."

"No thanks," I replied.

"I understand," she said.

What was unknown to the Japanese Students Club group was that the JCC five were out to wreak vengeance for my alleged violation of club decorum. The JCC group had refused to endorse any censure or punishment.

FIGURE 5. A graduate of Seattle's Broadway High School in 1932, where he played varsity baseball, Jimmie Omura was recommended and personally recruited by the assistant dean of students at the University of Washington. But with the nation in the grip of the Great Depression, Omura was unable to seek higher education. Accordingly, he sought employment in journalism, even though mindful of the lack of opportunities for Nikkei on mainstream newspapers and the dead-end prospects within the Japanese American press. Omura Papers, Green Library, Stanford University.

Two incidents had upset some members. The first was a water-splashing duel between two boats at a church picnic; the second was for my demonstration of levity at my own baptismal. Each time I was advised JCC members had considered the traditional reprimand of paddling but voted against it. Because the tip had come from a Rainier Valley member each time, I did not suspect the disenchanted were among the very group with whom I associated. The Japanese Commons Club five had devised their own punishment by not supporting my election.

To add more salt to the wound, I was approached by a different member and asked whether I would sell the pins and insignia of the club. I was in very great need of ready cash but refused on principle. I was a member of the club and none of the meetings should have been held without my knowledge. Besides, I was entitled to face my accusers. I had no use for the pins and insignias but the request was an insult.

The Japanese Students Club incident climaxed my already strained and weakening outlook on the Christian religion. I had begun to reach the conclusion that being a Christian was no better than being an infidel. Most parishioners were simply make-believe Christians burdened with the baggage of hypocrisy. If a religious fraternity such as the Japanese Commons Club finds the normal enthusiasm of a member so offensive to its society, it wasn't the sort of fraternity of which I wanted to be a part. I was at the time serving as a Sunday school teacher, coach of the Little Tots basketball team, and was also a member of the church's hard-court team. In a fashion, the JCC experience served as a catalyst to sour me on religion. My toleration for bigots and hypocrites had worn thin. This is not to say I lost any basic faith, but I could see only the hypocrisy of the faithful, not only demonstrated by JCC members but by the congregation as a whole.

I began my final semester at Broadway in the fall of 1932. By late October my finances had reached a critical stage. I was not aware that it showed— the worry of having to drop out of school. "Why do you look so worried?" Miss Foote asked one afternoon as I was passing in the hallway.

"I'm afraid I will have to drop out of school," I said.

This news disturbed Miss Foote. It was known among the faculty and the administration that I was in my graduating semester. She expressed confidence that a solution could be found. The next day she said, "Mr. Henderson has found a place for you." Mr. Henderson was the boys advisor. He sent me with a note to the Red Shield Boys Club in downtown Seattle.[41]

Miss Foote inquired ten days later and was appalled to hear that I had been sent to a transient refuge. She promised to find something better. I was walking down the hall at the end of my studies when a man sidled up to me.

"Miss Foote brought up your case in a faculty meeting," I was informed. "I share an apartment near the school. You're welcome to stay with us. I'm a history teacher, too. My name is Don Nylen. I room with a young man, a recent arrival from Scotland. Take the key and let yourself in. I've got a faculty meeting to attend."

The apartment covered half of the top floor. There was a small room off the kitchenette where I bedded down. Things went well until I came down with the flu.

Soon after my recovery, Don's roommate accused me of using a four-letter word and issued an ultimatum that I either leave or he would move to the YMCA. Don stuck with me but was unable to manage the rent himself. It required a move to the University of Washington district, where two sharp Nisei boys from down in the valley shared the downstairs floor at the Horsley residence. These were both straight-A students.

The midterm graduation was held at the Civic Auditorium. Don accompanied me to the ceremony. I looked around the auditorium before the lights were doused and could find no familiar faces. I prepared myself for a perfunctory courtesy applause but was completely overwhelmed when a thunderous applause greeted my appearance. It was exceeded only by the applause given the president of the student body. I was greeted warmly by the presiding official. It was a grand sendoff I had never anticipated. I still wonder about it.

Don soon departed for Europe. He had won a fellowship to the University of Vienna.[42] Having nowhere to go, I remained at the Horsleys'. One evening a visit was received from the assistant dean of men at the University of Washington. Sid Spear was a tall, lanky, darkish-complexioned man. He seemed to be east European.[43] He said I was highly recommended. For forty-five minutes he attempted to have me register at the university for the fall term. "If you don't go at least one quarter, you'll never go to college," he declared on his departure. I knew he was right but I couldn't swing it with the low income in the Alaska canning industry. The letter of recommendation was left behind and it definitely stated I would need university help. Mr. Spear never mentioned the subject.

THREE

Dateline California, 1933–1940

Convinced of the dim economic prospects in the Pacific Northwest, I headed for Los Angeles on the Greyhound Bus after returning from Alaska. I hit the Iwaki drugstore[1] in the heart of Lil' Tokio[2] at four in the afternoon and decided on a quick dinner before hunting for a place to stay. The streets were clogged with home-goers when I turned to leave. While I stood and watched the mass of people, I heard my name called and saw, snaking through the throng, the familiar faces of the Kadoya brothers, whose acquaintance I had made in Alaska. These were Kibei boys, well educated and quiet. I was escorted to their hotel and informed of an opening as English editor at the newspaper where they worked as Japanese typesetters.

I was hired the next morning by the *New Japanese American News* (*Shin Nichibei*)[3] and thereby inducted into the Nisei vernacular press. If I thought I was launched on a journalistic career, it certainly was not an auspicious beginning. The *New Japanese American News* was a morning newspaper. I went on duty at four in the afternoon. I started out at the magnificent wage of fifty cents per day; I also got a room at the Iowan Hotel and meals at an upstairs kitchen at East First Street and Weller Court. The total package could be estimated at around forty-five dollars per month. That was very slim picking, but this was in the depth of the Great Depression and it was better to have a job than to be idle.

Dust Bowl refugees from Oklahoma and Arkansas descended upon California, and "Hooverville" shacks had sprung up in rural districts.[4] Men stood for blocks in Los Angeles for handouts at innumerable "soup

kitchens."[5] Vendors peddled all sorts of wares on the streets of the southern city—fruits, neckties, toiletries, and so on. Those who inhabited "Hell's
Kitchen"[6] dished out ten cents for questionable stews. Hell's Kitchen was a
piece of downtrodden real estate between Los Angeles and Hill streets and
running from East First to Seventh streets. I was idly stirring a bowl of stew
when a dead rat showed up. It ended my patronage.

The city of Los Angeles was still recoiling from the impact of the Long
Beach–Los Angeles earthquake. Scars of the tremor were evident in downtown Los Angeles in October 1933, with cracked cement and streets, alleys,
and sidewalks strewn with large chunks of cement that had hurtled down
from above. Aftershocks were still rumbling through the city. The image of
tall buildings swaying perilously as if threatening to crash down on unwit-
ting passersby was a strange and awesome prospect.

Nisei journalism was sedentary in nature, seemingly at its embryonic
stage. It was unexciting, as no reporters appeared to cover events, even those
in which Nisei were participating. Walking into the Los Angeles Memorial
Coliseum press boxes or boxing matches was a lonely feeling. The leading
vernacular dailies were the *Rafu Shimpo* [*Los Angeles Japanese Daily News*][7]
and the *Kashu Mainichi* [*Japan-California Daily News*],[8] but Nisei editors
were conspicuously absent. All Nisei editors functioned short-handed, some
more than others.

News items came through the mail or by phone or were clipped from
other publications and rewritten to editorial specifications. Not even the
popularity of the Lumpe Lions, a skilled collection of midget football talents, performing between halves of Pacific Coast League football games,[9]
brought out the troops. Nor did a single Nisei editor or reporter attend
the mainland debut of Johnny Yasui, a Hawaiian Nisei boxer,[10] facing the
emergence of Ceferino Garcia, a fighter on the rise.[11] The job as editor was
a learning experience and an orientation to what was called Nisei journalism. It soon became abundantly clear that Nisei journalism was simply not
highly regarded in the world of journalism. It brought no income to the
publishers.

Getting acquainted in a new location and new job is normally frustrat-
ingly difficult, but the Nisei staff of the rival *Japan-California Daily News*,
edited by Lawrence Tajiri[12] and sidekick Brownie Furutani,[13] eased the way
in Lil' Tokio with a warm welcome on the first weekend of my editorial stint.
I was spirited to the popular Iwaki Drug, where introductions were made of

Nisei notables—Ken Matsumoto,[14] Masao Satow,[15] Kay Nishimura,[16] Ken Tashiro,[17] T. John Fujii,[18] and others—and escorted by Brownie to the Oliver Club.[19] We became a threesome, taking in the downtown movie palaces and afterward enjoying a gabfest over coffee and rolls.

When I ran a short item on the death of Sen Katayama, a Communist leader, in Moscow, I received the first contact from a Japanese Communist. Katayama was a convert of the People's Rights Movement in Japan and had fled to America to establish cells in Oakland, Los Angeles, and Seattle. He lived in San Francisco for a while and was internationally prominent. Although communism was not my brew, I considered his death as news.[20] I received the visit of the Communist contact at my Iowan Hotel room. He was an Issei and a mouse of a man and extremely furtive. Later I was approached by a young Kibei Communist. But in each case I was not favorably impressed. The Oakland Nisei Democrats[21] and Karl Yoneda[22] represented the Communist ideology in the Golden Gate districts, and the tribulations and travails of the Great Depression made it expedient for recruits among them.

One event of inspiring effect was the cherry tree planting at the Pasadena mansion of W. A. Alexander, the Pacific shipping magnate.[23] John Steven McGroarty, the poet laureate of California,[24] rendered a heartrending and specially written poem, "Japanese Cherry Tree Planting," for the occasion. I was so impressed by this poem that I requested a copy and the right to publish it. The poem stirred the muse within me, but after three years of effort I was unable to compose anything worthwhile.

Although my own creations were mediocre, I offered five of my poems for publication consideration to the *Japanese-American Courier* in Seattle. The associate editor was Bill Hosokawa.[25] He flipped through them cursorily and rejected them outright. The five poems were ultimately published in the *Japan-California Daily News* of Los Angeles.[26] Then one day a letter came from Alameda, California, stating: "Your poem SANCTUARY will be read during the 'Songs at Eventide' feature, Monday evening, September 17, 4:15 p.m., over K.R.O.W. in Oakland."[i] That was certainly an honor for a poem not deemed good enough for Seattle's *Courier*.

If I were to single out one person in Los Angeles I might call a friend, it would be Bill Kono, a slender, rather tall sort of Nisei. He dropped by one

---

i [Ed. See postcard dated September 16, 1934, addressed to Omura at the *New World News* in San Francisco, California (OP).]

evening and his visits became a nightly thing. It was through Kono that an interview was arranged with Toshia Mori (neé Ichioka), the winner of the Wampus Baby Star of 1932, sponsored by the U.S. Western Association of Motion Picture Advertisers, at her Boyle Heights residence. Toshia Mori (1912–95) made her mark in the film *Daughter of the Dragon* and also was cast as Chita in *Fury of the Jungle*. At the time of the interview, she was having a flap with Columbia Pictures and was trying to break a six-year contract. Kono was a family friend, and Toshia Mori's father, Dr. Toshio Ichioka, was a prominent Lil' Tokio physician and surgeon.[27]

Bill Kono was a commercial radio operator. When he landed a job, we went to Philippi's to celebrate. Philippi's was a popular after-dance eatery near the Los Angeles Memorial Coliseum. There we listened to soft music, sipped port wine, and munched on Polish sausage on Italian buns.[28] That weekend Bill went on a fishing expedition to Lake Arrowhead in the San Bernardino Mountains and was drowned in a boating accident. Years later I noticed his portrait on a mantel in a Jefferson Heights[29] home but did not inquire about it because of the coolness with which I was received. My thoughts have often wandered back to that night at Philippi's.

I resigned my editorial position with the *New Japanese American News* in February 1934 and took a standby job in Hollywood. Three weeks later I ran into a group in Lil' Tokio interested in resurrecting the *Pacific Weekly*.[30] I was urged to join the group.

"I can't come in without a job," I protested.

"We'll get you a job," declared Kay Nishimura. "There's plenty of fruit-stand jobs around."

"I'd also need a place to stay and eat," I added.

"That's no problem," Dick Takeuchi[31] spoke up. "You can stay with me at the Iowan. We can eat at the newspaper's communal kitchen." It appeared he worked for the *Shin Nichibei* after my departure.

These measures were to be temporary until the revival of the weekly. Others of the group were Howard Kakudo, a commercial artist;[32] Dick Nobuhata, a silkscreen painter;[33] Ruth Kurata, a secretary;[34] and Aki Miyagishima, a former Tacoma, Washingtonian.[35] The publisher was Franklyn Sugiyama.[36] I picked up day jobs at Los Angeles area fruit stands, and when the Kadoya brothers turned over a South Central San Pedro fruit-stand job to go to the country, I took over the work. I was fired two months later.

Franny Yamamoto, my buddy from Seattle,[37] arrived just at this time with a "swamper" prospect at the Ninth Street Wholesale Market.[38] This general assistant job came about in the nick of time. Dick was kicked out of the Iowan Hotel. Quarters were found at the Ohio Hotel on East First Street,[39] a couple of doors from the Miyako. I footed the rent and maintenance money and Dick shopped and did the cooking. The site became the stomping ground for the transplanted and the footloose. The *Pacific Weekly* did resume publication but it was short-lived.

The summer of 1934 turned out to be blistering hot in the Southland. The continuous heat wore me down physically. It seemed imperative that I find a cooler climate. On the insistence of T. John Fujii, an itinerant Yobi-yose[40] journalist, I stopped in San Francisco to look up a mutual Seattle friend at the *New World Daily*. The acquaintance was long gone and the man at the helm was young Yasuo Sasaki. Sasaki was all enthused about my succeeding him as the paper's English-language editor as he would be returning to his biochemistry studies at the University of Cincinnati in two weeks. He set in motion the machinery, which the editor in chief, Takeshi Ota, consummated. Sasaki was not unknown in the Nisei literary circles, as he had authored the quarterly *Reimei* publication in 1931 when he was living in Salt Lake City, Utah. *Reimei* published eight pocket-sized editions.[41]

The *New World Daily* was the oldest continuously published Japanese immigrant newspaper in the United States. It was inaugurated in 1894 by Hachiro Saejima, and in 1925, along with the *Japanese American News*, was the first vernacular newspaper to offer an English section.[42] The *Rafu Shimpo* of Los Angeles followed the next year, in 1926, when it lured UCLA student Louise Suski to edit an English weekly.[43] The *Japanese American News* started out with an Anglo editor, while the part-time editor of the *New World Daily* was Oski Taniwaki, a technical student at the University of San Francisco. Taniwaki, like Fujii, was a Yobiyose regarded as a Nisei journalist.[44]

Though I was not aware at the time I assumed the editorship of the *New World Daily*, I stood on the brink of the so-called Golden Age of Nisei Journalism. Lawrence Tajiri, the brightest star in the Nisei literary firmament, was lured to San Francisco by the rival *Japanese American News*, and his arrival in November 1934 ushered in Nisei journalism's golden era. I was at the *New World Daily*. The breakaway publication, *Hokubei Asahi*, was headed by University of Missouri graduate Howard Imazeki, a strong pro-JACL advocate.[45] The *Nichibei* was also a strong supporter of the Citizens League, but a natural antipathy existed between the two newspapers as the *Hokubei* was the result of a strike at the *Nichibei* plant.[46]

I had already earned the wrath of the JACL hierarchy by the time of Tajiri's arrival in San Francisco. Conflict then developed when the *New World Daily* published an editorial on "leaders."[47] The editorial was not aimed at any specific group, but that did not prevent the JACL leadership from taking umbrage at its theme. Public opinion might differ on this topic. However, since this editorial grew into a lifelong conflict between the Japanese American Citizens League and me, it is presented below.

The man who stands out from the crowd and refuses to trail along like a "little doggie" is often condemned. He is pointed out as a foolhardy, harebrained sap. It is not because the principles for which he stands are wrong. It is because he has the strength and courage to laugh at the sheepish beings.

Second-generation circles sadly miss capable leaders. There are a number of potential "headmen" in the growing army of the Nisei and Sansei. But they lack the power to become leaders because they cannot stand alone. They depend too much upon the emotions and sentiments of their little groups.

Only time will tell the destiny of the Americans of Japanese parentage on these soils. But today they are getting nowhere fast. Those in the second generation who are to become the pillars of these transplanted souls are yet in their adolescent stages.

There are the tomorrows. But must we look to those tomorrows to draw our strength for the realization of our aim? Should we, in the meanwhile, sit in the drawing room and silently hope that a "Gray Champion"[48] will rise to spur us on to victory?

The drama of the Dai-Nisei[49] is tragic. We are young, yes, but we shall not always remain young. Youth flies fast and the twilight falls swiftly. The strength, the energy, the very flower of young spirit dies before they can be tested.

The second generation has contributed little to the welfare of its own group. They have been engrossed too deeply with the fluttery bane of "little society." Like the moth that flits around the flickering flame, they have been caught in the undertow.

It is fear, the dread of public opinion, which silences the potential leaders. They would rather coddle to the good graces of "little society" than stand upright on their two feet and speak their piece. In the common language of the day, they lack the courage of their conviction.

Perhaps they are awaiting the opportune moment. But when will that time arrive? Will it be tomorrow? One seeks too far and looks too high and the moment will slip by unnoticed.

FIGURE 6. After a brief stint in 1933 as the English-language editor for the Los Angeles, California-based *Japanese American News*, in 1934 Jimmie Omura was named editor of San Francisco's *New World Daily News*. It was in this capacity, during 1934–35, that he first crossed swords with the Japanese American Citizens League leadership. Omura Papers, Green Library, Stanford University.

To be misunderstood is no crime. Precedent has shown that contemporaries seldom appreciate or understand. It remains to posterity to judge their works. Nor is it a disgrace to err. We are all fallible and prone to make mistakes. Should that be a deterrent? The path of the Dai-Nisei is cluttered with "jellyfishes."

Saburo Kido, the JACL's voluntary national secretary, found this piece offensive to the League. He expounded his opinion in a letter to JACL patriarch Jimmie Sakamoto.[50] He also criticized the *New World Daily* editor in the *Hokubei Asahi*. That prompted the *Hokubei's* editor, Howard Imazeki, to come steaming into the editorial sanctum of the *New World Daily* to read me a riot act on the function of an editor. I was compelled to listen in silence because of the force of his outburst. Not given an opportunity for response, the *New World Daily* came out with a scathing editorial titled "A CHUMP."[51] Imazeki's intrusion was resented and it seemed it took a lot of crust for him to lecture another editor. The ever-energetic Saburo Kido wrote another private communication to Jimmie Sakamoto. After predicting that I would lose my job should the rumored merger between the *New World* and the *Hokubei* come to pass as expected, Kido contemptuously added: "He sure is a fool to call his future superior a chump. I never heard such an asinine thing."[52]

It came as a surprise to learn that the Third National Biennial Convention of the Japanese American Citizens League was scheduled to be held in 1934 from August 31 to September 2 in Soko Town,[53] as the Japanese district in San Francisco was then called. I was delegated by the *New World Daily* to welcome Sakamoto to San Francisco. I found him, as directed, on Post Street near the Aki Hotel, but standing all alone while his wife Misao was conferring with the driver.

"Mr. Sakamoto, I'm Jimmie Omura," I said. "I was delegated by the *New World Daily* to welcome you to San Francisco."

"Why did they have to send *you*," he growled.

I was startled by his reaction. I gave him a long look, then turned and walked away. At this time I was unaware that Saburo Kido was writing negative reports to Sakamoto. Sakamoto was blind and had to rely on the opinions of others. His attitude was a portent of what was to come. One afternoon I approached the convention headquarters at Kinmon Hall,[54] in search of news items. The delegates were out on the raised cement patio on a break between sessions.

"Keep it up, Jimmie!" shouted a delegate from Stockton. It was Stuart Nakano,[55] whom I knew.

"Keep what up?" I asked somewhat startled.

"Keep up your criticisms," he responded.

"Why?" I inquired.

"I think it helps crystallize our national policies," Nakano declared.

"That's exactly what I was hoping to accomplish," I replied.

This repartee with Nakano was my first inkling that a motion had been offered on the floor of the convention to censure the editor of the *New World Daily*. The motion had been beaten back.

At the convention's conclusion, a delegate named Tokutaro Nishimura Slocum[56] paid a visit to the newspaper office. "You're the only Nisei editor to have the guts to go up against the JACL," he stated, and then asked me to serve as his confidante in the campaign to seek citizenship for Oriental veterans of World War I. "Tokie" Slocum was the campaign director. He was a burly sort of person, opinionated and forceful in speech. He was a Yobiyose and was adopted by the Slocum farm family of North Dakota. He had served in the same Rainbow Division as the celebrated Sergeant York and was his superior as sergeant major.[57] Gassed on the last day of the war, Slocum became a casualty. He had a habit of referring to his ethnic people as "Japs," a form of speech for which I had little use.[58]

The reaction of the JACL to the "leadership" editorial was extremely disturbing. This organization did not enjoy a good repute in the ethnic society and was regarded as a do-nothing group primarily concerned with propagating social elitism. I had not previously been caught up in any undue interest about the Citizens League, but the failed censure effort awoke in me a desire to look into this group.

Like the majority of Nisei, I was less than enchanted with the organization's fraternal approach to membership. Prospective members were preselected and handpicked and, of course, it was presumably representative of the "cream of the crop," although in actuality that was far from the fact. The League eschewed membership of common laborers and Nisei figures not known to be prominent, such as ordinary farmers and entrepreneurs. This practice thus invited the perception toward the group and the creation of its public image as elitist. Its primary objective appeared to be the tendency to sponsor gaudy dances at sites considered exclusive (but in poor taste by Great Depression standards), like the Seattle Yacht Club,[59] the Biltmore Hotel in Los Angeles,[60] the Fairmont Hotel in San Francisco,[61] and the *Chichibu Maru*.[62] Such flamboyant affairs did not sit well with the economically suffering majority Nisei, who saw them as a figurative slap in their faces. With the conclusion of the second Sayonara Ball at the luxurious Biltmore Hotel in Los Angeles,[63] it came to be described as the "Nisei 400," an emulation of high society's New York 400.[64]

Most Nisei envisioned the League as in the grips of the elite who, it was often contended, stood to make capital with their influences and affiliations. Not until Pearl Harbor would the JACL leadership become involved in community efforts to help alleviate the sufferings of the general Japanese American public. Then it took the shape in Los Angeles of the Anti-Axis Committee of the Southern District JACL Council, but this group fell victim of its *inu*, or collaborationist, activities.[65] The situation was somewhat analogous in Seattle with the Emergency Defense Council, headed by the sightless Jimmie Sakamoto and his cohorts in the Seattle Progressive Citizens League, which also participated in a similar *inu* operation with investigative authorities (as publicly disclosed at the Tolan Committee hearings).[66] Not as cooperative were the Bay District Nisei Americans.[67] Only five of fifty approached indicated any willingness to serve as "stool pigeons" until mid-March 1942, when FBI pressure was applied on the leadership of the satellite Japanese American Citizens League.

The unpopularity among Nisei of the JACL organization is evidenced in the defection of college graduates who increasingly shunned the group and joined hostile opposition groups or remained unaffiliated. This rapidly growing trend was exemplified in the Pacific Northwest by Seattle's Junior Chamber of Commerce;[68] in Los Angeles by the marketing industry, as represented by the AF of L labor union; and in the San Francisco region by the East Bay college intellectuals. In 1938 national JACL president Walter T. Tsukamoto[69] issued a public appeal to the "best and the brightest" of college graduates to join his organization and to work from within to improve and strengthen the group rather than criticize the JACL from without.

The weak link in the JACL armor was its bias against the common working Nisei who formed the majority element in the ethnic society. Unlike the Great Emancipator, Abraham Lincoln, who is said to have observed that "God must have loved the common people because he made so many of them," the hierarchy of the Citizens League cultivated only the upper echelon of its ethnic society—Nisei in the professions, scions of entrepreneurship, and large agricultural successes—and patterned its membership requirements to exclude all others. When a JACL official refused to intervene in antilabor legislation before the Washington state legislature with the tart retort that "the JACL is not a labor organization," its appeal to the Nisei society was sharply reduced. "What use is the JACL?" wrote an activist Yakima Valley[70] Nisei girl to Jimmie Sakamoto, the organization's founder. The incident occurred in the throes of the Great Depression when sixteen million people were without jobs and millions were trekking from coast to coast in search of work. The attitude of the JACL was not aimed at benefiting the general Nisei society but merely to grease the palms of the Nisei elite.

The League's asinine effort to censure the editor of the *New World Daily* prompted a study of the organization and its people to determine what made it tick. It was from this study that the *New World Daily* editorially concluded that the JACL was in fact a political organization.[71] To bolster that contention, it cited the organization's activities in the Oriental veterans citizenship campaign,[72] the Takahashi fishing case at southern California's Terminal Island,[73] and its observer status on the Cable Act in the nation's capital.[74]

Unexpectedly, the editorial brought forth vehement denials from the JACL national headquarters. Its refusal to acknowledge the obvious tended to confirm for me the oft-charged criticisms of the group that its leadership lacked a definitive policy and were intellectually confused. The *New World Daily* thereupon charged that without a political goal, the JACL had little excuse for existing.

To counteract the *New World Daily*'s political label, national headquarters sent out two speakers to promote its "non-political" agenda. The first speaker was Tamotsu Murayama, a police and waterfront reporter for the *Hokubei Asahi* newspaper, a fanatically pro-JACL publication.[75] "JACL is non-political!" he proclaimed in the Sacramento delta town of Walnut Grove.[76] Murayama's statement was echoed by Sacramento Nisei lawyer and future national JACL president Walter Tsukamoto when stopping in southeastern Idaho during an Intermountain District[77] tour. This reaction cemented deeper the publicly held belief of the group's indifference to the needs of the ethnic society in deference to its own self-aggrandizement.

It took slightly over a year for Saburo Kido, the linchpin in the national headquarters, to admit its error. I was accosted on the steps of the merged *New World Sun* building in December of 1935:

"Jimmie, you were right!" the admission was made by Saburo Kido. "We made a mistake. What we meant was 'nonpartisan.'" With Kido's admission, I dropped the subject but the "nonpolitical" theme did not die entirely, probably because of failure to pass it down to JACL subordinates. As late as February 1942 it popped up in a community newspaper in the Sacramento area. Then too on February 23, 1942, JACL spokesman Mike Masaoka also claimed the group was "non-political" before being prompted to correct himself by a member of the Tolan congressional panel.[78] Could it have been more than a slip of the tongue?

It was inevitable that my association with Tokie Slocum would be the cause of further rift with the JACL. This was particularly true because of Slocum's rather uncomplimentary regard for the group's leadership. His primary complaint was the lack of financial support being received from the organization in his campaign to gain citizenship for Oriental veterans of World War I. The *New World Daily* focused on this issue, which brought a rejoinder from the pro-JACL *Hokubei Asahi* that published statistics of contributions in the campaign. The *New World Daily* countered the published statistics as indicating contributions supplied by the veterans themselves, not the JACL. It charged that the Citizens League merely processed the contributions from the veterans but did not raise them. This charge stuck! Saburo Kido ridiculed the *New World Daily* editor, claiming he was being "cute" in thinking that he had "inside dope."[79] The matter so angered the JACL hierarchy that it refused to acknowledge Tokie Slocum's success in steering the Nye-Lea Act into law.[80] The citizenship measure had been devised by Slocum at the JACL's founding convention in Seattle in 1930 and executed by him to its successful conclusion with weak financial support from the Citizens League. Still, for better or worse, Slocum represented the JACL and therefore the JACL deserves credit for its auspices and its contribution to Japanese America.

The Okei memorial beautification controversy was the most aggravating incident of my editorial tenure in San Francisco.[81] Charging that the *New World Daily* item had besmirched his personal integrity, a stocky Nisei farmer burst into the editorial room and ranted and raved. He stomped out threatening a lawsuit. The man was so worked up that he failed to give his name or allow for a response. Larry Tajiri, editor of the rival *Japanese American News*, furnished his name. Tajiri called for a response, saying he had a statement from Thomas Yego[82] of Newcastle, which he intended to publish that afternoon. Jofu "John" Fujii had written the article in question, which I had not reviewed prior to publication. The best I could do, therefore, was to issue an oblique statement to the *Nichibei*. In the meantime, Saburo Kido called to inform me that he had Thomas Yego in his office. According to Kido, Yego wanted to file a libel suit and the national JACL was considering joining in the action.

Fujii had discussed writing the piece on the Okei beautification issue and I had given him permission. He was a veteran editor, having previously edited the *Hokubei Asahi* and the *New Japanese American News* of Los Angeles, and for that reason I felt it unnecessary to check his article. He was now gone and I realized that as I was the editor the article was my responsibility. The moment I read the article, I could see the problem. Instead of "drive," the word "fund" had been used. The matter was resolved by the issuance of an "Okay . . . Okei!" explanation.[83] Yego was an early devotee of the JACL movement and because of the *New World Daily*'s critical assessment of the League, he was worked up about a lawsuit to singe this editor's hide. It did surprise me that he had issued a statement to the *Nichibei* even before contacting the *New World Daily*.

The services of John Fujii became available when Michi Oka[84] quit as an assistant at the end of January 1935. Four months later, she sailed for Japan to take up a post as secretary of the YWCA in Tokyo. I was gratified to have Jofu as an assistant. In fact he was the reason I had become editor of the *New World Daily*. But two months later he too was gone.

In any event, Jofu had returned from his usual visit to the *Hokubei Asahi*, where he had once been an editor. He sat near the outer door. I was propped on the opposite end of the long editorial table, my chair leaning against the wall. It was our relaxed period, waiting for the first press run of the day's edition. Jofu brought up the issue of the JACL and we were discussing the matter in a desultory fashion and in normal tones. He rose after a bit and began pacing slowly toward the end of the table as if in deep thought. Upon reaching the end, he suddenly sprang at me with fists flailing. The blows were warded off on my arms, and even under attack there was no power behind it, a mere rat-tat-tat of a child. He stopped as suddenly as he had begun and rushed out of the editorial room.

"John's fired!" the editor in chief, Takeshi Ota, declared, getting out of his chair and coming forward. The entire staff of the Japanese Section had witnessed the incident. I considered Fujii a first-class assistant and strongly protested. This flare-up was a momentary thing and no physical injury had been intended. He was well liked but could be eccentric at times.

"No, he's fired! Mr. Ota reiterated.

In an analysis of the aforementioned "leadership" issue, the arrogance of the JACL came to the fore. Though the eventual Nisei Era was widely predicted, the reference I made to "jellyfishes" in my editorial was, as previously noted, to the Nisei generation as a whole and not to any single group. Obviously, the JACL felt it was the predestined leader and would not brook any criticisms. Its bullheadedness regarding its political bent indicated a fuzziness of its goal and an intellectual deficiency, as did its estimate of the Oriental veterans' campaign.

I possessed some personal knowledge of the JACL leadership. I first met Jimmie Sakamoto in the fall of 1930 and, as earlier foreshadowed, learned that he was a friend of my father. I served as a paid umpire in the *Courier* Baseball League[85] the following spring and when payment was not forthcoming wrote Sakamoto to make the collection. The fee was forwarded to an Alaskan site with a gruff note from Sakamoto stating he was not a collection service. The supervisor of umpires was Hito Okada, who during World War II served as the national JACL's treasurer and managed its wartime office in Salt Lake City before being elected to the JACL presidency in 1946.[86] In 1931 I made the acquaintance of Clarence Arai, a leader in the Seattle JACL chapter and the first Nisei attorney and politico of the Pacific Northwest.[87] Journalist Bill Hosokawa came along in 1935, but I had watched him play basketball for Waseda Nippons some years earlier.[88] Then there was the personable Ken Matsumoto, wartime vice president of the national JACL, whom I met in 1933 in Los Angeles along with Masao Satow, who joined the national JACL staff in 1946 and later served as national director, and Lawrence Tajiri, who would edit the JACL's newspaper, the *Pacific Citizen*, from 1942 to 1952.

The first Sunday of my editorial tenure at the *New World Daily*, Saburo Kido came for a look-see by inviting me to attend the International Institute's meeting with him. Our first meeting was mutually ineffective. Kido was a dapperly dressed, small man who favored a mustache and conveyed the impression to me as one not to be trusted. I knew at once that I had been sized up by him in a negative fashion. In his eyes, I was just a "kid," and so he wrote to Jimmie Sakamoto at the *Courier*.[89] He had very little to say on the way and we arrived too late for the meeting. A woman who I took to be Annie Clo Watson, the Institute's director,[90] greeted us in the hall. She took down three folding chairs and placed them into a semicircle and plunged immediately into a discussion with Kido as if continuing some interrupted conversation. I was not introduced, and even at the time of departure she gave no recognition of my presence. The walk back to the newspaper office with Kido was in silence. I was poorly impressed with both Kido, the obvious glue that held the national JACL together, and the institute's director. Their actions had been crude and inconsiderate.

It was not until the February 16, 1942, meeting of the Bay Region Council for Unity, which will be taken up in the next chapter of this memoir, that I came into direct confrontation with Mike Masaru Masaoka. I met numerous secondary leaders in other capacities, for lower-rung JACL leaders did not speak much about their affiliations with the organization. In fact generally none spoke of their membership, at least during my sojourn in San Francisco.

The Rossi-for-Mayor Candidate Night,[91] sponsored by the JACL at San Francisco's Kinmon Hall in 1935, was a political faux pas. The list of sponsors for the event contained the names of JACL luminaries in the San Francisco Bay Area. The campaign committee was composed of Nisei journalists of the three Nisei newspapers. Not a single person from the public attended. Four political speakers waited around forty-five minutes before departing. The only persons in attendance were Tamotsu Murayama, the chairman of the affair, Iwao Kawakami,[92] Curtis Otani,[93] and I; all of us were from the *New World Sun* and members of Rossi's campaign committee.

Long before Mike Masaoka appeared on the JACL horizon with his tainted "the end justifies the means" proclamation, JACL leaders were involved in lying to each other and engaged in filing untruthful reports. Chairman Tamotsu Murayama toasted the Rossi-for-mayor event in glowing terms: "The Rossi Nite went over big and gave a fine impression upon the Nisei. I think it was a healthy sign of the Nisei toward the American Life."[ii]

Lying to the Nisei public came easily to leaders of the JACL but apparently so also did lying to each other to enhance their image. In July 1943 Masaoka admitted fabrications of information he had communicated to national headquarters. He made this admission in the course of his examination by the Costello Subcommittee,[94] acknowledging that he did so to "impress the JACL with his importance."[95] His postwar public statements are riddled with such inaccurate assumptions and pure imagination. So too are the books by William Kumpe Hosokawa, the League's commissioned propagandist. My review of *JACL in Quest of Justice* touches upon a few of the instances.[iii]

Although the national officers were slow in acknowledging their errors, they also avoided any conscientious liaison with the general Nisei community. Their pet comeback was, "If you've got anything to say, join the League." JACL leadership seemed to think that they—and only they—had the answer to the Nisei utopia. The Citizens League functioned in a secretive fashion and maintained a secretive organization of selective members.

---

ii Tamotsu Murayama to Jimmie Sakamoto, November 4, 1935, Sakamoto Collection, Special Collections Department, Henry Suzzalo Library, University of Washington, Seattle, Washington.
iii James Omura, review of *JACL in Quest of Justice* (New York: William Morrow, 1982), by Bill Hosokawa, in *Amerasia Journal* 11 (Fall/Winter 1984): 97–102.

Much of the League's public releases were written primarily by Jimmie Sakamoto and Saburo Kido and were so inappropriate as to seem concocted on Mount Olympus. Community service of any magnitude was left up to the Japanese Association. The Citizens League became portrayed as a self-interested group that, in the opinion of Issei, was engaged in pursuit of such nonsensical matter as American-style dancing and boozing.

The Japanese American Citizens League was initially organized, funded, and backed by the Japanese Association, a situation dating as far back as the 1921 fight before the Washington legislature (which will be discussed later in this chapter). Only a year after the 1930 formation of the national JACL, Saburo Kido wrote of his dislike of the thought of the Japanese Association deriving credit: "Why let others do things for us and suck the cream when we, ourselves, can build up our organization on a sound and substantial basis? All the other races have such a plan working in their organization."[iv]

Despite its collaboration policy during the eviction and detention periods, the national JACL was not out of the investigative woods. Unknown to them, the FBI was conducting a surreptitious investigation by inducing knowledgeable members to serve as informers against JACL sources and by secret wiretapping of its headquarters and local outlets. JACL members, in other words, were finking on each other without the knowledge of its hierarchy. FBI director John Edgar Hoover issued the following directive: "All inquiries must be handled in the most discreet manner. It is believed the development of confidential informants within the various [JACL] chapters would probably be in the best manner in handling the investigations. . . . To date no indication has been made to the organization or to the leaders thereof that the Bureau is investigating the JACL."[v]

In the spring of 1935 as the imminence of a merger with the *Hokubei Asahi* neared, the rumor mills geared up. The focus of attention was on the English editorial staff. No one could see the melding of a pro-JACL staff with an outspoken critic of the organization. The *Japanese American News* editorially commented on the situation and predicted the discharge of the *New World Daily* editor. Letters of support came from the nation's capital, the first an offer to intervene, stating an asserted influence on the *New World Daily* management. The second included copies of letters to two prominent JACL

---

iv Saburo Kido to Jimmie Sakamoto, November 5, 1931 (Sakamoto Collection, University of Washington).
v John Edgar Hoover to Jay C. Newman, October 7, 1946, FBI file No. 100-31040-151, National Archives.

bigwigs.[vi] Acting unilaterally, however, equal recognition was obtained with the coeditor having autonomy of the second page. The two papers merged in mid-June of 1935 and took the name *New World Sun*.

The loyalties of the merged English staff of the *New World Sun* were divided and an undercurrent of unrest prevailed. But it was not until late December that pro-JACL advocates made any direct advances. The first open complaint came from Saburo Kido, who wrote the "Timely Topics" column on the front page of the *New World Sun* under contract with the newspaper.

"I'm being embarrassed by my friends," he said. "They read my columns and when they turn to your editorials, they say you write exactly the opposite. I'm embarrassed."

I listened to Kido's complaint without comment. Kido was a slick customer. I was aware of his desire to get rid of me and knew that he had been the one to leak the dismissal report about me prior to the merger. The next move was the publication of a highly critical letter in the special New Year edition regarding my functions and talents, presumably written by a Tom Okamoto of Stockton. The op-ed letter stated:

> Sir: The *New World Sun* isn't very bad, but I think the old *Hokubei Asahi* was much better in every way. If you are the same editor who used to edit the *Hokubei*, you are certainly falling down on the job. The *New World Sun* lacks that sparkle of personality the *Hokubei* used to possess. I don't know what . . . is the matter, but I know you have writers who don't seem to amount to very much: like Jimmie Omura who seems to think he is god or something—full of ego, and nothing else. You had better wake up and do something to revive the *Hokubei* personality. —Tom Okamoto, Stockton.[96]

Ten days later a Tom Okamoto of Stockton wrote the *New World Sun* disclaiming authorship of the critical letter and requesting a retraction. His friends, he stated, were ostracizing him and charging: "You don't know Jimmie Omura. How dare you write such a letter?" The disclaimer from Tom Okamoto, already linotyped, was called to my attention. It was clear the first Okamoto letter had been manufactured by a member or members of the *New World Sun*'s English staff.

The matter was discussed with the Japanese staff members of the former *New World Daily*. They were aghast! I was told that Shozo Abe, the publisher of the *New World Sun*, was a "fair and just man, who would resolve

---

vi Ibid.

the matter fairly." Encouraged by this report, I met with the publisher in his apartment and presented my views. He listened in silence to my grievance on the manufactured letter issue, and when I finished briefing him I noticed him in deep thought. He didn't speak for a while but then blurted out, "If you want to sue, go ahead!" I was flabbergasted and shocked. Nothing had been mentioned about a suit. What his attitude seemed to indicate was approval of an unpardonable breach of journalistic ethics. By implication he was not only condoning the violation but also defending it. This was too much!

I briefed the *New World Daily*'s Japanese Section staff members on the result of the meeting, and I informed them that I could not continue to work under a publisher of this caliber.[97] They assured me that a full-scale staff meeting would be called in a couple of weeks to thrash this matter out. I went on to Seattle and was informed by letter that the promised editorial meeting did take place. In May 1982, Howard Imazeki, then editor of the *Hokubei Mainichi*, recalled that board meeting with a touch of unbelief. "It was a blow-out," he declared. "Tosuke [Yamasaki] wrote that letter."

It came somewhat as a surprise that Tosuke was the culprit of the manufactured criticism letter. Our division of authority was separate and thus led to no personal confrontation. It has always been my feeling that the false letter of criticism was not the work of one person but the result of a threesome. It is also an indication of the extent to which devotees of the JACL attempt to go to throttle opposition while advancing the organization's goals.

In the aftermath of the torrid board meeting of January 1936, the English staff of the *New World Sun* was revamped.[vii] The editor-in-chief post went to Tamotsu Murayama. Tosuke Yamasaki, an associate editor, was dismissed and sailed for Japan. The balance of the staff was composed of Howard Imazeki, Iwao Kawakami, and Buddy Uno,[98] with Ann Oshima later joining as social editor.[99] The following year, Imazeki also departed to complete the total shake-up. Imazeki was in charge when the false op-ed letter was published and thus responsible for its publication.

The prewar Nisei journalists were decidedly conservative and on the whole adhered strongly toward the status quo. They were dependent on the largesse of Issei management and restricted by the paucity of opportunities in the economic mainstream. In large measure, their stewardship was

---

vii See *New World Sun*, January 27, 1936.

unimaginative and staid in character, ever careful not to offend the employing authorities or its readerships. Much of their space was devoted to dull
club activities and sports. Lead articles usually came from the Domei News
Agency,[100] which expressed the viewpoints of Imperial Japan on matters of
significance in the international field, or clipped reports of American wire
services. The best one can say about the Nisei media at that time is that it
copied a bulletin-board style of the community newspaper, which is so re-
sistant to literary maturation and journalistic excellence.

Not gifted with any great natural literary talent, I shored up this shortcoming by focusing on issues within the ethnic society avoided by other,
more gifted contemporaries. This meant venturing out on a wider horizon
than the restrictive racial borders of Nisei journalism. Unquestionably, this
would lead to confrontational journalism as it breached the communal ethics
of maintaining the status quo and kowtowing to cultural tenets. I viewed the
function of an editor and editorial responsibility not as a platform for public
popularity but rather—hewing to the wisdom of James Gordon Bennett,
the father of print journalism[101]—in advising aspiring reporters to be true to
their craft. In taking over the editorial reins of the *New World Daily* of San
Francisco, I tried to offer a prescient style of editorship that ultimately would
shake up the orthodox believers. The society itself was criticized and faults
that existed within it were accented, as well as the prejudice and discrimination that burdened efforts toward the ethnic group's upward mobility.

In resigning from the *New World Sun* in 1936, I had in effect left Nisei
journalism and its daily grind of hurly-burly rush that ill befitted a focus
on editorial writings demanding more than casual thought. I arrived in Seattle from San Francisco just in time to catch an address by Professor Yamato Ichihashi of Stanford University[102] to the Seattle Progressive Citizens
League. I was curious to hear this expert on Far Eastern studies propound
his views. At the conclusion of his speech, I rose and made this inquiry:
"What would you recommend should be the policies to be pursued by the
Nisei in the event of a war between Japan and the United States?"

His response was wholly unexpected and asinine. "You shouldn't," he
declared, "be thinking about foolish things like that!"

The audience erupted into jeering laughter at Professor Ichihashi's remarks. Thinking both his reaction and the jeers of the JACL audience to be
totally out of place, I walked out of the meeting and went directly to my
hotel room to type a blistering report. Later, feeling my criticism would be

more effective if aimed at a single target, I removed reference to the local chapter. My critique was published in the *Great Northern Daily News*'s next afternoon edition.[103]

Despite the professor's ridicule, the prospect of war in the Pacific was far from a "foolish thing" in 1936. The Nisei generation appeared to be oblivious to the impending war clouds. This was a far cry from even the itinerant Issei migrants. Since right after the end of World War I, they had begun to worry about just such a conflict.

It was not until the Easter vacation of 1921 when we moved to the Beach-front Bungalow on Eagle Harbor near the ferryboat landing at Winslow that I had firsthand contact with the Issei. Mainland Pacific Northwest Issei came in increasing frequency to our door, seeking to consult with Father, as did the berry farmers of Bainbridge Island. Those were anxious and eventful times for immigrant Japanese. Great concerns were expressed on a bill introduced in the state legislature at Olympia to bar the ownership of land to aliens ineligible for citizenship. To combat the legislation, the Japanese Association in Seattle[104] organized and financed an adult citizen Nisei group, small though they were in number at this stage, named the Seattle Progressive Citizens League.[105] Despite this fledgling effort, the Alien Land Law was enacted in the state of Washington in 1921.[106] Asian prejudice and economic discrimination against Asians were as intense in the Pacific Northwest as they were in California. If San Francisco was the epitome of racism, the Puget Sound region was its North America cradle.[107]

It was from this defeat in the legislature at Olympia that the theory grew into a conviction that the salvation of Japanese in America was integrally entwined with the emerging recognition of their citizen progenies, the Dai-Nisei, as having all the rights and privileges of equality, the same as other citizens. The Alien Land Law of 1921 grew out of the antipathy against the Japanese after the close of World War I when employers refused to discharge Japanese labor in preference to returned veterans. This added to the bigotry already established against Asians by the 1892 Exclusion Act against the Chinese. When immigrants from Japan began to replace Chinese labor, they were confronted with built-in prejudices due to their physical similarity to the Chinese. In 1882 a workingmen's group called the Knights of Labor had ousted the Chinese from the nearby city of Tacoma and was in the process of doing likewise in Seattle when a court order brought a halt. The alien Japanese fell victim to similar bigotry.

The talk of the elders in the early decade of the Roaring Twenties in the Pacific Northwest revolved around the Dai-Nisei as the bright hope to overcome the barriers of economic discrimination and racial prejudice that burdened their lives in America. The Issei spoke often and fondly about the coming of the Nisei Age. Their fondest dream was to see their progenies take their rightful place in the socioeconomic fabric of the nation. But this grand vision of the Issei was destined for disillusionment and doomed to failure. By the early 1930s, the chant had changed to "*Nisei wa dame,*" or "Nisei are no good."[108] What had caused this transformation? The rigors of the Great Depression could hardly be the culprit, since adversity normally steels the heart and allows people to rise above disasters.

The Seattle Progressive Citizens League went into hiatus after the passage of the Anti-Alien Land Act in the state of Washington. In early January 1928 it saw a revival when James Yoshinori Sakamoto, a prep sports hero of a sort,[109] returned from a relatively mysterious boxing career on the East Coast with badly shattered eyesight to establish a weekly publication he named the *Japanese-American Courier.* Sakamoto saw the wisdom of reviving the Seattle Progressive Citizens League as a promotional ploy to enhance the prospects of his newspaper venture. Then, in late August 1930, two and a half years later and using the Seattle Progressive Citizens League as his foundation, he formed the present national Japanese American Citizens League (JACL). From the outset, Sakamoto's ideology was "100 percent Americanism," which was diametrically opposed to the Issei concept of overcoming economic discrimination.[110] The JACL strategy was to impress the immigrant Issei, who held the purse strings, as being the best of the best, which it did. How the JACL performed was the gauge to judge the second generation. The embryo League, as earlier depicted, responded with social high jinks that included showy dance affairs held at lavish sites at which the ordinary Nisei were strangers. These affairs and the JACL's extravagant biennial conventions overshadowed any contributions, which were minimal, that the group performed for the ethnic communities. Its selective system of memberships and its nonproductiveness gave rise to criticisms of the creation of an elite class among the Nisei. The Citizens League was seen as not overly concerned with the practical problems, eschewing major issues of the day such as the difficulties in the labor market. The Issei were understandably unhappy with this trend and, ironically, measured the entire second generation society by the performances of the JACL.

The Citizens League's notion of U.S. patriotism tended to denigrate the emerging Nisei, for whom no need appeared to exist for any patriotic fervor. In the late Roaring Twenties, young Nisei were being educated in the American public school concepts and doing quite well in that regard. I was also in the public schools and did not feel the need for injection of further patriotism. Like any group that sets itself above the multitude, the Japanese American Citizens League steadily lost touch with the Nisei community and the common folks making up its majority numbers. The Citizens League's fraternal structure bred the essence of arrogance within its own ranks and developed its beliefs in its own preeminence.

It was from the immigrant Issei, the commoners who followed the migrant pathway of the West, that I developed the concerns of the inevitability of conflict in the Pacific. These farmers and simple laborers were better attuned to the times than their urban cohorts. They viewed war in the Pacific as a foregone certainty. Whether in the salmon canneries of Alaska, the berry farms of Bainbridge Island, the hop fields of Yakima, or the itinerant flow of California's agriculture, these ordinary members of the migrant West would lay down their vernacular newspapers in the evening after a hot day in the fields and discuss the looming probability of war in the Pacific. And it was then that I would sit and listen attentively to their talk and become inculcated in their farsighted wisdom. Nowhere in my wanderings did the subject ever come up in Nisei circles.

An example of this Issei concern occurred in a farm labor camp in the Stockton, California, area in 1938.

"*Nihon-to konokuni senso-ni ikku*-wa *aolashi ne?*"
(Isn't it foolish for Japan and America to go to war?)

"*Sorewa tottemi kanashimi-no koto.*"
(That could be a very sorrowful happening.)

"*Honto-ni* kuru-*to omaimus-ka?*"
(Do you believe it will truly come to pass?)

"So *omoto rashi-desu.*"
(I believe so.)

"*Kurushi koto.*"
(It's a bad thing.)

"*Senso-wa kure-wa shimin-wo tottemi kawai-so.*"
(If war comes, it would be very sad for the American-born.)

"*So ne!*"
(Isn't that so!)

"*Senso-wa kimashita, shimin-no shitto-wa konokuni-ni heitai-ni ikku-no-wo ataramashi.*"
(If war comes, American-born should properly serve in the United States services.)

"*Sorewa shittoru.*"
(That's understood.)

These common migrants of the immigrant era displayed a surprising perception of the Damoclean Sword that hung ominously over the Pacific, and an awareness of the Nisei status in such a conflict. Though the laws of the United States barred them from the enjoyment of citizenship, these migrant laborers were cognizant of their own status and far more concerned with the problems besetting the Nisei generation. Acutely aware of the prejudice and discrimination in this new land of their hopes, they pinned their hopes on the Nisei as their salvation. It seems unbelievable, therefore, that hostility—even hatred—existed between the generations, as some books tout the domestic situation during the course of the eviction and detention era of World War II. It is sad to contemplate that such was the case in the ethnic leadership of the Japanese American Citizens League. Though differences are a part of any family life, parental hatred is difficult to conceive.

That spring of 1936 I shipped out for Nushagak, off the Bering Sea,[111] for what was to be my seventh and final trip to Alaska. The seas were so rough that the kitchen crew took to bed and I was pressed into service at Cordova. The winds and the waves were so violent when we reached Squaw Harbor on Kodiak Island[112] that machinery had to be transferred to scows[113] for unloading. For all the lashing of the winds and the heaving of the waves, it was a welcome surprise when the ship crossed the Aleutians and the placid waters of the Bering Sea greeted us. The ship anchored in midchannel because of the low tide, and men and machinery had to be portaged several miles by tug-powered scows. The cannery to which we were destined was situated hard against a sharply rising cliff at the mouth of the mile-wide Nushagak River.

Only the enterprising would assay a climb up the steep cliff. Having the longing to view the celebrated tundra of the far north, I attempted the climb but was so exhausted and worn out in reaching the top that not much energy remained for discovery. Nevertheless, the climb was worth the effort, for over a short rise the view of the tundra covering a vast valley stretched into the far distance—an impressive sight. From this high perch, also, the broad reach of the Nushagak River meandered toward the northeast and the interminable stand of the spruce forests marched endlessly into the distant north.

There was no night, only pale twilight. Windows had to be draped with black cloth to woo sleep. The most magnificent spectacle is the Aurora Borealis or the Northern Lights. Each night their brilliance was awe-inspiring. Summer in the far north is not much different from summer on Bainbridge Island—hot and humid. It was not the frozen north all year around as our minds had been conditioned to believe.

But Nushagak was an ordeal in wrestling with the effects of hair loss disease, alopecia areata,[114] contracted in a Seattle barbershop. It was an embarrassing sight, seeing the hair being replaced by short, white fuzz. It was a task to treat the hair each night with a home remedy of camphor-kerosene, and recovery was exceedingly slow. Upon returning to Seattle, I received violet-ray treatment, but that too failed to speed up the recovery. Money was running low. It seemed the appropriate time to take a boxcar trip across the continent and not be a drag on the Yamamoto family of Beacon Hill where I was staying. I was asked to delay the projected trip until Thanksgiving. Franny Yamamoto was planning to attend a Thanksgiving dinner at the home of a friend in Portland, from where I could begin my odyssey.

Thanksgiving morning turned out to be miserable. Wet and thick fog blanketed the route. Visibility was down to less than thirty feet, and at times we could only inch along. It took us until evening to make Portland and we partook of Thanksgiving dinner at the home of Deeks Chin,[115] a former Seattleite with whom I was familiar. We then chatted for several hours until it was time to leave. Franny drove me out to the Portland railroad yard, and as we looked down on the yard from the vantage of a high cliff, he instructed me on how to avoid the "bulls," or railroad police.[116]

The moon was full, brightening the scene, and the air was crisp. When a freight train began pulling out, I ran around the yard and caught it as I had been told. The train stopped about an hour and a half later at a water tower, and I got off and stood in the tall weeds. A crewman came down that side and I moved across to the other side. There a uniformed man accosted me.

"I knew you were on this train," he said. "Where are you headed?"

"East," I said.

"It's dangerous to ride a loaded freight," he declared. "The load could shift and you'd be hurt. You should hit the highway. Someone will come along and give you a lift."

"Okay," I replied.

"Where were you riding?" he asked. "If you've been riding in those tubes, it could cut loose and hurt you. Take the highway. It's safer."

I inched very slowly toward the highway. The uniformed man went back to the engine. The train began to move. I made a dash for the freight. Someone yelled, "Hey!" I slid into a culvert on the left side. Two handlers came down and checked the culverts on the right side. I transferred over to the ones inspected. The two men returned and inspected the culverts on the left side. The freight trundled along eastern Oregon and across the sagebrush wasteland of Idaho and pulled into the yards at Pocatello. It had been a crisp, cold, miserable ride and I jumped off as it slowed going into the yards. When the train passed, I found myself looking straight at two tall, well-dressed *hakujin* [Caucasians].

"We've been waiting for you," one man said with a broad smile. "We had a report you were on this train way back in Portland. Let's go to the station office."

I followed them to an upstairs office. It was well heated and warm. One man soon disappeared when we reached the station.

"Where are you heading?" I was asked.

"Ogden!" I said, thinking of the nearest main stop.

"That's less than three dollars," I was told. "You can ride a warm coach. I know you've got money. I could search you but I'd rather not. I'll let you go if you pay the fare to Ogden."

"Okay," I said. "Let me go to the restroom."

He purchased a ticket to Ogden for me with the requested money. I remained in the warm office until departure. The train was a local, making many stops. It reached Ogden at eight in the morning. The station had a wide paved approach and I approached a workingman-type passerby.

"Where's the hobo jungle?" I asked.

He seemed perplexed at the question but a young fellow with a patch over his left eye overheard the inquiry. "I'm going there," he said. "I'll show you the way." The route he took was a trifle complicated. We would walk along a piece, drop down to a second tier and follow that for a bit, and then drop to the final level. "It's under the bridge," he said. I could see a high bridge spanning a wide ravine. The jungle was hidden behind some shrubberies. One man was tending a fire and four others were wandering about the perimeter.

"Want coffee?" the fire attendant asked.

"That'd hit the spot," I replied.

It was a miserably cold morning. The man poured black coffee heated in a stone pit. A man with a brown bag extended it to us. "Have a pastry," he said. The coffee and pastry went well on a cold morning. I was surprised by this camaraderie. But these men were not common hoboes. They were members of the millions of the unemployed on the move in the Great Depression decade, going from coast to coast in search of work. These were the outcasts of the jobless.

"Where are you going?" my young benefactor asked.

"Washington, DC," I responded.

"Why don't we travel together?" he inquired. "I'm going home to New Hampshire. I've been to the Coast in search of a job. Things are pretty rough out there, too. Just couldn't line anything up. Now, I'm going home. I can show you the ropes."

I knew teaming up on the road was risky business. But it was important to learn the ropes. I agreed to team up. We caught a freight heading east that afternoon. The December weather in Ogden was cold but it kept getting colder in the boxcar. Late that night the train pulled into a siding and stopped. We were the last to jump off and the wind was bitter cold. "The fellows are in the sand house. It's got a roaring fire going and it's warm," someone yelled. The fire was a little too much for me and I flopped on the pile of sand, which was on the hottish side. From talk going around, I gathered that the town I was in was Minturn, Colorado, and that we were on the eastern slope of the Continental Divide. We had been pretty well warmed by the sand-house heat when a red-haired fellow entered and announced:

"I need men to work at the icehouse. Anyone wanting to work will be paid five dollars per day. There's a warm bunk to sleep in and you can take your meals in the mess hall."

"How many men do you need?" a voice asked.

"I can use every man here," the hirer replied.

Clustered in the sand house were a dozen men. It was around 11 p.m. when he led us to the bunkhouse. Before we could settle in, a fistfight took place; a red-haired man pummeled a bigger but soused fellow to a pulp. Then in a belligerent tone he asked, "Anyone else?" I had no idea what the disagreement was all about, but I did not think it had been a fair fight. The bigger man was drunk and didn't even counter with a punch.

I was assigned to the dock, where I bucked two-hundred-pound blocks of ice transported in on freight cars. We wrestled the ice blocks with iron tongs and fed them onto a conveyor belt, which took them up into a storage warehouse. It was not an easy job and the wind was chilling, exposed as we were to its unceasing blast. The job was completed in a fortnight on eight-to-ten-hour daily shifts. To collect our pay, we were given passage on the Denver and Rio Grande Railway to the Mile High city and the office of the Denver Ice and Cold Storage Company.

We remained in Denver for ten days before catching a "reefer," or refrigerated car, headed east. I experienced a moment of panic when a trainman opened the trapdoor through which we had entered and then closed it. Had he locked the trapdoor, we would have been trapped inside. The reefer stopped in west Chicago and we started on a long walk across town when a friendly salesman gave us a lift two-thirds of the way. It was dark, and nine bells rang when we made it to the border town of Crescent City, Illinois, on the Indiana side, where we split up to bum for a sandwich. Spotting an upstairs Chinese restaurant and expecting a welcome reception, I tried my luck but was greeted hostilely upon entering. "Get out; get out!" the Chinese man shouted. Most other establishments were closed down for the night and I returned empty-handed to our meeting site.

"How'd you do?" I was asked.

"No good," I replied.

"Here, have a sandwich," he said. He handed me a big plastic-wrapped roast beef sandwich.

The weather was awfully cold and traveling was miserable. We caught a local train to Fort Wayne, Indiana, where we were told another local to Cleveland, Ohio, was about to depart. The cabman invited us to ride in the heated caboose. When we were dropped off at Cleveland, he wished us a Merry Christmas.

"Let's check in at the Y," said my companion. "They'll give us coffee and rolls and a warm bed to sleep on so long as we're not blacks." We were required to shower, which was a godsend. The man at the desk registered me as "white" and we were provided with blankets. We caught another local to Pittsburgh in the morning and tried our luck there at a steel mill. We were told to go down into the mill and wait for the manager, but he never showed up. We waited for hours, watching the men at work in the smoke-shrouded interior. I was not interested in working in such a polluted atmosphere.

With no sight of the manager, we gave up our vigil and walked across the city to McKeesport to catch an eastbound freight. We were told a freight train would come through at midafternoon but would merely slow and not stop, so we prepared to make a run for it. My companion barely made it and I was knocked down. I was dusting myself off just as a uniformed man came up. The uniform was not familiar but he was obviously some sort of an official.

"I saw you trying to hop the freight and get knocked off," he stated. "Where are you heading?"

"Washington, DC," I replied.

"Don't worry," he said. "There's a mail train coming by in half an hour. I'll get you on it." When the mail train came to a stop, the man addressed a train man, after which he called me over. "This man will see you'll be taken care of," he said. "Just climb up there and hold on."

Up there was a slight recessed spot behind the engine. I was to cling on to steel rungs. It was a frigid night and a real test to hang on when crossing the Cumberland Gap. My gloves stuck to the rungs and there were moments when I wondered whether I could hold on any longer. The wind was chilling. The train man came to check on me just once. The descent on the eastern side was a relief, the air growing increasingly warmer as the train descended.

"When you see a big road sign on the right, get off," the train man said. "The train will slow down at that point before it goes into the yard. You'll find a road just beside the sign. That road will take you into the center of Washington. Don't go into the station. The bulls are pretty mean!"

"How far do I have to follow the road?" I asked.

"About two miles," he said.

Those two miles seemed awfully long. The road wound through mostly darkened forests. It seemed like forever before I spotted a lit sign, which read "Rooms for Rent." I was cold, miserable, and hungry. Even though I found the rooming house rather low-class, I was in no mood to shop around at that ungodly hour. The following morning I transferred downtown to the respectable Adams Hotel,[117] which had a nice décor, spacious rooms, and maid service.

I looked up a friend and took in the sights of the nation's capital. Preparations were underway for President Franklin Delano Roosevelt's second inauguration.[118] What most impressed me was the Lincoln Memorial and the aura of history that seemed to exude around the statue of Abraham Lincoln. I spent ten days viewing the sights and then took a Greyhound bus into New York. I was finally in the "Big Apple."

My first instinct, after finding a modest hotel, was to look up Greenwich Village, much celebrated for starving artists living in attic quarters. However, I somehow missed seeing that spectacle. Nevertheless, New York proved to be a revelation. The immense canyons formed by towering skyscrapers and the storied sites recorded in books all came to life: Fifth Avenue, Central Park, Times Square, Union Station,[119] and the Bowery. Then there was Coney Island, closed for the winter but with some maids braving the chilly January 1937 morning to saunter down its boardwalks or push baby carts. Out in the chilly waters, a trio of snorkel men cavorted nearby a deserted jetty.

New York would not have been complete without a visit to the Statue of Liberty. Despite the blustery weather, a large crowd assembled to be transported to Liberty Island. It was not until the third steamer load before I made it to the statue. The steps up the statue were rickety and not altogether safe. The outer rope guard was perilous, as it was simply strung through frail stanchions in rather a loose fashion. Wide gaps were apparent in the casing of the statue through which the chill winds blew and the harbor could be seen far below. The guard stationed at the observation deck prevented our climb to the crown, pointing out the cracks on Liberty's brow. He spoke of the need to refurbish the Statue of Liberty because of the dangers imposed by the aging of its superstructure. But forty-five years would pass before any campaign to refurbish the Statue[120] would begin.[viii]

Below the hotel at which I stayed in New York was a workingman-type restaurant. I was drawn to it by a large sign on the window which touted a "New York Liberty Steak."[121] I went in and ordered it out of curiosity and discovered to my astonishment that it was just a plain hamburger steak with a fancy name. However, the steak came loaded with all the trimmings and

---

viii Distressed by the statue's deterioration and the impending need to maintain this great symbol of immigration, I was among the first in line in 1983 to donate to its restoration, an amount that Chairman Lee Iacocca considered substantial. Donations for restoration of the statue were at a standstill and Americans were slow in responding. In recognition of the contribution, a certificate of honor signed by Iacocca and then–U.S. president Gerald Ford was awarded to me.

a plentiful supply of coffee and bread or buns galore. The price was twenty-five cents, a standard price for restaurant fare in the Great Depression era of 1937.

The atmosphere in the restaurant was friendly and genial. I was interested in seeing other historic sites, especially in New England, and made inquiries while at the restaurant to the owner and some of the patrons. They all nixed the idea of my going to New England via Brooklyn, stating that railroad bulls were very mean there. They told stories of transients having their heads bashed in and advised that I take the Greyhound to New Jersey and from there hitch a ride with a trucker heading west. The truckers' stop, I was told, was just a block away from the bus station. I followed the wisdom of these well-wishers and approached a trucker having his dinner at the restaurant.

"Not here," the trucker said. "Go down the road until you see a big sign. I'll pick you up there."

I wandered down the road and came to this large lighted billboard and waited. Half an hour later, he came along and picked me up.

"I could lose my license for picking up riders," he stated. "There are insurance investigators everywhere. It would have been suicide to pick up anyone at the restaurant. How far west are you going?"

"All the way to the Pacific Coast," I answered.

"Well, I can take you as far as Pittsburgh," he said. "That's the end of my run."

He dropped me off in Pennsylvania half a mile from McKeesport. I headed to the station to check on freight departure when a young fellow came out from the station.

"You going west?" he asked.

"Sure!" I said.

"Just found out in the station there won't be any trains out today. It's Sunday. We might as well start walking," he declared.

"Where to?" I asked.

"Bellaire is the next city," he said. "It's about ten miles."

"Wow!" I exclaimed. "That's a long ways off."

"Some farmer may come along and we can hitch a ride," he assured me.

The region in which we headed was barren and consisted of nothing but endless stretches of prairie. We saw no signs of a farmhouse. No one came along to pick us up. We started out at eight in the morning and at nightfall the lights of a large city appeared on the distant horizon. The more we walked, the further the lights seemed to recede. It was well after midnight when we reached Bellaire. Ten miles? It was more like forty-five miles. We picked up a local that night and it circled Chicago and wound up at a town called Mankato in Minnesota.

We had nothing to eat for two days and split up to scrounge for food. I found a lighted kitchen, as instructed by my companion, and heard the rattle of dishes. I knocked and a large, middle-aged woman answered the kitchen door.

"I'll shovel snow for a sandwich," I offered.

I was invited in. The lady prepared a large dish of leftovers and I could feel her inspecting me on the side. She joined three others in the living room, two elder women and a small man with a cane. The man came over and sat directly opposite me, watching me intently as I ate. He never said anything. I felt uncomfortable and had a strong urge to get out of there as quickly as possible. There was plenty of snow but the walks didn't require shoveling. In fact, I had reneged on my shoveling offer just to get away.

We spent the night in the warm sand house and heard talk of a mission in town providing shelter and serving coffee and meals. The next morning we checked into the mission. The mission master discouraged our crossing the Rockies in the cold of winter and prepared a letter of recommendation to a Salvation Army major in St. Paul. We were told to wait in the downstairs workroom until the return of the major and his foreman. Half an hour after the workers knocked off work, we went back to the office to check. No one was about; the office was empty.

Disgusted with the experience, we walked back to Mankato and the mission. The mission master was astounded at the treatment accorded us. He was dead-set against our tackling the Rockies and stated we could stay at the mission until other arrangements could be made. My companion was adamant about going on but I was uneasy about Montana and its forty-below-zero winter temperature. I was not properly outfitted for that type of weather. My companion went on but I stayed at the mission for three more days. I was also restless to be on the move. The mission master steered me to the Santa Fe railroad line, believing it would swing south toward Arizona. Instead, it took the central route through Wyoming and deposited me in Pocatello.

I looked up the Okamuras and then went on to the Yamada farm, where I rested up for a couple of days. Mrs. Yamada parted with some loose change she had squirreled away from household expenses when I was about to depart. It came to a dollar and thirty-five cents and was of real help to tide me over. I caught a freight train out of Pocatello and wound up late at night in some little town in eastern Washington. It being cold and dark, I slipped into the station, knowing the waiting room would be heated. Half an hour later, I was startled by a state patrolman flashing a spotlight in my face. "You were seen entering the station," he said. "We're looking for a killer. We thought you might be him, but I guess not."

The patrolman checked my identifications and explained that a murder had been committed in Olympia, Washington. Satisfied that I was not the fugitive, he allowed me to sleep in the station. Next morning I caught the first freight out. It crossed the Cascades and pulled into Seattle's King Street Station, near J-Town, the following morning. No one seemed to be about so I rode the train all the way into the station. I cleaned up in the warm washroom and put finis to my transcontinental odyssey.

Franny had me stay with him at his family's Beacon Hill home. I went down to Kushi Contractor the next morning and was shocked to learn I had been totally blacklisted for cannery work by the Seattle Japanese Association. Prior to my transcontinental departure, I had filed a lawsuit against a barbershop for contraction of alopecia areata. I was being punished for that hair-loss lawsuit without consideration of the merit of the case. It appeared the barber was an influential member of the Seattle association. The word had been passed on to other association branches, so I was at wit's end.

In late July 1937, the prospect of acquiring the pioneer Yamaki Grocery Store for a nominal sum was brought up by Franny's father, Mr. Yamamoto. I was stymied by the need to speak fluent Japanese but Franny had a friend who could surmount that barrier. The deal meant that I would have to enter into a partnership, and though I was not keen about it, an agreement was reached. Not long after the partnership was completed, it became evident that the grocery store's route business was falling off instead of improving as I had hoped. Sales on the route represented the core of the business. With deterioration of this business, I offered to buy my partner out. He refused. I then asked him to buy me out, stating that we were otherwise headed for insolvency. He refused again. Despite my warning that we had to shut down the business, he stood steadfast. My brother Casey, who had just returned from a season in Alaska, refused to invest any funds in the store. I therefore closed the enterprise. "I told the former owner that you were footloose and you could go off to California. There was nothing he could do. Even if he found you, it wouldn't be worth anything, that you were broke," Mr. Yamamoto said.

Mr. Yamamoto was telling me to beat it for California. Casey had caught wind of celery work around Stockton[122] and offered to purchase a used car if I would accompany him. Having no better prospect, I agreed. He purchased a Reo coupe.[123] Before heading out for Stockton, he wanted to try a hop-picking job he had heard about in Yakima Valley in eastern Washington. The weather was hot in Yakima and our quarters were in a large community tent. For mattresses large bags were filled with hay, and we slept on the bare ground.

When management squawked at excess leaves in the pickings, the crew went on strike. Labor rates were cheap and the threat of downsizing the take was discouraging. The ranks of the pickers thinned as a number of men departed during the course of the strike. Although management relented after only three days, our trip to Yakima nonetheless proved unprofitable.

It was on to Stockton, and there we checked in at the Nishimoto Boarding House,[124] where we learned that prospects in the celery fields were not too bright. Production was controlled by a quota system that entailed frequent work stoppages. Employment was by day work. The damp, fog-covered conditions in the celery fields affected Casey and he coughed badly and took to bed. I thought it was just flu. Mr. Nishimoto sent us out on unproductive leads to the communities of Florin[125] and Lodi,[126] but work in winter was scarce. Casey was compelled to ask the boardinghouse keeper for credit, but just as we were at rock bottom, a job was found for us with a big farm operator.

That afternoon, George Uyeda, head of Uyeda Farms, led us to one of his fields at Rindge Island.[127] Within sight of the farmhouse, a large fallen tree blocked the road, which necessitated our leaving the cars and walking the remaining distance. Our immediate jobs were to work on the grading machine, separating marketable onions and potatoes. Fieldwork was at a standstill due to flooding caused by the drenching rains, overflowing the irrigation canals by a steady downpour. The field was not dry enough for us to begin sugar beet grading until late March 1938.

That first morning we set out for the field, Casey began to spit blood on the way and I insisted on his returning to the bunkhouse. He remained ill through the rest of my stay on Rindge Island. I was assigned to operating the truck and tractor in the field but in May was transferred to the 1,600-acre Webb farm in the Sacramento Delta and assigned to night plowing. But toward the end of the shift, I apparently got too close to the edge and the tractor sank gently down toward the canal. I was then reassigned to plowing a virgin section, progress at which was very limited because of the many roots and underbrush growing there.

In August 1938, unable to work, Casey came to Webb Island for fare to Seattle, where he felt he could obtain necessary treatment for whatever ailed him. He left that afternoon from Sacramento. His illness was diagnosed by the King County Health Department as tuberculosis and he was confined to the Firland Sanatorium at Richmond Highlands, just north of the city.[128] He was released as an arrested case seven years later and obtained a watchmaking certificate at a school in the eastern Washington city of Spokane. He practiced watchmaking only as a sideline, working mainly as a janitor for various Seattle hotels, the last being the Washington Athletic Club.[129]

Just for the mere purpose of checking how others would view my writing talent, during my Webb Island employment I entered the *Nichibei* literary contest under a pseudonym and was gratified in winning a cash prize. I wrote one other time; it was a rebuttal to a *New World Sun* article that had extolled the virtues of Issei farmers in the conduct of their agricultural enterprises. The op-ed letter criticized the poor living quarters provided the migrant workers, the severely depressed wage scale, and the general exploitation of ethnic workers. This letter elicited a "Good Comments" editorial footnote. These two literary efforts were convincing evidence for me that my writing had not grown rusty by disuse.

To fill the hours during the stop-and-go work schedule in the Stockton celery fields, I spent many hours in the town's library and there became acquainted with Russian writers. It was at this time that I read Tolstoy's *War and Peace* and the works of such great Russian writers as Fyodor Dostoyevsky and Maxim Gorki, as well as other classical writers of their era.

Breaking virgin ground at an adjoining acreage at Webb Island proved to be my Waterloo. Progress was slow due to the plow clogging with roots and underbrush. One day the foreman showed his displeasure and to demonstrate my lack of aptitude jumped on the tractor to demonstrate. It was a no-go. Various other makes of plow were tried in vain and the final solution was to borrow a spinner plow to cut the roots and not clog the plow. It was on this mission to borrow the spinner plow that the tractor hit a rise and veered left toward the river, striking a fisherman's parked car before coming to a stop. I drew my pay and left the ranch.

Back in Stockton, I signed to work with another farmer, a World War I veteran. His wife was grouchy, overworked, and unfriendly. Our work consisted of weeding sugar beet seedlings. When hearing about a coworker's sudden departure that morning, I became suspicious. I recalled that he had watched me intently one evening as I fumbled with my suitcase. I checked for my paycheck and found it missing. This young fellow had shown interest in a boot on display at the Rossi Shoe Store one Saturday night when we had gone window-shopping in town together. I promptly filed a complaint with the foreman and the contract boss came the next morning and drove me in to Stockton. I was taken to the Rossi Shoe Store and Mr. Rossi stated I was not the person who had cashed the check. Our next stop was to the office of the district attorney, who promptly issued a statewide warrant for the forger's arrest. The culprit was last seen in the Florin area, but I never heard the result of the case. Two weeks later the weeding work came to an end and so I had to move on.

I left for the central California town of Selma in the company of a vineyard foreman. The harvest proved poor and the foreman made good on his promise to find other fields to pick. We worked at another small vineyard in the adjacent town of Parlier, using Selma as the base camp. Then followed a stint in Visalia at the large J. B. Martin vineyards and warehouse, to which we commuted from Selma. I worked in the warehouse, packing grapes, a job for which I was not suited. I had difficulty filling the quota and was very distressed about this situation. Additionally, I was assigned to trucking boxes of grapes unloaded by field trucks, which provided me some relief from being monitored in the packing process.

Nevertheless, the working environment was not comfortable, as the other packers were all middle-aged housewives who tended to ostracize me socially. Visalia was noted as a hostile anti-Japanese area.[130] When I ran across an advertisement in the San Francisco *Japanese American News* for a drayage[131] helper, I applied by letter and was informed that the job required a personal application. I left on Saturday afternoon and found the owner taking a drunken nap. The owner's son suggested my returning Monday morning, but when I opened the door to the family establishment at the appointed day and time, he shouted out, "The job has been filled!" I considered the action improper and crude.

Ten days later, I caught on as a truck delivery driver for a wholesale florist, Western Wholesale Florists.[132] The Issei owner of the firm was said to be suffering an unstated illness and the business was managed by his Nisei wife. He came to help pack during the peak periods. My principal duties were to pick up cut flowers down on the peninsula. I was advised by the senior packer that the company hired drivers helter-skelter for the peak season only and then discharged them when the need expired. I took this warning to heart and decided to learn the packing trade, which might be useful in the shipping industry.

One morning the boss man called in sick and asked me to complete the pruning he had begun on an acacia tree, taking along a newly hired driver as ground help. The tree in question was a very large one, towering sixty feet into the air. He had pruned forty feet of it, leaving the upper twenty feet for me to prune. I had a phobia about heights, however, and was very leery about the job. He said the trick was not to look down but out. I followed his instructions and found tree pruning duck soup. I was confident that I had done an excellent job but the next morning was advised that the owner of the property had complained of my "butchering the tree." I drove the boss man to inspect the work. "That's a beautiful job," he exclaimed. That was the last I heard about it. Our acacia pruning took us to the Santa Cruz Mountains, where I took over for the last two hours. The blue waters of the Pacific were visible from my perch on the tree branch, but at 3:30 that afternoon strong, chilly winds forced us to abandon the work.

In the meantime I had become quite fast and adept at wrapping violets and took up cut-flower packing[133] with the help of the senior clerk. That knowledge, I felt, would qualify me elsewhere. Around Easter an incident occurred with another packer that precipitated a crisis. The senior packer went to bat for me when asked his opinion by the owner's Nisei wife about letting me go. "I told her not to because you are the fastest packer we ever had," he informed me. "You can pack three boxes to one over George." That lanky packer was then let go and later the truck driver as well.

I was not happy where I worked, and the boss woman was unhappy about my refusal to cover the flower market. Doing so meant having to get up two hours earlier. I packed until one o'clock during peak days. Nor did I consider the wages as commensurate with my production. Besides, working in the market amounted to picking up orders already filled and I disliked trailing her around like a trained chimpanzee.

The situation was headed for a collision and I put out feelers for other jobs. The first to come along was a driver–market salesman job with Ioki Greenhouse of Oakland.[134] I was tipped off to the availability of the prospect and went to Oakland for an interview. Mr. Ioki showed up at Western Wholesale Florists where I still worked and was dissuaded by the boss woman from hiring me. He stated to me he did not feel right about hiring someone employed by another Japanese firm. It would be against cultural courtesy. She spiked this opportunity but then again jockeyed for my discharge. Again deterred by the senior packer, she made an offer of a ten-dollar raise if I would cover the market. When I adamantly refused, the raise was honored without the condition.

The second opportunity for employment came along from the Economy Shippers, also of Oakland and a branch of a Salt Lake City firm.[135] On my second trip to Economy, the manager reacted angrily to my making a packing suggestion. I lost interest in working for this man and I have no doubt he lost interest in employing what he might have considered an upstart "Jap" packer.

On a Saturday morning in October, the boss woman said to me: "I'm going to sign a sales agreement. When I return, I'll make out your final check."

I wandered over to the corner drugstore for a coffee break. "Guess this will be the last time I'll be around," I told the druggist.

"Why?" he asked.

"Mrs. Furuya has sold the business," I said. "I've been notified that I'm to get the boot."

"Why don't you go to Amling's[136] over there," he said. "He's been having trouble with some of his help. He may be willing to hire you. It wouldn't hurt to ask!"

I looked over to the small Amling shop and drank my coffee and munched on a roll while I considered the druggist's suggestion. I had never seen Amling and was uncertain of the reception.

"Go ahead!" the druggist urged. "It won't hurt."

"Oh, what the hell," I thought to myself. "Why not?"

I went across to Amling's shop without too much anticipation. Mr. Amling came outside and talked to me on the street. I didn't know it at the time but he used to do that for the sake of privacy.

"How much do you want?" he asked.

"At least as much as I was paid at Western," I said.

"What was that?" he asked.

"One hundred and twenty-five dollars," I stated.

"I'll call you by five with the decision," he declared.

I didn't put much stock on the promise. I picked up my final check and went on home. But the call came in from Amling at 4:30. "Be at the office at ten in the morning," he said.

This instruction perplexed me. No one worked on Sundays during the slack season. Still, the next morning I reported right on time. Mr. Amling apparently was waiting for me. He came out of the door and locked it as I approached. "Hop in the truck," he said.

His pickup was parked in front the wrong way. He said nothing and I too kept mum. We drove over the Golden Gate Bridge into Sonoma County and finally stopped along a barren stretch of the highway. I watched as he inspected a four-foot acacia sapling beside the road. "It's a little too early," he mused, before turning back for the shop.

"Report at eight in the morning," he said.

I tried to figure out if I had undergone some sort of a test. The entire episode was strange. The next morning I discovered that a young fellow, who was a packer, and a gruff old fellow named Rossi, who specialized in ferns and decorative items, were the only two workers in Amling's shop. It was apparent that friction existed between Amling and Rossi and so I was caught totally unprepared when the young packer was dismissed at the end of the week.

Mr. Amling took me outside that first morning for a chat. "I ran into your former boss in the market," he said. "Guess that was sour grapes."

"I guess so," I agreed, not having the faintest inkling of what had been said but expecting the worst.

I knew that it had given Mrs. Furuya great pleasure to fire me. It must have galled her to hear that I had hooked on with a competitor. Under the terms of the sale, she was required to function as a buyer for a period of time to acclimate the buyers.

It was the second week when Mr. Amling sat down at a bench three spaces down from me and began packing. I noticed that he was going rather fast and so I raised my speed a notch to keep ahead of him.

Three days later he took me outside. "The other night I was testing you to see how fast you really are," he said. "You are fast. I hired you because you have the best reputation in the market. You have the reputation of being the fastest packer in the market. I checked you out!"

I had nothing to say. The fastest-packer label could only have been popularized by the crew of the railway express company who picked up the shipments. They were the only ones to cover the entire shipping industry. I wasn't aware of that reputation. I did know that I was a fast packer at Western from the statements of the senior packer. Two weeks after the dismissal of the young packer, a manager out of Cincinnati was hired. His system of bench layout hampered the efficiency in packing. Production dropped and became so noticeable that Mr. Amling inquired about the slowdown. I faulted the manager's layout system and declared I could not pack with any consistency. That led to exchanges of strong words and I fully expected to be terminated. But instead, at the end of the week the manager was let go. His departure devolved upon me the responsibility of packing off the order slips; the number of back orders puzzled me.

"Why are there so many back orders?" I asked.

"Because I can't get the merchandise," Mr. Amling replied.

"I don't see why not," I retorted.

Twenty minutes later, Mr. Amling came out of the office. "Jim, if you think you can get the materials, why don't you take over the market Monday morning," he said.

I took up the challenge and immediately found out what the bottleneck was all about. Mr. Amling was a new boy on the block and lacked credibility with the growers. "Jim, I'd like to help you out," a grower said, "but I have to sell to people who will take care of me in the slack season. If you can guarantee that Amling will take care of me, I can sell you the goods."

There was no way a guarantee of that sort could be given. I was nonplussed by his statement. While I was mulling it over, he apparently realized his request was too demanding and added, "I don't mean buy it when you have no orders, but take care of me when you have." I could live with that and I made my commitment, and he said, "We'll start with a couple of dozen and see how it goes."

The next grower was more concerned with Amling's credibility. "I don't know Amling," he said. "I want to be paid for my goods."

"Amling's checks have yet to bounce," I assured him.

Thus, I entered into buying in the wholesale floral industry. The Amling Company grew rapidly with the availability of merchandise. By summer it had established branches in Los Angeles and Jacksonville, Florida. My afflu-ence also grew with the company's growth. I received a twenty-five-dollar increase in pay along with a bonus of fifty dollars each week. Amling hired two managers, one for the office and the other for the shipping. But I had autonomy in the shipping warehouse, even though I seldom exercised it. The shipping manager was paid $345 monthly, and I drew from $350 to $400 per month. In a survey for the California Employment Service, the conclusion was that "wages are low" in the San Francisco Flower Market. This survey probably relied too heavily on book statistics furnished by the secretary of the Japanese Flower Growers Association, which it cites.[137] Nisei workers on Grant Avenue considered sixty dollars per month good wages at the period in question.[138]

While I was employed at the flower market, I was pressed by Larry Tajiri to initiate a column for the *Japanese American News*. That was in 1939, and after three months of appeal I consented. I made my bow with "The Passing Show" column,[139] which received good reviews. This writing stimulated and reawakened literary interest, and when an opening for an editor of a new magazine opened up, I mailed off an application.

One afternoon when I stopped at the *Nichibei* on request, I was told by Tajiri: "I hear you're going to be the editor of a magazine. I was inter-viewed for a recommendation. I gave you a good, strong reference. You're a shoo-in!"

Ten days later I ran across Iwao Kawakami, the linotypist for the *New World Sun*, on J-Town's main Buchanan Street thoroughfare.[140] "I think you're going to be the editor of a new magazine," he stated. "I was asked about you. I gave you a good recommendation. I'll probably be its part-time linotypist."

Though the recommendations were most encouraging, I had yet to hear from the prospective publisher. I believed at the time that I was the only qualified candidate. But the delay vexed me and I felt something was wrong. Six weeks later the reply came in. The decision was negative. The publisher, Ted Ogasawara,[141] stated that he had selected a girl from Reno, Nevada, named Ann Oshima to be the editor. The publication was not a monthly, but a weekly, to be called *Pacific Affairs*. While he did not indicate it, I felt certain my application had been skewered by the Japanese Ameri-can Citizens League.

FOUR

Showdown in San Francisco, 1940–1942

At the time the Ted Ogasawara prospect to edit a new magazine emerged, I had been thinking of establishing a Nisei literary magazine myself. In early summer of 1940 Larry Tajiri had departed San Francisco for New York to assume his duties there for the Domei News Service. Tajiri's departure doomed my column "The Passing Show"[1] for the *Japanese American News*. When one of my columns was submitted to that paper in support of funding for the Shonien, a Japanese orphan home in Los Angeles,[2] it was rejected by publisher Yasuo Abiko with a cryptic note reading, "The Chamber of Commerce of Los Angeles is not in San Francisco." Abiko was a board member of the Northern California JACL Council. I did not agree with the provincial type of editorial policies Abiko seemed to embrace.[3]

With this turn of events, it made the publication of a literary magazine a more serious consideration for me. Toward that end, submissions were encouraged and when a sufficient stockpile was on hand, the first edition of *Current Life* rolled off the press in October 1940.[4] In its initial year *Current Life* attracted the attention of prestigious universities, public libraries, secondary educators, and national associations across the land. Among its distinctions was a subscription from the Library of Congress, perhaps the first mainland Asian publication to be so recognized. It could also boast of an international readership with subscribers in Canada, Hawai'i, and Japan. *Current Life* was fortunate to earn favorable write-ups in vernacular newspapers and to receive helpful publicity in metropolitan presses such as the *Chronicle* and *Call-Bulletin* of San Francisco and the *Herald-Express* of Los

Angeles.[5] Although it acquired paid subscriptions of a mere five hundred in the first year of its existence, its circulation, thanks in large part to the publication's policy of providing potential subscribers with three complimentary issues, rose to approximately thirteen hundred per edition.

In the fifteen years of being on my own, I was unable to distinguish even a ripple of any material change in the depressed lot of the second generation in America. Nisei were still shut out from the main marketplace. Engineering graduates from such esteemed colleges as Yale, Harvard, Princeton, and Stanford were hawking fruits in Los Angeles public markets or, as some chronicler termed it, serving as "carrot washers." In such an environment, it was no wonder graduates of American universities were going overseas to pursue their careers in the land of their parents. The job prospects of the Nisei were at a standstill, which was made more difficult by the haughty no-labor attitudes of the Japanese American Citizens League.

The reasoning that propelled the establishment of *Current Life* was that if the upper echelon of educators and administrators could be tapped, they in turn could extract a significant measure of tolerance and interest among their students, the future captains of American industries, to transcend the economic barriers of racism. It was in a sense a trickle-down theory, to work from the top down. In the past the Nisei were trying to climb the economic ladder in the most difficult ways, through the competitive ranks of the common workers. Resistance toward other laboring groups was formidable. *Current Life* was dedicated to unlocking this gridlock and to bridging the racial abyss. Much less bigotry existed in the field of literature than in the workplace. The publication sought to showcase Nisei talents but it also endeavored to demonstrate that it was not entirely a one-way street.

While the Nisei press was simply an adjunct of the immigrant presses and thereby responsive to the influences of the cultural Japanese Association, *Current Life* was owned directly by a Nisei and was independent of ethnic limitations. Furthermore, the major English sections of the Japanese vernacular newspapers were controlled by the ascending JACL and performed as propaganda organs for the organization. An example of this was the role of Togo Tanaka, English-section editor of the *Rafu Shimpo* [*Los Angeles Daily News*] in Los Angeles, who was also the national publicity director for the JACL. In 1934 JACL journalists formed the Coast Nisei Press,[6] a JACL media cooperative embracing the *North American Times* of Seattle,[7] the *Japanese American News* of San Francisco, and the *Rafu Shimpo* of Los Angeles. Not invited to the conference were the *Hokubei Asahi* and the *New World Daily News*, both of San Francisco. The *Hokubei*, although strongly pro-JACL, was persona non grata as a breakaway unit of the *Japanese American News*. The *New World Daily News* was an outspoken critic of the JACL organization.

December 7, 1941, dawned just like any other Sunday in the Bay City. My usual procedure was to drive out to Daly City and South San Francisco to pick up cut flowers previously ordered. It was not unusual not to see any-one. I sensed something was wrong on my return trip when I noticed that traffic on Bayshore Drive seemed extremely light for a Sunday afternoon. Market Street, too, was deserted. I arrived at the Amling shipping shed and unlocked the door when the newshawks' shouts of "Extra! Extra!" struck my ears. The hawkers' words were garbled, but it was unusual for an "Extra" to be released on a Sunday. Something momentous must have happened and I was possessed by a premonition of dire consequences.

"Heard newshawks shouting 'Extra! Extra!'" I said to a Railway Express[8] driver who showed up at 3:30 p.m. "What was that about?"

"I don't know," he said. "I'll go check and find out."

This driver was a person unfamiliar to me. He did not come back. At 5:30 p.m., a covey of express men arrived. I put the question to the lead driver, whom I knew.

"Pearl Harbor has been bombed, Jimmie," he said. "We're at war!"

My heart sank. I was overcome by grave foreboding. The Sunday after-noon packing was hurried and I anxiously headed for Soko-town.[9] The dis-trict was deserted and strangely quiet. Doors were barred and lights were darkened. The Eagle Cafe,[10] where I took my meals, was about the only establishment open. It had no customers in sight and the owner kept to himself. I read the city dailies and was horrified at the unpreparedness of the United States at Pearl Harbor. The headlines in the media screamed "Sneak Attack," as if to add greater righteous anger to the attack. Rumors ran ram-pant about sabotage, subversion, and a "Fifth Column." The president of the United States, Franklin Delano Roosevelt, addressed a joint session of Congress and labeled the day of attack as a "day of infamy." This focused attention on the minority Japanese in the United States and led to their becoming victims of Japan's action.

I was probably the last person to hear about Pearl Harbor and was thus un-aware of what had occurred in J-Town. Graphically, that moment is described here by Charles Kikuchi, who was then a student in social work at the University of California at Berkeley.[11]

> In the San Francisco Japanese Section there is wild confusion this week. . . . Faces are stunned. Hundreds crowd the streets. FBI men have been swooping down into their midst and systematically extracting the "enemy aliens" . . . some who are innocent . . . in their dragnet. Uniformed police stand guard in the area. Radio cars patrol the streets. Only those with legitimate reasons—students—can get in or out. Groups of worried, frightened Nisei stand in nervous clusters on the corners. "What will become of us and our parents?" (they whispered). (At this place, an editor's note, handwritten in ink: "neurotic tendencies among the American-born Japanese. And then the war came.")
>
> (Other Nisei have their) ears glued to the radio. . . . Some students coming home from the campus find government men in their home. They can't go in. They can't communicate. So they go to the Japanese hotels to sleep. The hotels are raided. All documents seized; papers strewn all over the floors. Some are held for questioning. I saw one Nisei handcuffed and being hauled off while tearfully protesting: "Let me go! I'm an American citizen!"[i]

Kikuchi also described the scene that took place on the campus at the University of California.

> They were stunned . . . many of the Nisei became panic-stricken. . . . They wandered around dazed and with strained, worried expressions. . . . It verges on hysteria in some cases, particularly among the girls. The Nisei are on a spot and they know it. Some come to school with guilt feelings, although they have nothing to do with the political government of Japan, no ties except a distant racial affinity. They are reacting as Americans, yet they are painfully aware that faces turn to look at them as they self-consciously walk down the streets. . . . They are American, yes, but their faces are so conspicuously that of the enemies![ii]

Although I took my meals at the Eagle Cafe in J-Town, the editorial office of *Current Life* was beyond the Western Addition on Broderick Street.[12] The

---

i Charles Kikuchi, addendum ["Then the War Came"] to "Neurotic Tendencies among the Second Generation Japanese" (research paper, School of Social Welfare, UC Berkeley, December 5, 1941), 5–6, in JERS, BANC, UCB, Reel 096:0012-102:0645, Folder W1.80**. The addendum is dated December 8, 1941. [Ed. This document is not available in the digitized version of the JERS collection.]

ii Ibid., 3–4. This same material is also available in the Charles Kikuchi Papers (Collection 1259), Department of Special Collections, Charles E. Young Research Library, University of California, Los Angeles [hereafter UCLARL], Box 12, 4:1174.

FIGURE 7. In October 1941, *Current Life* commemorated its first anniversary with a sukiyaki party. Seen at this event with Omura and his wife, Caryl, the publication's business manager, is celebrated Armenian American writer William Saroyan, one of the magazine's notable contributors. Omura Papers, Green Library, Stanford University.

business manager of the publication, Fumiko "Caryl" Okuma,[13] was in Los Angeles on promotional business when Pearl Harbor occurred.[14] I received the message at 8 p.m.

"We're all frozen in the Miyako Hotel," Caryl reported. "They won't let us out. The FBI fingerprinted all of us. I don't know when I can get back. Travel is restricted."[15]

The situation at the San Francisco Flower Market[16] was chaotic on Monday morning. Growers of Japanese extraction were barred from entry. Groups of growers and customers were congregated at the entrances. When advised that I was a buyer for Amling Company, the big Italian guard asked me to wait "just a minute" while he went to consult his superiors. Fifteen minutes later he allowed me in, but the stalls were little occupied. Most of my business was transacted in the Terminal Grill,[17] where we gathered for breakfast.

Caryl had returned unexpectedly from Los Angeles, stating that American citizens had been cleared for travel. J-Town was still deserted the following day. Padlocks were on Issei-owned businesses and *Current Life* was affected by this procedure because of the padlocking of its printer, the Sutter Printing Company.[18] When the padlocks were removed ten days later, the publication was transferred to the Flatiron Building downtown to avoid any further hang-up. It was the wrong move. The Argonaut Press,[19] which was located in the Flatiron Building, seized the publication as a fallout of the Pacific War. Two Wells Fargo vice presidents were dispatched to seek the publication's release but were denied access and driven off. The publication not being under the jurisdiction of the War Relocation Authority,[20] an appeal to the government didn't seem likely. *Current Life* thus became a casualty of the Pacific War.

The news media reported that 770 Japanese, including some citizen Nisei, had been caught in the FBI dragnet in the first twelve hours of the war. Within the next few days, more than two thousand individuals were arrested and over five thousand subjected to questioning. Systematic criticisms began to rise about the incompetence of the FBI and the office of the attorney general. This led to a breakdown of confidence in the government's handling of the domestic situation on the West Coast.

In the meantime the Western Defense Command[21] ordered blackouts for coastal cities. Whenever radar picked up an oncoming plane, people were compelled to huddle in the darkness for hours until the blackouts were lifted. Air wardens patrolled the streets and could be heard shouting, "Douse your lights!" Sometimes they would cuss, "Get that damn light out, Goddammit!" But invariably the plane would be one of our own. In order to continue editorial work, it became necessary to purchase black cloth to shut out the light.

In the three weeks following Pearl Harbor, no immediate outcry arose against resident Japanese. I went about the business of my shipping duties and publication affairs in the normal fashion, riding the transit each day without incident. Sporadic anti-Japanese editorials did appear but were dwarfed by editorials and commentaries of a more tolerant nature. The attorney general of the United States, Francis Biddle,[22] lent his voice for tolerance and pleaded against committing reprisals upon resident Japanese. But the quiet was ominous due to the lack of activities of traditionally anti-Japanese proponents.

The hierarchy of the Japanese American Citizens League interpreted this ominous quiet as a good omen. Later, spokesmen for the League would admit publicly as having been "lulled into false security" by the tolerance being shown. While the activities of the JACL appeared to have been in limbo at this time, League officials were actually involved in promoting a brand of institutional self-preservation that would not become clear until well after the eventful episode.

The catalyst of the JACL program took active shape in late October 1941 when the United States and Imperial Japan were tussling over the prospects of oncoming conflict in the Pacific. The national JACL headquarters, then located in Saburo Kido's law office in San Francisco,[23] was visited by an emissary for President Roosevelt. The emissary, tapped by John Franklin Carter, the president's personal intelligence operative,[24] was Curtis Burton Munson, a member of the State Department's special investigative staff.[25] Munson was specially assigned to explore the national security interests on the West Coast and in Hawai'i. This visit was far more significant than either of the two Citizens League officials, Mike Masaoka and Saburo Kido, have been willing to admit. Bill Hosokawa claims that the two Nisei leaders were bound to secrecy "so as not to alarm the public."[26] That statement in itself is suspect, for secrecy was no longer justified after the issuance of Executive Order 9066 on February 19, 1942. Furthermore, all bets were off after disclosure of the Munson Report in the highly acclaimed and very influential *Years of Infamy: The Untold Story of America's Concentration Camps* by Michi Nishiura Weglyn.[iii] Secrecy after the mid-1970s by the JACL was not apropos. Munson spent three days in conference, primarily with JACL field secretary Mike Masaoka, and what transpired was far more than inspecting maps of Japanese communities in California, or the West Coast for that matter.

The Munson Report was released in 1946 at the sixth and final Pearl Harbor investigation. It is believed that this report was first referred to by historian Roger Daniels in his 1971 work *Concentration Camps USA: Japanese Americans and World War II*,[iv] but Daniels failed to mention the relevant JACL proposals or attempt to analyze the Munson Report. That task was

---

iii Michi [Nishiura] Weglyn, *Years of Infamy: The Untold Story of America's Concentration Camp* (New York: William Morrow, 1976), 33–53.

iv Roger Daniels, *Concentration Camps USA: Japanese Americans and World War II* (New York: Holt, Rinehart and Winston, 1971), 28.

left to Weglyn, a Nisei victim of the tragedy, who came along five years later with her eye-popping exposé. It is her account in *Years of Infamy* that provides posterity with what actually did occur at the Munson-Kido-Masaoka three-day conference in San Francisco in late October 1941.[27]

It was on the basis of these talks with the two JACL leaders that specific suggestions were offered by the special presidential emissary, including:

> The loyal Japanese citizens should be encouraged by a statement from a high government authority; their offer of assistance should be accepted . . . ; an alien property custodian should be appointed . . . ; accept investigated Nisei as workers in defense industries . . . ; put *responsibility* for behavior of Issei and Nisei on the leaders of Nisei groups such as the Japanese American Citizens League; and put *responsibility* for production . . . on Nisei leaders.[28]

The foregoing were all JACL programs enunciated over and over again to its ethnic community during the pre-eviction era. Beyond any debate, it clearly shows that the purpose of the Kido-Masaoka duo in seeking control of its ethnic society, with the backing of the federal government, was the seizure of the reins of power of the Japanese American community groups, and not simply the assumption of community leadership because of a vacuum caused by the arrests of Issei leadership, as the JACL has claimed orally and through the semiofficial writings of William Kumpe Hosokawa, the oracle of the commissioned JACL party line.[v] It will also be shown later how the JACL participated in aiding the government in the destruction of that Issei leadership.

Posterity is indebted to Michi Weglyn for bringing to the fore the Munson Report. She has perceptively characterized the Munson suggestion as an endorsement of "power-to-the-Nisei."[29] This point is clearly demonstrated in Munson's addendum to his report:

> In case we have not made it apparent, the aim of this report is that all Japanese Nationals in the continental United States and property owned and operated by them within the country be immediately placed under absolute Federal control.

---

v See the following books by Bill Hosokawa: *Nisei: The Quiet Americans* (New York: William Morrow, 1969, 2002), 240; (with Robert A. Wilson) *East to America: A History of the Japanese in the United* States (New York: William Morrow, 1980), 191; and *JACL in Quest of Justice* (New York: William Morrow, 1982), 138.

The aim of this will be to squeeze control from the hands of the Japanese Nationals into the hands of the loyal Nisei who are American citizens. . . . It is the aim that the Nisei should police themselves, and as a result police their parents.[30]

The Munson Report categorically says a great deal about the JACL for discerning Japanese Americans who are willing to shed their defensive cultural armor and stare the Citizens League in its face. The JACL leaders' craze for power is self-explanatory. The matter of policing their Issei parents was brought to the surface twice before; first, by the founder of the national JACL, Seattle's James Yoshinori Sakamoto, in his testimony before the Tolan Congressional Committee;[31] and subsequently, if it is to be believed, in July in San Jose, presumably by the JACL's field secretary, Mike Masaru Masaoka. This latter incident is a revelation of Masaoka's and remains unconfirmed for lack of any documentation. The field executive states that he wrote a letter to a General Richardson at the Western Defense Command.[32] Such a letter has failed to surface, and until it does Masaoka's suicide battalion theory should be considered merely a pipe dream.[33] Unfortunately, however, chroniclers appear to be taking Masaoka's suicide battalion theory at face value. The first statement to this effect, to this writer's knowledge, appeared in 1969 in *The Great Betrayal* by Audrie Girdner and Anne Loftis.[34] It is saddening to see that even in *Years of Infamy*, Masaoka's unconfirmed statement is seemingly treated as valid. I consider this statement by Michi Weglyn to be totally inaccurate: "In a desperate last-ditch effort to halt the mass uprooting, Nisei leaders proposed the formation of a volunteer suicide battalion."[vi] The alleged proposal was said to have been made in 1942 during the Fourth of July period, and by that time the Japanese American evictees were largely committed to Army-administered assembly centers. Furthermore, documents clearly indicate that mass eviction was endorsed by the JACL even prior to issuance of the presidential proclamation.

I also dispute the conclusions reached by Weglyn in *Years of Infamy*. She states, "Munson's suggested course of governmental action, which would have catapulted the Nisei into a position of leadership and control, might have proved sound had both the Issei and Nisei been permitted to remain at liberty as in Hawaii."[vii] In this particular case, as Munson himself

---

vi Weglyn, *Years of Infamy*, 38.
vii Ibid., 51.

declaimed, the Nisei leadership that he envisioned was then a small circle of ambitious Nisei under the banner of the JACL.[35] This group faced a monumental identity crisis, considered itself as ordained by destiny for ethnic leadership, and entertained the attitude that they knew best what was good for their community.[viii]

Munson, in his report to President Roosevelt, endorsed the loyalty of American-born Japanese. This finding was further endorsed by Lieutenant Commander Kenneth D. Ringle of the Office of Naval Intelligence (ONI).[36] According to U.S. Army historian Stetson Conn,[37] it was around February 1, 1942, that Ringle submitted an undated report to John J. McCloy, assistant secretary of War,[38] allowing as to how he "heartily agrees with the reports submitted by Mr. Munson."[ix] Ringle himself had arrived at a similar conclusion in his ONI reports to commanders of the three Pacific Coast naval districts. In banking on Nisei loyalty, Ringle reminded leaders of the Southern District JACL Council,[39] at a meeting held in Santa Ana, California,[40] that he was staking his reputation and career on Nisei loyalty.

The JACL scenario took off on November 28, 1941, a day after the Thanksgiving Day holiday. Masaoka left San Francisco abruptly on an unstated mission that took him to Colorado and Nebraska. His first public address, made at Fort Lupton, Colorado,[41] to a group of Nisei farmers, was both startling and significant. I have discussed this event previously in a multi-part critique that appeared in the *Rafu Shimpo* in 1989 and which was later excerpted within the JACL-commissioned yet unreleased Lim Report.[x] The relevant portion, in so many words, declared as follows: The most bizarre incident is Masaoka's mission to the Plains states right after Thanksgiving 1941, where at a congregation of Fort Lupton [JACL] chapter members,[42] he warned of impending concentration camps for all Japanese in the event of

---

viii It is not my intention to criticize Weglyn, but I would not be true to my craft if I did not dispute errors that I run across. I feel that I am more knowledgeable concerning such errors by consequence of my longer confrontations with the JACL hierarchy. Michi Weglyn and her husband, Walter, are in the forefront of those who have provided moral support to this writer, and to them and to all others who have done likewise, I am forever grateful.

ix Stetson Conn, *The Decision to Evacuate the Japanese from the Pacific Coast* (Washington, DC: Center of Military History, U.S. Army, 1990), 138.

x James M. Omura, "Debunking the JACL Fallacies" (four-part series), *Rafu Shimpo*, April 13, 14, 17, 18, 1989; Deborah K. Lim, "The Lim Report: A Research Report of Japanese Americans in American Concentration Camps during World War II" (hereafter cited as Lim Report), unpublished 1990 study prepared under the auspices of the national Japanese American Citizens League, ID-1, 24, 1989, and then mothballed. [Ed. For a discussion of the historical evolution of this report by William Hohri along with a copy of the report as originally submitted by Deborah Lim, see the following website: www.resisters.com/study/LimTOC.htm#IA1 (accessed on April 15, 2015).]

war. On his urging, the president of the chapter carried the message to Fort Morgan, Sedgwick, and other points, though expressing skepticism.[xi]

Deborah Lim, a special JACL-salaried archival investigator on Resolution 7, cited as evidence the original tape-recorded interview of Lee Murata of Brighton, Colorado.[xii] Passed at the 1988 Biennial Convention of the National JACL in Seattle, Washington, Resolution 7 mandated apologies to persons who had sustained injuries by the wartime policies of the organization.[43] Murata's recollection of the year [he mentions the possibilities of both 1940 and 1939] was confused, but not the contents of Masaoka's speech. Lim's conclusion on this matter appears to have been based upon limited background information, which her research did not disclose. She states: "The tape of Murata, of course, can be explained away as the reminiscences of a confused mind. However, while a listener could conclude that there was confusion on the dates, there was no confusion in the interview about Masaoka's message and presence."[xiii]

This conclusion of the JACL investigator on Murata's confusion of the year of occurrence fails to understand the sequence of the itinerary taken by Masaoka. To clarify, Masaoka departed San Francisco one day after the Thanksgiving holiday of 1941; spoke before the Fort Lupton, Colorado, JACL chapter on that weekend; and then went on to North Platte, Nebraska. He was arrested by FBI agents the morning of December 7, 1941, the following Sunday morning, while addressing a group of fifty Japanese Americans gathered from eastern Wyoming, southern South Dakota, and western Nebraska in the basement room of the North Platte Episcopal Church.[xiv] Pearl Harbor had been bombed by Imperial Japan and the nation had been plunged into World War II.

Lim did come to the Mile High City when conducting her research but unaccountably, although urged to by a historian,[xv] failed to contact this writer, whom she herself described and recognized as a "longtime thorn in the side of the JACL."[xvi] Had she done so, the discrepancy in her conclusion

---

xi See Omura, "Debunking the JACL Fallacies," April 17, 1989.

xii Lee Murata, past president, Fort Lupton JACL chapter president, interviewed by Joe Grant Masaoka, October 28, 1966, Buddhist Church Lounge, Denver, Colorado, Oral History Tape 249, Box 394, Japanese American Research Project, UCLARL.

xiii Lim Report, ID, "The Decision to Cooperate with Evacuation." [Ed. See relevant section in online version of this report, www.resisters.com/study/LimPartICID.htm#ID1 (accessed on April 15, 2015).]

xiv Bill Hosokawa, *JACL in Quest of Justice*, 131–32.

xv Professor Arthur A. Hansen of the History Department, California State University, Fullerton. [Ed. See postscript in Art Hansen, letter to Jimmie Omura, January 13, 1990, OP.]

xvi Lim Report, as cited in note xiii above.

would not have been as complicated as she makes it. Mike Masaoka was hired as a field secretary on September 1, 1941, and prior to his appointment had no reason to be representing the national JACL, which thus identifies his Fort Lupton dictum. Furthermore, Lee Murata was the then-presiding official of the Fort Lupton JACL chapter and, considering his capacity, is entitled to greater consideration than that accorded him in the Lim Report as to his confusion on the year.

Lim further notes in her report:

> This tape by itself would not amount to much in the way of support for Omura's contentions. However, taken along with an even more puzzling document referred to by Omura in Part Three of his "Debunking JACL Fallacies," one must pause to consider. On February 9, 1942, ten days prior to Roosevelt's issuance of Executive Order 9066, Attorney General Francis Biddle wrote a memorandum to his assistant James Rowe.[44] It states: "Please note the attached memorandum from Mr. Hoover to the effect that the Japanese-American Citizens League wants us to evacuate its members and alien parents. I think we should begin exploring with Mr. McNutt[45] the possibility of having some refugee camps for the Japs, which we will need."[xvii]

The national JACL headquarters shelved the Lim Report and issued a substitute report under the aegis of the Presidential Select Committee, nullifying its archival expenditures.[46] In response to the Biddle memoranda, the League fired back: "Critics of JACL have referred to the latter memo, without reference to the first one." This reference apparently is to the Hoover memo, which does no more than confirm the Biddle interoffice communication: "At a special meeting on January 30, 1942 at San Francisco, California, the National Headquarters of the Japanese American Citizens League passed a resolution to request the federal government to permit its members and their alien parents to evacuate the West Coast area voluntarily."[xviii]

Our basic interest is the original letter received by Mr. Hoover from the national JACL headquarters. In June 1992 I attempted to secure access to the National JACL Archives in San Francisco, but was refused access.[47] That fact raises the suspicion that the Citizens League continues to follow a policy of secretiveness to hide and to defend its blemished wartime role.

---

xvii Memorandum from U.S. Attorney General Francis Biddle to James Rowe Jr., an assistant to Biddle, February 9, 1942.
xviii Memorandum from J. Edgar Hoover, FBI Director, to Attorney General Francis Biddle, February 3, 1942, Washington, DC.

Lim deserves unstinting credit for her openness and objectivity in the production of her JACL report. The only problem might be the lack of depth in her research and a tendency to overemphasize initial preliminary proposals advanced [by the JACL] prior to the eviction. Thus, the Lim Report offers a clouded perspective on the matter of the Hoover revelation and is not focused forcefully on the memo's implication. What is actually implied is the suggestion by the national JACL headquarters of forsaking its ethnic society, thereby leaving it in the lurch. It is important to keep in mind that the request to Hoover was for the JACL's "members and alien parents," and had refugee camps been available we can only speculate as to the result. In another sense, the memo also endorses the JACL's approval of eviction of the Japanese ethnic minority from the West Coast. The bona fide membership of the national JACL at this time was 5,700, which represented roughly 4 percent of the total number of Japanese residing in the affected military zones. On the basis of the Hoover memo, the national JACL was prepared to abandon the bulk of its ethnic society. Abandonment was not such a farfetched ideology. In fact, a JACL leadership group in Monterey County[48] did exactly that, ditching their constituents and leaving them leaderless. This incident is noted in a WRA Community Analysis Report: "During the evacuation, this JACL chapter acquired a disreputable reputation amongst the people. It is reported that the JACL leaders were the first to leave Monterey for inland districts, thus exposing the residents to turmoil. They were left without an influential body to iron out the difficulties that arose during those trying periods."[xix]

Can the JACL be faulted for being concerned with self-preservation for its members and alien parents? Under normal conditions, it is the function of an organization to look after the interest of its own group. However, the oncoming eviction of its ethnic society was not a normal situation; furthermore, as early as October 1941, the JACL had proclaimed itself the legitimate leader of the Japanese American communities. Thus, it was incumbent upon the JACL to place its priority on the interest of its ethnic society over its own self-preservation. To even consider the abandonment of its ethnic society constituted a breach of responsibility and a grievous violation of acceptable and ethical conduct. The fact that the federal government had

---

xix Paul Higashi, Community Analysis Report No. 6, Colorado River [Poston] Relocation Center, March 16, 1945, 3, in JERS, BANC, UCB, File J 3.22. [Ed. Omura used the 1958 JERS finding aid. In the revised 1996 finding aid, the report cited is found within Reel J 3.21]. See also Lim Report, 1C, 21.

no refugee camps in place mitigated the JACL's request to Hoover. The first congressman to tee off against the Nisei Americans was Leland M. Ford of Santa Monica.[49] The California congressman, who had been pushing the attorney general and the War Department to take drastic action, took the floor of the House of Representatives on January 20, 1942, to blast the "Fifth Column" prospects of the California Japanese, declaring, "A patriotic native-born Japanese, if he wants to make his contribution, will submit himself to a concentration camp."[xx]

That suggestion outraged JACL founder James Sakamoto, who angrily rebuked the California congressman: "This is our country. We were born and raised here and have made our homes here and we are ready to give our lives if necessary, to defend the United States."[xxi] While Sakamoto's indignant retort was characteristic for an ultrapatriotic organization, the national headquarters had no comments to offer. Instead, its hierarchy was engaged in drawing up a blueprint to care for its own interests. Indeed, the request to FBI director John Edgar Hoover had come only ten days after the Ford proposal.

Voices of traditional anti-Japanese bigotry were heretofore conspicuously and ominously silent throughout the seasonal holidays after the bombing of Pearl Harbor. The hierarchy of the JACL incorrectly interpreted this inactivity as the product of its successful prewar propaganda campaign, badly underestimating the power and dedication of the racist groups. This attitude is reflected in the statement of Togo Tanaka, the national JACL's publicity director: "Throughout the three month [*sic*] period from December 7 to the second week in February, there appears to have grown an assumption on the part of the JACL leadership that the position of American citizens of Japanese ancestry had been secured by vigorous action."[xxii] Ten years later, Mike Masaoka, reminiscing about the events of eviction, wrote: "There is no doubt in my mind that these original pledges of confidence from those in high authority lulled many of us into believing our position to be secure."[50]

But all of the public relations work done by the JACL was dashed as soon as the New Year of 1942 dawned. The West Coast congressional bloc revved

---

xx [Ed. See Greg Robinson, *By Order of the President: FDR and the Internment of Japanese Americans* (Cambridge, MA: Harvard University Press, 2001), 92. See also Martha Nakagawa's entry for Ford in the *Densho Encyclopedia*, http://encyclopedia.densho.org/ (accessed on April 17, 2015).]

xxi [Ed. As stated by Bill Hosokawa, *JACL in Quest of Justice*, 144.]

xxii Togo Tanaka, "History of the JACL" [1945?], JERS, BANC, UCB, MSS T 6.25, Chapter 4, 45. [Ed. In the 1996 JERS finding aid, this document is listed as being on Reel 084.0340, Folder T 6.25.]

up its considerable political influence to call for the eviction of all Japanese from the West Coast. In early January Congressman Ford inserted an inciting letter from Hollywood actor Leo Carrillo[51] into the Congressional Record that set off the call for mass eviction. "Why wait until (the Japanese) pull something before we act? . . . Let's get them off the coast into the interior. . . . May I urge you in behalf of the safety of the people of California to start action at once."[xxiii]

Nine days later and only a day before the JACL's self-preservation letter to Hoover, syndicated Hearst columnist Henry McLemore[52] fired off a highly provocative column supporting mass eviction:

> I am for immediate removal of every Japanese on the West Coast to a point deep in the interior. I don't mean a nice part of the interior either. Herd 'em up, pack 'em off and give 'em the inside room in the badlands. Let 'em be pinched, hurt, hungry and dead up against it.
>
> Personally, I hate the Japanese. And that goes for all of them.[xxiv]

Such outlandish expressions were having a damaging effect upon large sections of the populace and served well to create public hysteria. Attitudes on the Pacific Coast were not helped any by repeated losses in the South Pacific. Still, no words came out of the JACL national headquarters. Joining the fray was the well-respected liberal commentator Walter Lippmann,[53] and his entry brought in another syndicated columnist, Westbrook Pegler,[54] who was preceded by Damon Runyon[55] and the Mutual Network commentator John B. Hughes.[56] Shockingly, the wartime president of the JACL, Saburo Kido, stated in a Japanese American Research Project (JARP) tape interview in 1967 that JACL leaders were not "conscious of the impact that mass hysteria would have on the decision to evacuate."[xxv] Clearly, it would be difficult to imagine that the Citizens League leadership was not cognizant of the effects wrought by the syndicated columnists.

---

xxiii Leo Carrillo, Hollywood, California, to Congressman Leland M. Ford, January 6, 1942; Jacobus tenBroeck, Edward N. Barnhart, and Floyd W. Matson, *Prejudice, War and the Constitution: Causes and Consequences of the Evacuation of the Japanese Americans in World War II* (Berkeley: University of California Press, 1973), 77.

xxiv Henry McLemore, *San Francisco Examiner*, January 29, 1942.

xxv [Ed. The 1967 interview with Saburo Kido signified by Omura was done on January 4 of that year in Los Angeles by interviewers Joe Grant Masaoka and Robert A. Wilson. Within the JARP project at UCLA, this interview is Tape 36 and is included in Box 381. For information about this interview as well as selected others within the JARP Project, see Gary Y. Okihiro's finding aid, "The Oral History Tapes of the Japanese American Research Project, Tape Numbers 1-112: A Survey," UCLARL.]

On February 3, 1942, the prospect of mass eviction was not on the mind of Lieutenant General John L. DeWitt. He reported to Chief of Staff General George C. Marshall via telephone that he was amenable to California governor Culbert Olson's[57] proposal for the establishment of camps in California's interior rather than to subjecting the resident Japanese American population to resettlement outside the state.[xxvi] Two days later, on February 5, 1942, Governor Olson summoned a group of Nisei from around the state to his executive chamber to lay out the framework of his proposal. He demanded that the Nisei submit themselves and their alien parents to self-imposed internment in the interior of California. These holding reserves were to be guarded by federal troops but the men would be allowed to go out each day, under military guards, to harvest the rich California agricultural crops. Olson further explained that participants were to be identified by stamping and branding so that they could be accounted for once they were out in the fields. The alternative to this arrangement, the governor warned, was ultimate dispossession outside the combat zone as defined by Military Areas No. 1 and No. 2.

Although unofficial JACL historian Togo Tanaka[58] acknowledges that "how the group had been selected was never made known," the majority of Nisei actually attending the February 6, 1942, meeting with Governor Olson were key national leaders of the Japanese American Citizens League.[xxvii] Walter T. Tsukamoto, who presided as JACL president before turning over the mantle of leadership to Saburo Kido, unabashedly endorsed the governor's proposal, as did most others, but reservations were voiced by Ken Matsumoto, the national JACL's vice president, and these were weakly concurred with by Saburo Kido and Masaoka.[59] Tanaka's account dances gingerly around the Olson proposal and avoids coming to grips with essential specifics. However, an echo of the governor's proposal appeared in San Francisco at the JACL's National Emergency Meeting, which I will deal with at its appointed time.

It is not crystal clear at what point the JACL embraced the concept of collaboration, but it is easier to determine when that crystallized into its subsequent form. That development occurred shortly after the conference with Governor Olson. By mid-February, the JACL went public, endorsing mass eviction, a policy decision that had yet to be determined. Masaoka

xxvi Daniels, *Concentration Camps USA*, 57–68.
xxvii See Tanaka, "History of the JACL." [Ed. Chapter 4, 25.]

appeared before a meeting of the Bay Region Council for Unity on February 16 in San Francisco, and again on the eighteenth at a mass meeting of an audience of over a thousand at the Maryknoll Auditorium in Los Angeles, to advocate for mass eviction. The legal scholar and *coram nobis*[60] expert Peter Irons states without equivocation that collaboration was "established well before the outbreak of war" and "fatally compromised the JACL."[xxviii] My analysis of the situation tends to confirm Irons's assessment, a point I will explore further at its proper time.

Surprisingly, no one seemed to question Masaoka's bald statement that "the end justifies the means." What he meant by that was that anything goes, and he was not shy about indulging in that philosophy. This phraseology is a remnant of the historical Jesuit policy of casuistry, which society ultimately felt compelled to reject. However, the Mormons, to which Masaoka belonged, seemed to have resurrected this outworn theory, and the JACL spokesman demonstrated his zealotry on his by-and-large passive ethnic constituents. In addition, both the League's founder and its national headquarters in San Francisco had pledged full support to President Roosevelt upon the outbreak of war in the Pacific. The JACL alluded to this pledge in implementing its "constructive cooperation" theory and in defending its organization from its critics.

From their responses to criticisms, it is evident that JACL leaders never had a clear perception of their organizational aims. The muddled state of the JACL mentality is reflected in the confusion of its founder, Jimmie Sakamoto, on the matter of loyalty in relation to obedience to laws. Sakamoto characterized men like Minoru Yasui and eight other Japanese Americans who violated the curfew as "negligent" and strongly declaimed: "There is no excuse for them. They knew the rule. Of course, all this reflects on the Japanese generally, but this is not the point. Loyalty is shown by obedience to the laws, and we can best prove our loyalty by obeying orders of those in authority."[xxix]

On the basis of Sakamoto's confusion regarding obedience to the laws as evidence of individual loyalty and thus Americanism, it is apparent that the JACL theory of collaboration dated as far back as the League's inception in Seattle on August 29–31, 1930. Given its origination at that time,

---

xxviii Peter Irons, *Justice at War* (New York: Oxford University Press, 1983), 81.

xxix James Yoshinori Sakamoto, *Japanese-American Courier*, April 10, 1942; Jerrod H. Takahashi, "Changing Responses to Race Relations: The Formation of Nisei Perspectives," *Amerasia Journal* 9 (1982): 29–57, esp. 39–40.

collaboration obviously did not crystallize until October 1941 and the issuance of the JACL Declaration of Policy.[61] It was further reinforced by Curtis Munson's visit toward the end of the same month and flowered into fruition with the Pearl Harbor attack.

It was a visit paid me from internationally famed sculptor Isamu Noguchi[62] that precipitated my participation in the wartime crisis. Noguchi arrived at the *Current Life* office in early February 1942. His purpose was to form a cell of the Writers and Artists Mobilization for Democracy.[63] Noguchi explained that he had established a direct line to Archibald MacLeish, Librarian of Congress and director of the War Department's Office of Facts and Figures.[64] He further stated that such a group as he sought to launch would operate under the oversight of the Hollywood Screen Writers Guild.[65] Noguchi admitted that his reception at the JACL's national headquarters was cool. I also had misgivings. It sounded too much like government propaganda. However, I kept my feelings to myself and agreed to participate, but only as an observer.

Not much is known about the Bay Region Council for Unity. It was short-lived and received only a brief mention in the *Japanese-American Courier* of Seattle but otherwise went unnoticed by the Nisei wartime media.[66] Because of this selective public scrutiny, it is cited here in greater detail for public knowledge. The Bay Region Council for Unity is notable for being the first Nisei group before which the Japanese American Citizens League unveiled its mass eviction policy responsible for producing the charge that the Japanese American community was "sold down the river" by the JACL.

The initial meeting of the Bay Region Council for Unity was called on February 11 at Noguchi's North Beach[67] studio. It was shocking to find only seven participants, all of whom except for me were either left-wing or out-and-out Communists. Nevertheless, I offered a motion to call the group the Bay Region Council for Unity, which to my surprise was accepted. This action totally changed Noguchi's stated agenda. Despite efforts to name Noguchi the chairman, Lawrence Tajiri, the JACL's front man, was easily elected. I then asked for adjournment until a larger and more representative group could be assembled. But prior to adjournment, I called attention to the speaking tour of Mike Masaoka down the California coast and indicated that Current Life Publications was receiving negative reactions. Tajiri assured the group that national headquarters was aware of the situation and was calling Masaoka back for rebriefing and might even write future speeches for him.ˣˣˣ

The second meeting of the group was held five days later, on February 16, and it was well attended. When notified by Noguchi, I briefly alluded to the Communist dominance in the group.

"Don't you think there are too many Communists?" I inquired.

"No!" he responded emphatically.

I said no more. Noguchi made his first organization attempt of the Writers and Artists Mobilization for Democracy in Los Angeles, but there saw his effort shattered on charges of domination of the group by Communists and left-wingers. It appeared to me the same situation was being repeated in San Francisco. I was to learn later that artists and writers in New York, the circle to which Isamu Noguchi belonged, were labeled as Communists or left-wingers.

There was a large audience at Noguchi's North Beach studio on the sixteenth. It was so crowded that people sat on the floor Indian fashion. "There's a chair coming your way, Jimmie," someone yelled, and I was watching the chair coming toward me hand over hand when the chairman, Larry Tajiri, rapped for order. Then came a stunner. "I move for the expulsion of Jimmie Omura," declared Tajiri. I looked to the right, where I had heard a quick second, and gazed directly into the eyes of Ernie Iiyama,[68] the leader of the Nisei Young Democrats of Oakland.[69] The silence that greeted the motion was absolute and a pin drop would have been startling.

"On what ground?" I asked Tajiri.

"*Current Life* is a publication," he stated. "It does not represent a group."

"On that definition, I would have to withdraw," declared Isamu Noguchi.

"I am in the same boat as *Current Life*," Karl Yoneda,[70] the Communist politico, added, after detailing his role as branch manager of the Los Angeles-based *Doho* newspaper.

"If *Current Life* is expelled, I'll be going, too," came the voice of Lincoln Kanai, executive secretary of the Buchanan YMCA,[71] from the far east corner of the room.

The Tajiri expulsion motion was overwhelmingly defeated on a call for a vote by Isamu Noguchi. I had been expecting something, but nothing like this. A report had seeped to *Current Life* in midweek of an ad hoc group

---

 xxx To Masaoka admirers this revelation might seem like a chink in the armor of this reputed forensic marvel.

walking down Buchanan Street to the Buchanan YMCA building for a meeting. "They're up to no good!" I remarked. It surprised me that Larry Tajiri was masterminding this expulsion. We had been close associates from Lil' Tokyo days in Los Angeles and he was the most broad-minded Nisei editor of prewar times. Now he was denying access to dissent, a total flip-flop.

I took the floor to pitch my ideology of resistance, hoping to raise the audience's awareness of the fact that their constitutional liberties were being violated. Suddenly, Mike Masaoka entered the room and unabashedly took a position in front of the group just eighteen inches from where I stood. He immediately plunged into his report of reckless shootings by night riders into homes of Japanese Americans and the murder of an aged farm couple by Filipinos in Imperial Valley. This was old news already carried in the daily media. Blocked by the speaker, I had to stand my ground and thus I noticed Masaoka's body trembling as he related the goings-on in east-central California from where he had just returned.

"This man is scared," the thought raced through my mind.

Masaoka declared: "We must all get out! We should all go quietly into internment. We can sit out the war in safety, under protective custody." It should be noted that this accession to mass eviction had come three days before Executive Order 9066. The suggestion was horrendous and shocking.

"We're being sold down the river," I objected.

"If you want to say anything, join the League," was Masaoka's tart rejoinder.

"This is a racial crisis," I pointed out, "and not a simple organizational problem. When it affects my own destiny, I have the right to speak out on the determination of that destiny."

"Under the circumstances, who would want to remain here?" he asked, turning his head to me.

"I would!" I responded simply.

Masaoka began his exit and then added, "If we go quietly, the government has promised to show future considerations."

"What future considerations?" I demanded. But Masaoka was gone into the darkness without a response.

After Masaoka's departure, Noguchi pressed the issue of remaining. "You'd want to remain here?" he asked.

"Yes," I replied.

"I don't think anyone would wish to remain here," he declared.

"I would," I repeated. "I think enough of my civil liberties to want to fight for them. If we aren't willing to fight to keep them, we shouldn't be entitled to have them at all. Whatever is worth the having is also worth fighting for."

"But don't you think mass evacuation is for our own protection?" Noguchi asked.

"I haven't observed much hysteria in San Francisco," I replied. "I'm willing to risk remaining here."

No one else offered any objection. Masaoka had played on the fears of his audience. "What Masaoka had just proposed," I wrote a friend later, "sounded strangely like the words of Congressman Leland Ford in his January 20th pronouncement on the floor of the House of Representatives to me."[xxxi] Ford's words were carried on the radio and widely disseminated in the news media. It seemed to me as if Masaoka had embraced the outrageous Ford concept.

The key recommendations proposed by Masaoka were that

1. In order to avoid mob violence, Japanese Americans should be evacuated under protective custody.

2. Japanese American families should be kept together.

3. Japanese Americans should sit out the war in internment camps under guard of federal troops.

As to the first recommendation, Masaoka voiced JACL opposition to the so-called voluntary relocation feature in deference to hostilities of inland people. This was a complete reversal of Masaoka's oft-repeated pre-eviction claim that the consequence of refusal to leave would be wholesale massacre by federal troops "with guns and tanks" for forceful eviction. This was simple demagoguery, for high administration officials had already stated that the remedy for noncompliance was unknown. Refuting the Masaoka "massacre" theory, I contended that the United States government could not afford to allow a massacre because of the threat of reprisal to Allied prisoners of war in the Japanese Imperial government's hands.

---

xxxi Jimmie Omura, Denver, Colorado, to A. Norman Depew, Los Angeles, California. [Ed. Omura provides no date for this letter to the enigmatic Depew. The letter in question, while the information rings true, does not appear to be included in the extensive correspondence file (contained in OP) between the two men from April 16 to June 22, 1942. For more on Depew and his relationship with Omura, see the May 13, 1942, memorandum in the same correspondence file that Omura sent to Mr. [?] Carpenter of the Denver FBI field office.]

Masaoka's second recommendation was a moral phobia based on the tragedy of the French people of Acadie, now Nova Scotia. After the French defeat by the British, the people of Acadie refused to pledge allegiance to their British king. The Acadians were dispersed haphazardly to French Louisiana, with husbands separated from wives, mothers and children divided, and lovers split asunder.[72] It was because of this historical event that the concept of family togetherness was conceived for the Nikkei, and not because of any appeals, as implied, that the Japanese American Citizens League might have issued.

Masaoka's final recommendation constitutes a contradiction in the wartime policy of the JACL. The fear of violence was accentuated by the Citizens League, and it became real to the majority of Japanese Americans. Although reports were played up on some actual incidents of killings and rapes by whites, Filipinos, and blacks, their total number was comparatively few and "sporadic," according to Attorney General Francis Biddle, who did not feel that they justified mass eviction. The JACL contradiction, in this matter, lies in the fact that personal safety was used as its criterion for mass eviction; on the other hand, the JACL was the leading ethnic force for sending Nisei soldiers into battle to be annihilated. Were we to accept the undocumented appeal for a suicide battalion, we could only believe the Citizens League apparently was splitting hairs between annihilation of the Nisei in domestic "massacre" and annihilation of them in the war. Thus, "sit out the war in safety" was merely a ploy, for the 442nd Nisei Combat Battalion made that "duration of the war" rather brief.

The next matter that came before the Bay Region Council of Unity was the status of the organization. Whereas the JACL's Larry Tajiri strenuously argued for affiliating the council with the JACL as a "sounding board," I warned the group that Tajiri's motion for such an affiliation was a kiss of death and that our only salvation was to remain independent. My warning notwithstanding, Tajiri and his left-wing supporters rammed through the sounding board measure. Lincoln Kanai, the executive secretary of the Buchanan Street YMCA, thereupon bolted the meeting and, shortly thereafter, I did likewise. The sounding board concept had made any personal participation by me a waste of time. As far as I was concerned, the Bay Region Council for Unity was doomed.

But before the council's institutional oblivion occurred, *Current Life* was again attacked at the group's third and final meeting held in the YMCA.

This time the motion for *Current Life*'s expulsion was offered by Ernest Iiyama, who previously had seconded the original Tajiri motion. Again the motion was defeated overwhelmingly.

Current Life was the lone opposition group to the JACL's "constructive collaboration" theory. However, its effort to drum up converts through public forums and its editorial stand proved fruitless. Fundamental rights were treated by the Citizens League as virtual anathema in the crisis, and the Nisei public, although noncommittal in public debates, appeared to have accepted the JACL's mass eviction proposal. Anti-Japanese exponents had used the Issei, who were aliens barred from citizenship, as a strategic inroad for inclusion of the American-born citizens in their drive for mass eviction. The attacks against people of Japanese ancestry were no longer simply confined to alien Japanese, but now included all Nikkei.

It cannot be properly said that when war came the Japanese American Citizens League truly represented the only functioning racial leadership. But to gain its preeminence as such, the JACL required the backing of the federal government. To achieve that backing, the JACL sacrificed its principles and betrayed the very people it purported to represent. Even though the JACL leadership preached quiet submission and docile acceptance of the harsh Roosevelt transgression to fundamental rights, in those times and in the climate of war it seemed to the general Japanese American populace that the JACL dictum represented the only thread of sanity left to which it could cling. Put another way, Masaoka's tenuous and illusory palliative appeared to be the Japanese American community's only hope. The number summarily evicted from Military Areas No. 1 and 2 was 112,235, all of whom went into captivity without visible protests. "Contemporary Americans may wonder," asked a University of California, Berkeley, oral historian many years later, "why Issei and Nisei went so quietly, standing in long lines to fill buses."[xxxii][73] Why, indeed, was acquiescence so complete?

It was made painfully aware that the Nisei public, at least for the most part, were not interested in standing up for their constitutional rights. However, I had no intention of being caged as a hostage within a concentration camp. In his address to the Bay Region Council of Unity, Masaoka had indicated the prospect of our becoming hostages. The surprising fact was that no one reacted to this statement except me. The issue was brought up again

---

xxxii Rosemary Levenson, an oral historian in the Regional Oral History Office at the University of California, Berkeley.

by Isamu Noguchi without causing a ripple. This lack of support for vested constitutional prerogatives was a frustrating spectacle for me to witness.

The hostage factor was also taken up in the *Current Life* office. "I can't understand the Nisei not protesting, and becoming hostages in these camps," I declared. "I'll be darned if I'm going to submit myself as a prisoner. I'm going to keep all the freedom I've got."

Two days later, on the eighteenth, similar appeals for mass eviction were made by the national JACL spokesmen at a public meeting in the Maryknoll Auditorium in Los Angeles that drew over one thousand people. Unlike the quiet reception in San Francisco, the reaction in the Southland was violent outrage against the theory of submission.[74] The rapidity shown in embracing the Leland Ford proposal indicates how the minds of the embryo JACL hierarchy had been conditioned for eviction before any removal had been fully contemplated.

Violation of constitutional justice was not in the public repertoire of Masaoka and in fact he opposed that of his own peers, who had the audacity to advocate the principles of the Bill of Rights. No plea was made for the vast economic and financial losses that loomed ahead and were to be incurred by his people. He was instead more eager to see them uprooted, as indicated in his "willingness" to go "gladly" on the order of the military.[xxxiii] Other JACL leaders echoed the Masaoka injunction, and supporting them were the Communist politico Karl Yoneda and his bedfellows, the Oakland Nisei Democrats. The irascible Tokutaro Nishimura Slocum, head of the Anti-Axis Committee of the JACL's Southern District Council, declared the Japanese would go "gladly," and the word "cheerfully" was added by Jimmie Sakamoto in the Pacific Northwest.

Under the situation of oppression by a repressive authority, it seemed peculiar to use such honeyed words of submission. These words debased the fundamental birthright of the American Nisei. At that moment no group of people held their constitutional privileges in such low esteem and in apparent contempt as to consider the ideology of eviction of their own ethnic society in such condescending terms. That is the legacy bequeathed by the JACL to succeeding generations of American Nikkei. It is a betrayal of a

---

xxxiii Statement of Mike Masaoka, National Secretary and Field Executive of the Japanese American Citizens League, Hearing before the Select Committee Investigating National Defense Migration, House of Representatives, 77th Cong., 2d sess. [hereafter Tolan Committee Hearings], San Francisco, California, February 23, 1942, Part 29, 11148.

people of remarkable proportion that has yet to be addressed. More than half a century has expired and spokesmen of the JACL still speak with pride and unconcealed arrogance of the correctness of its wartime policies. Nor will they concede that mistakes were made or that such policies contradicted the long-established moral concepts of human dignity, moral decency, and personal liberties that mankind forever seeks and cherishes. It is not the sort of pride shared by grassroots victims of this colossal human tragedy.

On February 19, 1942, President Franklin D. Roosevelt signed Executive Order 9066. In the words of Bill Hosokawa: "Its significance all but escaped the notice of JACL leaders. Only when it began to be implemented did the full horror of E.O. 9066 become apparent."[xxxiv]

Two days later, the hearings of the Tolan Committee got under way at the Post Office Building on Van Ness Avenue.[75] The matter of *Current Life*'s participation was discussed in our office; but in view of Executive Order 9066 it appeared to me that the committee could accomplish nothing of value, prompting me to declare that its proceedings would be "an exercise in futility." Precisely because the presidential proclamation could not be changed or altered or moderated by a congressional committee, *Current Life* decided to bypass the hearings.

The twenty-third day of February 1942 dawned clear and mild. It was a type of day that lures golf bugs out on the fairways and the common folks to revel at Ocean Beach. A soft, tempting zephyr breeze tickled the concrete wastelands of the Golden Gate city. It was an inspiring day, and a day beckoning for creative thoughts in editorial inclinations. Time ground slowly during this period of the slack season between holidays. It was 4:15 of that afternoon when the phone in the warehouse shipping department jangled. The caller was my boss, Harold Amling.

"Jim, you're wanted by a congressional committee," he stated. "You better get over here. There's a courier waiting for you."

It took five minutes to reach company headquarters. The courier was Caryl Okuma, *Current Life*'s managing editor. She briefed me quickly about the proceedings at the hearings, including Masaoka's outrageous behavior before the Tolan Committee and his refusal to seat himself according to protocol. Despite repeated requests to testify in a sitting position, Masaoka

---

xxxiv See Hosokawa, *JACL in Quest of Justice*, 145–46.

had delivered his testimony standing upright—his legs astraddle and his arms akimbo while pointing and gesticulating to emphasize certain items. Masaoka's antics had so disturbed the Tolan panel as to put it in a mood to hear an opposition opinion. The committee had received and read into the record an anonymous communication received from an East Bay student in which the Japanese American Citizens League had been roundly denounced. It said:

> I do not know what weight is given to testimony presented by representatives of the Japanese American Citizens League. However, I think that I can safely state that many thinking people have condemned that organization as a spokesman for the Japanese population. Its officials are notoriously fearful of answering questions directly or formulating upon policy which will reflect the desires and opinions as well as actions of the group which they are purported to represent. Moreover, it is a political organization and, hence, cannot be representative of those who prefer to hold their own political views.[xxxv]

The panel apparently was so nettled over Masaoka's arrogance that Congressman John J. Sparkman of Alabama[76] read this anonymous letter into the records of the proceedings. I was identified as the leading critic of the JACL and a call had been sent out for my appearance.

The wall clock over Amling's right shoulder stood right on the half hour as I opened the office door to inform him of my departure. I had some doubts of reaching the Post Office by the stipulated five o'clock. Thus Caryl and I set out promptly in a brisk walk, but we were stymied by homeward-bound office workers who clogged the sidewalk at Mission and again at the main thoroughfare of Market Street. Uniformed police further complicated matters by holding up pedestrian traffic for three signal changes while directing vehicular traffic. At last safely on the north side, we alternated brisk walking and intermittent jogging, and yet the tower clock at City Hall, across the street, read nine after the hour as we crossed the threshold of the Post Office Building.

We arrived at the rear of the auditorium just in time to see a panel of four religious leaders moving into their seats in the witness section. Thankful for this respite, I was able to compose myself and orient myself to the proceedings. The impression came over me, as I listened attentively to the

---

xxxv Tolan Committee Hearings, San Francisco, California, February 23, 1942, Part 29, 11142.

testimonies, that the chair appeared most condescending to the ministers as do-gooders rather than convinced of any beliefs they might hold.

I was the last witness, going on at 6:12 p.m. and unprepared due to the eleventh-hour request. In part, I testified as follows:

> I am strongly opposed to mass evacuation of American-born Japanese. It is my honest belief that such an action would not solve the question of Nisei loyalty. . . . I suppose you understand that I am in some measure opposed to what some of the other representatives of the Japanese community have said here before this Committee. . . . I specifically refer to the JACL. It is a matter of public record among the Japanese community that I have been consistently opposed to the Japanese American Citizens League. . . . I have felt that the leaders were leading the American-born Japanese along the wrong channels.[xxxvi]

"The wrong channels to which Omura referred were evident at the hearings," the coauthors of the historical documentary *To Serve the Devil*, an analysis of America's treatment of its minorities, would later declare. "All JACL representatives, including its national secretary, Mike Masaoka, testified that the Japanese Americans were willing to accept evacuation to prove their loyalty to the United States. 'I think sincerely,' stated Masaoka, 'if the military say "Move Out," we will be glad to move.'"[xxxvii]

In keeping with its traditional biases against what it considered as its primary critic, the *Pacific Citizen*, house organ of the Japanese American Citizens League, editorially blasted the position that had been taken by me with a double-column spread under the masthead of the newspaper's March 1, 1942, issue. Smarting from the evidence of opposition building against the Citizens League, the JACL struck out pell-mell under the editorship of Evelyn Kirimura.[77]

> The Congressional Committee had a surprise when they witnessed James Omura, the publisher of the Current Life, take the stand and testify against the JACL and its leadership.
>
> It may have been a grand gesture for a magazine with a circulation of 500 more or less, but it certainly did not do the Japanese, especially the Nisei, any good.

---

xxxvi Testimony of James M. Omura, Editor and Publisher, Current Life, San Francisco, California, February 23, 1942, Part 29, 11229–30.

xxxvii Paul Jacobs and Saul Landau, eds., *To Serve the Devil*, vol. 2: *Colonials and Sojourners* (New York: Random House, 1971), 166–67.

The tragedy of the whole thing is that simply because one puny publisher desired to make a show of himself, all the American citizens of Japanese ancestry are affected.[xxxviii78]

In actual fact, when I stepped into the marbled hallway I experienced a passing moment of having failed in not more clearly stating the position I desired to the Tolan Committee. It was a feeling that comes of wanting to have contributed some lasting words of wisdom or of value to posterity. Now the opportunity had been lost. I did not have long to dwell upon it, however, for within ninety minutes I had a scheduled conference with Commander [?] Lawrence of the Twelfth Naval District.

During that week and during interrogation of James Sakamoto at the Seattle hearings, Congressman Laurence F. Arnold, Illinois, confirmed the fact that the *Current Life* testimony had been requested. He stated:

> In San Francisco, we had two witnesses, whom we asked to appear, and they did not feel that their organization was properly represented by the president of your national organization [JACL]. . . . They thought that their group was not represented at all by you . . . and there was a magazine [*Current Life*] published in connection with it.[xxxix]

The actual circulation of *Current Life* stood in the neighborhood of twelve hundred to thirteen hundred, which was considered good for a starting publication in the Great Depression climate. The five hundred figure stated represented paid subscriptions, of which we admit to erring on the side of prudence. Contrary to the derogatory analysis of the JACL's *Pacific Citizen*, no single event has had a greater impact upon the publisher's life than that Tolan Committee hearing appearance. Remarkably, that testimony has gained increased stature in literary circles and brought me uncommon distinction in postwar literature. What has made this incident unique are the events that shaped it before and afterward. Had it not been for the Tolan Committee antics of Mike Masaoka, the panel would not have been upset and desirous of hearing an opposing view.

Obviously the JACL view is not the considered opinion of scholars and historians. For example, during an intermission in the 1983 International

---

xxxviii The *Pacific Citizen* editorial, as with many of the JACL charges against me, has no foundation in fact. Part of the confusion is due to my injudicious choice of words at the hearings. The words in the editorial attributed to Evelyn Kirimura, one of two volunteers putting out the paper, are strangely reminiscent of the language of JACL wartime-duration president Saburo Kido.

xxxix Testimony of Laurance F. Arnold, Congressman from Illinois and Tolan Committee member, Tolan Committee Hearings, Seattle, Washington, February 28 and March 2, 1942, Part 30, 11476.

Conference on Relocation and Redress held in Salt Lake City, historian Roger Daniels remarked to me, "You stand out like a sore thumb"[xl] (see Appendix 2).

Other historians have termed my Tolan Committee testimony "courageous," and still others have stated that the action was "very brave." But none of that entered into consideration at the time of my testimony. It was a matter of moral conscience that provoked my disagreement with the concept of eviction. I could not stand idly by while our own government was violating the basic principles of the Constitution, and the Bill of Rights was being made into a shamble.

The chancellor of a prestigious West Coast university described my action as "the lone voice of protest."[79] And yet the San Francisco session was the first of the Tolan Committee's series of hearings and the expectation was for a multitude of protests from other Nisei witnesses. I had not dreamt then that I would be the lone voice of protest before the Tolan Committee, and I am aghast now in reflecting upon this shameful fact. In investigating the archives, I found only two other dissident views: an Auburn, Washington, Nisei girl defending her constitutional rights in an op-ed letter to a Seattle newspaper;[80] and an editorial titled "For the Children's Sake" by *Rafu Shimpo* coeditor Louise Suski. A sixteen-year veteran plucked off the UCLA campus in 1926 to edit the first Southland English-language edition of a Japanese vernacular newspaper, Suski advocated resistance for posterity's sake.[81] Where Suski's and my approach differed, aside from the venue where our respective opposition was voiced, was that I continued to criticize the Roosevelt mandate.

It would be remiss of me not to provide one more quote from the documentary historians Jacobs and Landau, for this offering of theirs has gained greater currency than any others.

> He [Omura] spoke earnestly to the Committee, almost desperately pleading with them not to proceed with the plans to remove the Japanese.
>
> "It is doubtlessly rather difficult for Caucasian Americans to properly comprehend and believe in what we say. Our citizenship has even been attacked as an evil cloak under which we expect immunity for the nefarious purpose of conspiring to destroy the American way of life.

---

xl Roger Daniels, author of many books on the World War II Japanese American tragedy and coeditor, with Sandra C. Taylor and Harry H. L. Kitano, of *Japanese Americans from Relocation to Redress* (Salt Lake City: University of Utah Press, 1986), an anthology based upon the International Conference on Relocation and Redress held in Salt Lake City in March 1983.

"I would like to ask the Committee: Has the Gestapo come to America? Have we not risen in righteous anger at Hitler's mistreatment of the Jews? Then, is it not incongruous that citizen Americans of Japanese descent should be similarly mistreated and persecuted?"[82]

This last paragraph has been repeated in numerous chronicles of this sad Japanese American tragedy, beginning with Morton Grodzins, a University of Chicago political scientist, in 1949.[xli] A two-decade span ensued before Jacobs and Landau featured this Tolan Committee appearance of mine as a prologue to their documentary section on the "Japanese." In 1976 came Michi Nishiura Weglyn and her much-applauded *Years of Infamy*, which honored the quote as a chapter epigraph. Historian Richard Drinnon elevated it still higher in 1987 when he named me one of the nonconformists to whom he dedicated his book.[xlii] The latest is the playwright Frank Chin, one of four members of a literary group called CARP (Combined Asian American Resource Project), who authored the piece on the Heart Mountain Fair Play Committee, in which this writer figures, in the CARP-edited volume *The Big Aiiieeeee!*[xliii] In between, references have appeared in master's theses and in historical productions by Roger Daniels, Douglas W. Nelson, and Arthur Hansen, to name but a few. It is an amazing testimony that what was offered to the Tolan Committee was simply an ad-libbed framework, the gaps to be filled in upon questionings that never transpired. Although my disappointment was great and I grew obsessed at having frittered away a golden opportunity, the matter was done. It was not until receipt of the Tolan Report summary in June 1942 that I realized I had made an impact not anticipated while still in San Francisco.

Numerous books have been written on the Japanese American eviction but authors have been largely JACL leaders or League adherents. This explains why there has been a trend toward the glorification of its leadership. History is thus being written to uplift an organization that was so roundly condemned for its collaboration policies with a repressive government. Euro-American writers either are unaware of the cleavage that exists in the ethnic society or consider it unimportant. This gulf is irrevocable and not one to

---

xli Morton Grodzins, *Americans Betrayed: Politics and the Japanese Evacuation* (Chicago: University of Chicago Press, 1949), 196.

xlii Richard Drinnon, *Keeper of Concentration Camps: Dillon S. Myer and American Racism* (Berkeley: University of California Press, 1987).

xliii Jeffrey Paul Chan, Frank Chin, Lawson Fusao Inada, and Shawn Fong, eds., *The Big Aiiieeeee!: An Anthology of Chinese American and Japanese American Literature* (New York: Penguin, 1991), 52–92.

be resolved in the lifetime of the people involved. Perceptive academics do abound, though few in number, such as the historian Arthur A. Hansen, who pointedly condemned the WRA-JACL viewpoints that were manufactured for public consumption,[xliv] and Roger Daniels, another historian, who states, "The JACL-WRA view has dominated the writing of the evacuation's postwar history." He further adds that "others, more knowledgeable, have either consciously underplayed it [the division within the Japanese American community] or suppressed it completely, hoping thereby, in their view at least, to manage and improve the image of an oppressed people."[xlv]

I had not long to reflect on what I considered a debacle at the Tolan hearings. Slightly over an hour later Caryl and I were climbing the darkened steps of the Twelfth Naval District for a prearranged meeting with Commander [?] Lawrence. Walking down an unlighted hall to a small glob of light at its end was reminiscent of a cloak-and-dagger scene. We sat down on a bench provided just before a three-foot-high wooden balustrade. The glob of light was due to a brightly lit office in an alcove that shielded the reflections. No one was in the office and we had a wait of about five minutes. Then, as we watched, the alcove wall began to rotate and from within its fold stepped out a fully uniformed officer of stout, medium build. He took a seat at the desk.

"I am Commander [?] Kerrigan," he informed us. "I am taking Commander Lawrence's place. He was called away on urgent business." Hardly had he introduced himself when the telephone rang. It was a long call, about thirty minutes. The commander listened mostly and spoke in monosyllables. His face was grave when he faced us, and after several minutes of deep thought, he said:

"That was about a submarine surfacing at Goleta on the California coast and lobbing shells at the oil tanks on the hill. The shells all fell wide of the mark. No damage occurred."

Then the phone rang again. The conversation was somewhat shorter but lasted at least twenty minutes.

"Someone on the hill was signaling to the sub with a lantern," he said. "They sent M.P.s on two army jeeps to investigate. They'll get him!" he said with conviction.

---

xliv See Arthur A. Hansen and David A. Hacker, "The Manzanar Riot: An Ethnic Perspective," *Amerasia Journal* 2 (Fall 1974): 112–57.
xlv As quoted in Daniels, *Concentration Camps USA*, 129.

Then there was a slight pause. Suddenly, he leaned across his desk and with a ghoulish smile asked, "Do you know anything about this?"

I was outraged! I noticed the smirk that played across Commander Kerrigan's face. His eyes watched us intently. I had not come to Naval Intelligence to be insulted and I felt it was time to go. I turned to Caryl. "Let's go!" I said.

We stood up, turned, and departed without another word being spoken. Commander Kerrigan, still wearing his sickly smirk, watched us intently as we walked out down the hall. The walk back to the office of *Current Life* was in total silence. It was not difficult to speculate that I might have antagonized Naval Intelligence, and as I discovered many years later through inspection of Freedom of Information (FOI) documents, that was exactly the outcome of my action. The relevant FOI documents showed clearly that *Current Life* had been placed in an opposition category to the collaborationist JACL. And this became apparent later with a negative report from Naval Intelligence to Special Agent in Charge in Denver upon my so-called voluntary relocation there.

On the afternoon of March 3 a curious call came through from the executive secretary of the San Francisco JACL chapter, Henry Tani,[83] requesting my presence at the public meeting three days hence at Kinmon Hall. I knew Tani personally from his insurance sales work, but I tried to beg off due to magazine work and offered to send a staff member. He would have none of that or my conditional "maybe." Finally, in desperation, I agreed to attend. His persistence raised a red flag and I suspected something was in the wind.

Everyone appeared to be in their places and waiting when I reached Kinmon Hall. The podium was a makeshift elevated job that looked rickety and none too secure. Nearby, against the wall, was a single unoccupied chair that looked to be held in special reserve. I took possession of it, and a few minutes later Dr. Carl Hirota, who was known as a Soko-town dentist,[84] climbed aboard the rickety set-up, and Masaoka, the JACL spokesman, made his appearance on the Kinmon stage and began addressing the group a good thirty feet from the podium. Masaoka opened his speech with a surprise attack on "enemies" of the JACL. First to be named was Bishop Frank Herron Smith of the Methodist Church.[85] Next was Lincoln Kanai, executive secretary of the Buchanan YMCA. I was then provided with the distinctive label of "Public Enemy No. 1 of the JACL." All three of the named individuals had in some ways opposed the JACL's collaborationist policy, which appeared to have been the rationale used for their selections.

Advocates and protagonists of the JACL ideology have shown a penchant to cite that organization's prepared statement to the Tolan Committee,[86] while totally ignoring the oral interrogatory offered by JACL spokesman Mike Masaoka. However, the JACL's prepared statement is not a true measure of the Citizens League's position during the hectic period leading up to the eviction. This statement was the combined contributions of a number of persons. National president Saburo Kido played no part whatsoever, while Mike Masaoka's input was at best minimal. Beset with a rash of eviction problems, Masaoka's time to fashion an appropriate response for the Tolan Committee was strictly limited. The true attitudes and feelings of the JACL hierarchy at the time are best reflected in the Masaoka interrogatory by Alabama congressman John Sparkman, which is reproduced here because of its former deliberate omission.

> MR. SPARKMAN: Do I understand that it is your attitude that the Japanese-American citizens do not protest necessarily against an evacuation? They simply want to lodge their claims to consideration?
>
> MR. MASAOKA: Yes.
>
> MR. SPARKMAN: But in the event the evacuation is deemed necessary by those having charge of the defenses, as loyal Americans you are willing to prove your loyalty by cooperating?
>
> MR. MASAOKA: Yes.
>
> MR. SPARKMAN: Even at a sacrifice?
>
> MR. MASAOKA: Oh, yes; definitely. (Here he brings up "mob violence if permitted to remain.")
>
> MR. SPARKMAN: And it affords you, as a matter of fact, perhaps the best test of your own loyalty?
>
> MR. MASAOKA: Provided that the military or the people charged with the responsibility are cognizant of all the facts.
>
> MR. SPARKMAN: Certainly. That is assumed.[xlvi]

That in a nutshell is what the JACL wants to keep under wraps. The pain with which they seek to avoid public disclosure is beyond all common sense. It is printed in the Tolan Report and it is impossible for the JACL

---

xlvi Statement of Mike Masaoka, Tolan Committee Hearings, San Francisco, California, February 23, 1942, Part 29, 11148.

either to erase it or run from its implications. It was this concluding testimony of JACL spokesman Mike Masaoka that set off Dr. Frank Herron
Smith, who is said to have charged Masaoka in the marbled corridor of the
Post Office Building, grabbed his arm, and spun him around and, in a loud
angry voice heard throughout the corridor, accused: "You have betrayed
your people. They should ship you back to Utah!"

Smith was the first individual to indict the JACL for "betrayal" of its
ethnic people. Since the 1980s the most vociferous and vocal critic of the
organization's representation of the Japanese American community at the
Tolan Committee hearings has been Frank Chin, the highly touted Chinese
American playwright of Los Angeles. I have always believed in a similar
concept, having been there at the time.

The oft-quoted JACL rationale offered in the JACL's prepared statement
to the Tolan Committee, as previously noted, is believed to have been the
combined efforts of a number of contributors, among whom was Dr. Frank
Herron Smith. The statement itself seems to have been assembled by Lincoln Kanai, who at the time appears to have been one of the five board
members of the JACL in the Bay District. The claim of a Smith-Masaoka
collaboration was made to the FBI by wartime-duration JACL president
Saburo Kido, but Kido was the man-who-wasn't-there when the chips were
down. His law work for his Issei clients consumed his time, and direction
of the national JACL was left up to Masaoka, his twenty-five-year-old field
secretary. Even the Tolan Committee wondered at Kido's absence. Where
was Mr. Kido? He stated that he thought so little of the Tolan hearings that
he went off to his dentist. To FBI agents Kido characterized the Smith-
Masaoka duo as agents for the FBI. On the other hand, the Office of Naval
Intelligence (ONI) accused Smith as being a paid agent of Imperial Japan.
However, Dr. Smith is not known ever to have been restricted during the
war years, which in itself is ample evidence to question the credibility of the
ONI charge.

A report has surfaced that Taro Katayama was the basic author of the
JACL's prepared submission. That suggestion was advanced in June 1942 by
the Nisei social worker Charles Kikuchi: "Taro (Katayama) wrote most of
the statements for the JACL to present to the Tolan Committee. . . . Taro
got his M.A. in English at [the] University of Utah."[87]

Lincoln Kanai's name is not a household one, and he seems to have been
lost in the shuffle. But he was the only Nisei known to have challenged

Public Law 503, the military freeze order.[88] "The Department of Justice," notes Michi Weglyn in *Years of Infamy*, "thought that Public Law 503 was unconstitutional."[xlvii] Kanai came to Denver to confer with me and was quite convinced that eventually he would be apprehended by the FBI— which in fact he was, at Williams Bay, Wisconsin, on July 11, 1942, while attending a religious conference. Kanai was tried in San Francisco, where he was returned. Convicted to a six-month federal prison sentence, he served it at an eastern Oregon penitentiary located in the town of Dupont.[xlviii]

The agile mind of Masaoka concocted what he characterized as an "Enemies List" in order to rebut the increasing criticisms emerging out of the community. The Citizens League was at the time involved in selling its "constructive cooperation" theory of submission to the government. It was not amenable to non-JACL views and was definitely hostile to any type of opposition. To buttress his "enemies" theory, Masaoka threw out one of his fabricated, red-herring scenarios that JACL critics were "hirelings of Communist California Congressmen." He enhanced his charge by asserting that the FBI was investigating this linkage and the Western Defense Command would make known the findings on Monday morning.[xlix] This was three days prior to the pronouncement of the "Enemies of the JACL List" during the JACL-sponsored public forum at Kinmon Hall. The suggestion was shocking! It was the response of the JACL to strike back against its critics. The same rumor was repeated by a white minister on Sunday morning at a meeting I attended of the YMCA Coordinating Council held in the Buchanan Street YMCA's gymnasium. I was appalled to hear an unconfirmed rumor being broadcast.

"Did you confer with Mike Masaoka?" I asked.

The unexpected challenge from the floor seemed to fluster the minister. He appeared nonplussed. "Did you hear that from Masaoka?" I persisted. The minister seemed to be in a shock and at a loss for words.

"Did Masaoka tell you that?" I kept pressing.

"Yes," he answered weakly after my third inquiry.

---

xlvii See Weglyn, *Years of Infamy*, 73–74; and Hohri, *Repairing America*, 41.

xlviii Kanai was a 1930 graduate of the University of Hawai'i and came to the mainland in 1937. He was the organizer of the Coordinating Council of the Japanese YMCA and executive secretary of the Buchanan branch in San Francisco's Japantown. He was thirty-three years old in 1942 when convicted of disobeying the military freeze order. After his release, Kanai, who was married to a Euro-American woman, resided in Michigan until his death in the early 1980s.

xlix [Ed. There is no available documentation, apart from Omura's memory, for either the quoted passage that he attributes to Masaoka or Masaoka's alleged enhancement of same.]

That was enough. I walked out of the meeting. Monday came and went and, as expected, no disclosures ever occurred. The incident was considered a "JACL dirty trick." The strangest part of the public meeting format at Kinmon Hall was the statement-challenge concept invoked. Each time that Masaoka made a particular point, the chair would turn around for my response. It was clear by this method that the affair was a set-up. No one else interjected any thoughts, even though their fundamental constitutional rights were at stake. This nonreaction of the audience demonstrated to me that the Nisei had fallen under the spell of the JACL's intimidation, or perhaps that the Japanese American community had succumbed to the cultural mandate to accept submission even though that meant captivity. No one in those uncertain days after Pearl Harbor showed any willingness to defend their own constitutional rights. This was the saddest realization. My voice was only the sound of lonely wailings in the unheard wilderness.

FIVE

Denver Disputes and Concentration Camp Dissent, 1942–1944

In an honest appraisal and subjective study of what is now popularly described as the Japanese American Evacuation, the most significant and enduring factor denoting dignity and pride of racial origin is the "Resistance." Concededly, it was an atomized movement in which a miniscule 315 individuals participated, and yet the sentiments that emerged were widespread as to the injustice of the Roosevelt wartime administration. Most chroniclers have been inclined to dismiss this incident or to view and interpret the movement improperly because of its strong linkage to the military draft. Others, serving special interests, have blatantly alluded to the war resisters as "draft dodgers." Paradoxically, Nisei resisters were already imprisoned in desolate concentration camps, ringed by barbed wires and guarded by armed sentinels in watchtowers. Thus, a new category of war objectors of conscience was created. These imprisoned young Americans, from their incarcerated abodes, called into account the government's transgression of constitutional rights and demanded their restoration as a prelude to going into the army and making their supreme sacrifice for the nation. It could hardly be said that their goals were unreasonable. It was a position with which I empathized and in which a high government official concurred.[1]

The reinstitution of the draft was branded as immoral after racially motivated eviction and detention. Protests aside, the greater urgency of the Roosevelt administration was the depletion of American manpower and the necessity to call for utilization into the pool the idle Nisei under detention. The late January 1944 reinstitution of the draft followed hard on the heels of the aborted call for volunteers to staff the previously mandated and segregated Nisei combat battalion. It had provided just over eight hundred recruits, tarnished by the defective and controversial "loyalty questionnaires." Resistance was inevitable. But in only one camp—Heart Mountain, Wyoming—did organized resistance emerge, although sporadic individual opposition blossomed in other War Relocation Authority (WRA) camps. Resistance in Heart Mountain, though late in developing, was destined to leave a historic mark on the legal history of Wyoming as well as the detention itself.

Two notable trials grew out of the Heart Mountain resistance. The first of these was the trial of the sixty-three draft resisters, the largest mass trial in the state of Wyoming's history. These sixty-three resisters lost in the lower courts and the Supreme Court of the United States refused to grant certiorari. The sixty-three resisters were followed by twenty-five others from Heart Mountain. It is interesting to note that the eighty-eight at Heart Mountain were dwarfed by the one hundred and twelve who resisted at the Poston Relocation Center in Arizona. That story, along with the conspiracy trial of Fair Play Committee leaders (to be discussed later in considerable detail), is documented in the historical works of Roger Daniels and his former graduate student at the University of Wyoming, Douglas W. Nelson.[2] The saga of the Heart Mountain resistance is still incomplete as neither of these pioneering authors sought out any of the principals for pertinent information from their perspective, but instead relied entirely on archival records. To a large extent, public ignorance persists and the essential constitutional issue involved remains buried. However, currently a few crusading researchers are uncovering documents and interviewing participants, and they may yet illuminate this highly significant lost chapter of the detention era.

The story of my involvement in the conspiracy trial and the basic objective of the Fair Play Committee have been totally emasculated and misinterpreted through the deliberate propaganda of pro-JACL literary advocates and the careless conformity of historians and other scholars in survey books and monographs. Most have a tendency to view the struggles of the Fair Play Committee as a draft issue. It is regrettably true that the draft did predominate as a means toward a greater end. It was the last best program available for unification of universal protests. At the time, the *Rocky Shimpo* assisted the Fair Play Committee with editorial support. The militant group had already retained a Denver lawyer to pursue efforts through judicial and political avenues to clarify the Nisei's puzzling and ambiguous citizenship status. Often forgotten in the scramble to heap vituperation on the *Rocky Shimpo* is the fact that editorial support was based solely on legislative and/or judicial exploration of the issues involved.[i] It was not until somewhat later that the Fair Play Committee established its policy of resistance to reporting for pre-induction physical examinations. Unrelenting was the *Rocky Shimpo*'s support on the broader theory that a questionable ruling or law must be violated in order to test its validity.[ii] This was the sum of the positions advocated by me during my editorship of the *Rocky Shimpo* in the early months of 1944.

The struggles of the Fair Play Committee are not totally ignored in American literature. Their accounts appear not only in the works of Roger Daniels and Douglas Nelson, but a third historian, Richard Drinnon,[3] alludes briefly to them. Of the Japanese American chroniclers, William Minoru Hohri, the principal figure in a class-action suit against the government, mentions the Fair Play Committee in his account of the Japanese American redress movement, *Repairing America*.[4] There are also several degree-seeking theses, including Andrew Sakaye Nakahata's "A Lost Chapter of World War II" done at Wesleyan University in Middletown, Connecticut.[5] Also of note is a semifictional novel, *Heart Mountain*, by Gretel Ehrlich.[6]

The most definitive portrayal, however, appears in *The Big Aiiieeeee!*, an anthology of Asian American literature. The narrative section on the wartime resistance in this volume is written by Frank Chin (1940–), a fifth-generation Chinese American playwright, novelist, and short story writer of note.[7] Chin has not only produced the most authoritative scholarship on camp draft resistance but also stood out as the movement's strongest advocate. Although his historical depiction in *The Big Aiiieeeee!* is not free of mistakes, it is clearly the most insightful piece on the topic yet written. Having studied assiduously the archival materials on WRA camps and painstakingly compiled an impressive oral historical record of pertinent participants and observers, Chin is arguably the most knowledgeable person on draft resistance mounted from behind barbed wire. In 1981 he wrote a featured article entitled "The Last Organized Resistance" for the holiday edition of the *Rafu*

---

i See the following declaration within my April 7, 1944, *Rocky Shimpo* editorial, "The Rocky Shimpo Affirms Its Stand": "The support we accord the Fair Play Committee at Heart Mountain is predicated simply upon our desire for authentic and authoritative clarification of the legal status of the Nisei as citizens. We have at no time supported that organization on any other point." [Ed. See OP.]

ii See my editorial "Court Ruling May Affect Nisei," ibid., April 3, 1944: "And unless an act of the federal government is challenged in court, we have no assurance that the government would act to rectify a wrong." [Ed. See OP.]

Shimpo.[8] Until then, the Heart Mountain Fair Play Committee was a forgotten cause in Japanese America. Frank Chin is thus credited with rescuing the Fair Play Committee out of archival oblivion. In many respects, his reasoning on the exclusion and detention of American citizens of Japanese ancestry has a ring of truth that no other writer has been able to achieve.

In 1990, at its biennial convention in San Diego, pushed by Sansei elements, the JACL—the most vigorous detractor—offered a left-handed recognition of the wartime resistance as an alternative response; but the action did nothing to appease those hard-nosed critics of JACL's wartime betrayal.[9] Hesitancy still exists in the Japanese American community to embrace the ideology of resistance because it is at variance with the mainstream acceptance of the Nisei soldier as the epitome of military courage. But there are other types of courage besides military courage. And whatever happened to compassion, tolerance, and understanding for people victimized by their own government? There was another time and another occasion when eligible men fled their country to avoid conscription and another president of the United States pardoned these men.[10] How many other writers will rise to continue the erroneous characterization of the 315 Nisei resisters as "draft dodgers?"[11] Ignored also in court testimony is the assertion of an FBI investigating agent that not a single member of the Heart Mountain sixty-three—who some thoughtless Nisei soldiers have described as "yellow bellies"—refused to bear arms for the United States simply for the sake of refusal.[12] They all offered to serve, provided their rights and the rights of their parents were restored. That was not too much to ask for sacrificing one's life in the cause of this nation.

Wyoming signified the Teton Peaks, etched against the northeastern horizon—austere, imposing, and in a fashion awe-inspiring. It evoked the raw and fabulous Yellowstone; the noted chronicler of Western lore, Zane Grey, and his absorbing literary accounts of the Jackson Hole gang of outlaws, of gunslingers, of frontier marshals, and of cowboys; and Cheyenne, the state's largest metropolis on the eastern plains, a frontier outpost often mentioned in stories of the Old West. That was in my boyhood years in the late twenties while residing in the southeastern Idaho rail center of Pocatello. This concept of Wyoming abruptly changed in the spring of 1942 when the Corps of Engineers set to work to establish a concentration camp in the sage land of Park County, eleven miles southwest of the city of Powell.

The government named the compound Heart Mountain Relocation Center, inspired by the peak that loomed in the background, but there was no mistaking its concentration camp entrapments—watchtowers mounted with powerful searchlights, sentinels perched at the ready with rifles under orders to shoot any internee approaching within five feet of the barbed wire encircling the compound, and at the entry gate army personnel to monitor egress and ingress. All of this spoke of a prison camp. Heart Mountain housed nearly eleven thousand Japanese American inmates from the West Coast, of whom two-thirds were American citizens by birthright.[13] The only legitimate charge that conceivably could be lodged against these people was that of their racial origin. Despite the confinement of more than two thousand immigrant Japanese, who were aliens by U.S. laws, in Department of Justice internment centers, and the custody of 120,313 in so-called wartime "relocation camps,"[14] not a single prosecutorial case ever arose. Instead, the fundamental precepts of the Constitution and the Bill of Rights were twisted and frayed by President Franklin Delano Roosevelt and his administrative minions. In a further attempt to eliminate the Japanese presence in America, the Roosevelt administration resorted to congressional passage of a thinly veiled, hastily conceived denaturalization law.[15] Now whenever Wyoming is mentioned, it conjures up the memory of Heart Mountain and the Fair Play Committee, a courageous and militant citizens' organization born in captivity.

It is one of the great ironies of our time that the goals the Fair Play Committee sought have been virtually relegated to limbo. It is my belief that this Nisei movement deserves a much better fate. Its policies spoke to the moral conscience of a victimized people and in so doing constituted an integral and historic segment in the story of Japanese in American life. The reason for its obscure nature comes from a deliberate design to obliterate it as an act of shame and dishonor. Its own ethnic leadership has branded it as an evil commission against the wartime Roosevelt administration. However patriotic, it did not demand that a collaborationist leadership should loudly espouse every infringement of constitutional prerogatives by an authoritarian government. But the Japanese American Citizens League chose to run verbal interference for a regressive government and was allowed to serve as a stalking horse for the FDR entourage.

Harassment did not begin with my editorship of the *Rocky Shimpo* on January 28, 1944, nor did it end with my November 1, 1944, acquittal in the conspiracy trial of the Fair Play Committee steering committee and me, two developments which I will enlarge upon later in this memoir. In the fall of 1942 my wife, Caryl, opened a malt and sandwich shop in Denver, Colorado, at 2008 Larimer Street, next door to Harry Osumi's jewelry shop.[16] The enterprise was well patronized by furloughed internees until a month later, when persistent negative rumors began to circulate against the establishment. The office of the evacuee placement bureau I managed had been moved by then from its original Nineteenth Street address to a mezzanine site on the property of the malt and sandwich shop.[17] I thought it necessary to look into the first rumor and to put it to rest. The investigation identified the source as a driver for the Coca Cola Company. The result of that report was forwarded to the Denver Coca Cola Company. Our report had established that the driver had skipped town. To our dismay, other rumors surfaced periodically and badly damaged patronage. Consequently, in the fall of 1943 Caryl's Malt & Sandwich Shop was forced to sell out,[18] and it then became Ben's Place.

In late December 1945 Caryl picked up some revealing information about the damaging rumors in Denver of a few years earlier when she visited Phil Stroupe, the pre-eviction photographer for *Current Life* magazine, at his commercial studio in San Francisco. Stroupe is said to have stated to her that Nisei agents for Naval Intelligence were planted at Caryl's Malt & Sandwich Shop to instigate pro-Japan utterances. Furthermore, Stroupe allegedly told Caryl that he had obtained this information from a longtime personal Nisei friend in Naval Intelligence.[19]

The erroneous report of the Fort Lupton JACL rally on February 10, 1943, appears to continue to linger. In 1988 two researchers from the Japanese American National Museum based in Los Angeles paid me a visit and briefly alluded to the incident,[20] obviously having picked up some unsavory rumors in the community. Here is the story as I saw it. It all began with my overhearing two activist native Coloradans, Kazumi Miyamoto and Harry Matsunaka,[iii21] discussing excitedly a JACL dinner in the northern Colorado farm community of Fort Lupton. I requested being taken along and it was agreed upon on the one condition that I not speak out. That promise was given and kept.

---

iii Former Fort Luptonite Miyamoto was a radio operator and Denverite; Matsunaka, a past *Rocky Nippon* editor.

However, I was spotted from the head table, and after some consultation each attendee was asked to rise and identify him- or herself. When my turn came, I rose quickly, spoke rapidly and not too clearly, giving the name "James Matsu." Joe Grant Masaoka[22] at the head table heard it as "James Iwasa." The members at the head table held another long confab. I was seated two-thirds down at the long table. The person to whom Masaoka refers in his press article sat two chairs closer to the head table. Masaoka's story was not centered on some unknown attendee, but on me.[iv]

Few of us lingered near the long table after the dinner had ended. When an excited verbal ruckus broke out in the back of the auditorium, our group naturally drifted toward the commotion. Loud accusations were being tossed back and forth. Then, totally out of nowhere, Masaoka ended the confrontation with, "We're coming back with a bigger group, Jimmie!" I was standing at the fringe of the group and was not involved. The fireworks had been set off by Miyamoto and Matsunaka, the two activists whom I had accompanied to the rally. I had never formally met Joe Grant Masaoka, but to him I was undoubtedly a target.

Before departing Denver, Masaoka released his press article to the two Denver vernacular presses. The publisher of the *Rocky Nippon*, Tetsuko Toda,[23] provided me a copy for my information and comment. This was my response:

> I have looked over the report written by Joe Masaoka, Director of the Associated Members Division of the National Japanese American Citizens League, on the Buddhist Rally held in Fort Lupton last Sunday evening. I have given particular attention to the following passage:
> "In the Open Forum which followed, James Omura directed questions which indicated the lack of unanimity among a certain Nisei population. Masaoka gently rebuked the attitude and lethargy of such lackadaisical groups. The announcement of the volunteering [for military service] of the National Secretary of the JACL [Mike Masaoka] was roundly applauded and was [a] more than adequate answer to would-be carping critics."

I advised Miss Toda that "in the event this report is printed in full, we would like to request an opportunity to [provide a] rebuttal in the following

---

iv [Ed. The identity of the person whom Omura notes being mentioned within Joe Grant Masaoka's press release is unclear, though probably it is either Floyd Koshio, the president of Fort Lupton's JACL chapter, or Tad Hirota, executive secretary of the Young Buddhists and the meeting's chair.]

issue."[v] The *Rocky Nippon* did not publish the article,[vi] but apparently its rival, the *Colorado Times*,[24] did.[25] Neither of the Masaokas was a diligent purveyor of the truth.

It was 9:00 p.m. on June 10, 1943, when two plainclothes men entered Caryl's Malt & Sandwich shop on Larimer Street. One man locked the door and the other advanced on me. Caryl was cleaning the grill.

"It's been reported that a pro-Japanese statement was made in this establishment," he said.

"I don't know anything about it," I replied. "I wasn't here."

"We know," the detective acknowledged. "We're from the United States Attorney's office."

"What's this about?" I asked.

"We're asking the questions; you just answer them," he retorted a bit testily.

I kept backing away because he advanced uncomfortably close. I was backed into a back booth above which was a wall phone. When I tried to reach the phone, his hands screened me off without making any contact. His too-close proximity was unbearable.

"I have a right to call my attorney," I said.

But the detective prevented it. At that moment, Caryl made a dash for the private quarters before the second man could block the exit. There then ensued a long verbal sparring duel. No further mention was made of the pro-Japan remarks. I had been told a customer had made such a remark and the businesspeople on Larimer Street had alerted us that inquiries were being made in the community. It was only a matter of time before we would be approached directly.

Two hours later, the detective asked to see my Selective Service registration card. He quizzed me about the name and claimed it was registered illegally. Though he prohibited me from use of the phone, he contacted United States attorney Thomas J. Morrissey.[26] It was a long conversation, and after it was over the detective stated he had been instructed to allow me to call my attorney. I therefore dialed Robert McDougal[27] and informed him of the situation. McDougal spoke with Morrissey and later called me back.

---

v James M. Omura, Director of the Evacuee Placement Bureau, letter to English editor of the *Rocky Nippon* [Tetsuko Toda], February 8, 1943, Denver, Colorado. [Ed. See OP.]

vi [Ed. In fact, this item appeared within the *Rocky Nippon* on February 10, 1943.]

"Mr. Morrissey said if you would agree to be in his office at eight in the morning with your wife, he would call his man off."

"I agree!"

The next morning, June 11, 1943, we were ushered into a long oblong room with a high ceiling. Mr. Morrissey was the only occupant, but I could glimpse an adjoining lighted room. I suspected I was being monitored. I stated to Morrissey that I objected to being "hassled by his flatfoots." I was still hot under the collar.

"Look here," Mr. Morrissey declared, "I can have you locked up for seventy-two hours without any charge at all. I've got a good mind to do that!"

The questioning then proceeded. At its conclusion, he explained that he would have to check with my draft board in San Francisco. We were allowed to leave. In the 1980s, under the Freedom of Information Act,[28] I received a copy of this report. It appears my own attorney wrote this report.[29] Special FBI agents were sent out to Seattle and San Francisco. In Seattle the agent drew a blank. In San Francisco an agent so infuriated Phil Stroupe that he banged a set of *Current Life* issues on his desk and challenged the agent to find any pro-Japan articles in it. He told Caryl in December 1945 that the agent picked out an article about discrimination in the Red Cross and one other on eviction as being somewhat pro-Japan. These were struck out by J. Edgar Hoover in his summary.

Nat J. L. Pieper, the special FBI agent in charge at San Francisco,[30] wrote that no negative report on me had been uncovered. Every Caucasian contact offered sterling references. Agent Sterling F. Tremayne[31] interviewed my brother Casey at Firland Sanatorium, just north of Seattle. Long afterward and during the period I was out on bond, Casey wrote that Tremayne was particularly interested in my reported use of the name "James Iwasa."[32]

The name "James Iwasa" appeared in the complaint alleging a false registration charge in Selective Service records in San Francisco in 1940. United States attorney Morrissey, in declining to prosecute after extensive investigation, stated the action of his office had been predicated on a complaint from the Japanese American Citizens League.

It surprised me to learn the high degree of status I seemed to have enjoyed among the white community. The "white paper" was so complete of my San Francisco sojourn that I couldn't have asked for a better set of references.[vii] Though the FBI inquiries swirled all around me, I was never

---

vii Notations in the Daily Journal of James M. Omura, January 1946, Hillsborough, California. [Ed. See OP.]

directly asked about any legal name. The FBI did ask me about the "James Iwasa" name, which I disclaimed. In the witch-hunt activities of the JACL, I knew I would be a target, and I could feel the pressure. Shortly after the California Street Methodist Church public forum sponsored by the national JACL in March 1943 in Denver (which will be discussed below), I applied to legalize James Matsumoto Omura as my name, feeling it could be the Achilles' heel in an otherwise unblemished record. It was not difficult to unravel the JACL intent. The Fort Lupton faux pas, the Joe Masaoka obfuscation in the *Colorado Times*,[viii] the preplanned attempt at embarrassment at the California Street Methodist Church public forum, the Mike Masaoka/Minoru Yasui incident at the Denver Japanese Hall[33]—all pointed to dire things to come. This accounted for the legal name change, although it was not on that knowledge that the United States attorney declined to prosecute. There simply was no case.

On March 14, 1943, the national JACL scheduled a public forum at the California Street Methodist Church (CSMC) in Denver, Colorado.[34] En route to the meeting, I had been overtaken by a young Nisei lad who warned me to be on the alert for a JACL ploy intended to embarrass and publicly humiliate me. Thus, I was cautious, not knowing from what direction I would be hit. When Mike Masaoka invited me to respond to a *Rocky Nippon* article, I asked him whether he would yield the floor. Masaoka appeared at a loss at my inquiry and it took three repetitions before he reluctantly condescended to yield. The JACL plan then began to unfold. Four successive pro-JACL adherents rose to object: Larry Tajiri, editor of the *Pacific Citizen;* Jack Nakagawa, a Seattle YPCC [Young Peoples Christian Conference] leader; Joe Grant Masaoka, Mike's older brother; and Tad Hirota, a Buddhist leader.[35]

"Who is this man," Joe Masaoka asked. "He was James Iwasa at Fort Lupton. Who is he?"

The objections were interrupted by a YMCA delegate, returning to Heart Mountain from an organizational confab at St. Louis, and by a female representative of the American Friends Service Committee in attendance.

"Let this man speak," the man said. "I want to hear what he has to say."

"I want to hear him, too," chimed in the white woman.

---

viii [Ed. This "obfuscation," as indicated above in note vi, was also published in the *Rocky Nippon*.]

Masaoka's inquiry on a *Rocky Nippon* article was ignored and I spoke instead in opposition to the concept of the volunteer Nisei combat battalion; my remarks concluded the public forum.[36] The CSMC event was the outgrowth of the Fort Lupton disruption and was in response to alleged charges by the JACL of my being responsible for the brouhaha that culminated its fundraising dinner meeting. Though I had no hand in the matter, it obviously pleased the Joe Grant Masaoka–Tad Hirota duo to entwine me as a target. The elder Masaoka had kept his promise that he would return reinforced and, with a larger headquarters, would counteract this lone JACL critic. That it had to engage in a ploy stretches the imagination. The problem became greater because I had to relinquish the floor unwittingly.

FIGURE 8. Refusing to be imprisoned in U.S. government concentration camps, Jimmie and Caryl Omura, along with some five thousand other Japanese Americans, "voluntarily" migrated outside of the exclusion zone to interior resettlement sites. The most popular of these was Denver, Colorado, which soon sprouted a Japantown. Their plan, which was foiled, was to continue to publish *Current Life*. Instead, Jimmie Omura used funds amassed as a packer and buyer in the San Francisco floral market to launch a free employment service for other Nikkei resettlers pouring into Denver. The three signs gracing the ramshackle structure in front of which Omura is standing testify to his intentions, his humanitarianism, and his patriotism. Omura Papers, Green Library, Stanford University.

The chief spokesman for the JACL wasn't through yet. Mike Masaoka carried his vendetta before the Young Buddhists group that March 14 evening in Denver[37] and baldly stated, "Since Jimmie Omura isn't here, I can speak frankly." The same group invited me to offer a rebuttal without any briefing of what had been said by Masaoka.[38] The time seemed appropriate to outline the work of the Evacuee Placement Bureau and the defenses being made on the Pando, Fitzsimons Hospital, and Denver's Robbins Incubator discrimination cases.[39] Then Masaoka took his rhetoric to a meeting at the Japanese Hall in Denver, where I posed a question on the matter of our eviction. Masaoka was deterred from responding by the chair and I therefore charged, "You are avoiding the question!" Later, a Japanese-language journalist stopped by and agreed, "You are right, Masaoka is avoiding the question."[40]

In early January 1943, a conference was called in the office of John J. McCloy, assistant secretary of war, at which time he made an announcement relative to the use of Japanese Americans as combat troops: "There is a paper in the War Department relative to the use of Japanese as combat troops, upon which a decision has already been reached."[41]

Support came immediately from Captain Ellis Zacharias,[42] the acting director of the Office of Naval Intelligence (ONI),[43] who stated that the majority of the Japanese wanted to be loyal citizens but their loyalty might be impaired if action was not taken in the near future to assure them that the United States considered them loyal. Commander Cecil H. Coggins of ONI[44] also urged that a combat team should be formed and given lots of publicity so as to erase the impression that the army was discriminating against the Japanese American racial group.[ix] [45]

President Franklin Roosevelt emphasized the "political advantages" to be gained in this undertaking: "The memorandum to you from the Staff points out in the last paragraph that formation of such battalions would be strictly limited to cases where political advantages are to be gained. . . . Even if the numbers were small enough only for a company, the objective would be served."[x]

---

ix Colonel W. C. Crist, General Staff U.S. Army, memorandum to General George Veazey Strong, Assistant Chief of General Staff U.S. Army, January 4, 1943, Record Group [hereafter RG] 319-47-391, National Archives [hereafter NA].

x U.S. President Franklin D. Roosevelt, memorandum to Secretary of War Henry L. Stimson, November 17, 1942, Franklin D. Roosevelt Presidential Library and Museum, Hyde Park, New York.

The immediate effect in the WRA camps was a universal objection to the segregated nature of the proposed 442nd Combat Battalion and the limitation and restriction of service-oriented opportunities offered. The announcement by Secretary of War Henry Stimson[46] of the formation of a volunteer segregated Nisei combat battalion on January 28, 1943, was not greeted with much enthusiasm by either the inmates in the government camps or by wartime refugees who had relocated into interior America ahead of the military freeze. All of the community councils of the ten permanent concentration camps deluged authorities in Washington to complain of the discriminatory nature of the program, primarily objecting to the segregated feature of the combat battalion.

Resistance to military service actually began with the volunteer program and was then leveled against not only the mandated "loyalty registration" of the War Department but also developments occurring in the camps and in the military. The situation was further compounded by combining the War Department's loyalty registration with the War Relocation Authority's "leave clearance" program, which required the registration of all males and females seventeen years of age and older.[47] The WRA was already on its way to developing plans for mass registration and the army registration provided an opportunity to combine the two programs since the information required by each was similar.[xi]

The War Department set the quota at 300 volunteers per camp, plus 1,500 from Hawai'i, to stock the 442nd Nisei Combat Battalion. Volunteers in camp, however, totaled a mere 1,208, with only 805 able to pass their physicals. The slack was picked up by doubling the volunteers from Hawai'i, where nearly ten thousand had rallied to the U.S. cause,[xii] plus several hundred from those on the mainland living outside the camps. What contributed to the miserable showings in mainland camps were the ill-worded "loyalty questionnaires," the two most controversial questions of which are reproduced here:

---

xi War Relocation Authority, *The Relocation Program: A Guidebook for the Residents of Relocation Centers* (May 1943), 22. See Section 3, "War Relocation Authority: Washington Office," in Edward N. Barnhart, comp., *Japanese American Evacuation and Resettlement: Catalog of Material in General Library* (Berkeley: University of California General Library, 1958), 27, for listing of this pamphlet.

xii Japanese in Hawai'i were not incarcerated in the same manner as their counterparts on the U.S. mainland. The reason was econonmic: the 150,000 people of Japanese descent formed an important economic bloc in the civic affairs of the island. Those interned in Hawai'i were confined principally at Sand Island Detention Center in Honolulu Harbor and later at Honouliuli Gulch Internment Camp in central O'ahu, but most were transferred eventually to mainland detention centers. [Ed. Altogether there was a total of thirteen confinement sites on the islands of Hawai'i: four on Kaua'i, three on O'ahu, two each on Maui and Hawai'i, and one apiece on Moloka'i and Lana'i.]

No. 27: Are you willing to serve in the armed forces of the United States on combat duty, wherever ordered?

No. 28: Will you swear unqualified allegiance to the United States of America and faithfully defend the United States from any and all attack by foreign or domestic forces, and foreswear any form of allegiance or obedience to the Japanese Emperor, or any other foreign government, power, or organization?

Question No. 28 was the most vexing. For the U.S. government to ask the alien Japanese to foreswear their nationality while at the same time U.S. laws forbade their becoming American citizens was an injustice. To comply would cast them adrift as people without a country. To the adult Nisei of military age, foreswearing was seen as a prima facie acknowledgment of dual allegiance, which the vast majority disavowed. While no policy existed at this time for combat service for adult females, the questions conceived by the War Department had a shattering effect upon the entire family.

The call for voluntary enlistments clashed with dual investigations being conducted by Congress amid the clamor for tighter restrictions on the incarcerated Japanese. The people in the camps had become embittered by almost a year in captivity and with no opportunity to relocate under WRA guidelines. The WRA-Army loyalty registration was interpreted by many as additional discriminatory infliction rather than a means toward the restoration of rights. Not all of the confusion resided with the internees. As the government acknowledged, "Some of the appointed staff were also not sure of the meaning of this question [No. 27] . . . [while] other questions were also so phrased as to make them difficult to understand, [and] consequently difficult to answer."[xiii]

The army required the setting up of the Joint Japanese American Board, which was created on January 20, 1943.[48] In the meantime, a small but violent section of the press had created particular suspicion of Japanese Americans in the public mood. This inspired the federal Civil Service Commission to place into force special discriminatory regulations to limit employment of the Nisei by the government. The Japanese American Joint Board approved only 491 applications for war plant employment in the Eastern Defense Command[49] from a total of 37,423 cases referred by the War Relocation Authority, while 11,728 were disapproved. Leave clearance for the Eastern

---

xiii War Relocation Authority, *Relocation Program*, 23.

Defense Command totaled 21,167, and to the Western Defense Command 2,495, with 489 requests not acted upon. "The Joint Board," the WRA stated, "had functioned more as a detriment to relocation than as an aid as had been hoped."[xiv] Within ten months, project hearing boards and review committees had heard 9,177 cases, approving 7,184 for indefinite leave and denying 1,524, while deferring fifty cases and returning 436 for rehearings. But as of July 1, 1943, the large majority of inmates had been processed and declared eligible for indefinite leave. Fewer than ten thousand inmates had relocated, and eighty-five thousand who had been cleared for leave were still in the centers.

After the spring 1943 registration, the "Stop List" was established in leave clearance. The outcome of the loyalty registration was a reprisal in the form of segregation for all those inmates who refused to answer unqualified allegiance to the United States. These, including family members, numbered 18,000, of which 12,173 were transferred to the designated segregation center of Tule Lake;[50] the remainder of the inmates were left in their respective camps, under restrictions, for lack of available quarters at Tule Lake. Some 6,500 original Tuleans refused to move out of Tule Lake for a variety of reasons.

As already established, much opposition to the segregated concept of the 442nd Combat Battalion materialized within various concentration camps. Having in the past opposed vigorously the segregated conditions in economic workplaces, I found myself in full accord with the detainees. Segregation was inimical to our basic ideology of democracy. The clearest example was the Negro Division,[51] which was created during World War I and remained extant.[52] The concept was criticized by me in the *Rocky Nippon*,[xv] and the critique was followed by a letter of protest from me to Secretary of War Henry L. Stimson, which he acknowledged.[53] His response emphasized the need to highlight the achievements of the Japanese American soldiers, denied any policy of perpetuating racial segregation, and was silent about any adverse effects.

The positive outlook the secretary of war described had a good deal working against it. There was no correlative relaxation of stringent restrictions, either actual or promised. Also, there was no favorable dispensation

---

xiv Ibid., 27.
xv [Ed. See James Omura, "Nisei Life," *Rocky Nippon*, February 3, 1943.]

for volunteers who might be physically rejected. The program had all the earmarks of a one-way street. Nor did the promises of Secretary Stimson exude any feeling of confidence. It was Stimson who had lumped the citizen Nisei into a "non-alien" category with their alien parents as the most dangerous to national security to facilitate their eviction. In so doing, he had personally advocated special consideration for the Italians, including the alien-by-choice Italians, and would later ask for similar consideration for those of German ancestry.

Thus, Stimson was motivated by racism, giving priority status to "white" belligerents over citizen Nisei. In addition, the secretary of war had ordered that draft classification for the Nisei be demoted to 4-C, a category considered ineligible due to ancestry and therefore demeaning to Nisei Americans. There was little reason to believe in the secretary of war or have any confidence in his promises. Moreover, had it not been for the War Department, mass eviction of the Japanese population on the West Coast was unlikely to have happened.

The Stimson letter was published in the *Rocky Shimpo* as requested, but not without a companion response from me characterizing the 442nd Combat Battalion as a guinea pig unit.[54] There were good and valid reasons for this thinking. Sentiments being booted about in Congress favored the creation of the Nisei unit as a means of decimating the U.S. Japanese-ancestry population to simplify postwar reconstructions. In a public address in the 1980s, a decorated Nisei veteran reached the identical conclusion.[55] No army brass has ever acknowledged this purpose but the figures for the highest battalion casualties in the European campaign stand as mute testimony that the 442nd Combat Battalion was indeed intended as a guinea pig operation. Nisei soldiers were considered expendable. That they acquitted themselves with gallantry and courage under battlefield conditions is forever to their credit and the credit of their evicted contemporaries.

Historian Douglas Nelson viewed the army program from the Nisei standpoint:

> Many Heart Mountain Nisei, possibly a majority, remained highly
> skeptical of the Army program. . . . The early months of protests had
> strengthened the sensitivity of many Nisei to the government's continuing
> discrimination. Japanese American citizens, who had never given cause
> for their patriotism to be doubted, resented being subjected to a loyalty
> examination. Others objected to the unmistakable Jim Crowism in the

Army's plan to form an "all-Nisei" combat unit. . . . The suspicion of the government . . . was accompanied by growing doubts concerning the leadership of the JACL. Up to 1943, most Nisei had accepted the JACL argument that cooperation would best counteract the racism and prejudice in American public opinion. In this hope, they had endured evacuation and later detention. The evidence in 1943, however, suggested that despite the compliance of the inmates, anti-Japanese sentiment was growing in Congress, in the press, and in the attitude of the general public.[xvi]

As earlier pointed out, criticisms of the system were raised with Stimson by this writer. Of particular concern to me was the question of non-use of the 100th Infantry Battalion,[56] then stationed at Camp McCoy in Wisconsin,[57] as well as the nearly five thousand enlistees who had been unarmed and reduced to menial duties in interior military posts. The secretary of war's personal response to these complaints in his two-page letter of February 9, 1943, depicted the War Department's creation of the Nisei Combat Battalion as a "first step" in the theory of redemption for Japanese Americans within American society.

In subsequent communications, the War Department stated it was doing the Nisei "a favor" and the battalion creation was not predicated on any shortage of manpower, as I had indicated.[58] This view sharply contradicted the manpower director, Paul V. McNutt,[59] with whom I also maintained direct communication.[60] McNutt saw a critical shortage of able-bodied fighting men. Women were being hired in war plants as welders and for other specialized work formerly performed by men, who had been called into military service. The lowering of the age limit to fourteen-year-olds for recruitment in defense work was also under serious consideration. The volunteerism aspect of the War Department's proposal appeared to be the only saving grace.

In one camp, Heart Mountain, resistance to registration took the shape of a boycott under the banner of the Congress of American Citizens.[61] Its founder, Frank T. Inouye, an incarceree from Los Angeles,[62] was opposed to the Heart Mountain administration and also the JACL. A large number of inmates tended to agree with his antiregistration views and his declarations: "Our future certainly is no brighter. . . . Nor is there any reason for hoping it will be better when we have joined the colors." Inouye took the following

---

xvi Douglas W. Nelson, *Heart Mountain: The Story of An American Concentration Camp* (Madison: Historical Society of Wisconsin for the Department of History, University of Wisconsin, 1976), 102–3.

position: "We must demand that our name be cleared; and have it read to the world that there had never been a justification for our evacuation."[63]

On February 19, Inouye sent telegrams to each of the nine other administrations urging the formation of groups to lead a boycott of the registration.[64] No other camp developed the activism of the Congress of American Citizens. The boycott at Heart Mountain lasted through the month of February and brought an offer of concessions by the army to accept conditional loyalty responses, and the director of the War Relocation Authority, Dillon Myer, wired the Heart Mountain director, Guy Robertson, that he should "assure the evacuees" that the WRA would continue "to defend . . . citizenship rights" of the Nisei.[65] Inouye had also criticized the *Heart Mountain Sentinel* as a WRA-JACL kept press, and consequently that organ offered to be less biased. The boycott at Heart Mountain was broken in March and 3,829 Nisei registered, but one in nearly 7.6 registrants refused to cooperate. Of the eligible WRA camp population of 77,842, 74,588 registered. Of this number the Nisei constituted 40,194. Whereas 65,312 respondents replied "Yes," a total of 9,287 were considered uncooperative and subject to removal to Tule Lake, designated as a segregation camp, in reprisal for conditional responses or failure to answer at all. It is noteworthy that the government did not keep any of its promises to the Congress of American Citizens when the boycott ended. At the same time, this organization did have a strong impact on volunteerism in Heart Mountain, where only a meager 38 Nisei responded to the call as opposed to the anticipated 360.

Inouye is of no further importance in this discussion. He faded from the scene and relocated to the Midwest and later moved to Hawai'i. But the concept of resistance that he fathered became a significant factor in a successor organization, the Heart Mountain Fair Play Committee. Moreover, Inouye's most ardent lieutenants, Robert Kiyoshi Okamoto[66] and Paul Takeo Nakadate,[67] would play prominent leadership roles in the Fair Play Committee in early 1944.

One factor that inhibited volunteerism by camp detainees was the high-handed intimidation practiced by some members of the WRA leadership and army recruiting team. The *News-Courier* at Gila River Relocation Center declared, "Project Director Leroy Bennett warned citizens that an answer 'No' to questions 27 and 28 will probably result in the loss of citizenship."[68] More bluntly put at Gila River was this statement from Captain Norman Thompson: "It is my duty here to see that every registrant states his honest opinions, not anyone else's. I am not asking you; I'm telling you. You cannot tamper with the United States Army."[69]

What the army achieved was 26 percent of its goal, a sobering reality of the perniciousness of arbitrary detention. This sort of army pressure had its intended effect in Gila River, as it later became one of only two camps where no resistance [to the military draft] took place.[70] Objections also arose [in Gila and the other WRA detention camps] to the four-page Statement of U.S. Citizens of Japanese Ancestry, DSS Form 304A, with assertions being voiced that it was a discriminatory survey aimed only at Japanese Americans. The Selective Service Board threatened to file legal suit for those not answering the survey.[xvii]

I further charged in my communications to the War Department that Nisei soldiers would be used as cannon fodder,[71] a theory that was then being freely booted about on the floor of the House of Representatives. Congressional bigots expressed hopes of decimating the Japanese Americans through battlefield casualties to simplify postwar rehabilitation. The attitude was reminiscent of the pre-eviction proposal to corral all resident Japanese on a Pacific island and then blast the island to kingdom come. The collaborationist editor of the *Pacific Citizen*, Larry Tajiri, ridiculed the army's guinea pig intent and portrayed the dissidents as those who "tend to make ridiculous the wild speculation in some quarters of any attempted decimation of Japanese Americans through the device of using them as spearheads in attacks on the Italian front."[xviii]

The loyalty registration ignited the intense resentments smoldering among the incarcerated people. They had been beguiled into passive submission to captivity by their own ethnic leadership on the theory that it would demonstrate their loyalty to the United States. The government consideration promised by the JACL had not been fulfilled and instead more stringent restrictions were being applied. Outside their barbed-wire compounds, racial antagonism in the United States grew more intense, and within, the WRA's restrictions became more onerous. Inmates were not only being treated as prisoners; in actuality, they were.

---

xvii Selective Service Board No. 97, San Francisco, California, to James M. Omura, Denver, Colorado, May 15, 1944. [Ed. See OP.]

xviii Larry Tajiri, "Nisei USA," *Pacific Citizen*, March 11, 1944. [Ed. This column is not one of the many included in Greg Robinson, ed., *Pacific Citizens: Larry and Guyo Tajiri and Japanese American Journalism in the World War II Era* (Urbana: University of Illinois Press, 2012), but a copy of it exists within OP.]

Tule Lake was another scene of registration resistance, where it started out with a trickle on February 10. WRA officials met with a citizens' group on February 15 and told them that any interference with registration was punishable under the Espionage Act[72] by fines up to ten thousand dollars or twenty years of imprisonment, or both.[xix] Two-thirds of the all-male residents of Block 42 declined to report. On February 21 WRA officials, accompanied by MPs with machine guns and bayonets, hustled the dissidents off to jail. A Christian minister and a Kibei translator for the camp newspaper were beaten and a JACL leader was spirited out of the center for his safety.[xx] The center attorney was informed by FBI agents that refusal to answer the registration questionnaire was not a violation of the Selective Service Act. After checking with the War Department, WRA director Dillon Myer was advised that registration was not considered compulsory. The WRA, however, kept this advice secret, although an army document posted in the mess halls stated that a "Yes" answer to Questions 27 and 28 would mean liability to induction.[xxi] Further arrests were made.

One-third of the people in Tule Lake, including three thousand Nisei, did not register. Another 1,238 replied "No" and only 59 volunteered for the army. Project director Harvey Coverley[73] transferred about a hundred Kibei who defied an order to register to an isolated CCC camp. He also issued a bulletin stating that nonregistrants "will be considered as having violated the orders of the War Department and the War Relocation Authority and subject to such penalties as may be imposed."[xxii]

Belatedly, Question 28 was changed to read: "Will you swear to abide by the laws of the United States and to take no action which would in any way interfere with the war effort of the United States?" That solved the nationality issue of the Issei and a majority changed their answer to "Yes." But there remained a knotty issue of leave clearance, with some Issei suspecting that a response in the affirmative could result in forced "relocation."

In all ten WRA detention camps registration aroused fear and created emotional strains. The press and radio attacks promptly branded the "No-No" group as disloyal and dangerous. Demand for segregation arose in Congress. California state senator Clarence C. Ward of Santa Barbara

---

xix   Dorothy S. Thomas and Richard S. Nishiomoto, *The Spoilage* (Berkeley: University of California Press, 1946), 73–75; Allen R. Bosworth, *America's Concentration Camps* (New York: Norton, 1963), 172.
xx   Thomas and Nishimoto, *Spoilage*, 79, 81, and 82.
xxi   Bosworth, *America's Concentration Camps*, 173.
xxii   Thomas and Nishimoto, *Spoilage*, 81–82.

stumped the state, urging their detention and eventual deportation.[74] Racist elements sounded the drum for deportation of all Japanese.[xxiii] The WRA itself came under investigation by two subcommittees of Congress, the Senate Committee on Military Affairs, and the House Dies Committee. In early July 1943, a Senate resolution asked the WRA "to take such steps as may be necessary for the purpose of segregating persons of Japanese ancestry in relocation centers whose loyalty to the United States is questionable or who are known to be disloyal."[xxiv] In Administrative Instruction No. 100, on July 15, Tule Lake was designated as a segregation center.[xxv] One month later, Coverley was replaced by Raymond R. Best as Tule Lake's project director.[75]

The loyalty registration was conducted during the month of February 1943 and extended into March because of inmate delays in responding.[76] It precipitated the most crucial and the largest act of resistance that occurred during the imprisonment years. It was the most traumatic incident to confront the evicted people; it tore family units apart and destroyed friendships established over the years. In the eyes of the constituted authorities and politicians and racists, the result came out as "loyals" and "disloyals." Out of 77,967 qualified respondents over the age of seventeen, 9,679 would be designated as "disloyals." They became known as segregants for their refusal to answer "Yes" to Questions 27 and 28. This category included those who qualified their answers, those who refused to reply at all, and those who simply answered "No" out of pure frustration. In 1987 the segregants were recognized as constituting the "Resistance Movement in Wartime America" by the prestigious Smithsonian Institution in its bicentennial exhibition: A More Perfect Union—The Japanese Americans and the United States Constitution.[77] Similarly recognized were the draft resisters of the Fair Play Committee of Heart Mountain and the twenty-eight military resisters of Fort McClellan, Alabama.[78]

Soon after the 442nd Combat Battalion was activated on February 1, 1943, recruits converged on Camp Shelby, Mississippi.[79] On April 13, 1943, General John DeWitt went before the House Naval Affairs Subcommittee[80] in San Francisco to make his now infamous charge, "A Jap's a Jap."[81] On that very same day, 2,686 Nisei enlisted men arrived at Camp Shelby from

---

xxiii Bosworth, *America's Concentration Camps*, 177.
xxiv Thomas and Nishimoto, *Spoilage*, 84.
xxv Ibid., 84–85.

Hawai'i, while in the continental United States only 1,208 signed up, with 805 passing their physicals. The army's recruiting campaign was considered a miserable failure.[xxvi]

During the period of Japanese American confinement just prior to the formation of the segregated Nisei combat team and the correlated loyalty registration, the government of the United States, in concert with its ethnic acolyte,[82] had made every effort to portray the manifestation of resistance in the WRA camps in terms of un-American reactions. Such labels as "pro-Axis," "un-American," "disloyals," and "troublemakers" were employed to denigrate the incarcerated people and to incite the public press, thereby washing its own blotched linen. Contrary to its image-building purpose, more damage than good resulted from this policy. These incident labels gave credence to the American press's assertions that eviction of these confined people was truly for the security of the West Coast areas. Whether leaders of the Japanese American Citizens League knew it or not, this labeling harmed the image of Japanese America far more than all the wartime protestations of loyalty made by its leadership had possibly helped it.

The first major incident of internal dissension in a permanent concentration camp occurred in late November 1942 at the Poston 1 detention center,[83] where the beating of a JACL leader triggered a community-wide strike.[84] Kay Nishimura, an Imperial Valley rice broker,[85] was seriously beaten after the arrest of two popular individuals, George Fujii[86] and Isamu Uchida,[87] both of them acclaimed judoists. Demand for the release of the two individuals arose in the community, and to emphasize its demand the Poston No. 1 camp went on strike. The interesting development was that both of the arrested individuals were eventually released. Other beatings occurred, including the national president of the Japanese American Citizens League, Saburo Kido.[88] Kido was spirited out of Poston[89] and the WRA made concessions for Kay Nishimura so that he would not have to return to camp.

The next significant camp uprising dividing the inmate population took place in early December 1942 at the Manzanar concentration camp in the Owens Valley of east central California.[90] It also took the shape of a physical beating administered by inmates to a JACL leader, one who was considered

---

xxvi See also Bosworth, *America's Concentration Camps*, 169–71.

an informer or, culturally, an *inu*.[91] The seriously beaten individual was Fred Tayama, a strong southern California Citizens League figure and former proprietor of the U.S. Cafes chain in Los Angeles.[92] In Manzanar various shadow groups emerged, colorfully described as San Pedro *Yogores*, Blood Brothers, and still other names.[93] Fear of these shadow groups became so strong that the Manzanar administration was forced to spirit away a large group of sixty targeted individuals for protection to a CCC camp outside the perimeter of the concentration camp.[94] The project administration dubbed these shadow groups as "pro-Axis" when in reality they were "anti-JACL." Those most notably earmarked for beatings [or worse] were Tokie Slocum, Togo Tanaka, Joe Grant Masaoka, and Karl Yoneda. Every one of these individuals appear in either FBI or Naval Intelligence documents as "informers."[95] The beating of Fred Tayama resulted in the administrative arrest of a kitchen crew leader named Harry Y. Ueno.[96] Ueno's arrest led to mass protest, and thereafter Ralph Merritt, the camp's leery project director, called in the army's military police detachment to maintain control. Trigger-happy soldiers fired into a crowd of unarmed protestors, killing two and injuring nine others.[97]

The shooting of unarmed protestors and the spiriting out of reputed *inu* to protective security appeared to have cooled the ardor of the Manzanar dissidents, but the beatings of JACL leaders and other imputed collaborationists reverberated in still other WRA camps.

At Jerome, Arkansas,[98] Dr. T. T. Yatabe, founder of the American Loyalty League, was beaten and hastily removed out of camp,[99] and a minister of procollaboration leanings, the Reverend John Yamazaki, was beaten.[100] Beatings also occurred at the central Utah camp at Topaz,[101] where a former University of California art instructor, Chiura Obata,[102] was a victim, and at Minidoka in southeastern Idaho,[103] where JACL leaders were silenced by grassroots threats, particularly against the blind founder of the JACL, Jimmie Sakamoto.[104] The beatings of JACL leaders and adherents were so intimidating that only one camp, Gila River Relocation Center in Arizona,[105] was able to establish a JACL chapter, which fell apart after a shaky year of existence.[106] Membership in the national JACL organization dwindled to around 1,800, of which approximately 900 were associates or bleeding-heart white liberals. Had it not been for the financial contributions from the Intermountain District Council, located outside of the evicted area, the League could not have existed.[107]

Still, quite apart from these dramatic acts of dissent and protest, the overriding submissive reaction of Japanese Americans toward their captivity was greatly surprising and disappointing. It would seem that in a crisis of this magnitude people ought to resist their poor treatment. The government's attitude was reminiscent of the iron fist of feudal Europe: do what you are told, or else. That attitude persisted throughout the detention era and became starkly evident in the policies pursued in the draft reinstitution. What is most galling to contemplate is that meekness in accepting eviction was interpreted by government officials as submission, and that the Japanese American people didn't have the guts or intestinal fortitude to oppose the dictates of government and had thereby vacated their honor and pride as members of the human family. Anglo-Saxon authorities in government already regarded themselves as superior to colored people of the world and had developed the arrogant attitude that Japanese Americans could be handled like slaves. The attitudes and practices of government officials toward Japanese Americans were those of keeper toward prisoners, not the enlightened policies of a benevolent government. Despite being betrayed by their ethnic leadership, few of the Nikkei victims appeared to realize it in their anxiety and desire to place primary onus on government and overlook the evil that lurked in their own society. They thus failed to grasp that the JACL's basic tool was deception, the purpose of which was to seal its goal of proving its own importance and influence at the expense of its racial community.

The result of the controversial loyalty registration notwithstanding, the War Department switched signals and announced the reinstitution of selective service on January 20, 1944. Army recruiters had indicated that failure of volunteerism would lead to the reinstitution of the draft. The *Pacific Citizen*, the mouthpiece of the Japanese American Citizens League, declared baldly: "Those among you who do not volunteer but are of the right age and physically fit will probably be taken into the military service in due time."[xxvii]

The background to the reinstatement of the Nisei draft is instructive. Milton Eisenhower, who had resigned in mid-June 1942 as the first national director of the War Relocation Authority,[108] had taken an assistant's job under Elmer Davis at the Office of War Information.[109] Davis was a close

---

xxvii *Pacific Citizen*, February 10, 1943.

associate of President Roosevelt, and Eisenhower prevailed on Davis to use his influence. Davis sent a memo to the president, associating Eisenhower with its contents and stating: "It would be hardly fair to evacuate people and then impose normal draft procedures, but voluntary enlistment would help a lot. Moreover, as citizens ourselves who believe deeply in the things for which we fight, we cannot help but be disturbed by the insistent public misunderstanding of the Nisei."[xxviii]

Davis and Eisenhower were not the only officials disturbed. There existed at the time a coterie of midline officials who favored the employment of Nisei Americans in the armed services and worried about the negative aspects of the government program. It would appear that Milton Eisenhower was the first important official in government to advocate the draft of the Nisei, which he began during his brief stint as the WRA's director in San Francisco. This policy was carried forward by his successor, Dillon S. Myer. Though the input of the Japanese American Citizens League was no doubt important, it is highly unlikely that reinstitution could have occurred solely on its representation, and too great an emphasis has been placed on this group in the Japanese American community concerning its impact. It is however true that at the JACL's November 1942 Emergency National Meeting at Salt Lake City a resolution was passed and sent to Roosevelt urging the use of the Nisei in the armed forces.[110] Still, it is inappropriate and inaccurate to give major credit for the reinstitution of selective service to the Japanese American Citizens League. The JACL was a mere addendum in a larger perspective. Nor was the draft reinstated in the fashion that was requested by the ethnic organization.[xxix]

The Davis-Eisenhower memo was referred by President Roosevelt to Secretary of War Henry Stimson, and after strong persuasion by Assistant Secretary of War John McCloy, Stimson sent this handwritten note to Chief of Staff George C. Marshall: "I am inclined strongly to agree with the view of McCloy and Davis. I don't think you can permanently proscribe a lot of American citizens because of their racial origin. We have gone to the full

---

xxviii Elmer Davis, Director of Office of War Information, memorandum to the President [Franklin Delano Roosevelt], October 2, 1942, NA, RG 407.

xxix Secretary of War Henry L. Stimson, undated letter, to Chief of Staff George C. Marshall, NA, RG 407; memorandum to Stimson from John J. McCloy, Assistant Secretary of War, October 15, 1942, NA, RG 107; and (draft) memorandum from McCloy to Stimson, October 28, 1942, NA, RG 407.

limit in evacuating them."[111] Marshall approved the Stimson recommendation on January 1, 1943.[112]

General Staff was not convinced of the use of the Nisei as an appropriate policy but bowed to pressure from those involved in the so-called relocation program concerning the wisdom of returning the confined Japanese Americans into useful postwar lives. In August 1943 Captain John M. Hall[113] described the situation this way:

> At the time of the establishment of the Japanese American combat team last February, the General Staff was definitely in favor of a segregated unit for military reasons. There was widespread lack of confidence in their [Japanese Americans] loyalty. . . . Mr. McCloy, however, was more interested in establishing a symbol which would call the country's attention to the fact that there were loyal Japanese Americans ready to fight. He thought that the creation of a separate unit with a high esprit de corps would go further in helping the relocation program. . . . He also had in mind the psychological warfare aspect [of the situation].
>
> As was to a certain extent foreseen, there was an immediate and violent reaction by the evacuees in the relocation centers against the formation of a separate unit. There were cries of discrimination, segregation, and cannon fodder.
>
> From the point of view of the welfare of the evacuees, almost everybody familiar with the relocation program is strongly in favor of the general reinstitution of selective service for all persons of Japanese descent. However, the General Staff has serious doubts whether our military assets would thereby be increased, wholly apart from whether or not it would be the best thing for the evacuees.[xxx]

Opposition to the Davis memo arose from Navy secretary Frank Knox.[114] Still engrossed with his twisted logic of spies and saboteurs at Pearl Harbor, he "suggested that everyone's time could be better spent handling the 'problem' of Japanese sympathizers in Hawaii."[xxxi] Also vehemently opposed was the Western Defense Command, which was firmly persuaded that loyalty could not be distinguished among Japanese Americans.

---

xxx John M. Hall, Captain, F.A., Assistant Executive, War Department, to Lieutenant General George W. Bicknell, Pentagon, August 13, 1943, memorandum (substituting for Colonel [William P.] Scobey), ASW 342.18, J.A. Infantry 442nd, Doc. 000046.

xxxi Letter from Frank Knox, Secretary of the Navy, to President [Franklin D.] Roosevelt, October 17, 1942, NA, RG 107; also memorandum from General John L. DeWitt, Commander of the Fourth Army, to Chief of Staff George C. Marshall, January 27, 1943, NA, RG 107.

In spite of such opposition, however, Secretary of War Stimson was correct in declaring that the opening of the draft to the Nisei was urged from a number of quarters concerned about the effect long confinement would have on the postwar adjustment of Japanese Americans.[xxxii] "Immediately after my first field trip in July," WRA director Dillon Myer admitted in an interview, "I began talks with Mr. McCloy, urging that the Nisei be drafted into the Army through regular procedures of Selective Service. McCloy agreed with my viewpoint, and he immediately started procedures to get it under way."[xxxiii]

One year after the controversy over the loyalty registration and the debacle of the volunteer enlistment program, the unrelenting War Department announced the reinstitution of the draft for Nisei Americans on January 20, 1944. There were obvious warning signs of Nisei reactions. The controversial loyalty registration of February–March 1943 and the results of the volunteer program could not have failed to alert the authorities.

In the Heart Mountain camp an activist organization called the Fair Play Committee formed. It was the most faithful advocate of constitutional principles during the period of incarceration. In contrast to the meek submission with which Japanese Americans in general greeted eviction, the Fair Play Committee restored a degree of ethnic pride and dignity to a racial-ethnic community oppressed by the hammer of authoritarianism. The father of the Fair Play Committee was Robert Kiyoshi Okamoto, who in October 1943 formed at Heart Mountain what he fashioned as a "Committee of One" to fight camp injustices and make representations to federal officials. Okamoto conducted public forums in camp but was not too successful because of his use of vulgar language and his intemperance. In a late December 1943 public meeting, Okamoto stood up to challenge a Nisei minister, the Reverend Donald Toriumi,[115] who had spoken in favor of compliance with registration. In the audience were several Nisei who were impressed with Okamoto's knowledge of constitutional affairs. One in particular was a prewar San Fernando grocer, Frank Seishi Emi, who despite two years of college education admitted his ignorance of the Bill of Rights until hearing Okamoto's explanation.[116] Emi asked to talk further with him

---

xxxii [Ed. Source of this quoted passage by Omura is undisclosed and undetected.]

xxxiii Notes on September 29, 1943, interview with Dillon S. Myer by Morton Grodzins, JERS, BL, UCB, Folder E 2.10.

on the subject, which led to an invitation to Okamoto's barrack. Besides Emi, the group that eventually gathered at Okamoto's quarters in February 1944—after the announcement of the Nisei draft restoration—is believed to have included a Los Angeleno named Isamu Horino,[117] and an Issei named Guntaro Kubota, a language schoolteacher from Mountain View, California.[118] Emi, Horino, and Kubota were all judo experts.[xxxiv] Except for Horino, the others were married. Emi was the father of two children, and Kubota of one.

At this meeting Okamoto agreed to turn over his one-man organization to this young group, conditioned on his being made its chairman. He suggested their getting in touch with Paul Takeo Nakadate, the former secretary of the Congress of American Citizens, who was conducting a speakers' forum in the center. With the Okamoto transfer, the Fair Play Committee took on an organizational format with its primary purpose to seek judicial and or legislative clarification of the suspended constitutional rights of the American Nisei. After this meeting with Okamoto, signs were posted on laundry rooms and latrines, raising questions on the resumption of the Nisei draft.

In February 1944 the Fair Play Committee retained a Denver attorney named Samuel Menin[119] to pursue grievances through legal channels against the U.S. government for its reinstitution of the Nisei draft in the previous month. I agreed to their procedure and it was supported by my newspaper, the *Rocky Shimpo*. It was in this sense that I became associated as an editor in the program of the Fair Play Committee. Having intimated in the editorial of February 28 a willingness to support judicial and/or legislative inquiry into the muddled constitutional situation caused by the removal and exclusion of people of Japanese ancestry from the Pacific Coast,[120] I could do no less.

The first evidence of the existence of the Fair Play Committee (FPC) in the Heart Mountain Center occurred on February 24, 1944, when the group distributed a mimeographed circular in both English and Japanese throughout the community.[xxxv] The circular needled the Community Council for its

---

xxxiv Kiyoshi Okamoto: "The Committee of which I claimed to have been chairman was founded around October of 1943. Then, around February 1944, three or four people came to me when this draft issue came up." [Ed. Omura neglected to supply the source for this information, which certainly rings true based upon written and oral evidence I have examined.]

xxxv Report of Harry W. McMillan, p. 7, WRA central files, Washington, DC, April 24, 1944, 7, NA, RG 210 17-2, made [?] by Asael T. Hansen, Community Analyst, Heart Mountain Relocation Center, Heart Mountain, Wyoming.

inaction and called the people's attention to the Topaz and Rohwer camps where the councils are "genuinely interested in clarifying the draft issue."xxxvi When stronger measures were later proposed, Okamoto strongly opposed direct draft confrontations yet found himself overruled by his fellow leaders and the wishes of FPC members. In its third mimeographed bulletin, the Fair Play Committee took a stronger stand: "The Fair Play Committee hereby refuses to go to the physical examination or to the induction when we are called in order to contest the issue."xxxvii

And with that declaration, the organization crossed the military Rubicon. It was the basis on which the government filed a conspiracy charge of aborting the Selective Service Act. The only involvement that I had with the committee was in my capacity as a newspaper editor. Here was a legitimate committee that had retained a lawyer with the stated objective of seeking judicial and/or legislative remedies for their clouded citizenship status. It was because I empathized with this objective that editorial and moral support was offered in the *Rocky Shimpo* for achieving this goal. With the Fair Play Committee taking a firmer stand to resist the draft, the *Rocky Shimpo* recognized that rectification of constitutional wrongs by the government could only occur by breaking a relevant law. The Tenth Circuit Court of Appeals ruled that "two wrongs do not make a right" in an appeal of the sixty-three draft resisters, and condemned the second while overlooking the first. On the judgment of justice, the question ought to be measured on which of those two wrongs was the greater evil. I would beg to differ with the court. The Fair Play Committee case would not have arisen had not the government violated the fundamental principles of the United States Constitution and the Bill of Rights. The principal culprit was the government. Nor was there a need for mass eviction, for it was known the military chiefs of staff had previously ruled that no possibility of enemy invasion existed on the West Coast. Thus, not even the argument of war powers could have been justified.

To put the Fair Play Committee in its proper perspective, the trial of the sixty-three draft resisters was not merely the greatest mass trial in the legal history of the state of Wyoming, but also the largest mass trial of the Nisei during the World War II period. The trial of the Fair Play Committee

---

xxxvi [Ed. The same situation obtains here as with that indicated in note xxxv above.]
xxxvii [Ed. This pronouncement is cited by Muller, *Free to Die for Their Country*, 84, with primary source documentation provided by the author in chap. 5 ("Reaction"), 208n35.]

leaders on charges of conspiracy was one of four successful court challenges won during the eviction era. Three of the cases were grounded in the draft in one fashion or another. The fourth was the most significant—the habeas corpus case of Mitsuye Endo, a former civil service clerk for the state of California.[121] It was the Endo case that brought an end to government detention after being ruled unconstitutional by the Supreme Court. The ruling opened the exclusion gates for the return of the Japanese people to the Pacific Coast.[122] Despite its importance, the Endo case seems almost forgotten by the Japanese American community in the uncommon acclamation that was given to participants of the failed Supreme Court test cases—Hirabayashi, Korematsu, and Yasui—none of which had any impact on the alleviation of the Japanese American tragedy. Could it be that there is more glory in failure than in success?

The first resister case that went before the Ninth Circuit Court in the northern California site of Eureka was that of the Tule Lake twenty-seven, *United States v. Masaaki Kuwabara et al.*[123] The judge in the case was Louis E. Goodman.[124] It was dismissed, and the court, in an unusual burst of oral outrage, berated the government prosecutors: "It is shocking to the conscience that an American citizen be confined on the ground of disloyalty and then, while so under duress and restraint, be compelled to serve in the armed forces or be prosecuted for not yielding to such compulsion."[125]

SIX

Rocky Mountain Resistance, 1944

On the evening of January 13, 1944, I was visited at my modest home in Lakewood, a western suburb of Denver, by two representatives of the Japanese Publishing Company in Denver,[1] who offered me a job. At that time I was employed as a ladle operator for the United States Foundry Corporation,[2] which was producing armaments for the American military. All I knew about the Japanese Publishing Company was that it published a triweekly called the *Rocky Shimpo*.[3] I conferred with my wife, Caryl, then a student at Denver University[4] while supplementing her income as a cook for a Denver oilman's family in Park Hill.[5] Caryl opposed my accepting the job offer but provided no substantive reason for her opposition. So, three days later I accepted the offer, subject to my release from war work at the U.S. Foundry. Then, on January 28, 1944, I took up my dual role of the Japanese Publishing Company's publicity director and the *Rocky Shimpo*'s English editor.

At the time I assumed my editorial post, the *Rocky Shimpo* was under the supervisory control of the Office of the Alien Property Custodian.[6] This situation had occurred as a result of the internment of its publisher, Shiro Toda, following his publication of a patriotic Japanese poem and other allegedly pro-Japan materials (a subject touched upon within the previous chapter). It should be noted that its rival, the *Colorado Times*, although having published the same poem, was not similarity treated. With Shiro Toda's internment, the newspaper changed its name from the *Rocky Nippon* to the *Rocky Shimpo* and transferred ownership to Toda's eldest daughter, Tetsuko, who was named publisher. The government, however, balked at any change in its parent company, the Japanese Publishing Company.

While the problems of the newspaper were unknown to me at the time of my employment, it is important to more clearly grasp the paper's wartime status. The Japanese division of the newspaper underwent tremendous opposition during the war years and was subjected to calls for reform. Critics might well wonder why the government did not heed their recommendation. It may serve the interest of such critics, therefore, to understand better the actual situation, as depicted through the following contemporary documentation:

> A review of that file [the *Rocky Nippon*, Internal Security Alien Enemy] reflects that investigation, concerning the publication *Rocky Nippon*, was initiated as the result of the publication of a pro-Japanese poem entitled "The Day of Our Remembrance,"[i] which was contained in the June 8, 1943, issue of the *Rocky Nippon*, the publication of The Japanese Publishing Company, a corporation chartered by the State of Colorado on March 10, 1932. . . . Shiro Toda, a Japanese alien, was President, Manager, and Editor of the *Rocky Nippon*.[ii]

On February 25, 1943, Thomas J. Morrissey, United States attorney for Colorado, had submitted a recommendation for the arrest of Shiro Toda, the alien proprietor of the Japanese Publishing Company, to Edward J. Ennis, director of the Alien Enemy Control Unit of the Department of Justice.[7] Then, on March 2, 1943, Toda's arrest was ordered by Attorney General Francis Biddle under a presidential warrant. Toda appeared before an alien hearing board that convened in Denver, Colorado, on April 29 and was ordered interned at Old Raton Ranch in northern New Mexico (Santa Fe Department of Justice Internment Center).[8] Over two years later, on December 13, 1945, the Repatriation Hearing Board[9] ordered the deportation of the Issei publisher. However, Tom C. Clark,[10] who replaced Francis Biddle[11] as attorney general of the United States on June 27, 1945, rescinded

---

i "The Day of Our Remembrance," poem by "Seijiro," Santa Anita Assembly Center, Santa Anita, California, May 29, 1942. It was translated by Mr. [?] Oki, California Interior Security, Turlock, California, 100-2235-A (3).

ii Gordon A. Nicholson, special agent in charge, Denver FBI Field Division, September 8, 1943, Denver, Colorado. File No. 100-154244. [Ed. Unfortunately, there is no record of Gordon A. Nicholson's tenure of service as an FBI agent in either *Society of Former Special Agents of the FBI* (Paducah, KY: Turner Publishing, 1998), or National Law Enforcement Museum, *FBI Oral Histories* [of Former Special Agents], www.nleomf.org/museum/the-collection/oral-histories/index.jsp?page=11 (accessed on September 10, 2015).]

Toda's deportation order as of February 23, 1946, thereby allowing him to reunify with his wife and four children in Denver.

In early September 1943 the special agent in charge of the FBI's Denver field office had observed that "there were published in five issues of the *Rocky Shimpo* dated May 26 to June 4, 1943, an article entitled 'Awake From the Bad Dream' signed Bainro which strongly urged the Nisei to combat the materialism of America with the spiritual qualities of Japan. This article was strongly pro-Japanese and declared that the Japanese are a superior race." Also singled out was the July 14, 1943, issue that "contained an editorial entitled 'New Signs in East Asia' which described the Asiatic War as constructive and for building a Greater East Asia."[iii]

Following the translation and analysis of "New Signs in East Asia," the Office of Censorship condemned the publication. This action was referenced in a September 8, 1943, communication to FBI chief J. Edgar Hoover from the Office of Censorship.[12] "We do not require a recommendation as indicated in our letter of August 24, 1943 because the publication [*Rocky Nippon*] has now been condemned."[iv] In late October 1943 Hoover advised that the Criminal Division of the Justice Department felt that since the Alien Property Custodian had assumed control of the *Rocky Nippon* on October 16, "the control is sufficiently stringent to insure no further questionable material being published."[v]

Contrary to accepted public perception, the onus of what the Roosevelt administration considered un-American wartime journalism applied to all three of the existing vernacular newspapers and not only to the *Rocky Nippon/Rocky Shimpo* style of coverage. Various concerns were raised against the type and treatment of these newspapers throughout the war years, as illustrated by comments from the Department of Justice.

> Numerous reports are being received at the Bureau concerning the
> pro-Japanese character of the captioned Japanese language newspapers
> (*Rocky Shimpo*, *Utah Nippo*, *The Colorado Times*). . . . It is observed that
> a memorandum dated November 29, 1943, was forwarded to Assistant
> Attorney General Tom C. Clark regarding the "Utah Nippo" and the
> reply of December 4, 1943 indicated no action was warranted. . . . It is

---

iii J. Edgar Hoover, FBI director, to Tom C. Clark, assistant attorney general and head of the Justice Department's Criminal Division, October 2, 1943.

iv Letter to J. Edgar Hoover by J. P. Wolgemuth, executive liaison officer, Office of Censorship, September 8, 1943.

v J. Edgar Hoover, director of FBI, to Special Agent in Charge, Denver, October 22, 1943.

also observed that on July 7, 1942, a memorandum was forwarded to Mr. Lawrence M. C. Smith, Chief of Special War Policies Unit, with regard to the "Colorado Times."[vi]

Despite Office of War Information subsidization, the *Colorado Times* was denied distribution in Department of Justice internment centers, as well as prisoner of war camps, since November 1942. The *Utah Nippo* of Salt Lake City[13] likewise did not escape unscathed. The complainant there was the Civil Affairs Division of the Western Defense Command,[14] which made a translation of articles in the Utah paper by its editor, Taro Azuma.[15]

The *Rocky Shimpo*'s editor in chief for its Japanese division, Noboru Hiraga, was also removed in conjunction with my withdrawal in April 1944 as the paper's English editor, and he became the object of eleven anonymous complaints to the Special War Policies Unit of the Justice Department.[16] These letters began on April 22, 1944, only days after his removal, and continued to May 18, 1945; they were signed variously as "A Young Nisei" and "A Loyal Japanese American Nisei," but mostly as "A Japanese American." The War Division determined by analysis and comparison of the writer's habits that the anonymous writer was a *Rocky Shimpo* staff member.[vii]

The question is then posed that with all the complaints from the Nisei Communists in New York, the Japanese Desk of the Overseas Branch of the U.S. Department of State, a multitude of federal agencies, and the Japanese American Citizens League and its bleeding-heart liberals, why the lack of government crackdown on Japanese vernacular newspapers? The explanation lies in a decision reached in November 1942 in the office of the attorney general, attended by representatives of the War Department, the Office of War Information, and others. It was decided at that time to take no immediate action. In mid-April 1943 Tom Clark related to Thomas Morrissey the basis for this decision:

> It was mentioned . . . that the condition of the four remaining independent Japanese newspapers was helpful to the Office of War Information and the War Relocation Administration authorities in that it helped in preventing circulation of unfounded rumors. In this connection the War Department

---

vi J. Edgar Hoover, FBI director, to Assistant Attorney General Herbert Wechsler, June 13, 1945, 100-1582-20. The source is the Japanese Communist group in New York, according to FBI Special Agent in Charge, 2279-7, New York, memorandum to J. Edgar Hoover, FBI director, April 23, 1945, 14-1582-109.
vii Elizabeth C. Ito, for Jesse M. MacKnight, War Division, no date.

had subscribed to 200 copies of the "Rocky Shimpo," partly as a subsidy, and for use in their Japanese language schools.[viii]

I had been in Denver from the beginning of April 1942, but neither of the two vernacular newspapers paid any attention until the [Pacific Coast Evacuee] Placement Bureau relocated to 2008 Larimer Street, the site of Caryl's Malt & Sandwich Shop. The editor of the English section of the *Colorado Times* then took notice and began a daily visit to pick up news. Her name was Bea Kaihara and she was the daughter of the publisher, Fred I. Kaihara.[17] Before long she requested that I write a regular column. Two months later I became suspicious that comments in my column on the WRA-JACL programs were being censored. I then wrote a test column critical of the JACL and when that, too, went unpublished, I stopped writing my column. In the late summer of 1943, I received a request from the *Rocky Nippon* to conduct an editorial column for that newspaper. I agreed, providing that a suitable heading outlined by me could be furnished. I then approved the "Know the Facts" logo. I didn't know at the time that the *Colorado Times* had become a puppet of the U.S. government, although it had been whispered in the Japanese community that the paper was being subsidized by the government at three thousand dollars per month. This rumor was acknowledged in 1983 by a Utah-born journalist,[ix] and reference to it also appears in an oral history conducted for the UCLA-based Japanese American Research Project (JARP) in the 1960s.[x] [18] Nor was I cognizant of the previously noted *Rocky Nippon*'s difficulties with federal authorities, which simply multiplied after I climbed aboard as its English-language editor in early 1944.

Selection of the *Colorado Times* as a government propaganda organ did not come as a first choice. The search began in early January 1942 when the war closed down the West Coast's Japanese vernacular presses. Under Director Archibald MacLeish of the Office of Facts and Figures,[19] assisted by

---

viii Tom C. Clark, assistant attorney general, to Thomas J. Morrissey, United States attorney for Colorado, April 19, 1944, airmail, File No. 14-1582-19.

ix On special request for discussion at his Denver, Colorado, home in Park Hill by Kibei journalist [Art] Iwasaki, circa 1983. [Ed. The "discussion" alluded to by Omura was in fact a tape-recorded interview with Iwasaki; see OP for this interview. Tatsumi Obelle ("Arthur") Iwasaki (1914–2000) was born in Ogden, Utah, and died in Denver, Colorado. During World War II he was incarcerated at the Santa Anita Assembly Center, the Granada Relocation Center, and the Tule Lake Segregation Center.]

x Oral history interview of Joe Koide, by Joe Grant Masaoka and John Modell, April 19, 1967, Japanese American Research Project, Tape 33, Box 381, University of California, Los Angeles.

Alan Cranston (later a California senator),[20] a search was launched for a replacement forum. The initial attempt was Isamu Noguchi's drive to form an Artists and Writers Mobilization for Democracy. However, both of his endeavors failed. In Los Angeles in late January, his Southland effort collapsed on charges of Communist domination. His second try in San Francisco in mid-February also was frustrated when the organization was converted into a community group and later voted to become a subsidiary of the national JACL, a sure guarantee for its demise.

In the meantime, a New York firm, Starr, Park and Freeman, was enlisted in the search. C. V. Starr, head of the group, reacted to the proposal "that such a newspaper project would be an outlet for government propaganda and should be underwritten by the Government."[xi] The Starr Group's choice, if it could pass FBI muster, was a new organization in New York calling itself the Japanese American Committee for Democracy.[xii] This group not only failed to gain approval by the FBI but wound up on its list of Communist organizations.[21]

Cranston had shifted his search to New York after the failure of Isamu Noguchi to establish the Artists and Writers Mobilization for Democracy in California. The two leading West Coast newspapers, the *Rafu Shimpo* of Los Angeles and the *Nichibei* of San Francisco, were considered too costly.

> As far as the *Rafu* and the *Nichibei* are concerned, the difficulty there is that both these papers have too big an overhead. The *Nichibei* costs between $10,000 and $11,000 monthly to publish; subsidizing a newspaper with the organization and overhead of the *Nichibei* or the *Rafu* would run to more than $100,000 and would be quite an expensive proposition. . . . It is feared that *Doho*[22] has a too-pronounced leftist tinge, so that most people are still afraid to read it. . . . Two dailies (four to six pages) where cost could be reduced to about $2500 a month, although this is the minimum figure [, is affordable].[xiii]

At this point *Colorado Times* publisher Fred Kaihara agreed to a government pact with Bradford Smith, the director of the Office of War Information (OWI).[23] This fact was attested to by documents uncovered at Suitland

---

xi Randall Gould of the Starr Group to Alan Cranston, chief of the Foreign Language Division, Office of Facts and Figures, March 24, 1942, RG 208-3A-1, "G" 1942.

xii News Letter No. 45, addressed by Randall Gould to Executives of the Starr Group and Friends, March 14, 1942, 3-4, RG 208-3A-1, "G" 1942.

xiii Alan Cranston, chief of the Foreign Language Division, Office of Facts and Figures, to Randall Gould, Starr, Park and Freeman, Inc. of New York, March 20, 1942, RG 208-3A-1, "G" 1042.

Record Center, a branch of the National Archives, in nearby Maryland in 1987.[24] This agreement was cemented at the very time that the *Colorado Times* was censoring columns being written by me. Gene Cervi, publisher of *Cervi's Business Journal*, was delegated to supervise the *Colorado Times*. It is indicated by documents that Kaihara was in the habit of making daily trips to Cervi's office.[25]

"The Office of War Information," stated Bradford Smith, "is responsible for forwarding news stories to Japanese language newspapers and is responsible for guiding the editorial policy of such papers."[xiv] The broader role of the OWI, though, was to place a lid on public consumption of developments in the WRA centers. In a June 1944 memorandum,[xv] the OWI affirmed that it had obtained the "use of restraint in playing the stories of the Jap relocation" from Cranston Williams[26] and the secretaries of the Inland Press Association and Southern Newspaper Publishers Association.[27]

In the role of a rubber stamp for the government, the *Colorado Times* published the Kaz Oka article, a stinging rebuke to this writer.[28] I made a formal request to refute the charges in "the same forum" where the charges had been made. The request was refused. Bea Kaihara, the English Section editor, informed me that the Oka article, according to postal marks on the envelope, had been routed through the national office of the JACL in Salt Lake City. Actually, though, it was forwarded as an individual criticism out of Poston, Arizona. Oka, the records confirm, was an FBI informer at Monterey, California.[29] The *Times*' refusal brought Togo Tanaka, a columnist for the publication, into the picture. He offered his column as a forum. I accepted his invitation but requested a deferment due to being swamped. Feeling inclined to make public my response, which had been a private communication, Tanaka ridiculed me, his fellow journalist, in several inane columns. I knew Tanaka only by reputation, but this experience taught me to be very wary of JACL officials. Tanaka was also a government stooge and had to be spirited out of Manzanar Relocation Center after the December 1942 riot there, for the good of his health.

The issue of the moment when I took over the helm of the *Rocky Shimpo* was the Anti-Japanese Alien Land Proposal of Colorado.[30] The

---

xiv Memorandum from P. V. Hodges to Mr. [D. M.] Ladd of the FBI, December 15, 1942, 100-154244-5. [Ed. Special Agent Ladd's years of FBI service are undetermined.]

xv Office of War Information memorandum to John Herrick of the Planning Review Board of the Starr Group, June 24, 1944, Office of Facts and Figures, RG 208-E26-30, Folder: Julian Woodward.

Thirty-Fourth General Assembly had adjourned without taking any action on the measure and Governor John Vivian,[31] considered by some to be a tool of Western Slope landed gentry, had to consider its passage. Despite the counsel of the regional office of the JACL to remain away from the Legislative Hall to avoid physical violence, the situation in Colorado did not impress me as that rowdy. In fact, I had an invitation from Speaker of the House Homer Pearson[32] to meet with legislators in the well of the House between recesses to discuss opposition to the measure. The atmosphere I encountered was normal. Later I went to the gallery for a better view of the proceedings. Other Nisei obviously followed the JACL dictum and only two persons were in attendance, a young Nisei lad in the right back aisle and a woman huddled far back in the center gallery. Although the House passed the Anti-Japanese Alien Land measure 42 to 13, it was killed by the Senate 15 to 12. Proponents of the bill then used the petition route for a vote of the people in the general election. There the measure was defeated, fueled by the opposition of the Christian clergy and liberal elements. Contrary to other reports, the JACL was not a factor in its defeat.

The concern over the pending Anti-Japanese Alien Land Proposal led me to the *Rocky Mountain News*,[33] a subsidiary of the Gannett Newspaper Syndicate,[34] to consult with Lee Casey, a well-known columnist and a vice president.[35] It was a gloomy day when I was directed to the third floor, where I found Casey alone, a tall, spare, gray-haired person of thoughtful but personable persuasion. He was of the opinion that the Anti-Japanese Alien Land Proposal would not pass. That settled, our discussion covered wide-ranging subjects on the Japanese American difficulties, among which was the issue of the Nisei draft.

"I'm opposed to it!" I informed him.

"Isn't everybody subject to the draft?" he asked

"Not everybody!" I replied.

"Who?" he asked, after a long moment of thought.

"The convicts at Cañon City,"[36] I declared.

"Why do you oppose the draft?" he asked.

"I don't think it is fair to strip the Nisei of their constitutional rights, evict them from the West Coast, confine them behind barbed wires with armed guards in watchtowers and then without restoring any of their violated rights to demand that they give their lives for the nation. The Nisei are confined in these camps, which are little more than concentration camps. They are in the same boat as the convicts at Cañon City."

Casey did not respond immediately. I followed his eyes to the large window and noticed the lowering skies, threatening a deluge. I wondered if I would be able to beat it back to the *Rocky Shimpo.*

"You are right," Mr. Casey said at long last. And then he added a statement I would always remember: "When the war is over, the American people will regret what it has done to your people. The sober second thought of the American people will triumph in the end."

I was to meet Lee Casey once more. He was the main speaker at a public forum sponsored by the regional office of the Japanese American Citizens League in the Midland Bank Building.[37] The audience was cautioned by the chairwoman not to question Casey but simply to listen to him.[38]

"The Anti-Alien Land Law won't pass," Casey assured the group.

"They passed an alien land law in Arkansas," piped up my companion."[xvi] [39]

"It was signed by the governor," I chimed in. "The Arkansas measure applies to all persons of Japanese ancestry. Governor Homer Adkins[40] signed it. It is on the books. The law is unconstitutional but as long as it's on the book, it is the law of the state. We don't want the same thing happening in Colorado."

"I didn't know that!" Mr. Casey admitted.

It was not until the third week of February 1944 before I took cognizance of the resistance to the draft when I read in the *Denver Post* the sensational proclamations of five Nisei resisters from the southeastern Colorado encampment of Amache claiming loyalty to Imperial Japan. These five were the first to refuse to report for their physical examinations. Their proclamations, I felt, were a product of the frustration of confinement and their immaturity. It was rather disconcerting to read in the *Denver Post* the caption: "JAPS RESIST DRAFT AT CAMP; TELL DISLOYALTY."[xvii] The headline quoted project director James G. Lindley[41] as stating that an eighteen-year-old had declared: "I don't think I owe the United States anything after the way they have been treating us—and I don't see my future in the United States." Another eighteen-year-old was quoted as saying: "I feel no loyalty to the United States. When we came to the Center, we lost all civil rights. The Constitution says that in the United States all men are created equal. . . . I can't call this democracy."

---

xvi George Matsumonji (1914–96), a broker in the Denargo Market, Denver, Colorado.
xvii Associated Press report, Lamar, Colorado, February 22, 1944.

I was not inclined to believe that these expressions of disloyalty of the Amache Five[42] were anything but frustrations, and empathized with their dilemma. However, such proclamations of disloyalty had a tendency of simply feeding into the racist grill. What was needed was an appropriate and fundamental basis for the actions of all others who were bound to follow. That week brought an Associated Press report of thirty others at the southeastern Idaho project of Minidoka renouncing their citizenship in protest of treatment.[43] This negative trend was deeply troubling and the problem of finding an appropriate solution consumed my entire weekend. The issue of resistance was a thorny one. People seemed more intent at condemnation rather than understanding and compassion. No matter how much I struggled to find an answer, I could find but one solution: to focus on the constitutional aspects of their violated civil rights. With that in mind, and in the wish that it would give them the counsel they needed but were not getting, the initial editorial, "Let Us Not Be Rash," was published on February 28, 1944. I hoped that it would serve as an anchor in the resistance.[xviii] This editorial was the first on the subject of the draft and was to become the most scrutinized, analyzed, and quoted of all editorials I ever wrote. (See Appendix 3.)

Saburo Kido, the wartime president of the JACL, offered the lone detraction, terming the editorial "weak" and accusing the *Shimpo* editor of using it as a shield against any attacks.[44] The editorial was carefully written and the Criminal Division of the Justice Department[45] was unable to find legal justification for prosecution, and thus riveted attention more on what was not said than what the editorial actually did say. Other federal bureaucracies took their turns, trying to figure out its meanings. The head of the Justice Department's Criminal Division and Assistant Attorney General Tom C. Clark called the "Let Us Not Be Rash" editorial a "clarion call" for resistance. The editorial loomed large in government analysis, but it was the editorial support accorded the Heart Mountain Fair Play Committee that became a lively matter of contention for both the government and its racial cabal.

This first editorial of mine prompted a visit to the *Rocky Shimpo* editorial office by a Caucasian woman. It was a warm Friday afternoon and the visitor wore a sleeveless white dress, appeared nervous, and carried a sheaf of documents in her hands.

"My name is Sylvia Toshiyuki,"[46] she announced. But when the name failed to draw recognition, she added, "My husband, Frank,[47] runs the San

---

xviii *The United States vs. Kiyoshi Okamoto, et al.*, Criminal Case No. 4230, the alleged Wyoming Conspiracy Trial, National Record Center, Denver Federal Center, Denver, Colorado.

Kwo Low restaurant on Curtis Street." I had never been in that particular establishment but had noticed its neon sign on journeys uptown.

"I'm a friend of Kiyoshi Okamoto," she continued. "He is in Heart Mountain. These documents were written by him. I think he is a genius. Here, I want you to read them." She thrust the documents into my hand. "I'm double-parked and have to go." With that, she was gone.

FIGURE 9. Sylvia King Toshiyuki and her husband, Frank Toshiyuki, and their interracial child Kenny Toshiyuki were imprisoned at Wyoming's Heart Mountain Relocation Center in 1942–43 before taking a short-term work leave in Montana, where this photo of Sylvia and Kenny was taken, most likely by Frank. In 1944, while the now resettled Toshiyukis were operating a Denver Chinese eatery and Jimmie Omura was using the *Rocky Shimpo* to support Heart Mountain's organized draft resistance movement on constitutional grounds, Sylvia gave him a sheaf of writings by Kiyoshi Okamoto, the Heart Mountain Fair Play Committee leader, telling Omura she believed Okamoto to be a genius. Toshiyuki Family Archives.

While awaiting the press run of the day's edition, I began to read the twenty-nine-page proclamation addressed to Attorney General Francis Biddle. Okamoto, I thought, wrote very well, but I became conscious of the fact that he seemed to have a bad habit of repetition, stressing the same point in various different ways.[48] I could not feature a busy attorney general having the patience to plow through Okamoto's bulky and lengthy proclamation. I gave up at page thirteen. Okamoto did not impress me as any sort of a literary genius. That evening at my Lakewood home, I sifted through briefer documents and became alert at the announcement of the formation of an organized group—the Fair Play Committee. Its import was immediately recognized as news of value. The organization, the article stated, had retained a Denver lawyer and planned to pursue judicial and/or legislative process to seek clarification of citizenship status and the restoration of constitutional rights. It was an appealing goal. Therefore, on March 6 the *Rocky Shimpo* announced the formation of the Fair Play Committee in Heart Mountain. Thereupon, Heart Mountain's community analyst, Asael T. Hansen,[49] reported that the arrival of the *Rocky Shimpo* with a banner headline proclaiming this development had been greeted with great interest and, moreover, "it seemed to give legitimacy to the embryo FPC group, which was the outgrowth of a 'One Man' organization initiated by Kiyoshi Okamoto back in October of 1943."[50]

Okamoto's basic purpose, as I understood it, was to pursue "evacuation grievances" by means of the Fair Play Committee, and to restore rights and achieve indemnification. It is unknown whether responses were received to the forty-odd letters he claimed to have sent out, except for the American Civil Liberties Union opinion by Roger Baldwin,[51] which was also received at the *Rocky Shimpo* and published.[52] The ACLU refused to intervene in the Fair Play Committee case and took the position that leaders of the group had no legitimate legal case. It was the identical position of the Japanese American Citizens League. It is speculated by historian Richard Drinnon that the Roger Baldwin opinion was distributed at the urging of the national JACL.[53]

The lead article of the March 6, 1944, *Rocky Shimpo* that captured Asael Hansen's attention was subtitled "Report Says Organization May Seek Congressional Action for Full Restoration of Rights." In response, the *Heart Mountain Sentinel*[54] instituted an attack on the Fair Play Committee, calling the group "Janus-faced" and turning its hostility against the *Rocky Shimpo* for supporting a constitutional exploration of the issues.[55] The *Shimpo* article stimulated a flow of releases from leaders of the group; but unfortunately, an untruthful report of a camp-wide strike was forwarded by an FPC leader and appeared in the *Rocky Shimpo*.[56] This article ignited charges of manufactured incidents for the purpose of sensationalism. The *Rocky Shimpo* was not the only publication to receive this report. Similar reports were distributed to the *Billings Gazette*, the *Denver Post*, the *Chicago Tribune*, and other mainstream newspapers. When alerted by the Denver Field Division of the FBI that the report was false, I promptly requested guaranty of accuracy and was advised not to accept any publicity except from Frank Emi, who had been designated as the FPC's official publicist. Emi stated that the FPC would stand behind all future releases submitted by him.[57] The Fair Play Committee was very active in Heart Mountain, holding meetings almost nightly.[58]

When the first five members of the Fair Play Committee refused to appear for their physicals, they were not immediately apprehended since no procedure to deal with such action had been established. It was only later that the United States attorney at Cheyenne, Thomas Blake Kennedy,[59] decided to make arrests and place the draft offenders in county jails.

> Although it is true these individuals in the Centers are already confined and that it would, therefore, not be necessary to issue complaints, but their cases could be presented directly to a federal Grand Jury, the procedure in this district has, nevertheless, been to file complaints promptly in each individual case and to remove the Subjects from the Relocation Center. . . . It was felt that to allow Selective Service violators to remain at liberty in the Center after refusing to comply with the Selective Service Act would bolster the position of the Fair Play Committee and would encourage further wholesale resistance.[xix]

The question has been raised by historians, and must also rise in the mind of the public, why a responsible Nisei writer and editorialist would run the risk of tarnishing his good name and reputation by supporting a militant faction behind barbed wires. Furthermore, the leaders of the Fair Play Committee were unknown to the editor. The answer lies somewhere in the arena of a person's conscience. Though the resistance was overshadowed by the draft itself, the actual issue was much greater than the mere refusal

---

xix Special Agent in Charge, Denver to FBI Director, May 1, 1944, FBI file No. 100-164195-41.

to knuckle down to army demands. It raised the very large question as to the propriety of the government to demand adherence to Selective Service requirements after having violated basic constitutional rights without any correlative rectification of wrongs so inflicted. The irony was the betrayal of the victims by their ethnic leadership into believing the false credo that "quiet" submission would be regarded by the government as evidence of loyalty to the United States and thus their treatment would be "reciprocally" rewarded. The fallacy in this theory was twofold: supine submission was inclined to confirm suspicions of the thorny "disloyalty" viewpoint. And also, why should treatments be benevolent when due process was not invoked and legal charges not filed? The government's action violated the constitutional guarantees accorded to all American citizens and nonbelligerent aliens (and, in this particular case, aliens due to the mandate of restrictive U.S. laws).

I had been drawn into the FPC case on a thinly disguised prosecution effort to discredit dissent, since I had championed the cause of the Fair Play Committee. Mounted against the militant leaders of the FPC were not only the forces of the government but the leadership of its ethnic acolyte, the Japanese American Citizens League, adhering to public image over good laws and the fundamental tenets of justice.

On November 1, 1944, the federal court jury in Cheyenne, Wyoming, returned a verdict for me of not guilty of conspiracy on the basis of the defense's freedom-of-the-press First Amendment right. As noted in the previous chapter, government harassment of me neither began with the draft issue nor ended with the jury's verdict. Documents retrieved by me under the Freedom of Information Act merely confirm earlier rumors about the persistence and extent of the government vendetta, but they are nonetheless shocking and astounding for another reason. In any subjugated society, it is totally inappropriate and undignified for victims to greet eviction with such honeyed words as *happily, gladly, willingly, cheerfully,* and *welcome,* which tumbled unrestrainedly from the lips of JACL leaders such as Mike Masaoka, Jimmie Sakamoto, Hito Okada,[60] and Tokie Slocum in a litany of racial betrayal. In a democracy such as that in which we live, these words besmirch the pride and dignity of free people. This dishonored mantle was redeemed in some measure by the resistance. Meekness had in the past brought only harsher treatment, cumulative violations of rights, and demands for servility. It was a case of now or never for Japanese Americans to take a resolute stand under their constitutional principles.

The government that had denied Japanese Americans their rights was now demanding that they offer their lives to the nation without any correlative rescinding of restrictions, no offer of freedom for their loved ones, and no release from barbed-wire confinement. The JACL viewed the entire resistance episode in negative fashion as damaging to their public image and insisted that Nisei must prove entitlement to constitutional rights by the privilege of being Americans through shedding their blood on the field of battle. By the terms of the Constitution, it is not required to prove anything. The JACL was prostituting its own version and not what is contained in the Bill of Rights. The right to be an American was conferred at birth and for noncitizens by naturalization. The theory that a birthright is a privilege that can be given or taken away at the pleasure of a government is an inept reading of the Constitution and a JACL dogma. Birthright is a vested right that no arbitrary power is empowered to alter. What the Heart Mountain Fair Play Committee draft resisters asked for were the fundamental rights to which they, their brethren, and their kinfolk were entitled.

The ideology of the JACL that Nisei Americans must first shed their blood before being entitled to the fruits of democracy is in fact one altogether without foundation. It is an arcane, totalitarian concept of conquerors. Under this false belief that the destiny of Japanese Americans teetered in the balance, many thousands of Nisei Americans marched into battle bearing the banner of JACL patriotism. There is no intent here to denigrate the heroism of the Nisei soldiers or to question their long-lasting contribution of patriotism. But not even for all their gallantry did they demonstrate fidelity to the Constitution. That honor went to those in the resistance who fought so bravely to uphold their fundamental precepts. There is a difference between fidelity and patriotism in the context of the Nisei dilemma. Although the resisters were compelled to pay an enormous price—nothing worthwhile, of course, comes cheaply—they preserved their own individual dignity and the dignity of their ethnic people. Blind patriotism of the JACL had nothing to do with our right to live in America, a right guaranteed by the Constitution.

Thousands of Nisei soldiers became infected with the JACL-promulgated disease that those in the resistance were either disloyal or less than courageous, or both, and hence to be despised. This is the saddest of all chapters of brave men whose battle training somehow lacked sensitivity, tolerance, understanding, and compassion. They felt that marching out of the barbed-wire imprisonment, leaving their family and community behind to be guarded by shotgun-toting sentinels, was the most gallant of all acts, and they convinced themselves that the destiny of Japanese Americans is owed to them alone above all others. No greater fallacy can hard-nosed JACL-ites and the fanatic Nisei soldiers revel in. Testifying in the Cheyenne, Wyoming, June 1944 mass trial of the sixty-three Heart Mountain draft resisters,[61] Henry L. McMillen, a special agent of the FBI, stated that not a single resister had indicated any unwillingness to serve the country in combat upon return of their constitutional rights and the release of their kinfolk and brethren.[62]

The support given the Fair Play Committee by the *Rocky Shimpo* was on the single basic issue of clarification of citizenship status through restoration of constitutional rights as a prelude to military service. This position drew ever-increasing criticism from various government agencies, the administration-controlled *Heart Mountain Sentinel,* and arch enemy the *Pacific Citizen,*[63] a house organ of the Japanese American Citizens League. Both the *Sentinel* and the *Pacific Citizen* and JACL president Saburo Kido, in his in-house publication, *JACL Reporter,*[64] placed the blame for camp resistance sharply on our doorstep.

The editorial wizard of the *Pacific Citizen*, Lawrence Tajiri, reached the height of absurdity with his editorial blast, "The Bitter Harvest," against the Heart Mountain Fair Play Committee.[xx] Tajiri's loyalty to the JACL leadership knew no bounds, which seems somewhat surprising since we had been close associates in Los Angeles and San Francisco before the war. Tajiri inveighed against the *Rocky Shimpo* as follows: "It must bear heavy responsibility for the fact that twelve, and possibly thirty, Japanese Americans at Heart Mountain Center face prison terms for the violation of Selective Service regulations." Tajiri then chides the *Rocky Shimpo*:

"The English section of the *Rocky Shimpo* has editorially supported an attitude which would make a bargain-counter of loyalty, and it has magnified the protests of a small minority out of all proportion to their worth and influence."

This editorial of Tajiri's is laced with totally false assumptions. He states that the number taking similar steps in other camps was considerably smaller, but of course this was not true, as Poston came in with 112 resisters.

---

xx [Ed. See Larry Tajiri, "Bitter Harvest," *Pacific Citizen*, April 8, 1944.]

He also declares that there "is no report that any Japanese American, residing outside the relocation camps . . . has refused." There were three in Fort Lupton, Colorado, alone, and nineteen in all, according to WRA figures. Tajiri then goes on to call to task the Spanish Consul at San Francisco[65] for what he terms "unwarranted intrusion." Thereafter follows his condemnation of the *Rocky Shimpo*, the last sentence of which is gobbledygook.

> Similarly, the editorial attitude of the Denver newspaper, the *Rocky Shimpo*, has been such as to encourage the step toward sedition. It is tragic coincidence that Heart Mountain and the Granada camp in Colorado, which has had the next largest number of draft resisters [*sic*: Granada was fourth in the list of draft resisters], are the two camps which lie in the eastern intermountain area served by the *Rocky Shimpo*. The English section of the *Rocky Shimpo* has failed its editorial responsibility to serve the very great majority of the Japanese Americans whose loyalty today is above question.

Much of the Tajiri statement is pure malarkey. The *Rocky Shimpo* had strong subscriber interest in all of the ten relocation centers, not merely in the nearby projects of Heart Mountain and Amache. Nor is it true that the loyalty of the great majority of Japanese Americans were "above question" in the war year of 1944. Tajiri was dispensing nonconfirmable rhetoric, not facts, to bolster the JACL position. It makes me wonder now if much of what Tajiri wrote before the war might not require reexamination, or whether his credibility suffered only by his association with the JACL.

The trial of the sixty-three Heart Mountain draft resisters was far from being the insignificant event portrayed by Tajiri. It went into the legal history of Wyoming superseding the famous Teapot Dome Scandal as the state's biggest mass trial. The trial drew the attention of a leading Cheyenne newspaper, the *Wyoming Eagle*,[66] which in a front-page editorial made this observation:

> At issue in the case are the civil liberties of citizens as guaranteed by the federal constitution and the degree to which these civil liberties may temporarily be abrogated by a government at war.
>
> Probably no federal court has been called upon to hear a more "vital" case or one in which the issues are more momentous than the case now being heard. . . . The legal fraternity throughout the nation and statesmen will have their ears attuned to the proceedings.[xxi]

---

xxi "Civil Rights," *Wyoming Eagle* editorial, June 13, 1944.

Nor did former Supreme Court Justice and Truman Amnesty Board chair Owen J. Roberts[67] consider the case and its significance as miniscule. When pardoning 282 Nisei, 263 of whom had been incarcerated in government camps, Justice Roberts described the resisters as a "small but not insignificant" group.[68] In Japanese America, the resistance was not an insignificant event either, although strong efforts have been brought by ethnic image builders to bash this group and thus elevate the Nisei soldiers as the correct and only appropriate response in the Nisei dilemma.

Close scrutiny of archival records would indicate that the Citizens League and its adherents focused their attacks on the *Rocky Shimpo* editor rather than on the activities of the Heart Mountain Fair Play Committee. In all of the mudslinging engaged in by the *Pacific Citizen* and the *Heart Mountain Sentinel*, the restrictive nature of the *Rocky Shimpo* editorial support for the Fair Play Committee seemingly was lost in the public debate. No blanket support to the committee was offered. Then too throughout this ordeal, both the *Pacific Citizen* and the *Sentinel*, its WRA ally, insisted that no issue existed. It was obvious that a substantial issue did exist relevant to the reinstitution of the draft. Certainly, every camp felt impelled to forward petitions to Washington, thereby raising a multitude of questions. From the hindsight of history, an FPC leader now muses that refusal to submit to preinduction physicals was a mistake,[69] but without that stand having been taken, the FPC would not be what it is today in a historical sense—a revolt against a patronizing government over rights fundamentally conferred by the Constitution.

The militant stand of the FPC had great appeal as Nisei activism. After opposing eviction from the Pacific Coast in February 1942 before the Tolan Committee in San Francisco, I had attempted to institute suit against the government for massive violations of constitutional liberties.[70] In what looked like total ethnic submission to injustice, this "Last Organized Resistance" of the FPC, as described by playwright Frank Chin, was a shining light in a dismal world.[71] The merits of this resistance deserve the consideration of Japanese America, for in its own fashion it exemplified the spirit of the many thousands being strangled under the yoke of impudent governments.

The Wyoming grand jury indictment against the *Rocky Shimpo* targeted several instances of alleged editorial improprieties. Anti–*Rocky Shimpo* advocates took delight in thus castigating its editor. What such publications did not reveal to the public was the government's withdrawal of the charges prior to its prosecution in the conspiracy trial. The editor of the *Rocky Shimpo* was personally informed by Special Agent Robert G. Lawrence[72] of the withdrawal of the charges, following an FBI investigation that uncovered the source of the information.[73]

One such charge zoomed in on a *Rocky Shimpo* headline, "Wyoming Draft Resistance Has Authorities Stumped," of March 10, 1944. This was branded as "Misleading Article in *Rocky Shimpo*," by Saburo Kido in his "Timely Topics" column of the *Pacific Citizen*. He considered the report "reprehensible" journalism and declared:

> Merely because a person who does not report for induction is not yanked out of the relocation center immediately and placed in jail does not necessarily mean that the authorities are stumped. . . . This type of news reporting of draft dodging by the *Rocky Shimpo* is a reprehensible thing. . . . He [Jimmie Omura] should know better than to state that the authorities were stumped.[xxii]

Mr. Kido should have stuck to his legal knitting instead of passing judgment on the ethics of journalism. Government bureaucrats were lending a strong ear to the expressions of the national JACL president. The Office of Alien Property Custodian, a supervisory regulator of the *Rocky Shimpo*, assigned a Denver lawyer named Edward V. Dunklee[74] to make an objective assessment of the editorial "Let Us Not Be Rash" and two news articles, "Wyoming Draft Resistance Has Authorities Stumped" and "Camp Disturbance Pending." Following that examination, it was stated, "Mr. Dunklee concludes he sees no objections to any of these articles."[xxiii]

This conclusion did not satisfy the Office of Alien Property Custodian in Washington, which was seeking an adverse analysis. Charles J. Hedetniemi, supervisor of the Japanese Publishing Company–*The Rocky Shimpo*,[75] then produced his own analysis, which largely focused on the subject of intent rather than actual statements.[76] Also ignored was the *Rocky Shimpo* policy of offering both sides of the issue: the lead story by lawyer Minoru Yasui, the top billing accorded Roger Baldwin, head of the American Civil Liberties

---

xxii Saburo Kido, "Timely Topics," *Pacific Citizen*, March 25, 1944.
xxiii Analysis of *Rocky Shimpo* articles by Edward V. Dunklee for the Office of Alien Property Custodian. Copy also submitted to Federal Bureau of Investigation. [Ed. The content analysis by Edward V. Dunklee of selected *Rocky Shimpo* issues is incorporated into a letter from Edward V. Dunklee, Attorney, to Hon. Chas. J. Hedetnimi, Alien Property Custodian, April 4, 1944 (OP).]

Union, in rejecting the Heart Mountain Fair Play Committee's request for intervention, and the pro-JACL statement of the head of the Ogden JACL chapter. The *Rocky Shimpo* also invited national JACL president Saburo Kido to offer an objective analysis. Responding to a reader of the *JACL Reporter*, Kido acknowledged receiving the invitation but declared, "I don't want to get down in the mud and wrestle with Omura."

Although the "Stumped" article appeared in the indictment, the prosecution stipulated as to its veracity. United States attorney Carl Sackett[77] made admission of his being confused as to what procedure to follow. He viewed the violators as already in incarceration while confined within the Heart Mountain War Relocation Authority project, and for all practical purposes in jail. The prosecutor acknowledged that it was not until several days later that he reached the decision to take the five resisters out of the center and confine them in county jails to solve his troubling dilemma. It would have been more appropriate for Nisei legal beagles such as JACL's Saburo Kido to have first consulted with Carl Sackett before mounting an attack on the integrity of the *Shimpo* editor.

Not included in the indictment, but a matter drawing considerable publicity, was a request for a retraction demanded by the Heart Mountain Community Council. Considerable fuss was made of the request in the *Pacific Citizen*.[78] The JACL house organ was strangely silent when the *Rocky Shimpo* rejected the request on the basis of documents at hand.[xxiv] In a letter addressed to the chairman of the Heart Mountain Community Council, S. Nakashima, it stated, "I am in possession of documentary reports which inform us that the Community Council dispatched a letter to Washington requesting Mr. [Guy] Robertson's removal."[79] This was the statement requested by Nakashima that the *Rocky Shimpo* retract.

The thought should be kept in mind that draft-age Nisei were confined behind barbed wire, guarded by a detachment of army infantry divisions, and intimidated by armed sentinels stationed in watchtowers. These were the government's "non-aliens" and captives without due process. No charges were ever filed, but they had been stripped of their basic constitutional rights and protection of the Bill of Rights. Was it not appropriate for them to question their clouded citizenship status and to demand restoration of those rights as a prelude to sacrificing their lives on the field of battle? The

xxiv "Omura Turns Down Plea for Retraction," *Rocky Shimpo*, April 19, 1944.

ethnic JACL could only see these wartime resisters as tarnishing the institutional public image it was so vigorously attempting to enhance. To these ethnic traitors, the dissidents were to be condemned as evidence of disloyalty and pro-Axisism. The Citizens League, joined by its satellite *Heart Mountain Sentinel*, did its utmost to demean and to damage the Fair Play Committee resisters and to blacken their names. It was not beyond the illusory use of wording to defame the nonconformists, describing already confined men as ordinary "draft dodgers" and predicting dire consequences for them in postwar America. Through its house organ, the *Pacific Citizen*, it committed irreparable damage in making inaccurate and, in fact, conscious attempts to sully the reputation for integrity of an opposition journalist.

The JACL alone hammered away at the legal analysis of the *Rocky Shimpo* on the matter of wartime resistance. Saburo Kido seemed to imply that only a lawyer-writer like himself could properly express editorial opinions on legal cases. His argument, repeatedly made, that a non-lawyer was advising the Fair Play Committee, ignored completely that the group had retained a Denver lawyer for that purpose. The idea of the JACL was to use the *Rocky Shimpo* as a target, because of the editor's long-standing criticisms of the League. Though it is true that the War Department credited the *Rocky Shimpo* as "the single most influential voice in camp resistance,"[80] it did not regard the publication as an opposition element to the draft. No authority in the government was ever known to have made such a charge. But to the ethnic supporters of wartime government actions, such a terminology was merely incidental and could be employed with abandon. The *Pacific Citizen* made certain that only derogatory materials concerning its nemesis would be fed to its readership.

Moreover, even in the closing decade of the twentieth century the Citizens League continues to insist that its wartime policy was "correct" and has declined to apologize for its role. On August 10, 1988, President Ronald Reagan publicly apologized to the Japanese American public for the Roosevelt era debacle.[81] It is strange, then, that the JACL takes an opposite stand.

It would be a mistake to assume that the Fair Play Committee activities comprised all of the news in the *Rocky Shimpo*. When James Markham was installed as the Office of Alien Property Custodian,[82] he issued a long telegram demanding that the *Rocky Shimpo* reverse its stand and condemn the

Heart Mountain Fair Play Committee. This was, of course, out of the question. The Markham telegram read:

> To an increasing extent you are following a policy with respect to the application of Selective Service to Nisei which could reasonably be construed as indirect incitement to resistance to the draft. This policy is evidently . . . the extremely favorable publicity and support accorded in both your news and editorial columns to the articles of the Fair Play Committee. You are directed to effect an immediate and unequivocal revision of the policy of the *Rocky Shimpo* on this question.[xxv]

The custodian should have been well aware that compliance to his directive would result in the loss of journalistic credibility. Two letters, both unanswered, were addressed to Markham for a moderation of his order.[83] On April 5, 1944, I sent a letter to Supervisor Charles J. Hedetniemi, Office of Alien Property Custodian:

> I am in receipt this morning of a lengthy telegram from a James E. Markham, instructing us to "effect an immediate and unequivocal revision in the policy of the *Rocky Shimpo*" on the question of Selective Service.
>
> It shows a lack of confidence in our prudence under his custodianship and raises a doubt as to our personal loyalty to our government. I would like to say here that my reply to any question of loyalty is my public record dating back to the fall of 1933. I would not hesitate to lay down my record alongside that of any citizens of the United States.
>
> Mr. Markham's order also implies enforced subjection. I somehow resent the thought that I would support the government of the United States only because I have been ordered to do so. I have always supported the theory of democratic government—not once, but many times in the public press.
>
> The general tone and context of Mr. Markham's telegram are so peculiarly coincident with the views expressed by Mr. Saburo Kido, national president of the Japanese American Citizens League, and the views we know Mr. Harold Tarvin, reports officer in the Denver WRA Office, hold.[xxvi]

Markham's order, which was interpreted as bureaucratic oppression, revealed his contempt for any person of Japanese origin. This was an example of a government agency having issued its order and any person of Japanese

---

xxv Part of a two-page telegram from James E. Markham, Office of Alien Property Custodian, to the publisher of the *Rocky Shimpo*, March 30, 1944.

xxvi Jimmie Omura, editor of the *Rocky Shimpo*, to Supervisor Charles J. Hedetniemi, Office of Alien Property Custodian, April 5, 1944.

origin was expected to dutifully obey. Japanese Americans enjoyed rights only at the pleasure of the governing power and not as inherent rights—a throwback to the mid-nineteenth-century treatment of Chinese immigrants.

At this time, the Office of Alien Property Custodian had no solid information on me, although it had made an inquiry as far back as September 16, 1943, to the director of the Federal Bureau of Investigation, shortly after the initiation of my "Know the Facts" column in the *Rocky Nippon* [*sic*].[84] The FBI itself lacked any information.[xxvii] In fact, it was not until mid-April 1944 that Hoover provided additional materials to Lloyd Shaulis, the Alien Property Custodian's secretary.[xxviii] Thus, the JACL influence here seems rather apparent.

Well aware that it was like waving a red flag before a charging bull, the *Rocky Shimpo* issued an editorial, "The Rocky Shimpo Affirms Its Stand," in which I quoted from the paper's position in my first editorial.[85] By implication, the *Rocky Shimpo* rejected the custodian's directive.

Predicated on this support for the FPC, efforts were mounted in various agencies of the government to shut the *Rocky Shimpo* down. Its Japanese-language division had long been considered pro-Japan in tone and now the English editorial section was characterized as an incitement to resistance. Ignored completely was the basic fact that camp resistance had begun prior to any discussion of the topic in the *Rocky Shimpo*. Shutting down the newspaper would not bring a halt to resistance because the core of the problem lay in the eviction of Japanese Americans from the West Coast and subsequent strictures of detention. The real culprit was the Roosevelt administration, and scapegoating a Nisei vernacular publication could not change that equation.

In the vanguard of this attack being fomented against the *Rocky Shimpo* were white proxies allied with the policies of the JACL. They spoke at public forums or wrote denunciatory letters in the hope of affecting the discharge of the *Shimpo* editor without revealing their ties with the JACL organization. In this way, their official position was used to establish an aura of influence to tip the scale to the Citizens League's viewpoint.[xxix] [86]

---

xxvii Lloyd L. Shaulis, secretary of Alien Property Custodian, requests data on James M. Omura from FBI Director J. Edgar Hoover, September 16, 1943. Further data sent to Francis A. Mahoney, Alien Property Custodian, October 23, 1943.

xxviii J. Edgar Hoover, director of Federal Bureau of Investigation, to Lloyd L. Shaulis, April 15, 1944.

xxix A prime example was the two-page letter, April 12, 1944, addressed to Tetsuko Toda, the publisher of the *Rocky Shimpo*, by Utah University professor of anthropology and archeology, which expressed censorious concern over the newspaper's editorial policy in respect to the reinstitution of selective service to Americans of Japanese ancestry.

Markham's nonresponse to my letters was pure arrogance. The eviction from the West Coast had been predicated upon the same principle. To white officialdom, we were just "Japs." And that explained the wartime atmosphere.[xxx] Markham's silence was a studied policy of the Office of Alien Property (OAP) Custodian not to recognize the authority of individuals outside of its immediate control. When I was hired as public relations director for the Japanese Publishing Company, the OAP supervisor, Charles J. Hedetniemi, filed an objection to an outsider handling the company's affairs. In response, the attorney for the newspaper, Edward Dunklee, wrote of the desirability and the necessity for this arrangement. "Mr. Omura is the actual responsible party in charge and fully understands all the conditions under which the paper is operated, and it will be a great deal simpler for all concerned if the communication could be signed by him. . . . Unless there is some reason unknown to us we would appreciate it if this system could be adopted."[xxxi] I was never aware of any further communication on the matter from Washington. However, Hedetniemi thereafter dealt directly with the publisher, Tetsuko Toda, and it was my duty to respond to his letters. This made for an awkward situation but one that the OAP maintained throughout.

Charges that the *Rocky Shimpo* fabricated lurid articles surfaced in Saburo Kido's *Pacific Citizen* column, and these accusations were followed by an editorial bashing in the WRA-controlled *Heart Mountain Sentinel*. A case in point was the previously referenced *Rocky Shimpo* headline of a pending camp-wide strike. "Although no real general strike materialized," states historian Douglas Nelson, "enough workers quit their jobs to alarm [project director] Guy Robertson."[xxxii] This information was supplied by Paul T. Nakadate, then acting chairman of the Fair Play Committee, and was distributed widely to many newspapers other than the *Rocky Shimpo*. On the basis of the distribution, it appeared to me to be legitimate. Although agents of the Denver FBI field office determined that Nakadate was the cul-

---

xxx The *Rocky Shimpo* had no agreement with any group for coverage. Historian Douglas Nelson's statement, in *Heart Mountain*, that "He [*Rocky Shimpo* editor James Omura] quickly agreed to cover the activities of the Fair Play Committee in his paper" (122) is simply literary liberty and without sound basis.

xxxi Edward V. Dunklee, attorney for the Japanese Publishing Company, to Charles J. Hedetniemi, supervisor-in-charge, Office of Alien Enemy Custodian, February 23, 1944.

xxxii The *Rocky Shimpo*, March 20, 1944; Guy Robertson to Dillon Myer, April 1, 1944, WRA Collection, Bancroft Library; Nelson, *Heart Mountain*, 133n56.

prit and absolved the *Rocky Shimpo* of any blame of false reporting or news manufacturing,[xxxiii] the cancellation of the charge was not published in either the JACL organs or the government-controlled *Heart Mountain Sentinel.*

On the morning of April 18, 1944, the publisher of the *Rocky Shimpo*, Tetsuko Toda, received a telephonic ultimatum from Supervisor Hedetniemi threatening to shut down the publication unless I was separated from the newspaper. This matter was brought to my attention, in my capacity as the public relations director of the Japanese Publishing Company, and I volunteered to step down to prevent harm to the newspaper. That evening a farewell dinner for me was conducted at a Larimer Street[87] locale. Most of the Japanese section staff had come and gone by the time I arrived with the publisher. I had never seen any member of the Japanese staff, which was in the back room. I had imbibed a little too much sake and was a bit woozy.

"Do you want me to make out a check as agreed?" the publisher asked.

"Tomorrow morning would be okay," I replied.

It was a big mistake. When later requested, the excuse was that "Hedetniemi has forbidden any payment." The separation pay was never honored. Moreover, the *Rocky Shimpo* subsequently refused to contribute toward my defense fund.

The following morning I came in to the *Shimpo* office to clear out my desk and pick up my final paycheck. Precisely at that moment Hedetniemi appeared and demanded my turning over all correspondence to him, stating that "it was the property of the Japanese Publishing Company." I demurred, as some of it was personal, but to no avail. Hedetniemi promised to return the letters after making copies of those he considered pertinent for taking to Washington, DC. Several days later, I asked through the publisher for the return of the correspondence. These letters were never returned. Unbeknown to me, Hedetniemi had given the publisher a receipt with the instruction that they could be retrieved upon written request. This message was never conveyed to me, and many years afterward, even under the Freedom of Information Act, not all seized letters were returned, on the excuse of inability to locate them. Later Hedetniemi would claim the technicality that no formal request had been made by me.

---

xxxiii FBI interrogation of Editor James Omura, *Rocky Shimpo*, by Special Agent in Charge Robert G. Lawrence, Denver, Colorado, circa April 1944.

On a Friday evening in mid-April 1944, the newspaper had been visited by the JACL's Minoru Yasui, a Nisei lawyer. He was accompanied by Jiro Tani, a café proprietor and occasional interpreter for the Denver courts. *Rocky Shimpo* publisher Tetsuko Toda sat in on this office visit but she and Tani were silent. Yasui complained of the lack of opposition articles in the newspaper and the strong emphasis on activities of the Fair Play Committee. I pointed out to him that our function did not require our seeking out opposition views and that lack of such materials was due to the simple fact that we had received no submission. I assured him that if he cared to write such views, as long as what he submitted was objective, it would receive appropriate editorial consideration. I responded to every question posed by Yasui and he appeared subdued, and by the discussion's conclusion I thought him amenable to our position. I was wrong!

"I'm going to see that you go to prison one way or another," he blurted out unexpectedly at the street door exit.

I was shocked! Yasui's threat remained with me over the weekend and his "one way or another" phraseology seemed to me disturbing. On Monday morning, I confided my suspicion to the publisher.

"I think Min Yasui is an informer," I said.

"I think this could be confirmed by calling the FBI and asking for Min Yasui." The publisher volunteered to make the call, having previous acquaintance with an agent. She then relayed the response.

"Min Yasui hasn't come in yet," the telephone clerk replied. "Try the marshal's office. He usually reports there first. He doesn't come in until a little later."

I dialed the marshal's office and received this information: "Mr. Yasui hasn't come in yet this morning. He is a bit late. Why don't you try the FBI. He sometimes reports there first."

We had the confirmations. The supposed champion of civil rights was an informer. The Min Yasui–Joe Masaoka duo visited the Amache resisters in the Denver County Jail. An Amache resister stated that Yasui attempted to link the editor of the *Rocky Shimpo* to their refusals. The pair also visited Heart Mountain draft resisters in the Wyoming County Jail in Cheyenne and issued an official JACL report to the FBI and the WRA.[88]

These visits had the government's approval and were presumably initiated in an effort to change the resisters' mind. Only seven Fair Play Committee members condescended to be interviewed by the Yasui-Masaoka

investigators. None changed their minds. Because there was so little participation, the report cannot be considered as reliable.

We had now established that Min Yasui's daily routine began at the U.S.
marshal's office, followed by a visit to the FBI. It is believed that his next
stop was to Naval Intelligence, which kept a dossier on me. In the afternoon, Yasui visited the regional director of the War Relocation Authority's
Denver office. It was from this office that Yasui wrote a crocodile letter of
commiseration at the occasion of my dismissal.[89] Yasui was later nominated
as director of the Denver Human Rights Commission by then-mayor Tom
Currigan and served through the Bill McNichols administration until his
defeat by Federico Peña.[90] Yasui was the recipient of the Justice Department's highest civilian award[91] and undoubtedly his "informer" activities
had much to do with it.

The name Minoru Yasui was not unfamiliar as he was the Portland Nisei
attorney who had been reported to have deliberately violated the wartime
curfew presumably to test its constitutionality. The arrest report stated he
went around Portland asking to be arrested. This action appeared uncom-
monly strange to a publisher such as I was then. I had no quarrel with his
asserted objective, merely his method. Although Yasui was apparently a person of some importance in Portland, his name was unknown in California
circles. He was confined in the Multnomah County Jail and it was during this confinement that this Portland–Hood River Nisei contacted me.
Whether because of his isolation and having nothing to do, Yasui sent me
this hostile letter:

> It is well-nigh libelous to assume that your [Pacific Coast Evacuee Place-
> ment] Bureau is engaged in this work singlehandedly. . . . I refer in par-
> ticular to the statement . . . "They represent the only people of Japanese
> extraction to demand equal consideration and treatment as citizens of the
> United States and to fight for their rights." I wonder if you have heard of
> Mary Asaba Ventura of Seattle?[xxxiv]

No response to this letter was sent by me to Yasui, considering his remarks as unbecoming an asserted champion of civil rights. Mary Ventura
was the first Nisei to file an antieviction case, which the court rejected as
premature. Her work among Seattle people was in connection with an

---

xxxiv Letter from Minoru Yasui, November 19, 1942, Multnomah County Jail, Portland, Oregon, to
James Omura, Denver, Colorado. [Ed. Only the first page of this letter is archived in OP.]

organization [ACLU].[92] The [Pacific Coast Evacuee] Placement Bureau in Denver was independent of all ties and supported financially only by its director. This was the first intimation that Yasui's curfew violation might not be what it appeared to be.

Yasui was tried before Judge Alger Fee of the Multnomah County District Court.[93] Not only was Yasui convicted of curfew violation but his American citizenship was ruled invalid by the presiding judge due to his being an agent for Imperial Japan. Yasui had served in a propaganda fashion in the Japanese Consulate in Chicago. The Supreme Court restored his citizenship but upheld the curfew conviction. Under the coram nobis procedure, Yasui's conviction was nullified, but a further appeal for clarification became moot in 1986 upon his death from cancer.

It was in the mid-1980s that I ran across a DIO (district intelligence officer) inquiry of Yasui stating that had he been General DeWitt, he would have evicted the Japanese from the West Coast in the same fashion as him.[94] I brought this memo up before a prominent Sansei attorney aligned in the Yasui case, and upon reading up in Yasui's Portland trial record, he disassociated himself from the case.[xxxv][95] Yasui also indicated his regret for his violation of the curfew within forty-eight hours of his arrest to two FBI agents, both fellow law students at the University of Oregon. His statement to that effect also appears in the trial record of Minoru Yasui.[96]

Yasui was a man of complex character and impressed the coram nobis expert, Peter Irons, as such. He is regarded by his critics as a simple opportunist. The transcript of his Portland trial discredits his self-proclaimed civil rights status. Yasui spent nine months in the Multnomah County Jail and was released to the Minidoka Relocation Center at Hunt, Idaho. From that point on, he functioned as a government stooge and took a strong stand against Nisei refusing military service. He was later relocated to Chicago and subsequently established himself in the Mile High City of Denver, just about the time selective service had become a hot topic at Heart Mountain and various other camps. His sister, Michi Yasui Ando, and his brother-in-law, John Ando, also an attorney, had relocated to Denver during the so-called voluntary evacuation period.[97] There might be some who would claim Minoru Yasui was talked into becoming an "informer or *inu*" in order to rid himself of his tarnished reputation as a propagandist for a foreign nation. He was

---

xxxv Dale Minami was the lead attorney in the Yasui Case.

extremely hard on the wartime resisters and upon those who supported their endeavors, which seems totally out of place for an advocate of civil rights.

Mr. Yasui wrote his invited article and it was published as a lead story in the *Rocky Shimpo*.[98]

On the twentieth day of July 1944, I arose at 4:30 a.m. with the notion of getting an early start on the gardening route, and to enjoy an extended weekend to take our show dog[99] for a run in a mountain meadow, and to rest. One thing was certain, it would be hot again. The sun had beaten down relentlessly since the coming of summer. I had felt the need to recharge my battery from this intense heat wave. Breakfast dishes had been cleared, the dog fed, and as I picked up the dish to give the dog water, a surprise knock came at the cabin door. It was still dark outside and I wondered who would be knocking at the ungodly hour. The man at the door identified himself as an FBI agent. I could barely make out the shadowy figures of three other men behind him.

"James Omura?" the man asked.

"Yes," I said.

"We're FBI agents and United States marshals. You're under arrest."

He then held out a sheet of paper before him and someone behind him held a flashlight so he could read. While the agent read the opening indictment, the Doberman Pinscher nudged forward against my right leg and I lightly grasped the collar to restrain him.

The count on which I was charged, along with the leaders of the Fair Play Committee, was conspiracy to aid and abet violation of the Selective Service laws. The action was brought by the United States attorney in Cheyenne in a secret indictment issued by the grand jurors of Wyoming on the tenth of May. The actual case got under way on October 23, 1944, in a federal district court in Cheyenne, Wyoming.[100] Coincidentally, American troops were advancing upon the homeland of Japan, following a death blow administered to the Imperial fleet in June 1942 at Midway.

"Can I give the dog water and chain him up outside?" I asked, and the agent assented.

The two marshals and an agent disappeared out of sight. The lead FBI agent entered the house and began a search of the boxes, taking a slender bundle of documents. (Later I was provided with a list of materials removed from my home.) As I locked the door, I noticed that the next-door neighbor's kitchen light was on and I was given permission to have her provide water for the Doberman. It was going to be a hot day. As I crossed over to Mrs. Severson's house I spied a second FBI agent guarding the back of the house.

Though I had resigned as English editor the evening of April 18 (not, as generally stated, on the nineteenth), it was not considered enough by Tom C. Clark, assistant attorney general. My voice had to be discredited. Conviction was a sure method of discrediting me. It was what the Japanese American Citizens League had been clamoring about. The government bureaucrats were strongly influenced by what appeared in the *Pacific Citizen* and took their lead thereby.

I was driven to the United States marshal's building by the two FBI agents, fingerprinted, and confined in a freestanding cage on the top floor. There were cages lined in a circular fashion around the north and east walls. There were two freestanding cells and I was held in the closest to the entrance. I asked to use a phone but was refused. Each time the deputy marshal came around I repeated the request. Forty-five minutes after being caged, a *Denver Post* reporter showed up. He was a short, slender person and wore a disconcerting smirk on his face. He walked slowly around the cage, watching and sizing me up.

"So, you're a fifth columnist," he inquired.

"I'm not guilty of the charge," I responded.

"That's what they all say," he retorted. I didn't like this reporter. He was back a half hour later. "I'd like to take a picture of you," he said.

"Not in this condition," I stated, not having shaved.

"You people are all alike," he asserted, taking his leave.

Here was a reporter with a closed, racist mind. In fact, the newspaper he worked for was also bigoted. The *Denver Post* was a carbon copy of the Hearst "yellow journalism" of California.[101]

At 1:30 p.m., a deputy marshal escorted me to the City and County Building in Denver, where I was motioned to take a seat halfway down the courtroom. The courtroom was split in half with bright sunlight in the back and the front half in gloom. Barely discernible was a figure of a man on the bench. I could make him out by the white shirt he wore. He was leaning to his left, conversing with some people below him. They were visible only briefly when someone opened the rear door to exit.

"Mr. Omura, do you understand what you are charged with?" the judge asked.

"Yes," I replied.

"How do you plead?" he asked.

"Not guilty of the charge," I answered.

More discussions were held at the bench. I was then led out by the deputy marshal. "There's a bank of telephones to the right near the entrance," he said. "You can make your phone call now."

I made my call to Caryl at the Button's residence, where she was employed. I informed her of the situation and asked her to call our lawyer, Sidney Jacobs,[102] and see to the dog. I was returned to confinement.

Twenty minutes later I was taken out again, placed in a car, and whisked from Denver to Cheyenne, Wyoming, by a marshal and a deputy. We stopped only once, on my request to relieve myself, at a small cluster of buildings that included a general store. The deputy accompanied me to a rear privy but wouldn't allow me to close the door. It was 5:15 p.m. when we arrived at the Laramie County Jail in Cheyenne. There I was rudely received and cussed at by a deputy and placed in East Row among a group of about a dozen inmates. I was taken out less than five minutes later and placed in solitary confinement upstairs within a vacant woman's quarter. The windows were screened off with metal grills and plastic strips with about one inch of space between them. Toward the top of the windows, however, the strips were separated by up to a foot. This allowed for a restricted view of the sky. The room contained a bed and a commode in a far north corner; a basin and a pitcher of water but no towel; and a bureau from which the mirror had been removed. The entry was a metal grill with a foot-square opening eighteen inches from the floor for passage of food and so on. I made requests for shaving articles, pencil and pad, and reading materials, but all were denied. "The only thing we can let you have are cigarettes," I was told. The hours were long and boring.

The indictment stated,

The Grand Jurors for the United States of America, selected, empaneled, sworn and charged in the District Court of the United States for the District of Wyoming, at the May Term of said court in the year 1944, on their oaths and affirmations respectively do present.

It then charged that I had

unlawfully, willfully, and knowingly combined, conspired, confederated, and agreed together [with leaders of the Fair Play Committee and] divers other persons . . . to evade the requirements of the Selective Training and Service Act of 1940 and the rules, regulations and directions made pursuant thereto and to counsel, aid and abet . . . other citizens of the United States of Japanese descent who had registered . . . to evade service in the land or naval forces of the United States.

On the fifth day, I was standing by the window and caught a glimpse of five Nisei being escorted into the jail. I reasoned that these must be the leaders of the Fair Play Committee. That assessment was confirmed the next afternoon when a jailer slipped me a cigarette and a couple of bars of candies. "The boys downstairs asked whether you were here," he said. "They sent these up for you."

Caryl came up to see me on the ninth day and I was taken out to the office anteroom for the conference. I was informed by her that Sidney Jacobs had been retained and that the family Studebaker was sold for six hundred dollars, which I thought was a trifle low, to make the down payment. Before her departure and unbeknownst to me, Caryl went out and bought a new razor set and some magazines that I was never to see.[103]

Mr. Jacobs came to see me on the fifteenth day, on Friday, August 3. He was very brief and seemed to be in an awful rush to get back to Denver. He remarked that he had retained L. C. Sampson, a secretary of the Wyoming Bar Association, as a stand-in attorney at fifty dollars per day.[104] He stated that he had agreed with Caryl to take my case for one thousand dollars and promised to work hard on it. My opinion was not asked. He emphasized that the important thing was for me to get out on bail to help him with the case. He sloughed off my complaints regarding solitary confinement. "Take it up with Mr. Sampson when he comes to see you Monday," he said.[105]

I couldn't believe it. His somewhat cavalier attitude shocked me. Here I had been in solitary for fifteen days. I had gone along with Sidney Jacobs, a civil lawyer, because of my conviction that the government did not have a case. The Fair Play Committee had hired Abraham Lincoln Wirin, an ACLU attorney in Los Angeles who also doubled as attorney for the JACL.[106] Caryl had rejected an offer for inclusion from the Fair Play Committee in order to maintain independence.[107]

Mr. Sampson was outraged to hear of the treatment accorded me when he arrived Monday morning. He immediately lodged a complaint with the sheriff. This prompted a deputy sheriff to provide a used safety razor, a small mirror, and other shaving paraphernalia. The sheriff's excuse was that I was being held in solitary to protect me from the other Japanese prisoners. I was transferred to the East Row with leaders of the Fair Play Committee the next afternoon, nineteen days after being in solitary. The reading and writing materials were furnished by Mr. Sampson himself. I was greeted with enthusiasm by the five FPC leaders and taken in tow by Paul Nakadate. I wanted to interview Kiyoshi Okamoto, the leader, who had a cell at the other end.

I found that Okamoto was not as young as his compatriots. He was in his fifties. He wore eyeglasses, was dark-complexioned, small, thin, and favored graying whiskers. Okamoto had been lying down on his bunk but got up at my approach. "I was the first to demand rectification of this injustice!" were his first words.

I was shocked. I had been led to believe by Paul Nakadate in his letter that Okamoto didn't care about glory,[108] and here was a prime example of a man fishing for credit. "No, I don't believe that's true," I replied. "There are others who predated you. I was one!"

My comeback didn't set well with Okamoto. He seemed to have bristled at being contradicted. Without a word, Okamoto curled up in his bunk and clammed up, signifying that the interview was over. He was to continue this stance even after our transfer to the Albany County Jail in Laramie. I would not consider him a good companion in captivity. Nor did he impress me as a leader. He was withdrawn and uncooperative. When a request came from Wirin to bail a leader out, he shouted, "Count me out!" When Mr. [Katsusaburo] Kawahara, a wealthy San Jose, California, farmer,[109] asked for opinions of the type of Japanese food we would like him to send in, Okamoto promptly declared, "Don't consider me!" He reminded me of a spoiled child. I was informed by Paul Nakadate that Okamoto had not expected to be indicted and was attempting to divorce himself from the rest.[110] Paul himself appeared to be somewhat detached from his cohorts. It was apparent that personality conflicts abounded, but on the issues of restoration of constitutional rights and clarification of their citizenship status, they were as one.

Caryl initiated a defense fund among Larimer Street merchants and through letters to contacts in my file.[111] The former efforts proved especially futile as merchants avoided her on the streets by jaywalking to the opposite side upon her approach. One merchant tossed her an envelope containing five dollars and showed her the door with a request not to return. An Issei launderer of long standing and, previously, a staunch supporter asked her to take her business elsewhere. One young solicitor was gang-beaten in an alley and another was warned by a JACL leader not to make his rounds in the agricultural area because of the possibility of bodily harm. Since responses to letter solicitations were also negative, the defense fund collapsed.

Three major factors seemed to have resulted in turning the Japanese community against the defense fund. The first was the visit by national JACL president Saburo Kido to the office of the *Rocky Shimpo* and the rumor that he spread about my having done irreparable harm to the U.S. Japanese by testifying before the Tolan Committee in San Francisco.[xxxvi] The second was the charge that I had drawn excessive public attention to the Japanese community of Denver, which preferred to bury its head in the sand until the war blew over.[xxxvii] The third reason, which was not uncovered until the early 1980s, was a transcription of an article in Japanese in the *Colorado Times* that urged Issei not to contribute to a "draft dodger."[xxxviii] The attitude of the Japanese community in Denver is perhaps best illustrated by an Issei woman, a prewar resident of Walnut Grove, California, who in 1948 advised me not to do any more for the Japanese people because they did not appreciate the efforts. "I talked to many Issei people," she said, "and they all didn't want you to do anything anymore."[xxxix]

Wyoming stand-in attorney L. C. Sampson had succeeded in lowering my bail from $5,000 to $1,500. When I appeared before the U.S. commissioner in Cheyenne, he said to me: "I've read your case. If I were determining your case, I'd throw it out of court."[112] It was a big lift to hear this. When the case was over, I wrote and thanked him. Sampson came often to consult, and once when we were in the outer office, we heard people up on the roof and noticed a canister-type object lowered by a pole near the windows. "They're eavesdropping," Mr. Sampson said. "When you see that thing, talk in low whispers." The information was passed on. Eavesdropping was conducted at regular intervals.

Caryl's next trip to Cheyenne was August 11, the twenty-third day of my arrest. She reported that Rex, our Doberman Pinscher show dog, had been sold to Evergreen Fox Farm due to her inability to take care of him. She was selling anything of value to raise bond money and attorney's fees.[113] We did not have a great deal of money because I went broke the year before while

xxxvi Report of (?) Hikida to James M. Omura, circa October 1944, Denver, Colorado.

xxxvii Interview of George Matsumonji of Mission, Texas, by James Omura at Matsumonji's Denver, Colorado, home, August 16, 1985.

xxxviii War Relocation Authority transcription, Bancroft Library, Berkeley, California.

xxxix Mrs. Ioka, formerly of Walnut Grove, California, to James M. Omura, Denver, Colorado, circa 1948. [Ed. This letter is not included within the correspondence files of OP.]

running the free Placement Bureau. With the defense fund's demise, she had obtained a second job with Safeway Bakery in North Denver to raise the bond fee.

I was visited by Mr. Sampson three mornings per week and told not to send letters out through the usual channel as they were being opened and read. We were allowed one letter per week but all my letters were smuggled out by Mr. Sampson or Caryl.

On Caryl's second trip I told her about the mediocre food served and the lack of reading materials and urged her to write to the director of the Bureau of Prisons, James V. Bennett.[114] An inspector was dispatched on this first complaint and I noticed the inspector go into the sheriff's office and depart without visiting the cell blocks. Bennett wrote Caryl that the reason for prohibiting reading materials was because the inmates insisted on burning newspapers to heat their coffee.[115] I told Caryl that this rationale was a farce as we were never allowed to make coffee in the cells. I also told her to write Bennett about his inspector's faulty inspection. In the meantime, we were warned by a deputy that if we continued to complain, we would be placed on "bread and water."

Jacobs was insistent that I be bonded out to prepare the case. None of the bonding companies in Denver would touch a draft case. Caryl responded to Bennett's letter, citing me as the authority, and it led to his sending a second investigator, which resulted in some improvements. Shortly thereafter, Sheriff [Norbert] Tuck transferred to the Highway Patrol.[116] Kiyoshi Okamoto also filed a complaint through his attorney, A. L. Wirin, who communicated with Attorney General Francis Biddle. Wirin never received a reply but told Okamoto that the transfer of four people, which included Okamoto, myself, and two resisters, to Albany County Jail in Laramie, Wyoming, was the result of his representation. Okamoto informed the two resisters that the move was engineered by him. I kept my own counsel for the sake of peace and tranquility. The transfer occurred on September 13, 1944.

We had the northernmost half of the floor, overlooking the treetops of Wyoming's interminable evergreen forest. There was plenty of room to stretch our legs and a long table for mess, topped with magazines and newspapers. In addition, a local Issei restaurant operator graciously provided Japanese cuisine to appease our appetites. However our confinement there lasted only ten days, and on September 23 we were bonded out by Frank Cooper of the Arizona Bail Bond Agency of Phoenix.[117]

Wirin, who had been handling the Poston resistance as well,[118] agreed to an arrangement with Cooper to bail out the Fair Play Committee leaders on a 10 percent premium bond. Prior to my being bonded out of the Albany County Jail, Frank Emi had been bonded out, with Wirin volunteering to await payment of Emi's fees until he could pay. Issei in Heart Mountain were reluctant to give additional contributions. Later Guntaro Kubota was also bonded out by his friends.

I returned to Denver in the company of Frank Cooper. We visited the United States Fidelity and Guaranty office and were rudely met by its manager, Mr. David [?] Jacobs. He made his antipathy obvious to any draft cases involving Japanese. He virtually tossed us out of his office. We next went to the Colorado Council of Churches to see the Reverend [Clark P.] Garman.[119] It surprised me to see a hundred Nisei girls sitting at typewriters. The minister was out but the Nisei girl in charge repeatedly urged us to leave to avoid physical violence. It was shocking that a minister of the cloth would entertain such an attitude. Cooper chose to leave.

When Cooper returned to Phoenix, he was called to the regional office in Los Angeles on a complaint lodged by Mr. Jacobs regarding the infringement upon his territory. He was forbidden to write any new bonds in the Colorado-Wyoming district. It was learned through the American Civil Liberties Union that a Connecticut firm would furnish bonding at 3 or 4 percent. After the conviction of the FPC leaders in the lower court this information was passed through to Paul Nakadate, but he was advised that they desired to serve out their sentences while on appeal. I did not agree with this decision and concluded that they had given up any hope of overturning the conviction.

Immediately after my release on bond, I met briefly with my attorney, Sidney Jacobs, in his office. He requested that I not bother him for two weeks in order to clear his desk of pending cases. In the meantime I was to write a summary for him. The summary was written. Caryl had received no such admonition from Jacobs so had dropped in on him unannounced on several occasions. On her first visit, she found Jacobs in conference with Sylvia Toshiyuki, and on her second visit, with Kiyoshi Okamoto. I was told through her that both of these people were trying to help my case. Caryl also stated that Jacobs was attending the treason trial of three Nisei sisters in order to study the defense strategy.[120]

Kiyoshi Okamoto ambled by while I was waiting for Caryl at the former Pacific Coast Evacuee Placement Bureau building at Nineteenth and Curtis streets. He assured me that he was conferring with Jacobs to help my case. In that conversation I told Okamoto to forget the others and concentrate on his own case. I would later rue that advice for it would come back to haunt me. While confined in jail, Okamoto had separated himself from the other leaders and isolated himself. But it appears that he was responsible for what later developed in the lobby of the Windsor Hotel in Cheyenne and at the FPC meeting the afternoon before.

On Friday evening, October 20, my attorneys viewed the letters seized by the Office of Alien Property Custodian at the United States attorney's office. I had to sign some papers on the prosecutor's desk. "Jimmie made a mistake," Sackett said. "He needs someone to look after him so he doesn't get into trouble." I didn't pay any attention to what he said since he was the prosecutor. But I believe Sackett's words made a strong impression upon Caryl, to whom he was speaking, for later developments seemed to bear this out.

After looking over the seized letters, we headed for Sampson's office. We were just approaching an intersection and I was remarking about a phase of the case.

"You've been keeping things from me," Jacobs angrily accused. He was furious and his face was red with rage.

"No, I haven't," I declared. "It was in the summary I made for you."

"In the editorials you wrote, you could have been clearer," he retorted.

"What do you mean?" I asked.

"You could have condemned draft resisting," he said. I couldn't believe what I was hearing. He was acting like a prosecutor. "You knew there was no alternative except to violate the law," he continued with visible anger in his face and tone.

"That's not true," I responded.

"What other way is there?" he demanded.

"Petition for a declaratory judgment,"[121] I replied.

"That won't work!" he said.

"It would work," interjected Sampson, who had listened in silence. "I found an authority on it. It's an obscure Oklahoma law. It's among the laws that I looked up."[122]

Jacobs settled down after Sampson's statement. I welcomed this support for I was aware that my attorney was berating me. When we arrived at Sampson's office, his desk and the secretary's desk were covered with open law books. Jacobs went to the main desk and stood reading standing up.

"Looks like I've got the night cut out for me," he remarked.

"The office is yours," Sampson said. "Just turn off the light and lock the door when you leave." Then turning to me, he said: "Let's leave Mr. Jacobs to his study. I'm going home to bed." We parted at the intersection, Sampson going east and I straight south to the Windsor Hotel.

The next afternoon, which was Saturday, I was informed by Paul Nakadate of a meeting being held by the Fair Play Committee and he urged me to attend it with him. Paul went in first and faded quickly to the right back. I was so surprised to see a sizable audience that I stopped in front of the group. I glanced back at the clicking of the closing door and saw Wirin sitting before a desk facing the group. He was in semidarkness. A large number of people were sitting on the floor cross-legged and I spotted Mr. [?] Doi, an Issei lawyer,[123] perched on the arm of a sofa chair in which sat an aged Issei.

As I met Frank Emi's glance, he spoke up. "Okay, Tom," he said. Tom Kawahara[124] stood up.

"Let's go, Jim, follow me," he said.

I followed Tom out another door to the street. At the corner, he turned right and at the next intersection turned left and down the opposite street. At the next intersection, I said, "Guess I'll go to the hotel." During the walk-around, Tom hadn't said a word. I wondered at the reason for this strange behavior. It was clear the walk-around had been premeditated.

Paul later stopped by and stated that Jacobs was at the meeting.

"What did he say?" I asked.

"He wanted to know if you were a member of the Fair Play Committee," Paul said. "Of course he prefaced his question with, 'I believe Jimmie is telling the truth to me but I wanted to know in my own mind.'" I just thought to myself that if he really believed me he wouldn't have asked the question in the first place.

Late Sunday afternoon, Paul came around to tell me that the group was going to have a last dinner. I argued that after what happened the afternoon before, I was in no mood to go along.

"Forget about that," said Paul, a very insistent speaker. "This is the last time we'll be together and it'll be our 'Last Supper.'"

Paul and his wife, Alice,[125] had a room on the upper floor. They were the only Fair Play Committee people staying at the Windsor Hotel. Caryl and I led the procession down to the lobby. As I approached, Sam Horino, one of the FPC leaders,[126] blurted out, "You're a spy!"

"You spy!" intoned Guntaro Kubota[127] at Horino's shoulder. I was non-plussed. I looked around and saw Frank Emi at the cashier's window. He appeared to be writing a check. He looked up toward the Horino-Kubota duo and then caught my eye. I heard him say softly, "Yeh."

It was then that Paul came to my defense. The instant he finished, the voice of Okamoto rose also in defense. Okamoto was out of sight, shielded by a planter. There was no mistaking his views and he cleared the awkward situation. Caryl and I retired toward the stairs. I had lost my appetite. Again Paul talked me into attending the dinner. We sort of dillydallied and were the last to reach the restaurant.

Caryl ordered a hamburger sandwich. "We come to a high-toned restaurant like this and she orders a hamburger sandwich," Frank Emi shouted to loud, embarrassing guffaws. I ordered the standard T-bone steak, although I had no appetite, simply to avoid another scene. I did not eat the steak and piddled with my dinner. On our way back to the hotel, I declared we had better go it alone and forget the FPC.

It was devastating, first abandoned by the Denver Japanese community and now an apparent outcast of the Fair Play Committee. This trial was taking a lot out of me as to my faith in the Nisei generation.

The trial got under way the next morning at ten o'clock. Sampson sat beside me throughout. On the third day, Jacobs remarked: "Why is Sampson hanging around? He isn't being paid to." I gave no answer but I think Sampson stood by me for moral support. He pointed out the weaknesses and the strong points in the testimonies.

The seven Fair Play Committee leaders were tried first. Then it was my turn. The prosecutor was Assistant U.S. Attorney John Pickett.[128] He attempted to tie me into the FPC conspiracy by using implications in my *Rocky Shimpo* editorials and the letters seized from me. Our defense was based on the First Amendment principle of freedom of the press.

The late Indian summer sun shone down brightly on the eastern plains city of Cheyenne. In the streets, a strong gust blew down from Utah's distant Soldier Summit. The national banner atop the tall courtyard spire streamed resolutely toward the Great Plains. The wind had an edge to it, a harbinger of severe wintry weather in the offing. Within the Cheyenne district courtroom that twenty-third morning of October in the war-torn year of 1944, a case of more than academic significance was set to begin. Eight persons of Japanese descent faced an indictment issued by the grand jurors of Wyoming, charging them with aiding and abetting resistance to the Selective Service Act of 1940 and counseling others to resist. Seven of the leaders were reputed leaders of a militant organization formed in captivity at the Heart Mountain War Relocation Center known as the Fair Play Committee.[129] The eighth defendant was this author, a government-deposed editor of a Denver vernacular newspaper. The case was narrowly construed as a draft conspiracy prosecution, thus diminishing the basic purpose of the indicted men, who sought restoration of their fundamental constitutional precepts and freedom for their kith and kin. In actuality, two great constitutional issues were at stake: first, whether persons denied their constitutional rights could be compelled to fulfill their military obligations; and second, whether freedom of the press should and could be maintained even during the hysteria of war.

During a short recess in the hallway, I caught the eyes of the jury foreman and he winked and smiled. I considered that a good omen. Between sessions, Vern Lechliter, a *Wyoming Eagle* reporter,[130] attached himself to me. He was not only very friendly, but he expressed his opinion of my innocence. On the morning of November 1, 1944, a federal district court jury acquitted me by returning a verdict of not guilty. It convicted the seven leaders of the Fair Play Committee. The foreman of the jury requested I send him a copy of my editorials so that he could read for himself what I had written. Agent Lawrence of the FBI stepped out of the judge's chambers for a smoke and, seeing me at the end of the hall, rushed all the way over to congratulate me on my acquittal. He was the agent who interrogated me on a number of occasions but surprised me by not testifying against me. It was Agent Lawrence who had informed me that the FBI was withdrawing all charges of inappropriate editorial conduct. I was grateful for his reaction upon my acquittal. I left Cheyenne immediately.[131]

After the verdict, Nisei war hero Ben Kuroki, who had been a government witness, told the press: "These men are fascists in my estimation and no good to any country. They have torn down (what) all the rest of us have tried to do. I hope that these members of the Fair Play Committee won't form the opinion of America concerning all Japanese Americans."[xl] Kuroki was a Nebraskan and was never subject to incarceration.[132]

Attorney A. L. Wirin filed an appeal on behalf of the Fair Play Committee leaders contending that there was insufficient evidence to convict them.

---

xl Ben Kuroki statement in *Wyoming State Tribune*, November 3, 1944.

The Tenth Circuit Court of Appeals, in a 2 to 1 decision, reversed the district court conviction, citing the Supreme Court's Keegan ruling as setting a precedent, and remanded the case back to the district court.[133] The Justice Department, however, declined to contest the ruling. Thus, after eighteen months, five of the FPC leaders were released from serving the remainder of their Leavenworth stretch and set free.[134]

I kept in touch with Paul's wife, Alice, during the pending appeal. I attended and listened to A. L. Wirin's arguments before the Tenth Circuit Court of Appeals, and I informed Alice that I was confident of a reversal.[135] My confidence was strengthened by a front-page *Wyoming Eagle* editorial that had raised the question of imprisoning Japanese Americans while setting the Bundists free in the exact same type of issue. Upon my acquittal, Vern Lechliter, a reporter for the *Wyoming Eagle*, opined, "If you were convicted, I wouldn't know what journalistic justice was all about."[xli] The *Wyoming Eagle* summed up the ten-day trial this way:

> A federal district court jury here last night convicted seven of eight Nisei tried on charges of conspiracy to violate the Selective Service Act, and found James Matsumoto Omura, former editor of the English section of the *Rocky Shimpo*, Japanese language newspaper printed in Denver, not guilty after almost six hours of deliberation.
>
> In opening his argument to the jury, Jacobs, counsel for Omura, referred to Pickett's long discussion about his client and said, "The smallest amount of evidence and the largest amount of argument was put forth against Omura. I submit that means the government feels it has a weak case against him."
>
> In summarizing the government's case, U.S. Attorney Carl Sackett stated that "knowing of the Fair Play Committee conspiracy to fail to report for the draft, Omura backed them with his editorials."[xlii]

The anti-Nikkei *Denver Post*, which had gleefully headlined my arrest as a "Fifth Columnist" on its front page, shunted my acquittal far back between pages 30 and 40,[xliii] while the *Rocky Mountain News* noted that "Mr. Omura testified he had registered for the draft, complied with all draft board requests and notified them he would serve if called."[xliv]

---

xli Vern Lechliter, *Wyoming Eagle* reporter, to Jimmie Omura, ex-editor of the *Rocky Shimpo*, November 1, 1944.

xlii "Seven Nisei Are Convicted Here," *Wyoming Eagle*, November 2, 1944.

xliii "Ex-Denver Editor of Jap Paper Freed of Draft Charges," *Denver Post*, November 2, 1944.

xliv "Seven Are Guilty in Draft Case," *Rocky Mountain News*, November 4, 1944.

Though not intended for publication, the *Wyoming Eagle* requested my permission to print a letter I had sent that paper. This request I promptly granted.[xlv] "The *Wyoming Eagle*," ran the ensuing article, "was praised yesterday by the only one of eight Japanese Americans to be acquitted in a federal court conspiracy case held here last October, for having upheld 'the highest traditions of newspaper reporting' by the 'very impartial treatment' of its coverage." The article then quoted from my letter.

> I wish to thank the *Wyoming Eagle* for the very impartial treatment of its coverage to the recent conspiracy trial in Cheyenne. In particular, the reporting by Vern Lechliter of your staff was outstanding for its objective nature.[136]
>   I feel that the type of reporting given the trial had considerable bearing in determining the verdict in my particular case. My greatest fear was that the jury would include me in a landslide verdict. The fact that they did not sustains my faith in the American jury system and raises my personal estimation for the people of the State of Wyoming.]
>   The verdict of the jury in acquitting me leaves unimpaired the Freedom of the Press [see Appendix 4], one of the most important of our constitutional rights.[xlvi]

Following the acquittal, the defense counsel went into the chamber of Judge Rice and subsequently informed me, "Judge Rice told me in his chamber after the trial that had the jury convicted you, he would have sustained the verdict even though he knew it could be overturned on appeal."[xlvii] The judge had also denied all motions entered by Jacobs. One, a request for a directed verdict of acquittal, raised criticism by legal observers in attendance. "The court erred," declared L. C. Sampson, a secretary of the Wyoming Bar Association who was part of my defense team. "He violated judicial procedure, which requires a directed acquittal whenever the evidence of innocence is as strong as evidence to support the case. He should have issued a directed verdict of dismissal." The court ruled the decision would be up to the jury. The jury voted for acquittal.

In April 1944, the *Heart Mountain Sentinel* had berated the *Rocky Shimpo* and charged, "It has prostituted the privileges of the freedom of the press

xlv [Ed. See letter from James M. Omura, November 29, 1944, to Mr. R. F. MacPherson, Editor, *Wyoming Eagle*, Cheyenne, Wyoming (OP).]
xlvi [Ed. A copy of the published letter in the *Wyoming Eagle* is not included in OP.]
xlvii Sidney Jacobs, lead defense counsel, to his client, November 1, 1944, Cheyenne, Wyoming.

FIGURE 10. This photo of Jimmie Omura was taken around the time of the late October, early November 1944 conspiracy trial of the Heart Mountain Fair Play Committee leaders and him at the federal courthouse in Cheyenne, Wyoming. While Omura was exonerated, the FPC steering committee members were convicted and imprisoned, although they later had their convictions overturned upon appeal. Omura Papers, Green Library, Stanford University.

to advocate an un-American stand that strikes at the very institution that grants it freedom of expression."[xlviii] Championing constitutional grievances through court proceedings could hardly be considered "un-American." The *Rocky Shimpo* was practicing the proper function of print journalism, which is supposedly the watchdog of individual freedom infringed upon by the government.

Then, in an excess of irrationalism, the *Sentinel* had stated, "James Omura will be inducted (*sic*) as the number one menace to postwar assimilation of the Nisei."[xlix][137] Strong language indeed! The *Sentinel*, however, was but the mouthpiece of the WRA and an adjunct of the Japanese American Citizens League, a collaborationist arm of the U.S. government.

---

xlviii Editorial, "Facing the Future," *Heart Mountain Sentinel,* April 8, 1944.
xlix Ibid.

SEVEN

Down and Out in Denver, 1944–1945

I moved into Denver from suburban Lakewood after the acquittal and set about rebuilding my depleted finances. Though I was exonerated by a court of law, I was not vindicated in the eyes of the Denver Japanese community. I was beset by harassment of the Nisei in an effort to deny me occupation. The first prospect was at the Gallagher Freight Company. I was asked to wait for fifteen minutes, and while I waited a Nisei came out of a van being loaded and ran across the dock to the office, his face averted. I found myself confronting a young, red-haired personnel director, his face beet red and his eyes filled with anger.

"Have you changed your mind?" he asked.

"Why should I?" I inquired.

"You still think the way you did before?" he pressed.

"I don't see why not," I shot back, nettled at his inquisition.

"You haven't changed?" he asked.

"I was acquitted," I informed him.

"Well, if we decide to hire you, we'll let you know," he concluded.

I knew the job was out the window. I was seething inside. Is that all acquittal meant? I resented this inquisition. I knew the Nisei had bad-mouthed me. What I didn't know was this attitude would hound me at every turn.

Several days later, I ran into another prospect. I was hired and instructed to report at eight in the morning. In the afternoon, I answered a phone call. "It's better if you don't show up in the morning," the man who had hired me said. "I've got three Japanese boys working here. Feelings are pretty strong against you."

This sort of incident dogged me wherever I turned. I should have known other Nisei worked for these companies that initially hired me, but I had no way of knowing this. I finally caught on with a Jewish firm about three months later. Ten days later, when the Nisei office girl was hours away from returning to California, she told me the other Nisei office girl, who quit the next day, had reported me to the office. I was never told this by my employer, and the younger son who managed the firm never intimated his knowledge. He always treated me in fine fashion.

It was tough sledding until the first payday. I had shot my wad searching for work for three months. Just to save a ten-cent carfare, I walked to and back from work across several miles of the city. I was so exhausted at the end of the day that I nearly threw up halfway home on more than one occasion. I gutted it out and finally got over the hump. Hardest to understand was this job harassment of the Nisei. The instant reaction was anger but an insistent voice whispered that people of Japanese origin owed me nothing. I had acted upon my moral conscience and I would have to bear the cross as best I could. I pitied the Japanese people for their infidelity to constitutional doctrine and their submissive willingness to accept government dole, dictations, and oppression. I was also ashamed of my people.

On my shelf were two poems I had displayed because I liked their meanings. Now, in these difficult days, they came to be a solace. Each time I was in anguish, I'd read them over and over again. The first of these was Rudyard Kipling's "If."

> If you can keep your head when all about you
> Are losing theirs and blaming it on you;
> If you can trust yourself when all men doubt you,
> But make allowance for their doubting too;
> And so hold on when there is nothing in you
> Except the will which says to them: "Hold on!"

This poem had the power to give me a lift. The second poem was "Thinking," by an author unknown.

> If you think you are beaten, you are:
> If you think you dare not, you won't;
> If you'd like to win, but you think you can't
> It's almost a cinch, you won't.

No one confronted me face-to-face or in any physical way, although one came very close. It was in their attitudes that surfaced whenever an incident did occur, such as the bowling league rushing down to the ABC asking whether I had been suspended for not having bowled for five years. Other incidents continued to crop up and I finally gave up bowling as not worth the trouble. Then, in 1948, a Nisei doctor told me, "You're welcome in my home," as if I was persona non grata in most Japanese homes. There was also the evening I was asked to stick around for a trip to the practice range, and then isolated alone, by myself. These little things came to bother me and eventually I turned my back on the ethnic society.

Acquittal in the conspiracy trial, I felt, represented a confirmation of the propriety of journalism I had pursued. The Japanese community of Denver thought otherwise. It would seem the community might show some measure of remorse for its negative emotionalism and prejudgment. But the community set a stigma, which was noticeable even among those who appeared more tolerant and understanding. The trial had been a tremendous drain upon my finances and I needed a job badly. Employed Nisei saw to it that job hunting would be difficult, and there was an irony in that for I had placed countless numbers in jobs in the Denver area through the no-fee Pacific Coast Evacuee Placement Bureau. I searched for work as a truck driver as I had no taste for stationary work. Nor was I in the mood to fraternize with ethnic people who had deserted me in my hour of need.

I couldn't understand the Japanese community at first, but reading and rereading them many times clarified for me what was happening. No one had given me a mandate to champion the cause that I did, and thus the community owed me nothing. This did not prevent me from feeling ashamed of the Japanese people in America and particularly the local Japanese in Denver, whom I pitied for their lack of understanding of true historical issues.

Afterword

"Who Writes History?"

FRANK ABE

If the World War II internment of Japanese-Americans was a chapter of shame, what was done to James M. Omura remains a footnote of disgrace.

—Sharon Noguchi

Jimmie Omura would often wryly observe, in a matter-of-fact tone, that he didn't expect to be recognized for his accomplishments by his own ethnic community until fifty years after his death. For the better part of his life, this was a realistic expectation.

The decades of the 1950s and 1960s were a desert for anything Japanese American. The nation still grieved the young men lost to World War II, and few distinctions were ever made between Americans of Japanese ancestry and the wartime enemy. The best the Nisei could expect from the mass media was sympathetic coverage of cultural exchanges with Japan or the planting of cherry trees as offerings of peace. Any mention of the wartime eviction was swiftly shouted down by veterans and widows with variations of the cry, "Remember Pearl Harbor."

It was therefore no surprise that Jimmie's story and that of the Heart Mountain Fair Play Committee were omitted from the first popular history of Japanese America written by a Japanese American, Bill Hosokawa. But Hosokawa was no stranger to Omura: both attended high school in Seattle; Hosokawa edited the camp newspaper at Heart Mountain before leaving for the *Des Moines Register*, and he later resettled in Denver, where Omura already lived.

Every Nisei family at the time owned an obligatory copy of Hosokawa's 1969 *Nisei: The Quiet Americans,*[1] most likely ordered through an ad in
the *Pacific Citizen,* the JACL house organ in which Hosokawa held court
weekly under the banner of his "From the Frying Pan" column. My father
bought one of those books. It was brand-new; he probably looked through
it once and put it on the shelf, next to his copy of Dillon Myer's memoir
of the machinery of incarceration, *Uprooted Americans.*[2] During a college
break one summer, I opened Hosokawa's book and was shocked to read that
the Heart Mountain my father sometimes mentioned as a camp in which he
spent the war years was not some sort of benign summer camp, as he made
it sound, but an American concentration camp where he and ten thousand
others had been imprisoned for the duration.

Even as I read that book, however, something felt missing. From the text,
one would believe that Japanese America's response to eviction and incarceration was embodied by two phrases: *shikataganai,* Japanese for "it can't be
helped," passive resignation in the face of injustice; or *go for broke,* Hawaiian
pidgin for "go all out, give 110 percent," patriotic self-sacrifice to prove one's
loyalty. Surely there had to be some among those 120,000 people across ten
camps who spoke out in protest. But whenever I or any of the other Sansei, or third-generation, children would ask, "Mom, Dad, why didn't you
resist?" we'd be patted on the head and admonished, "Times were different
then; you weren't born yet; don't go applying your 1960s Berkeley civil rights
activism to the 1940s—you can't judge us."

Who writes history? "History is usually written by the winners," as Roger
Daniels reminds the viewer in our film, *Conscience and the Constitution,*
"and in the short term the JACL, or people who believe in that point of
view, the people who want to improve the image of the Japanese American
people, in the short run they controlled the history. That's obviously no
longer the case."[3]

The rehabilitation of James Omura and the recovery of his legacy began with a 1970 history master's thesis by Douglas Nelson at the University
of Wyoming, under the direction of his mentor, Professor Roger Daniels.[4]
Daniels, in turn, drew heavily from Nelson's thesis for his 1971 *Concentration Camps, USA: Japanese Americans and World War II.*[5] It was likely the
first time since the war that the organized resistance of the Heart Mountain
Fair Play Committee and the support provided by Omura's *Rocky Shimpo*
columns had been discussed in print. Michi Weglyn in her 1976 *Years of*

Infamy included Jimmie's "Has the Gestapo come to America?" as the epigraph to her chapter on the decision for mass eviction. As Frank Chin would write, seeing that quotation was the first clue he had to Omura's existence.

Out of his own pocket, Chin flew Frank Emi and James Omura to Seattle in 1983 to meet with Seattle redress activists and local resisters. After working with Chin to ignite the redress campaign with the first "Days of Remembrance," it was a relief for me to finally meet Emi and Omura. Their resistance was the missing link I had been seeking.

Chin arranged for Emi and Omura's introduction to academia at the 1988 Association for Asian American Studies Conference at Washington State University in Pullman. By this time, I had begun a career as a radio news journalist, and to help bring the story of resistance into the mainstream of Japanese American thought, I wrote about Omura's critique of the JACL for the JACL's *Pacific Citizen*.

As I got to know Jimmie, I found him to be a guarded figure, at times sullen, occasionally irascible, but also capable of incisive wit and a gentleman's grace. Despite my earnest desire to tell his story, he would often needle me and my generation, perhaps just to amuse himself, for not knowing our own history and what he considered a lack of journalistic guts.

Later in 1988, the national JACL conveniently held its annual convention in Seattle, where I hoped to ask Mr. Hosokawa to join a panel with Omura on the Heart Mountain resistance for an upcoming convention of the fledgling Asian American Journalists Association (AAJA). He had declined once before. After the Sayonara banquet, I caught up with him, surrounded by Nisei women trying to take his picture, and asked him to autograph my now dog-eared copy of *Nisei*. "Oh my gosh," he exclaimed, and seemed genuinely pleased. He signed it thoughtfully, and with a broad smile presented the book back to me, opened to his inscription. I chose that moment to ask him to reconsider appearing on the AAJA panel. His eyes suddenly burned and he growled in his deep voice: "What I resent is that Jimmie Omura turned a bunch of impressionable young boys, who didn't know any better, against the draft. They went to trial and were convicted, but HE GOT OFF"—punctuating the last three words by jabbing his finger toward my chest.

That was a taste of what James Omura had to endure in Denver, living among not one but two Nisei icons, who even forty years after the end of World War II still wished he had served time in prison. Whenever Bill Hosokawa or Min Yasui looked at James Omura, they saw an unconvicted felon.

It was in this context that I was pleased to be in a position within the AAJA to lobby for creation of a Lifetime Achievement Award to recognize courage and commitment to the principles of journalism, and to win support for Jimmie as its first recipient. Jimmie flew to San Francisco in April 1989, thinking he was to speak on a panel. Instead, we brought him into the grand ballroom at the Hyatt Regency Hotel, where AAJA president Lloyd LaCuesta and I presented Jimmie with the award in front of a roomful of young journalists. Jimmie was visibly moved. So was I. A friend exclaimed, "We should do a documentary on him!" And out of that moment, *Conscience and the Constitution* was born.

In Seattle a few years later, Jimmie's older brother Casey, with whom he had lost all contact, passed away. I helped Jimmie close up Casey's estate and drove him north to Monroe, Washington, to visit the widow of his oldest brother, Yoshito Ohmura, who had also become a stranger to him. For these and other kindnesses, Jimmie would often profusely thank me. In his papers, we found a letter I had written to him. I'm glad I said these words to him while he was alive, and not fifty years after his death:

> I don't want you to feel like you owe me for any past benefaction. On the contrary, I feel I owe you a lot for befriending me and sharing your story with me, and in a greater sense providing me with a history I can point [to] with some pride. I only wish I had known about you when I was trying to learn about Japanese America by reading Hosokawa's first book, and not being able to find myself in it. I felt like saying, "those people aren't me." No wonder so many of my generation turned away from Japanese America; there was nothing to be proud of.[7]

It was an honor and a privilege to have known Jimmie, to have his sense of conviction guide me in my work, and to be able to share his story in our film. When he died in 1994, his family displayed the AAJA award at his memorial.

Jimmie embodied true courage in journalism by daring to write about the resistance at Heart Mountain, which was a classic act of civil disobedience in the American twentieth century. As I write this, in the twenty-first century, the freedom of the press for which James Omura stood is, unbelievably, under attack from the highest levels of government, by the very people elected to lead this nation. A proposal for creation of a national registry of all Muslims in America was floated by an administration surrogate—a database whose only useful purpose would be to enable another retaliatory mass roundup. The mass evictions executed in the name of national security by the Western Defense Command in 1942 are disturbingly echoed by the deportations carried out today by Immigration and Customs Enforcement. The issue of guilt by association and the limits on presidential authority examined by the Supreme Court in its review of FDR's Executive Order 9066 are the same ones the High Court is being called upon to review again in connection with Executive Order 13780, banning travel by nationals from six Muslim-majority nations. As the parallels multiply daily, the cautionary question James Omura posed in 1942 resounds today: "Has the Gestapo come to America?"

Acknowledgments

Because this book project has taken its author, James Omura, and its editor, me, nearly four decades to complete, both of us became deeply indebted to a great many people and institutions for their much-appreciated assistance. Although naming all of these benefactors is impossible, it is earnestly desired that those whose identities are elided will pardon us for our unintended oversight.

In the interval in which James Omura researched and wrote his memoir, from 1981 until 1994, the help he received is documented in his correspondence and daily diary entries. Based on these records, the following are the acknowledgments I believe he would have proffered:

The five individuals who emerge as Omura's indispensable supporters are Frank Abe, Frank Chin, Lawson Inada, Michi Nishiura Weglyn, and Aiko Herzig Yoshinaga. Without them, Omura likely would not have completed his memoir.

Right behind these backers was a steadfast band of Fair Play Committee leaders and draft resisters, headed by Frank Emi, Tak Hoshizaki, Mits Koshiyama, Yosh Kuromiya, and George Nozawa, and extending through Sam Horino, Dave Kawamoto, and Jack Tono.

Next in line was a group of adherents who composed a veritable "resisters circle." Within it were Jim Akutsu, Violet de Cristoforo, Sue Kunitomi Embrey, Itsuko Emi, George Fujii, Kiku Funabiki, Leo Gruip-Ruiz, Jack Herzig, William and Yuriko Hohri, Hannah Tomiko Holmes, Fred Hoshiyama, Barbara Joe Hoshizaki, Amy Uno Ishii, Brooks and Sumi Iwakiri, Art Iwasaki,

Hiroshi Kashiwagi, Suzy Katusda, Toshi Kawamoto, Nelson and Taka Kitsuse, Mizue Koshiyama, Gloria Kubota, Irene Kuromiya, Paul Minerich, Henry Miyatake, Kay Ochi, Raymond Okamura, Miya Okawara, Chizu and Emiko Omori, John and Merry Omori, Kozie Sakai, Yoichi Shimatsu, Cedrick Shimo, Marge Taniwaki, Mary Tomita, Paul Tsuneishi, Harry Ueno, Kiku Uno, Clifford Uyeda, Walter Weglyn, Kenzo Yamamoto, Michael Yasutake, Grace Kubota Ybarra, and Ken and Kay Yoshida.

Because James Omura sought a memoir solidly grounded in scholarship as well as memory, he took counsel with a legion of multidisciplinary academics. This group encompassed Shirley Castelnuovo, Roger Daniels, Richard Drinnon, Russell Endo, Chris Friday, Stephen Fugita, Jim Hirabayashi, Yuji Ichioka, Peter Irons, King-Kok Cheung, Deborah Lim, John Liu, Franklin Odo, Gary Okihiro, Glenn Omatsu, Robert Sims, Peter Suzuki, Jere Takahashi, Rita Takahashi, Karen Umemoto, Alan Wald, Jack Wills, Shawn Wong, and David Yoo.

Omura was aided as well by media organizations and individuals. For the former, there was the *Amerasia Journal, Asian Journal, Asian Week, Bainbridge Nikkei, Bainbridge Review, Chronicles Magazine, Denver Post, Eastwind Magazine, Hawaii Herald, Hokubei Mainichi, Honolulu Star Bulletin, Pacific Citizen, Rafu Shimpo, Reader's Digest*, and *Washington Post*. For the latter, there was Dwight Chuman, Loni Ding, Naomi Hirahara, Arnold Hiura, Harry Honda, Robert Ito, George Johnston, Gary Kawaguchi, Russell Leong, Julia Matisoo, Takeshi Nakayama, Sharon Noguichi, Richard Oyama, Alan Parker, Michael Rosen, Sumi Seki, Bob Shimabukuro, Gwen Terasaki, George Yamada, J. K. Yamamoto, and Diane Yen-Mei Wong.

Finally, Omura was abetted by family members, friends, and associates, including Nancy Araki, Ernest Besig, Wayne M. Collins, Caryl Gertler, Fumiko Hayashida, Ernie and Chizu Kitano Iiyama, David Ishii, Mac Kaneko, Toyo Suyemoto Kawakami, Gaye Kouyoumjian, George Matsumonji, Vera Matsumura, Jim Matsuoka, Yuriko Mita, Brian Niiya, Miya Okawara, Gregg Omura, Karen Haruko Omura, Wayne Omura, Shosuke Sasaki, Eddie and Doris Sato, and Oski Taniwaki.

During my 1995–2017 span of editing the Omura memoir for publication, I too incurred a substantial debt to many people. Michi Nishiura Weglyn named me to undertake the project. Omura's oldest son and the executor of his estate, Dr. Gregg Omura, transferred the Omura Papers to my custody and worked with me to deposit them at Stanford University's Green Library. There I was aided by a succession of capable archivists: Tomas Jaehn, Alicia Maria Gámez, and Benjamin Lee Stone. Thanks to a 1999 California Civil Liberties Public Education Program grant, provision was made for the preservation and processing of the Omura Papers plus the preparation in 2001–2 by Rebecca Guillan Manley of a comprehensive finding aid for this collection. Manley was among the 125 graduate students enrolled in five Historical Archives classes sponsored by the San José State University School of Library and Information Science that in 1997–99 undertook the collection's preliminary organization under the guidance of my wife, Debra Gold Hansen.

Simultaneously with this activity, two people very familiar with James Omura's story, Steve Yoda and Mary Kimoto Tomita, volunteered their services to critique and copyedit the final draft of Omura's memoir, which he had provisionally titled "A Shattered People." Yoda wrote his 1999 senior honors thesis, a biography of James Omura, at Stanford University under Dr. Gordon Chang's direction. Tomita, the author of a 1995 Stanford University Press volume—*Dear Miye: Letter Home from Japan, 1939–1946*—in the "Asian America" series edited by Chang, not only assisted Omura in writing his memoir but also let me conduct a tape-recorded interview with her; and she turned her correspondence with Omura over to me for deposit at Stanford's Green Library.

Two other people close to Omura, Michi Nishiura Weglyn and Aiko Herzig Yoshinaga, generously passed along their correspondence with him to me for inclusion in the Omura Papers.

Among my corps of chief benefactors were Frank Chin and Frank Abe. Beyond penning the Foreword and Afterword to this volume, they helped me in countless ways throughout its protracted gestation. Additionally, they deepened my understanding of Omura's pivotal role in the Heart Mountain draft resistance movement through the stimulating interview they jointly conducted with me for Abe's 2000 film *Conscience and the Constitution*.

Another person earning my gratitude for bountiful assistance is journalist Martha Nakagawa. She gave unselfishly of her vast knowledge, overtaxed time and energy, and exemplary sleuthing skills to respond to my parade of requests for both information and insights.

A number of individuals connected with the Heart Mountain Fair Play Committee draft resistance movement were of invaluable help to me. Foremost among them were Frank Emi, Mits Koshiyama, George Nozawa, Tak Hoshizaki, and Yosh Kuromiya (plus his wife, Irene), who also contributed the

Preface to this volume. I was aided as well by draft resisters from camps other than Heart Mountain: Jim Akutsu (Minidoka), Noboru Taguma (Amache), Ken Yoshida (Topaz), and Joe Yamakido (Jerome).

I was fortunate to transact oral history interviews with people who knew Omura and possessed useful knowledge about him. These narrators were Wayne Omura, Jim Mita, Travis Mita, Cheryl Gertler, Marge Taniwaki/Leo Gruip-Ruiz, Sumi Takeno, Tak Terasaki, George Masunaka, Roy Nagai, Fumiko Hayashida, Sam Nakai/Tatsu Moritani, and Joe Yamakido. In Denver I also did off-tape interviews with Russell Endo and Carolyn Takeshita, who along with her husband, Mickey, led me on an enlightening tour of significant sites in World War II-era Japanese Denver. I furthermore interviewed two people for the renowned Tom Ikeda-led Densho oral history organization in Seattle who had interacted with Omura: Jim Akutsu and (with Frank Abe) Tetsuko Toda Matsunaka.

I enjoyed solid support for my work from two southern California institutions: the Center for Oral and Public History (COPH) at California State University, Fullerton, and the Los Angeles-based Japanese American National Museum (JANM). COPH colleagues who abetted my work were Ben Cawthra, Wendy Elliott-Scheinberg, Natalie Fousekis, Lawrence B. de Graaf, Cora Granata, Ray Rast, and Allison Versally, but most particularly Kathleen Frazee, Kira Gentry, Stephanie George, Trangdai Tranguyen Glassey, Gail Gutierrez, Garnette Long, Natalie Navar, Sharon Owen, Shirley Stephenson, and Suzanne Walter.

Many JANM colleagues provided me material and moral support, but those who actively promoted my research on Omura were Nancy Araki, Darcie Iki, Lloyd Inui, Sojin Kim, and Allyson Nakamoto.

Three other archivists who deserve recognition here are Nancy Hunter Caudill, Pollak Library, California State University, Fullerton; Rosemary Evetts, Aurora Library Archives and Special Collections, Denver, Colorado; and Karl Matsushita, Japanese American National Library in San Francisco.

Scholars who were in my corner when needed included Matt Briones, Shirley Castlenuovo, Sucheng Chan, Roger Daniels, Richard Drinnon, Louis Fiset, Diane Fujino, Jim Gatewood, Lane Hirabayashi, William Hohri, Yuji Ichioka, Tetsuden Kashima, Cherstin Lyon, Mike Mackey, Daryl Maeda, Eric Muller, Gail Nomura, Gary Okihiro, Chizu and Emiko Omori, Greg Robinson, Paul Spickard, Jere Takahashi, Barbara Takei, Eileen Tamura, Linda Tamura, Ellen Wu, Alice Yang, and David Yoo.

I also express my thanks to Kenji Taguma, president of the Nichibei Foundation, and Hiroshi Shimizu, president of the Japanese American National Library's board of directors, for arranging generous financial aid to Stanford University Press for the memoir's publication.

I profoundly thank Gordon Chang both for encouraging me to move forward with this project two decades ago, and then for shepherding its publication into his distinguished Asian America series. In this connection, I would like to applaud the entire Stanford University Press staff, most notably Margo Irvin, editor, but also the following individuals: Nora Spiegel, assistant editor; Gigi Mark, production editor; Stephanie Adams, marketing manager; Kate Templar, sales and exhibits manager; Rob Ehle, art director; Jeff Wyneken, manuscript editor; and Nancy Ball, indexer. All of them provided me with sage counsel and patient and compassionate guidance. My profound appreciation is also extended to the trio of anonymous peer reviewers of my manuscript for their altogether insightful and constructive critiques.

Lastly, I extend my deep appreciation to a very special Sansei friend, Kurtis Nakagawa. More than any other person, apart from my wife, he was the one who put the wind into my editorial sails.

Appendix 1

"Too Much Flag-Waving"

A P P E N D I X   1 :   Editorial, "Too Much Flag-Waving," *Current Life*, November 1941. Reproduced by permission from Omura Papers, Green Library, Stanford University.

Appendix 2

Letter, James M. Omura to Professor Roger Daniels, April 12, 1983

1455 S. Irving Street
Denver, Colorado 80219
April 12, 1983

Professor Roger Daniels
Department of History
University of Cincinnati
360 McMicken Hall (#373)
Cincinnati, Ohio 45221

Dear Prof. Daniels:

I did not return to Denver until evening of March 26th, having been routed to Seattle for a two-day meeting on request and remaining a full week for additional research.

Now that I have caught up with the most pressing portion of three weeks of neglected mail and have put my annual tax duties to bed, I shall endeavor to respond to the question you posed.

It would seem to me that the appearance I made before the Tolan Committee in San Francisco in 1942 has received greater recognition than it ordinarily should deserve. Of course, it cannot be said that I am not flattered by the attention it has received in the literature of the Evacuation. I thought then and I believe today that this was a monumental tragedy that was unnecessary to the security of the Pacific Coast and the action violated our fundamental concepts of constitutional government.

At the 1983 Relocation and Redress conference at Utah University, I was asked if it did not take "courage" to oppose the Evacuation. The thought never occurred to me in that term. I felt it was a natural thing to do. I was at work at the Amling Corporation when I was urged to hasten to the hearings to testify following Masaoka's provocative testimony. I had been certified to appear as the final witness. In Seattle later, a committee member stated that I was asked to testify by request.

I believe unequivocally that the position I took was the only proper stance to take by those who avow their Americanism and profess their loyalty to Old Glory. I had no illusion about my place in America. As a small boy of six years old I had been given a choice of being a Japanese in Japan or an American in the United States. I chose America. I remembered that every morning we would begin our class exercises by facing and saluting the Stars and Stripes and with our hand over our heart pledging allegiance to the United States. I suppose it imbued me with a feeling that the Constitution embraced all of us.

I remembered, even after the Evacuation, when I went to watch the El Toro Marines play at Folsom Field in Boulder how emotionally I felt when the National Anthem was sung as our flag fluttered in the breeze. It never entered my mind that our constitution, imperfect as it is, was anything else but color blind. I believed we all enjoyed its protective shield to individual liberties. In that belief, I saw the only proper response to the uprooting of resident people of Japanese ancestry who habited the Pacific Coast was to protest.

The position I took at the Tolan Committee should not have been an exception. There should have been a multitude of similar objections. In reading the testimonies of my fellow Japanese Americans, I am struck by the uniformity of attitudes implied and it evokes a painful feeling of sadness that such negative idealism should endure as a stark reminder of the Nisei heritage. That we should be remembered in our darkest and most critical hours [for] our docile and spineless acceptance of tyranny. It forever tarnishes our image in the historic context as free men.

The only mitigating factor that evolved was once the shock of Pearl Harbor and parental concerns wore off in the concentration camps, there came an awakening and an assertive protest of their plight. Most significant of Nisei protests was the Heart Mountain Fair Play Committee which advocated refusal to take physicals unless their constitutional rights were restored. By this militant stand, the honor of free men was salvaged to some extent and reduced the sting of shame that followed its bartering away by those who professed to furnish leadership and who functioned as such by the grace of an oppressor government.

The [Japanese American] Citizens League exercised no real impact in the Japanese American society at the time of Pearl Harbor. It was an ineffectual organization, primarily viewed as a social group engaged in perpetuating a Nisei elite class. It is not surprising, therefore, that its leadership was demonstratively weak and its belief in the basic tenets of our democratic system was fragile at the most. The Citizens League was not representative of its racial society but demanded conformity to its policy of collaboration and the oppressor.

I do not believe patriotism demands or requires that any group of people, whatever their race or ethnic background, yield up their rights that are embodied in the Constitution even in times of national peril. The call for national unity should not and must not be premeditated on the use of scapegoats for the creation of a war psychology through racial animosity as was carried out in 1942. We should learn, if we have not yet learned, to march shoulder to shoulder in mutual comradeship to thwart all enemies of our nation.

It is abhorrent and de-humanizing to realize that we were spurred on into internment camps with such guileless expressions as "cheerfully" by Jimmy Sakamoto; "gladly" by Tokie Slocum; and "willingly" by the national field secretary, Mike Masaoka. Those words stand as a hallmark of our shame. It remains as incontrovertible proof of Japanese America being sold down the river. The march to the internment camps proceeded with a sense of betrayal and the recognition of the futility of resisting at that late hour General DeWitt's armed military. They had been sold like cattle for what Masaoka characterized as vague "future considerations" and the presumed safety of protective custody which he touted.

The Evacuation is an historic blot upon democracy. It cannot be removed. But the honor of the nation can be assuaged through monetary redress. It is true that money cannot bring back those lost years, the sufferings from physical and mental anguish, and the monetary losses stemming from lost properties and economic opportunities. But money, however insufficient, can serve as a symbol of a nation's regret and remorse for wrongs committed against its innocent citizenry and resident aliens. It can restore to the Japanese Americans, who were affected, its pride and a feeling of human dignity re-conferred.

This is probably not what you wanted but it speaks my own personal sentiments. Perhaps I am a rebel or a nonconformist in the tradition of Emerson. I was interviewed for a radio newsletter after the meeting in Seattle and have accepted a taping session for an Oral History Project in California. Perhaps if I participate in such affairs sufficient times I will be able to boil down my thoughts in lesser words.

Sincerely yours,
[Jimmie]
James M. Omura

Appendix 3

"Let Us Not Be Rash"

Let Us Not Be Rash

THIS department has been queried as to our opinion in regard to the petition movement in war-born relocation centers. Our reply is simple. We are in full sympathy with the general context of the petitions forwarded to Washington by the Amache Community Council and the Topaz Ciizens Committee. We do not necessarily agree on all the points raised, however.

Insofar as the movement itself is concerned, the Nisei are well within their rights to petition the government for a redress of grievances. Beyond that, it would be treading on unsure footing. We must not forget that we are at war. This department does not encourage resistance to the draft.

It is reported that five at Amache and thirty at Hunt are guilty of resisting the draft. There will probably be more before this matter is finished. We cannot conscientiously believe that by these sporadic actions anything concrete and fundamental can be achieved. Those who are resisting the draft are too few, too unorganized and basically unsound in their viewpoints.

(continued on page 242)

A P P E N D I X 3 : Editorial, "Let Us Not Be Rash," *Rocky Shimpo*, February 28, 1944. Reproduced by permission from Omura Papers, Green Library, Stanford University.

(continued from page 241)

EXPATRIATION is not the answer to our eventual redemption of democratic and constitutional rights. Unorganized draft resistance is not the proper method to pursue our grievances. Expressions and feelings of disloyalty, purely because democracy seems not to have worked in our particular case, are neither sound or conducive to a healthy regard of our rights.

We agree that the constitution gives us certain inalienable and civil rights. We do not dispute the fact that such rights have been largely stripped and taken from us. We further agree that the government should restore a large part of those rights before asking us to contribute our lives to the welfare of the nation—to sacrifice our lives on the field of battle.

BUT those who have grown bitter with the evacuation must not forget that "eternal vigilance is the price of liberty." We have not been vigilant. We cannot condemn democracy for our present unhappy predicament. Democracy is not only a form of government, but it is also a spirit. If there is no spirit of democracy in our governmental leaders, we would not have democracy in action. Let us therefore not condemn democracy but the men who manipulate public affairs and the masses who sympathize and condone undemocratic ideals.

We should at all times stand firm on our God-given rights. We should let our voices be heard whenever an attempt is made to abridge such endowed privileges. But ours should not be an act of rashness or haste. We should think the matter through and in the ultimate end retain a proper regard for the implications and repercussions that in all probability would arise from our acts. There is no reason why we should not petition for a redress of grievances, but there is every reason why we should not resist the draft in the way it is being done now.

Appendix 4

"Freedom of the Press"

Freedom of the Press

DOES freedom of the press exist in War Relocation Centers? It would not seem so, if our opinion were to be based on the editorial expressions of camp organs. Instead, it would indicate a controlled press.

The editorials and the prominence given to certain types of news tend to reflect the views and policies of the W. R. A. rather than real attitudes and true opinions of the vast majority of west coast evacuees who are under temporary confinement in these centers. The editorials represent the minority and pro-administration views.

The highly controversial issue of the reinstitution of selective service for American-born citizens of Japanese parentage has more than ever emphasized the striking variance of evacuee opinions with the editorial stands of camporgans.

For example, the Heart Mountain Sentinel is extremely inconsistent on Nisei draft. In its much-quoted editorial—Selective Service Limited—it sounded a ringing denunciation of the restrictive and discriminatory features of the current selective service program. On March 11, it made a right-about face in maliciously attacking the Issei population of Heart Mountain and the Fair Play Committee, the latter militantly fighting for restoration of constitutional rights as a prelude to military induction.

(continued on page 244)

APPENDIX 4: Editorial, "Freedom of the Press," *Rocky Shimpo*, March 29, 1944. Reproduced by permission from Omura Papers, Green Library, Stanford University.

(continued from page 243)

THE Minidoka Irrigator, for instance, has the same wavering policy, now one way and then another. It technically took exception to the current draft procedures and then turned turn-coat with a hallelujah chorus, urging Nisei to respond to selective service and rapping those who opposed the draft.

The petitions forwarded to Washington are far more indicative of the majority sentiments prevailing within relocation centers as well as without. The great majority of such petitions have been approved by the community councils, which represent the people of each center.

Then again, in the matter of the Japanese American Citizens League, it is a well established fact that that organization's strength has been broken in relocation centers. It is believed that at least 90 percent of the people in the centers are opposed to the JACL.

THE Manzanar Free Press editorially supports the JACL. The citizens of Manzanar are strongly opposed. In fact, the Manzanar citizens recently forwarded a resolution to Washington asking for withdrawal of W.R.A. recognition of that organization as applying to their center. The Topaz Times is also in a somewhat related position.

The W.R.A. has indulged in widespread suppression of the true facts of conditions in War Relocation Centers. It has attempted to indicate to the general outside public that it is doing a competent job and whatever news that tends to discredit their program is suppressed wherever possible. The wave of draft criticism has not been permitted to be publicized generally and any individual or groups within the centers who express dissatisfaction to the present procedures are vigorously condemned, persecuted and coerced into silence. The incident in Amache and the current situation in Heart Mountain are glaring cases in point.

Notes

ABBREVIATIONS OF ARCHIVES

JERS, BANC, UCB, MSS   *Japanese American Evacuation and Resettlement Study*, Bancroft Library, University of California, Manuscript

OP   Omura Papers, Stanford University

RG, NA   Record Group, National Archives

UCLARL   Department of Special Collections, Charles E. Young Research Library, University of California, Los Angeles

INTRODUCTION

1. For a comprehensive overview of Omura's life, replete with bibliographical references, see my entry for "James Omura," in the *Densho Encyclopedia*, http://encyclopedia.densho.org/ (accessed on May 21, 2016).

2. See Arthur A. Hansen, "Return to the Wars: Jimmie Omura's 1947 Crusade against the Japanese American Citizens League," chap. 7 in Sucheng Chan, ed., *Remapping Asian American History* (Walnut Creek, CA: AltaMira Press, 2003), 127–50. This chapter (particularly 132–33, 142–47), along with Arthur A. Hansen, "Peculiar Odyssey: Newsman Jimmie Omura's Removal from and Regeneration within Nikkei Society, History, and Memory," chap. 13 in Louis Fiset and Gail M. Nomura, eds., *Nikkei in the Pacific Northwest: Japanese Americans and Japanese Canadians in the Twentieth Century* (Seattle: University of Washington Press, 2005), 278–307 (esp. 288–95), serve as the basis for the opening section of the present Introduction.

3. See Brian Niiya's "Rocky Shimpo" entry in the *Densho Encyclopedia*, http://encyclopedia.densho.org/ (accessed on August 19, 2015).

4. For information about the Heart Mountain Relocation Center, see Mieko Matsumoto's entry in the *Densho Encyclopedia*, http://encyclopedia.densho.org/ (accessed on April 25, 2015). On the Heart Mountain Fair Play Committee, see Eric L. Muller's entry in the *Densho Encyclopedia*.

5. For information on Fumiko "Caryl" Okuma Omura, see note 13 in Chapter 4.

6. Jimmie Omura, "Nisei in U.S. Labor," editorial, *Rocky Shimpo*, June 14, 1947; and "The Right to Work," editorial, *Rocky Shimpo*, July 30, 1947.

7. See esp. Jimmie Omura, "Optimism in Interracial Relations," editorial, *Rocky Shimpo*, August 28, 1947; and "Remedy Is from the Top," September 15, 1947.

8. See the editorials by Jimmie Omura in the *Rocky Shimpo*: "Nisei and Communism," May 26, 1947; "Henry Wallace and Russia," June 17, 1947; "A Dangerous Measure," July 9, 1947; "Is the JACD Communist?," October 11, 1947; "Builders of Hysteria," November 14, 1947; "JACL and Communism," December 10, 1947.

9. Jimmie Omura, "JACL and Communism," *Rocky Shimpo*, December 10, 1947.

10. See "Colorado Times" entry by Brian Niiya in the *Densho Encyclopedia*, http://encyclopedia.densho.org/ (accessed on August 19, 2015). For information on Togo Tanaka, see Brian Niiya's entry on him in the *Densho Encyclopedia*, http://encyclopedia.densho.org/ (accessed on May 28, 2016).

11. Jimmie Omura, "The Facts and Mr. Tanaka," letter, *Rocky Shimpo*, August 12, 1947.

12. Joe Oyama, "If He Were Mr. Omura, He'd Quit," *Rocky Shimpo*, September 11, 1947.

13. Togo Tanaka devoted his entire December 27 *Colorado Times* column to the Omura-Yasui confrontation. Tanaka interpreted Omura's resignation coming so quickly on the heels of Yasui's threatened libel suit as a cause-and-effect situation. It was a question, opined Tanaka, of a landscape gardener-writer being no match for a lawyer-writer. Tanaka confessed that initially he had greeted the resignation of the "windmill-tilting" Omura with glee but on reflection had softened his opinion because "Omura, our adversary in public print, was quite friendly in private correspondence."

14. For information on Harry Ueno, see the *Densho Encyclopedia* entry on him by
Arthur A. Hansen, http://encyclopedia.densho.org/ (accessed on May 28, 2016). This entry also encompasses the topic of the Manzanar Riot.

15. Bill Hosokawa, *Nisei: The Quiet Americans* (New York: William Morrow, 1969).

16. Robert A. Wilson and Bill Hosokawa, *East to America: A History of the Japanese in the United States* (New York: William Morrow, 1980).

17. Bill Hosokawa, *JACL in Quest of Justice* (New York: William Morrow, 1982).

18. Mike Masaoka with Bill Hosokawa, *They Call Me Moses Masaoka: An American Saga* (New York: William Morrow, 1987).

19. Wilson and Hosokawa, *East to America*, 243–44; Masaoka with Hosokawa, *They Call Me Moses Masaoka*, 179.

20. Hosokawa, *JACL in Quest of Justice*, 273–74.

21. See esp. Masaoka with Hosokawa, *They Call Me Moses Masaoka*, 179.

22. Hosokawa, *Nisei*, 361–62. For a superb biographical study of Kurihara, see Eileen H. Tamura, *In Defense of Justice: Joseph Kurihara and the Japanese American Struggle for Equality* (Urbana: University of Illinois Press, 2013).

23. Roger Daniels, *Concentration Camps USA: Japanese Americans and World War II* (New York: Holt, Rinehart and Winston, 1971).

24. Ibid., x.

25. Ibid., vii–viii.

26. Ibid., 128–29. On Omura's perspective on the limits of superpatriotism, see Appendix 1.

27. Michi Weglyn, *Years of Infamy: The Untold Story of America's Concentration Camps* (New York: William Morrow, 1976).

28. See Raymond Okamura, "The Concentration Camp Experience from a Japanese American Perspective: A Bibliographical Essay and Review of Michi Weglyn's *Years of Infamy*," in Emma Gee, ed., *Counterpoint: Perspectives on Asian America* (Los Angeles: Asian American Studies Center, University of California, Los Angeles, 1976), 27–30.

29. See Weglyn, *Years of Infamy*, chap. 3, "'So the Army Could Handle the Japs,'" 67.

30. On the isolation centers at Moab and Leupp, see Arthur A. Hansen's *Densho Encyclopedia* entry, http://encyclopedia.densho.org/ (accessed on May 28, 2016); on the Tule Lake Segregation Center, see the riveting entry pertaining to it in the *Densho Encyclopedia* by Barbara Takei, http://encyclopedia.densho.org/ (accessed on May 28, 2016).

31. See Glen Kitayama, "Collins, Wayne Mortimer (1900–1974), Attorney," in Brian Niiya, ed., *Encyclopedia of Japanese American History: An A-to-Z Reference from 1868 to the Present*, 2nd ed. (Los Angeles: Japanese American National Museum, 2001), 140–41. See also the discerning entry on Collins by Brian Niiya and Greg Robertson in the *Densho Encyclopedia*, http://encyclopedia.densho.org/ (accessed on May 28, 2016).

32. For the summary of the hearings, see Commission on the Wartime Relocation and Internment of Civilians, *Personal Justice Denied: Report of the Commission on Wartime Relocation and Internment of Civilians* (Washington, DC: U.S. Government Printing Office, 1982). In the interview Omura transacted on August 16, 1985, with family friend and supporter George Matsumonji (Omura Papers, Stanford University; hereafter cited as OP), Omura shares the following information:

> Now in 1981, I attended the Commission on Wartime Relocation and Internment in Seattle. At that time, I was feeling pretty bad. I had been feeling pretty bad for six years and had been in and out of hospitals. And doctors and cardiologists couldn't handle it. I came from Bainbridge Island, close by Seattle, so I thought to myself I'd take that in and go see my island home. It would be probably the last time I'd ever see it. I hadn't been there for thirty–forty years. Something like that.

33. See Michi Weglyn letter to James Omura, June 3, 1987 (OP).

34. See January 27, 1994, entry, Redress Diary of James Omura (OP).

35. See "James Matsumoto Omura," in *Book of Dedications* (Cambridge, UK: International Biographical Centre, 1989), 294.

36. See Jimmie Matsumoto letter to "Dear Brother" [Kazushi Matsumoto], November 27, 1928 (OP). This letter's postscript notes as follows: "Say I've changed my name again."

37. See Jimmie Hollingworth Royal letter to Kazushi Matsumoto, March 7, 1929, ibid. The letter's postscript reads: "Translated [Jimmie Hollingworth Royal] means Jimmie Royal. I'm studying a little Japanese. Here's how to write my real name."

38. For the sequential progression of these names, see the cache of correspondence between Omura and his brother Kazushi ("Casey") covering the years 1927–29 within ibid.

39. See "James Matsumoto Omura," *World Biographical Hall of Fame* (Cambridge, UK: International Biographical Centre, 1990), 1.

40. An appreciation of the relationship between Casey Matsumoto and James Omura can be gained through their extensive, informative, stimulating, intelligent, and sometimes confrontational correspondence in OP.

41. In a letter from James Omura to Michi Weglyn, June 28, 1984, ibid., Omura notes: "Yes, I was vilified by the JACL. It was a hazard of occupation that I had to accept. What rankles deep is the animosity of the Japanese [American] community of Denver and the contiguous environs that led to a self-imposed exile from the Asian [American] world."

42. For a nice encapsulation of this situation, see James M. Omura letter to Miya Okawara, December 15, 1983, ibid., where Omura writes: "I am an

old iconoclast who had resigned myself to travel the rest of the way unsung, unknown, unappreciated—my cross to bear alone. I had lost step with the times in my seclusion from Asian [American] events."

43. The quoted language here is appropriated from the dust jacket description of the Masaoka autobiography.

44. See Omura's review of *JACL in Quest of Justice*, in *Amerasia Journal* 11 (Fall/Winter 1984): 99.

45. See James Omura, "Another JACL Hoax," *Rafu Shimpo*, June 14, 1994. This letter to the editor was perhaps the last published piece of writing by Omura.

46. That constitutional matters were vitally important to Jimmie Omura during World War II is captured in an exchange he had during his 1944 tenure as editor of the *Rocky Shimpo* with a reader named Ikuo Okuma from Glendale, Arizona. Writes Okuma to Omura, February 26, 1944: "I just read your editorial by the title 'Let's Call a Spade a Spade.' I want to congratulate you. You are the only Nisei editor yet that's got the guts to stand up for our rights. Rest of the sons-of-bitches are nothing but weak-kneed pussyfooters and I mean it. They do not understand the basic reason why this war is fought." Responds Omura to Okuma, April 7, 1944: "I believe in constitutional democratic government. The treatment accorded the Nisei is not in accordance with the highest principles of our federal constitution. It is regrettable that there are not more Nisei who would willingly sacrifice their own personal consideration for the greater principles involved." See OP. Even earlier, in a May 15, 1943, letter from James Omura to California attorney general Earl Warren, Omura begins his letter thusly: "I am interested in the legal and constitutional rights of the U.S.-born Japanese and would like to ask an official ruling as to recourse and indemnity entitled them as a result of their forced evacuation from California." Earlier still, on January 28, 1944, Omura had written a letter to Warren that strongly protested the consideration by the California State Assembly of two bills which "seek to memorialize the President and the Congress to enact legislation disenfranchising the U.S.-born Japanese." For these letters, see OP.

47. In a December 30, 1985, letter from James Omura to Merry Omori, he writes: "The stories of military resisters and prewar draftees give greater meaning to the draft resistance in the concentration camps. Their stories have been shoved into the closet as incidents of racial shame rather than . . . a token of rare courage . . . and a symbol of fidelity to the fundamental tenets that form our system of constitutional government." See OP.

48. The best treatment of Omura's response to the Smithsonian exhibition, as viewed within the context of the activist Nikkei community, is found in Alice Yang Murray, *Historical Memories of the Japanese American Internment and the*

Struggle for Redress (Stanford, CA: Stanford University Press, 2008), 384–96; it is to this account that my own closely adheres, including the quoted passages. For Omura's critique of the exhibit script mailed to Tom Crouch on January 13, 1987, see OP.

49. See Eric L. Muller, *Free to Die for Their Country: The Story of the Japanese American Resisters in World War II* (Chicago: University of Chicago Press, 2001), 69–70.

50. See James M. Omura, interview by Arthur A. Hansen, August 22, 23, 24, 25, 1984, in Arthur A. Hansen, ed., *Japanese American World War II Evacuation Oral History Project, Part 4: Resisters* (Munich: K. G. Saur, 1995), 301. For the context in which this voiced threat by Yasui occurred, see ibid., 299–301.

51. This quote derives from Muller, *Free to Die for Their Country*, 98–99. Similarly, my treatment of this topic is based chiefly and heavily upon Muller's chap. 5, "Reaction," in ibid., 64–99, esp. 68–70 and 92–99. See also Martha Nakagawa, "Analysis: A Look at JACL's Role during WWII, Stance on Resisters," *Pacific Citizen*, July 16–22, 1999, available online at www.resisters.com/news/PC_7-6-99.htm.

52. As a supplement to this book, I have prepared an edited and annotated version of James Omura's Redress Diary, entitled "James Omura's 'Return to the Wars Diary, 1981–94,'" for use as an open-source electronic document, which is posted on the UCLA Asian American Studies Center-sponsored Suyama Project, www.suyamaproject.org/, since it is consistent with this project's mission "to preserve the history of Japanese American resistance during World War II."

CHAPTER I

1. In 1868 the Tokugawa shogun ("great general"), Japan's feudal period ruler since 1639, fell from power when the emperor was restored to the country's supreme position. Because the emperor took the name of Meiji ("enlightened rule") as his reign name, this transformative event became widely known as the Meiji Restoration. The Meiji era officially ended in 1912.

2. Since Omura never traveled to Japan in his lifetime, this "prophecy" proved self-fulfilling.

3. This designation was given to the youth selected by the ship's captain to attend devotedly to his assorted needs.

4. For a discussion of peasant uprisings happening around this time, see Misiko Hane, *Peasants, Rebels, Women, and Outcastes: The Underside of Modern Japan* (New York: Pantheon Books, 1982), 21–27.

5. On evasion of and resistance to the policy of universal military conscription in Meiji era Japan, see ibid., 18–20.

6. This formal agreement between the United States and Japan, although never codified into congressional law and ultimately nullified in 1924, was precipitated

by the San Francisco School Board's 1906 decision to segregate the city's Japanese-ancestry students into an existing segregated school for Chinese-ancestry students.

7. Kazushi Matsumoto's death date was November 12, 1990.

8. The legal paper referenced here does not appear to be contained within OP.

9. A 1932 graduate of Seattle's Broadway High School, Omura was personally familiar with the Edison facility. In 1921 a two-floor annex to Broadway High had been opened to house vocational/technical education classes.

10. In 1903 this southeast Bainbridge Island town supplanted Madrone, which had been first homesteaded in 1878 and officially named in 1890; by then it consisted of farms, small businesses, and a steamer dock. The name change to Winslow honored the recently deceased Winslow Hall, a community founder.

11. During the twentieth century's dawning, when the Hall Brothers Marine Railway and Shipbuilding Company was getting too big for its Port Blakely site, owner Henry Hall, in 1903, purchased acreage on Eagle Harbor near the settlement of Madrone (later Winslow) to expand the shipyard's operation.

12. An alternative explanation for Wilkes's naming of Eagle Harbor is that he was influenced by the distinctive birdlike shape of the harbor at Winslow.

13. Vancouver named this east-facing southern Bainbridge Island headland to honor King Charles II (1630–85), who in 1660 had been "restored" to England's throne.

14. This treaty between the United States and assorted Puget Sound area tribes, bands, nations was signed in 1855.

15. On March 31, 1854, Perry, acting on behalf of the United States, signed the Treaty of Kanagawa with Japan. It marked the end of shogunate-enforced Japanese isolationism that had held sway since the early sixteenth century.

16. This county recorded 2,065 people by 1883.

17. Climaxing some three decades of escalating racism in the United States against people of Chinese ancestry, the Chinese Exclusion Act of 1882 banned Chinese immigration. For detailed information on this act, see Mieko Matsumoto, "Chinese Exclusion Act," in the *Densho Encyclopedia*, http://encyclopedia.densho.org/ (accessed on September 14, 2014).

18. The term "picture bride" refers to the early-twentieth-century practice of immigrant male workers (chiefly Japanese and Koreans) in Hawai'i and the U.S. mainland's West Coast selecting brides from their home nations via a match-maker, who relied upon family recommendations and photographs to pair prospective mates. For a splendid topical amplification of picture brides, see Kelli Y. Nakamura, "Picture Brides," in the *Densho Encyclopedia,* http://encyclopedia.densho.org/print/ (accessed on September 11, 2014).

19. See certified copy of birth certificate, No. 10564, for Utaka Matsumoto, Washington State Department of Health, Division of Vital Statistics, Record No. 67, Special File Vol. #3, Registered No. 267, February 2, 1940 (OP).

20. This Japanese folklore term has achieved recognition in art, literature, and drama and can also be rendered in English as "demon," "ogre," or "troll." *Oni* are typically depicted as humans but of enormous size, prodigious strength, and frightful appearance and often with peculiar characteristics like horns, extra fingers and toes, or odd numbers of eyes.

21. This line derives from Whittier's 1855 poem "The Barefoot Boy."

22. This fairy tale, which is one of Japan's most famous, has variations based on geographical regions. The version that derived from the Edo period (1603–1868) is very likely the one Harue Omura related to her children. For a compact and cogent representation of this fairy tale, see Frank Chin, "Storytime for Children: Momotaro, The Peach Boy," in *Born in the USA: A Story of Japanese America, 1889–1947* (Lanham, MD: Rowman & Littlefield, 2002), 61–62.

23. Rather than a specific folktale, this word, which in Japanese means "fox," depicts a common subject in Japanese folklore. Stories about *kitsune* customarily represent them as clever, long-lived, possessing magical capabilities, and endowed with the ability to assume human form. Quite often presented as tricksters, *kitsune* are generally portrayed as women, particularly seductresses, with men being their prime victims.

24. This story, which dramatizes the quintessential rendition of the samurai code of honor, *bushidō*, is widely deemed Japan's "national legend." The incident at the heart of the story occurred at the start of the eighteenth century. It revolves around a group of samurai who were left leaderless (became *ronin*) when their feudal lord (*daimyo*) was coerced into committing ritual suicide (*seppuku*) for physically attacking Kira Yoshinaka, a court official. The *ronin* later killed Kira and in so doing avenged their master's honor. This act in turn forced the *ronin* to commit *seppuku* as the price for their murderous deed. If this story held special salience within the Meiji era, it was likely due to the pervasive, if unconscious public feeling that while the nation was undergoing the upheaval of rapid modernization, fidelity to Japanese cultural roots provided a much-needed psychological counterbalance.

25. This term's literal meaning is "a thing that changes." The transformation can involve a ghost, but an *obake* more frequently refers to a living thing or a supernatural being that has experienced a temporary transformation.

26. The version of the Weeping Willow Tree story that Omura told to Frank Chin during the 1982 interview Chin conducted with him in Los Angeles appears in Chin, *Born in the USA*, 12. See James Omura, interview by Frank Chin, May 14, 15, 16, 26, 1982, tape recording, Frank Chin Oral History Collection, Manuscripts, Archives, and Special Collections, Washington State University, Pullman, WA. See also James M. Omura, interview by Arthur A. Hansen, August 22, 23, 24, 25, 1984, interview 1765, tape recording and transcript, Japanese American

Project, Oral History Program [Center for Oral and Public History], California State University, Fullerton, Fullerton, CA. For a published edited and annotated version of the Omura-Hansen interview, see Hansen, *Japanese American World War II Evacuation Oral History Project, Part 4: Resisters*, 131–43, esp. 176–77, where Omura recounts the Weeping Willow Tree story.

27. Two comparatively recent Japanese American historical studies have employed this (variously spelled) word, and the context of each use deserves close attention here. First, Frank Chin, in *Born in the USA*, relates that during a taped interview of his with Nobu Kawaii (a contemporary of James Omura raised in the southern California city of Pasadena) and his wife, Miye, the Kawaiis engaged in this relevant dialogue: (Nobu) "We had snide remarks of being 'Japs' or 'skibbies' directed at us." (Miye) "I heard that when I was growing up. Skibbies. I would be walking up a street and a couple of young boys would say 'skibbies!'" (Nobu) "I don't know what it means." (Miye) "I don't either" (56). Second, Yuji Ichioka, in "The Meaning of Loyalty: The Case Study of Kazumaro Buddy Uno," chap. 7 in Gordon H. Chang and Eiichiro Azuma, eds., *Before Internment: Essays in Prewar Japanese American History* (Stanford, CA: Stanford University Press, 2006), 166, quotes Uno (a pre–World War II Japanese American vernacular-press colleague of Omura's in San Francisco) explaining resentfully to a white American correspondent that "I was treated like a yellow skibby and not an American citizen. . . . So I decided, the hell with the United States. I'd go to Japan where my knowledge of the States would be appreciated." Enlarging upon this quotation, Ichioka writes: "According to a dictionary of slang in the American West, *skibby* has the meaning of a Japanese prostitute. In using the term to describe his racial experience, Uno was saying essentially that he had been treated like a yellow whore by white men."

28. For the details of this biblical story, see Samuel 1:17.

29. In Japan, May 5 is "Children's Day," a day when Japanese families celebrate the Boys' Festival or Boy's Day, which is termed Tango-no-Sekku. On this particular day, a large cloth streamer representing a carp—considered the most spirited of fish because of its ability to fight its way upstream—is flown from bamboo poles on residential rooftops to celebrate the healthy growth and development of all the sons in the respective families. Japanese Girl's Day, called *hina-matsuri* (Japanese doll festival), is March 3; on this special day families display a set of *hina* dolls on a shelf to wish household daughters health and happiness. Japanese American families within Hawai'i and mainland U.S. communities widely observed these customs during the pre–World War II years.

30. According to Andrew Price Jr., in *Port Blakely: The Community Captain Renton Built* (Seattle: Port Blakely Books, 1990), 112, Dr. Frank Shepard "established himself in Winslow in 1912," the very year of Omura's birth, and was the owner of Bainbridge Island's first car (a Model T).

31. Florence Rumsey came to the greater Seattle area in 1915 and served the Japanese Baptist Church of Seattle for over fifty years in its missionary activities, which extended on Bainbridge Island to Port Blakely and Winslow. See "Japanese Baptist Church of Seattle, History," www.jbcseattle.org/history.html (accessed on June 13, 2010). For Omura's recollections of Rumsey, see the Omura-Hansen interview, in Hansen, *Japanese American World War II Evacuation Oral History Project, Part 4: Resisters*, 172–73.

32. The Apostolic Faith Church (AFC), a worldwide Pentecostal Church headquartered in Portland, Oregon, traces its roots to the 1906 Pentecostal movement in Los Angeles, California. That same year, the AFC first published its magazine, *The Apostolic Faith*.

33. In 1881 Winslow (then known as Madrone) opened a one-room schoolhouse. It was replaced in 1908 by Lincoln School on donated land. Thereafter, this school would grow one grade at a time until, in 1914, it added a twelfth grade, thereby giving Bainbridge Island its own high school and sparing high school students from having to commute daily to Seattle. Interesting in this connection is the following observation by Stefan Akio Tanaka, in "The Nikkei on Bainbridge Island, 1883–1942" (master's thesis, University of Washington, 1977): "Adequate roads were not built until the 1920's. Until that period it was easier for the residents of Port Blakely to go to Seattle on the steamer than to Winslow, a distance of only three miles" (102).

34. Ibid., 96.

35. This cannery was destroyed by fire in 1997. That this cannery was established in 1917, as Omura contends, is problematic; other pertinent sources suggest that the cannery was constructed in the late 1920s. Omura is assuredly correct as to the location of the cannery; however, the date he provides, 1917, applies instead to the opening in Seattle of the National Cannery Company, which was thereafter utilized by Bainbridge Island growers.

36. See Tanaka, "The Nikkei on Bainbridge Island, 1883–1942," 96.

37. For cursory information about the pre–World War II Japanese schools on Bainbridge Island, see ibid., 121.

38. Nippon, or Japan, the Land of the Rising Sun.

39. A neighborhood in Seattle, located east of Beacon Hill and west of Mount Baker, the Rainier Valley was noteworthy in the early 1900s for its Italian-ancestry population.

40. A Japanese syllabary (i.e., a set of symbols that represent or approximate syllables), *hiragana* is one component of the Japanese writing system, along with *katagana*, *kanji*, and *Romaji* (the Latin alphabet).

41. Chikara's death date, in Katsusa, was November 6, 1920, seventeen months after his birth. The epidemic, which lasted from March 1918 to June 1920, spread

around the world and killed anywhere from fifty to one-hundred million people. In the United States, about 28 percent of the population was afflicted, while between 500,000 and 675,000 died.

42. July 17, 1920.

43. Tom Loverich emigrated from Austria to Winslow in 1902. In 1921 he and his wife, Christina, purchased the Winslow Dock Grocery store at the foot of Madison Avenue (where the steamer landed) and went into the grocery business. The family lived above the store until they sold it in 1931.

44. Prior to 1964, the U.S. Mint made "silver" dollars from silver alloy, and these "cartwheels" were commonly used by casino customers in Nevada for slot machines and table games.

45. This colloquialism of unknown origin means "on the quiet."

46. This situation originally was discussed at some length by James Omura in a 1929 letter he sent to his brother Kazushi from his then-residence in Pocatello, Idaho. The key section states:

> Now as I look back and the past recalls back to me the shameful deed of disgracefully taking the old man's hard cash on the bureau I feel no regret. Rather I feel that I was justified in taking that money. Why? It's simply because the low state of poverty I was in and even though he had the money to furnish me with better clothing he disdained to do so. . . . I'm not a thief and am perfectly trustable.

Jimmie Hollingworth Royal [James Omura] to Kazushi Matsumoto, March 7, 1929 (OP).

47. The Alien Land Act became law in that same year, 1921, and it prevented noncitizens and those ineligible for citizenship from owning, leasing, or renting land. It was not repealed until 1966. For an examination of alien land laws aimed at Japanese immigrants in a national context, see Cherstin M. Lyon, "Alien Land Laws," in the *Densho Encyclopedia*, http://encyclopedia.densho.org/print/ (accessed on September 12, 2014).

48. Information on James "Jimmie" Sakamoto (1903–55), who founded the *Japanese-American Courier* in 1928, is substantially developed in Chapter 3. For a succinct and useful biographical overview of Sakamoto, a leader of the Seattle Progressive Citizens League, see Brian Niiya, "James Sakamoto," in the *Densho Encyclopedia*, http://encyclopedia.densho.org/ (accessed on September 12, 2014).

49. Founded in 1905 in Chicago, the IWW (whose members were dubbed "Wobblies") by 1908 had become influential in the Pacific Northwest region. The IWW was an industrial union in that it welcomed and organized both skilled and unskilled workers within particular unions, and it owed its existence in part to opposing the craft unionism of the American Federation of Labor (AFL).

50. In addition to providing crew quarters—modest shared quarters and bunk areas—for enlisted crew and junior officers, small-to-medium-sized vessels would maintain captain's quarters, which typically included an office, living room, bedroom, and a small pantry, much in the manner of an efficiency apartment.

51. Eagle Harbor Congregational Church, the first church on Bainbridge Island, was founded in 1882, but it lacked a building for worship until 1896.

52. Bainbridge Island's first library was located above the mill store in Port Madison and came into existence in 1863. During the first half of the twentieth century, an array of small libraries, supported by ladies' society "silver teas," appeared on the scene. One of these libraries was the Winslow Library, which was started in 1913 by the Winslow Library Association in the Knights Templar Building. It closed in 1947.

53. Open to the public in 1895, Seattle General Hospital, the city's second private hospital, was formed by a group of civic-minded women as a Protestant hospital. In 1900 a five-story facility was constructed on Fifth Avenue, and this structure continued in existence as Seattle General Hospital for seventy-one years.

54. The German word *scholle* is translated as "clod" in English. As used in American English, "clodhoppers" commonly conveys the British English connotation of clumsiness.

55. Edward FitzGerald (1809–83) is best known for his English translation of the *Rubaiyat of Omar Khayyam* (1859), a selection of Persian poems.

56. Available evidence points to the Issei man in question here being Isekichi Kunimatsu. As for the plant managed by him, according to John N. Cobb, *Pacific Salmon Fisheries*, 3rd ed., Bureau of Fisheries Document No. 902 (Washington, DC: U.S. Government Printing Office, 1921), 141, "at present [the plant of] the Japanese-American Fertilizer Co. on Lummi Island . . . operate[s] quite largely on the offal from the [Puget] Sound salmon canneries."

57. This small community is located near Winslow on the eastern part of Bainbridge Island.

58. There is confusion attendant upon this statement. In a letter dated June 29, 1932, from James Omura to Kazushi Matsumoto, Omura writes: "It might be a surprise for you to know that grandmother [Saiyo] is dead. She passed away on May 7th. Our sisters—Hanako and Taeko—wish to join us in America. They are staying with Dad's sister at present." However, the postmark on the envelope correlated with this letter carries the date of June 29, 1937. In any event, neither Hanako nor Taeko ever came to the United States. See Jimmie Omura to Kaz Matsumoto, June 29, 1932 [1937] (OP).

59. This particular letter from Hanako to James Matsumoto Omura does not exist in the at Stanford University. The only two letters between them archived

within the Omura Papers are in the correspondence file marked "Hanako": the first, from James Matsumoto Omura to Hanako (neé Matsumoto), is dated February 9, 1992; and the second, from Hanako (neé Matsumoto) to James Matsumoto Omura, was received by him on May 28, 1992. The communication between the two siblings was never direct owing to the first not knowing English and the second lacking facility in Japanese. The interaction between the two of them and the context in which it occurred can best be tracked through two Omura Papers documentary sources: Omura's Redress Diary and the July 5, 1989, to December 26, 1993, correspondence between James Omura and Mary Tomita.

60. Originally worn only by men, *hakama* later came to be worn as well by women. Tied at the waist and falling nearly to the ankles, this traditional Japanese article of clothing is typically worn over a kimono. *Hakama* come in two types: divided and undivided.

61. *Koseki* is a census register or registration, while *touhon* means a copy, a transcript, or a duplicate. A *koseki touhon* refers to one's entire family registry, which includes the names of relations beyond one's own parents and siblings. Often people leave their birthplace but still consider it their "real" home, and so they may choose to maintain their *koseki* in their hometown or place of birth. See "Family Registries: *Koseki Touhon* and *Koseki Shouhon*," www.rootsweb.ancestry. com/ (accessed on June 28, 2010).

62. Based on the teachings of the thirteenth-century Japanese reformist monk Nichiren (1222–82), Nichiren Buddhism is an inclusive term encompassing several major schools and a large number of subschools, as well as several of Japan's new religions. It had great influence among Kyoto merchants in Japan's Middle Ages and among some ultranationalists during the pre–World War II period. Nichiren Buddhism is also noted for having an evangelical streak and for opposing other forms of Japanese Buddhism, particularly those considered as different from Mahayana Buddhism orthodoxy.

63. For a very useful and quite detailed short history of this Seattle-area institution (which operated between 1911 and 1973), replete with an assortment of photographs, see Paula Becker, "Firland Sanatorium," in HistoryLink.org, *The Free Online Encyclopedia of Washington State History*, www.historylink.org/index .cfm?DisplayPage=output.cfm&file_id=3928 (accessed June 28, 2010). For a more detailed treatment of Firland Sanatorium, see note 128 in Chapter 3 of this book.

64. Gene Dennis to K. Matsumoto, April 24, 1940 (OP).

65. See note appended to letter, Kazushi Matsumoto to Miss Matsushita, May 3, 1940, ibid.

66. Ibid.

67. It is difficult to ascertain which historical researcher Omura had in mind when making this observation, but perhaps it was Stefan Tanaka, who in his

previously noted study, "The Nikkei of Bainbridge Island, 1883–1942," 102, declared that on Bainbridge Island "adequate roads were not built until the 1920s."

68. The birthday of the reigning emperor, Tenchō Setsu, has been a national holiday since the 1868 restoration of the Meiji emperor. It was a religious holiday until just after World War II. In 1948 it was renamed the Emperor's Birthday.

CHAPTER 2

1. Labor contractors, according to one reliable source, served as "an essential bridge between the [Asian] . . . crews and the cannery managers . . . responsible for recruitment, provisioning, establishing working conditions, and setting pay scales for their gangs, all without oversight by the cannery owners. The system was open to kickbacks, favoritism, inadequate provisions and living conditions, and to the blacklisting of anyone who complained." See San Francisco Maritime National Historical Park, "Asians in the Salmon Canning Industry," www.nps.gov/safr/historyculture/asiancanneryworkers.htm (accessed on July 6, 2010). Kushi Brothers and Company (headed up by Tanejiro Kushi), along with George Nishimura and A. B. Company, comprised the major labor contractors who recruited predominantly Japanese labor crews for the Alaskan salmon canneries. See Jack Masson and Donald Guimary, "Asian Labor Contractors in the Alaskan Canned Salmon Industry: 1880–1937," *Labor History* 22 (Summer 1981): 395. Two books that provide an assessment of the laboring class within the canned salmon industry in Alaska and the Pacific Coast region are Donald Guimary, *Marumina Trabaho ("Dirty Work"): A History of Labor in Alaska's Salmon Canning Industry* (Bloomington, IN: iUniverse, 2006); and Chris Friday, *Organizing Asian-American Labor: The Pacific Coast Canned-Salmon Industry, 1870–1942* (Philadelphia: Temple University Press, 1995).

2. Alaska's southeastern-most sizable city, Ketchikan has long been known as the "Salmon Capital of the World." The city is located on Revillagigedo Island, 679 miles north of Seattle and 235 miles south of Juneau, Alaska's capital. Ketchikan's history dates back to 1883 with the construction of a salmon saltery. As late as 1927, Ketchikan, with a population exceeding six thousand, outstripped Juneau as Alaska's largest city and it was viewed by other Alaskan communities as a Seattle "suburb." See Dave Kiffer, "1927: When Ketchikan Was the Largest City in Alaska," *SitNews*, April 30, 2007, www.sitnews.us/Kiffer/Ketchikan/043007 _ketchikan_1927.html (accessed on September 6, 2013).

3. The term "schoolboys" is not used here by Omura to designate the common practice among young Issei and Nisei (including himself) to take on live-in domestic work as a means to earn a livelihood while going to school, but rather to describe the large number of Nikkei high school and college students who labored to earn money for themselves and their family through summer employment in Pacific Northwest canneries.

4. It is possible that Omura, a onetime sports writer and a lifelong enthusiast of competitive athletics, might have confused the first name of the individual identified here with that of Julius Nicholas Boros (1920–94), the celebrated Hungarian American professional golfer.

5. Established in Philadelphia in 1869, the Knights of Labor (also known as the Noble and Holy Order of the Knights of Labor), pursued the following organizational goals: (1) an eight-hour workday; (2) abolition of child labor; (3) termination of the convict labor system; (4) establishment of cooperatives to replace the traditional wage system and help moderate capitalism's excesses; (5) equal pay for equal work; (6) government ownership of telegraph facilities and railroads; (7) a public land policy designed to aid settlers and not speculators; and (8) a graduated income tax. In contrast to the Knights' harsh policies toward Asians, this union was receptive to accepting blacks and women as members. By 1886 this industrial union claimed over seven hundred thousand members, but the growing repression of labor unions in the United States after that date, combined with the rise of the American Federation of Labor, a skilled trade or craft union, precipitated the sharp decline of the Knights of Labor, so that by 1890 it counted fewer than one hundred thousand members.

6. Around 1900 the *Star* (which started out and continued for much of its life as a steadfast workingperson's newspaper) was Seattle's largest paper, but by 1942 (when it became heatedly anti-Japanese, especially toward Japanese Americans in the Seattle area) it had the smallest circulation among Seattle's three general circulation dailies.

7. The *Times* began its publication life, albeit under another name, in 1891. It remains one of a handful of independently owned and operated family newspapers in the United States and has long boasted an international reputation for its investigative journalism.

8. With a founding date of 1863, the *Post-Intelligencer* (or simply the *P-I*) was purchased by Randolph Hearst in 1921. In the 1930s the paper's editorial policy was New Deal oriented, but during World War II the paper, with a change in publishers, turned increasingly conservative in its political persuasion.

9. There are several distinct stages involved in the "processing process" employed within Alaskan salmon canneries. The second of these stages occurs at the "slime table." See "Alaska Salmon Processing Jobs," *JobMonkey*, www.jobmonkey.com/alaska/html/salmon_processing.html (accessed on September 6, 2013).

10. The U.S. Hotel in Seattle was located at 315 Maynard Street in the area now designated as the International District.

11. Built between 1904 and 1906 by the Great Northern Railway and Northern Pacific Railway, the King Street Station is located in the Pioneer Square neighborhood of Seattle. Its construction improved Seattle's connections between

land and sea and signified that the city had become the Pacific Northwest's primary shipping port.

12. The Hotel Bannock was located at 111 S. Arthur Avenue in Pocatello.

13. There does not appear to be a Bannock River. Perhaps Omura had in mind the Portneuf River, a tributary of the Snake River, since that river flows through downtown Pocatello and enters the Snake River approximately ten miles northwest of the city.

14. For a photograph of this truck, see "Bannock County Images," in *Idaho Digital Resources*, http://idahodocs.contentdm.oclc.org/cdm4/browse.php?CISOR OOT=%2Fp2003coll1&CISOSTART=1,81 (accessed on July 8, 2010).

15. Theodore F. Turner (1868–1951), the husband of Lucy P. Turner, was "one of the most prominent men in the political life of the county [Bannock]." In addition to serving as Pocatello's mayor, he was a state senator and state auditor for Idaho. See Bannock County, Idaho AHGP [American History and Genealogy Project], "History of Pocatello, Bannock County, Idaho," www.idahogenealogy. com/bannock/history_pocatello_bannock_county.htm (accessed on September 16, 2014).

16. An abstract company customarily provides abstracts, title searches, lien searches, title insurance, and closing services for residential, commercial, industrial, and governmental real estate in the county or counties it serves. Theodore F. and Lucy P. Turner's oldest son was born about 1894.

17. Pocatello's first junior high school, Franklin opened in 1924 as a one-story "bungalow" style structure.

18. The national institution of American Legion Baseball was launched in 1925 for high school-aged players. In 1926 the first American Legion World Series was held in Philadelphia, Pennsylvania, where a team from Yonkers, New York, beat a team from Pocatello, Idaho.

19. A major figure in the American labor movement, William Dudley Haywood (1869–1928), more commonly known as "Big Bill Haywood," was a founding member of the Industrial Workers of the World, which championed industrial unionism. The IWW's most notable leader, he was embroiled throughout his career in violent conflict. In 1918 Haywood was convicted for violating the 1917 Espionage Act. However, during an appeal of his conviction, he fled to Russia (where he spent the remainder of his life). Upon his death, half of his ashes were buried in the Kremlin wall in Moscow, while the remaining half were sent to Chicago and buried near a martyrs' monument commemorating the 1886 Haymarket Riot, an event which had stimulated Haywood's early involvement in the labor movement.

20. Idaho's fourth governor and the first non–Republican Party member, Frank Steunenberg (1861–1905), a nominee of the Democrats and the Populists,

served as the state's chief executive from 1897 to 1901. In 1905 he was killed outside his Caldwell, Idaho, home by a bomb rigged to his front gate.

21. First published in 1864, the *Idaho Statesman* is a daily newspaper serving the greater Boise area.

22. Civil War veteran, lawyer, and political leader Robert G. Ingersoll (1833–99) was the New York-born son of an outspoken abolitionist Protestant minister. Because of his spirited defense of agnosticism, Ingersoll earned the sobriquet "Great Agnostic." In the silver-tongued speeches he delivered on his frequent lecture tours, Ingersoll lampooned religious belief while advocating humanism, free thinking, and scientific thought. Bertrand Arthur William Russell (1872–1970), a brilliant philosopher, logician, mathematician, historian, and social theorist, was a dedicated socialist and pacifist in word and deed. Although he was born and died in Wales, Russell spent most of his life in England. In a series of pamphlets, Russell advanced his notion of agnosticism, declaring that his readers should "stand on their own two feet and look fair and square at the world [with a] fearless attitude and a free intelligence."

23. In the 1920s, the Long Bell Mill in southwestern Washington was the world's largest sawmill. Timber baron Robert A. Long built the preplanned city of Longview, with paved streets, utilities, stores, churches, a school, and the opulent Columbia Theater. See R. A. Long Historical Society, "Longview, Washington," www.ralonghistoricalsociety.org/lgviewwa.htm (accessed on July 13, 2010).

24. An estuary located southeast of Ketchikan on the Pearse/Portland Canal, Hidden Inlet became the home in 1911 of the Hidden Inlet Cannery. For historic images of the Hidden Inlet Cannery during its heyday, see Alaska State Library, "Alaska's Digital Archives," http://vilda.alaska.edu/cdm4/results.php?CISOOP1=a ny&CISOFIELD1=CISOSEARCHALL&CISOROOT=/cdmg21&CISOBOX1 =Packing (accessed on July 13, 2010).

25. The inventor Edmund A. Smith (1878–1909), of Bellingham, Washington, developed a machine in 1903 that could butcher and clean salmon for canning fifty-five times faster than human workers. This innovation, which he called the "Iron Chink," was so named because it replaced the Chinese workers who then formed the backbone of the Northwest cannery workforce but had diminished sharply in number with the passage of the Chinese Exclusion Act of 1892 (allegedly two years after the word "Chink" came into existence as a racial slur for a person of Chinese ancestry). See David Wilma, "Automated Salmon Cleaning Machine Developed in Seattle in 1903," essay, HistoryLink.org, www.historylink. org/index.cfm?DisplayPage=output.cfm&File_Id=2109 (accessed on July 13, 2010).

26. Perhaps here Omura is thinking of the Fort Peck Indian Reservation, which comprises parts of four counties and is the ninth-largest reservation in the United States.

27. For a very useful historical overview of Seattle Japantown and ongoing contemporary efforts to preserve and interpret its significant remnants, see Trevor Griffey, "September 2003: Preserving Seattle's Japantown," www.historicseattle. org/preservationseattle/neighborhoods/defaultsept2.htm (accessed on September 17, 2014).

28. Acquired by Masahiro Furuya in 1914, the Beikoko Toyo Ginko or Oriental American Bank was located in Seattle's Japantown at Fifth Avenue and Main Street. In 1928 Furuya merged the Japanese Commercial Bank with the Oriental American Bank to create the Pacific Commercial Bank. See Seattle.gov, Department of Neighborhoods, "Historical Sites: Furuya Building," http://web1.seattle .gov/DPD/historicalsite/QueryResult.aspx?ID=1655591672 (accessed on July 15, 2010).

29. Since 1923 the *Bainbridge Island Review* has covered every aspect of life on Bainbridge Island. The paper is most notable for the courageous stand taken by its World War II editors Walt and Millie Woodward condemning the exclusion and detention of 227 Bainbridge Islanders of Japanese ancestry. See Mary Woodward, *In Defense of Our Neighbors: The Walt and Milly Woodward Story* (Bainbridge Island, WA: Fenwick, 2008).

30. Opened in 1902 under the designation of Seattle High School—the first building specifically constructed as a high school in Seattle—the renamed Broadway High School (after the avenue it faced) came into existence in 1909. Known for its diverse class and racial student body and its night classes, Broadway ceased to function as a high school in 1946. See "Broadway High School, Seattle's First Dedicated High School Opens in 1902," in HistoryLink.org, *Free Online Encyclopedia of Washington State History*, www.historylink.org/index. cfm?DisplayPage=output.cfm&file_id=3204 (accessed on September 11, 2013).

31. An American labor leader, Dave Beck (1894–1993) grew up in Seattle and attended Broadway High School (as would Jimmie Omura some years later). In 1917 Beck organized Local 566 of the International Brotherhood of the Teamsters. In 1927 he became both the president of his local and a full-time organizer for the international union. Eventually, he served as the union's president.

32. The president of the United Mine Workers of America from 1920 to 1960, John Llewellyn Lewis (1880–1960) was the dominant voice shaping the U.S. labor movement in the 1930s.

33. For information about Daisho "Dyke" Miyagawa (1915–89) and George Kiyoshi Takigawa (1916–n.d.) at the onset of the U.S. entry into World War II, see the confidential report prepared by the Counter-Subversion Section, Office of Naval Intelligence, dated December 24, 1941, and entitled "Japanese Tokyo Club Syndicate, with Interlocking Affiliations," http://home.comcast.net/e09066 /1941/41-12/TokClub.html (accessed on September 17, 2014). See also Daisho

Miyagawa, letter to "Big Bill" Hosokawa, "describing efforts to unionize Japanese and Filipino workers in the Pacific Northwest in the 1930s," sent on February 25, 1969, in the University of Washington Libraries, Digital Collections (Pacific Northwest Historical Documents Collection), http://digitalcollections.lib.washington.edu/cdm/ref/collection/pioneerlife/id/9596 (accessed on September 17, 2014).

34. In an interview with historian Chris Friday on March 25, 1988, in Pullman, Washington, Omura referred stingingly to the summer-time college and high school Nisei Alaska cannery workers as "Boys of Summer," for having a cavalier attitude toward their seasonal employment. The felicitous phrase employed by Omura, a passionate sports fan, was likely appropriated from Roger Kahn's book on the Brooklyn Dodgers, *Boys of Summer* (New York: Harper & Row, 1972). See Friday, *Organizing Asian American Labor*, 244, fn74.

35. For biographical information about Clarence Takeya Arai (1903–63), see Special Collections, University of Washington Libraries, "Guide to the Clarence T. Arai Photographs circa 1949–1951," http://digital.lib.washington.edu/findingaids/view?docId=AraiClarencePH2010_008.xml;query= (accessed on September 16, 2014).

36. An AFL affiliate founded on May 1, 1905, the Seattle Central Labor Council (SCLC) was comprised of over one hundred labor unions. Its labor base consisted primarily of craft unions and skilled middle-class white men.

37. George Takigawa, like Jimmie Omura, was a graduate of Seattle's Broadway High School, with the former graduating in 1933 and the latter in 1932. Whether they knew one another in high school is a moot point.

38. The Union Bay Cannery was established at Union Bay, Alaska, in 1916. Up to 1945 local fishermen sold their catch to this cannery—situated some forty miles northwest of Ketchikan—which in turn sold in bulk to Japan.

39. The friendship between Omura and Franny Yamamoto is discussed in Chapter 3 and Chapter 6 of this book.

40. In the early 1900s, because there were no hotels or rooming houses to provide safe and decent housing for the three thousand or so single Japanese women in Seattle, Mrs. Yoshi Okazaki, the wife of the pastor of the Seattle Japanese Baptist Church, determined that something needed to be done for these women. Commissioned in 1903 by the American Baptist Home Mission Society to work half-time on behalf of these female Issei newcomers to the city, Mrs. Okazaki opened the "Fujin Home" the following year. See Seattle Japanese Baptist Church, "History," www.jbcseattle.org/history.html (accessed on July 21, 2010).

41. The reference here appears to be to a youth organization run by the Salvation Army in many U.S. cities. Its mission is "to inspire and enable all young people, especially those from disadvantaged circumstances, to realize their full potential as productive, responsible, and caring citizens."

42. Donald Axel Nylen (1906–95) was born of Swedish immigrant parents in Des Moines, Iowa, and died in Seattle, Washington. Prior to World War II, he received his BA and MA from the University of Washington; after teaching at Seattle's Broadway High School, he studied and traveled in Europe, taking post-graduate work at the University of Berlin and acquiring his doctor's degree at the University of Vienna.

43. Sidney David Spear (1909–44), the son of Jewish American parents, lost his life during World War II at age thirty-five while serving overseas in the U.S. military. See "Washington State Roll of Honor, Part 8: University of Washington Interrupted Journey World War II Memorial," www.historylink.org/index.cfm ?DisplayPage=output.cfm&file_id=7108 (accessed on September 17, 2014).

CHAPTER 3

1. Before World War II, Iwaki Drug was located on the southeast corner of E. First Street and S. San Pedro Street. See Ben Pease, "Heart of Little Tokyo, E. First and San Pedro Sts., Japanese American Businesses of 1940," *Japantown Atlas Maps*, http://japantownatlas.com/map-littletokyo3.html (accessed on July 22, 2010).

2. For historical information on the Little Tokyo district in Los Angeles, California, see the following: Hillary Jenks, "'Home Is Little Tokyo': Race, Community, and Memory in Twentieth Century Los Angeles" (PhD diss., University of Southern California, 2008); and Mike Murase, *Little Tokyo: One Hundred Years in Pictures* (Los Angeles: Visual Communications, 1983).

3. For information about the *New Japanese American News* and Omura's brief editorship of it in 1933–34, see the published transcript of the 1984 oral history interview recorded by Arthur A. Hansen with James Matsumoto Omura, 193, as cited in Chapter 1, note 26, of the present book. See also the entry by Eiichiro Azuma for "Nichibei Shimbun," in the *Densho Encyclopedia*, http://encyclopedia. densho.org/ (accessed on October 9, 2014).

4. Shantytowns, consisting of shacks or tents, constructed by homeless people during the Great Depression were sarcastically named in honor of then-U.S. president Herbert Hoover, who was saddled with the blame for the nation's economic decline.

5. Located in the lower-income areas of cities and typically staffed by affiliates of volunteer groups, soup kitchens provided free-of-cost or very inexpensive meals for impoverished people.

6. This appellation has been assigned to any urban neighborhood in the United States characterized by poverty and crime.

7. For a concise version of the pre–World War II background of the *Rafu Shimpo*, which started publication in Japanese in 1903 and added an English-language section in 1926, see Eiichiro Azuma, "Rafu Shimpo," in the *Densho Encyclopedia*, http://encyclopedia.densho.org/ (accessed on October 12, 2014).

8. For a recent documentary film about this newspaper's founding publisher and editor, Sei Fujii, see the official website for *The Lil Tokyo Reporter*: www .ltreporter.com/blog/history/ (accessed on October 9, 2014).

9. See Haruo Imura, "Lumpe Lions—Lovable Lil' 'Leven," *Japanese American News*, January 1, 1936 (copy available in OP). According to Imura, the players on this team, coached by Frank Lumpe, were all Japanese Americans except for one Negro scout; they ranged in age from eleven to fourteen and weighed around ninety pounds.

10. Born outside of Honolulu on the island of Oʻahu, Johnny Yasui (1911–97), a bantamweight, had his first fight in 1929 and after compiling a career record of twenty-three wins (eleven by knockouts), four draws, and seventeen losses, retired from the ring in 1935.

11. Among his cohort of Filipino boxers, welterweight/middleweight Ceferino Garcia (1906–81) was allegedly the hardest hitter.

12. On Larry Tajiri (1914–65), see in particular Greg Robinson, ed., *Pacific Citizens: Larry and Guyo Tajiri and Japanese American Journalism in the World War II Era* (Urbana: University of Illinois Press, 2012); and Greg Robinson, "Larry Tajiri," in the *Densho Encyclopedia*, http://encyclopedia.densho.org/ (accessed on October 11, 2014). For a comparative treatment of Tajiri with Omura as World War II Nisei journalists, see David Yoo, *Growing Up Nisei: Race, Generation, and Culture among Japanese Americans of California, 1924–49* (Urbana: University of Illinois Press, 2000), 124–48.

13. Born in Honolulu, Hawaiʻi, in 1908, Brownie Noboru Furutani died in Hilo, Hawaiʻi, in 1990. During World War II Furutani was editor for the Tulare Assembly Center newspaper, the *Tulare News*.

14. Ken Matsumoto (1910–83), who in the pre–World War II years was president of the Los Angeles JACL chapter, held the position of vice president of the national JACL at the outset of the war. He actively collaborated with federal agencies following Pearl Harbor, including being a board member for the JACL's Los Angeles-based Anti-Axis Committee. This controversial committee is covered in a number of sources, including Deborah K. Lim, "The Lim Report," as reproduced on the "Conscience and the Constitution" website, www.pbs.org /itvs/conscience/who_writes_history/looking_back/lim-toc.html (accessed on October 15, 2014); Brian Niiya, "Tokutara Slocum," in the *Densho Encyclopedia*, http://encyclopedia.densho.org/ (accessed October 15, 2014); and Robert Shaffer, "Tolan Committee," in the *Densho Encyclopedia*, http://encyclopedia.densho.org/ (accessed on October 15, 2014). For the Anti-Axis Committee's statement of purpose, meeting minutes, and script of a radio program the committee presented on January 12, 1942, on the "Fight for Freedom" program, see OP.

15. For a biography of Masao Satow (1908–76), see Brian Niiya, "Masao Satow," in the *Densho Encyclopedia*, http://encyclopedia.densho.org/ (accessed on October 15, 2014).

16. Kazuo Kay Nishimura (1911–88) lived before World War II in the Imperial Valley, California, in the city of El Centro. Detained at the Poston concentration camp during the war, where he was active in community affairs and identified closely with the Japanese American Citizens League, his beating as a suspected informer by other detainees led to the arrest of George Fujii, his former brother-in-law, and Isamu Uchida, which in turn sparked the Poston Strike of November 1942.

17. Kenji Munn Tashiro (1906–67). Born in New Haven, Connecticut, "the first pure blooded Japanese baby born in New England," Kenji and his wife, Teruko, and their son, Kenneth, lived in Los Angeles prior to World War II. During the war the Tashiros were detained at the Gila River concentration camp in Arizona, where Kenji was the founding editor of the camp newspaper, the *News-Courier*, and a moving spirit in Gila's JACL chapter (the only one in the ten War Relocation Authority detention camps). Departing Gila in March 1943 to resettle in Cincinnati, Ohio, he shortly thereafter enlisted in the U.S. Army.

18. T. John Fujii (1913–?) was a journalist who worked on the English sections of Japanese vernacular newspapers in Los Angeles and San Francisco, including the *New World Sun* with Jimmie Omura. The son of a minister, Fujii was born in Japan's Shizuoka Prefecture but immigrated in 1914 with his family to the United States. He was educated at Pomona College and Southern Methodist University. In 1939, after resigning his New York-based position as a foreign correspondent for Japan's Asahi newspaper chain (and with the help of Nisei journalist Bill Hosokawa), Fujii secured a position on the *Singapore Herald*. With the outbreak of World War II, he was interned in a British concentration camp for ten months. Released in exchange for British prisoners, Fujii worked with a number of news agencies in Japan.

19. Nellie Grace Oliver (1861–1947) taught at the Amelia Street School and was the superintendent of the Stimson Lafayette Industrial Institute on Hewitt Street, both within Los Angeles' Little Tokyo.

20. An early member of the American Communist Party and cofounder, in 1922, of the Japan Communist Party, Sen Katayama (1859–1933) came of age in his native Japan at the height of the "people's rights" movement. An active unionist—he founded Japan's first labor paper, the *Rodo Sekai* (*Labor World*)—and socialist, after the Bolshevik revolution in Russia of 1917–18 Katayama became an active Communist and a Comintern officer. Upon his death, he was buried within the Kremlin walls.

21. To gain an enlarged perspective on this group, see Jere Takahashi, "Japanese American Responses to Race Relations: The Formation of Nisei Perspectives," *Amerasia Journal* 9 (Spring/Summer 1982): 29–57, esp. 42–48.

22. For a trenchant portrait of this Kibei activist, union organizer, and author, Karl Yoneda (1906–99), see Glenn Omatsu's entry in the *Densho Encyclopedia*,

http://encyclopedia.densho.org/ (accessed on October 11, 2014). See also Karl
G. Yoneda, *Ganbatte: Sixty-Year Struggle of a Kibei Worker* (Los Angeles: Asian
American Studies Center, UCLA, 1983).

23. Most likely the individual Omura meant to indicate here was H. F. (Hubbard Foster) Alexander (1879–1952). From 1916 to 1930 he was president of the
Pacific Steamship Company, operating the well-known fleet of the Pacific Coast
passenger and freight ships.

24. John Steven McGroarty (1862–1944), in addition to being an author, poet,
lawyer, educator, dramatist, and journalist, served as a Democrat in the U.S.
House of Representatives from 1935 to 1939. For a succinct yet thorough overview of McGroarty's life, see Francis J. Weber, "John Steven McGroarty: From
the Green Verdugo Hills," *Journal of San Diego History* 20 (Fall 1974): 33–37. See
also the sketch of McGroarty by Kevin Starr in *Inventing the Dream: California
through the Progressive Era* (New York: Oxford University Press, 1985), 87–89.

25. See Gil Asakawa's biographical entry for Bill Hosokawa (1915–2007) in the
Densho Encyclopedia, http://encyclopedia.densho.org/ (accessed on December 23,
2014). Hosokawa is treated later in this chapter and also in Chapter 4.

26. For four undated published poems that may be among the five referred to
by Omura here—"Farewell," "The Eternal Gift," "In Memoriam," and "Sanctuary"—see OP.

27. The Ben Pease map designated "Los Angeles Little Tokyo: Japanese
American Businesses of 1940," http://japantownatlas.com/map-littletokyo3.html
(accessed on October 11, 2014), indicates an office for a doctor with the name of
T. Ichioka located on 102.5 East First Street. Although available articles on Toshia
Mori are scant about details other than her birth and death dates and her film
career, it is clear from public records that she was the daughter of Dr. Toshio
Ichioka, an Issei who appears in the 1930 U.S. Census as living in Los Angeles
with four daughters (all born in Japan), of whom at eighteen Toshia is the oldest.
During World War II Ichioka and his wife were confined in Arizona's Gila River
concentration camp, leaving in summer 1944 to resettle in Denver, Colorado,
where they affiliated with the Denver Clinic and where Toshio Ichioka also
worked as a reporter for the *Colorado Times*' Japanese section.

28. Omura devoted his April 18, 1935, *New World Daily* "Drift Tides" column
to memorializing the last evening he spent with Bill Kono the previous year at
Philippi's. For an undated copy of this column, see OP. Although the masthead
designation for what Omura consistently labels the *New World Daily* is the *New
World Daily News*, I have followed his name for this paper.

29. Here Omura is likely referring to one of two Los Angeles neighborhoods,
Jefferson Park or Arlington Heights.

30. Information was undiscovered for either this publication's earlier existence
or its alleged later revival.

31. Richard Chihiro Takeuchi (1919–97) was a graduate of Seattle's Franklin High School, where he was a reporter on the school newspaper. At the University of Washington, which he attended just prior to World War II, he was a reporter on the *University of Washington Daily*. During the war he was detained with his family at the Puyallup Assembly Center, where he edited the *Camp Harmony Newsletter*. See Louis Fiset, *Camp Harmony: Seattle's Japanese Americans and the Puyallup Assembly Center* (Urbana: University of Illinois Press, 2009), 107, 127; on the latter page, Fiset notes that prior to entering Puyallup, "Dick Takeuchi published the English section of the now defunct *Great Northern Daily News*."

32. Evidence suggests that Howard Kakudo (1909–?) was born in Japan and in 1912 immigrated to Los Angeles. During World War II, he was imprisoned at the Poston concentration camp in Arizona, where he taught in the Poston Art School. In 1948 he was credited as an animator for the Disney Company's "Rudolph the Red-Nosed Reindeer" film.

33. Tsuyoshi Dick Nobuhata (ca. 1916–?) lived with his wife, Sylvia, in Los Angeles, California, at the time of the 1930 U.S. federal census (according to information accessed via ancestry.com on October 31, 2014). During World War II, Nobuhata, being fluent in both English and Japanese, served as an interpreter in a Japanese Imperial Army prisoner-of-war camp in Mukden, Manchuria.

34. Ruth Margaret Kurata (Yamazaki) (1914–75) is described by Karl Yoneda, a close friend and ally, in *Ganbatte*, as "a very attractive Nisei newspaperwoman who was active in the Los Angeles Young Nisei Democratic Club" (23). A reporter on the *Kashu Mainichi*'s English-language section, she married Tomomasa "Tom" Yamazaki (1913–46), a pre–World War II English-language reporter for the *Shin Sekai* and a University of California, Berkeley, student who was incarcerated at the Manzanar War Relocation Center in California; there, along with Ruth, he joined the *Manzanar Free Press* staff. Following the 1942 Manzanar Riot and their short protective custody stay at Death Valley's Cow Creek Camp, the Yamazakis in 1943 both became *sensei* at the U.S. Navy Japanese/Oriental Language School on the University of Colorado, Boulder, campus.

35. Relevant information on Aki Miyagishima failed to materialize during research for this study.

36. Born in the state of Washington, Franklyn Shinichi Sugiyama (1906–67) was married in 1940 at a time when he lived in Los Angeles. In May 1942 he was imprisoned, along with his wife, at the Poston Relocation Center in Arizona. During his year of confinement, he served as a law clerk in the project attorney's office, although he listed his primary occupation as author/editor/reporter with secondary occupation as salesman and potential occupation as commercial artist.

37. Francis "Franny" Yamamoto (1915–79) had met Omura in Alaska. When Omura was enrolled in Seattle's Broadway High School, he was asked by the mother of Yamamoto if he would monitor her son's behavior. When in 1933

Omura came to Los Angeles, he ran into Franny, who had moved there earlier along with his father; the two Yamamotos secured positions in the Ninth Street wholesale market, which in turn led to Omura landing a similar job through their intervention. See Omura/Hansen interview, 196–97, for details.

38. Located at the corner of San Pedro and Ninth streets in the Little Tokyo district of Los Angeles, the Ninth Street Market was opened in 1909 so as to ease the cramped conditions at the existing Third Street Market. By the early 1930s about 50 percent of all transactions at this market involved Japanese, while the overwhelming majority of the stalls were occupied by Japanese; still, only four out of forty-four commission merchants were Japanese. See "Ninth Street (Produce) Market," in Niiya, *Encyclopedia of Japanese American History*, 307–8.

39. According to Omura, the Ohio Hotel was on the corner of East First and San Pedro streets, "and right underneath it was the Iwaki Drug Store." See James M. Omura, interview by Arthur A. Hansen, in Hansen, *Japanese American World War II Evacuation Oral History Project, Part 4: Resisters*, 196.

40. When I interviewed Omura in 1984, he was unfamiliar with the term "Yobiyose" (see Omura/Hansen, 144–45) notwithstanding that many of his friends and associates in Washington, California, Alaska, and Colorado were Yobiyose. In Niiya, *Encyclopedia of Japanese American History*, an entry for this generational designation contains a useful definition: "Japanese American term for pre-1924 Japanese immigrants who came to the U.S. as children to join their parents, older siblings or other relatives. Though they are Issei, Yobiyose often have much in common with Nisei, representing a sub-generation between the Issei and Nisei" (362).

41. Among the many stunning portraits of Nikkei writers and artists produced by historian Greg Robinson for his "The Great Unknown and the Unknown Great" column in the *Nichi Bei Weekly* is one in the issue of October 18–31, 2012, titled "Pioneering Nisei Writer and Physician, Yasuo Sasaki, Fought for Reproductive Freedom." Robinson establishes that Sasaki (1911–2008) was born in Idaho but raised and educated in Utah. In 1931 Sasaki cofounded "Reimi, the first Nisei literary magazine," for which he also submitted poetry. Moving to Los Angeles in 1933, he took part in a group styled the Nisei Writers Group and served as a coeditor for a fledgling magazine named *Leaves*. Sasaki later enrolled as a student at the University of Cincinnati, from which he received a PhD in biochemistry in 1936, and four years later an MD from the university's medical school. All during this period he contributed his writings for publication in West Coast vernaculars.

42. For the rise of English-language sections in Japanese vernacular newspapers in California, see Yoo, *Growing Up Nisei*, 70–73.

43. For a biography of Louise J. Suski (1905–2003), see Patricia Wakida, "Louise Suski," in the *Densho Encyclopedia*, http://encyclopedia.densho.org/ (accessed on November 6, 2014).

44. In the Omura/Hansen oral history interview, Omura comments:

He [Japan-born Oski Sasaki Taniwaki (1904–86)] was editor of the *New World Daily* before my time. In fact, he was a pioneer editor of that publication; he had started the English-language section, and had worked there for years. According to a document [oral history interview no. 1517 of Oski Taniwaki by Joseph Manly, August 15, 1976] over at the university [Center for Oral and Public History, California State University, Fullerton], I read that Oski Taniwaki had started it and that he had worked for the *New World Daily* for ten years. Then I guess Jimmy Hirai was editor for a while, and then Yasuo Sasaki, and then came me. (276)

During World War II, Taniwaki was a founder of the *Granada Pioneer* (the inmate newspaper at the Amache Relocation Center in Colorado), which in 1942–43 he edited.

45. See entry on Howard Imazeki (1907–94) by Brian Niiya in the *Densho Encyclopedia*, http://encyclopedia.densho.org/ (accessed November 11, 2014).

46. For particulars of the *Nichibei* strike, see Azuma, "Nichibei Shimbun."

47. See Jimmie Omura, "Drift Tides," *New World Daily*, June 8, 1935. Prior to the January 15, 1935, issue of the *New World Daily*, Omura used the first name of "Jimmy" for his "Drift Tides" column.

48. This reference is to a heroic ghost figure from the New England Puritan world in Nathaniel Hawthorne's 1835 short story "The Gray Champion" and published two years later in the first volume of his *Twice-Told Tales* (Boston: American Stationers, 1837). In the story, the Gray Champion makes a brief appearance in pre–Revolutionary War eighteenth-century America to protest a British officer's power abuses. His action symbolizes the colonists' defiance to the British king and his appointed colonial governor and presages the hope that such behavior will inspire colonists to stand up for their liberty rather than bow to authority.

49. This Japanese term translates into English as "second generation." It was typically used in the phrase *dai nisei mondai* to denote "the problem of the second-generation" as viewed from the Issei generation's perspective. In this connection, see Yuji Ichioka, "*Dai nisei mondai*: Changing Japanese Immigrant Conceptions of the Second-Generation Problem, 1902–1941," chap. 2 in Yuji Ichioka, *Before Internment: Essays in Prewar Japanese-American History*, Gordon Chang and Eiichiro Azuma, eds. (Stanford, CA: Stanford University Press, 2006), 10–52.

50. See letter from Saburo Kido to Jimmie Sakamoto, June 6, 1935, Sakamoto Collection, Special Collections Department, Henry Suzzalo Library, University of Washington, Seattle [hereafter cited as Sakamoto Collection, University of Washington].

51. See Jimmie Omura, "Drift Tides," *New World Daily*, April 26, 1935. Without specifically naming Howard Imazeki, the column is clearly directed at him.

It ends with these words: "He considers himself a 'champion' of the niseis. He is rather a 'chump,' . . . a champion of nothing."

52. See letter from Saburo Kido to Jimmie Sakamoto, April 26, 1935 (Sakamoto Collection, University of Washington). In this same letter Kido writes: "[In his column] Jimmy [Jimmie Omura] . . . stated that Howard [Imazeki] was a chump. So Howard went over [to the *New World Daily* office] and slapped him in the face. . . . I guess Jimmy [Jimmie Omura] will be out of a job sooner or later because there is no question that he is not reliable in his judgment of things."

53. *Soko* is the abbreviated Japanese name for San Francisco. In his 1930s newspaper writings and correspondence, Omura eschewed the term "Japantown," and interchangeably used Soko Town, Soko, and Lil' Osaka for the city's Japanese commercial and cultural area.

54. Within the six-room Kinmon Gakuen, translated as Golden Gate School, there was an auditorium, which accounts for Omura's designation of Kinmon Hall. Completed in 1926, this building housed the institution that since 1911 had served as the Japanese educational system for elementary through high school-level Nikkei students in San Francisco. The building, located in Japantown on Bush Street, was where in 1942 San Francisco's Japanese American population registered for their wartime exclusion and impending detention.

55. Lawrence Satoshi "Stuart" Nakano (1909–89) was born in California's Sacramento County. In the mid-1930s he was a farm manager in Stockton, California.

56. See Brian Niiya's entry on "Tokutaro Slocum" in the *Densho Encyclopedia*, http://encyclopedia.densho.org/ (accessed on November 14, 2004).

57. The nickname of the U.S. Army's 42nd Infantry Division was the Rainbow Division. It was created in August 1917 shortly after the United States entered World War I. Its name reflected the division's composition of soldiers drawn from the National Guards of twenty-six states and the District of Columbia. However, Tokie Slocum and Sergeant Alvin York (1887–1964) were not in the 42nd but rather the 82nd Infantry Division, which carried the moniker of the All-American Division owing to its being comprised of soldiers from all of the then-forty-eight U.S. states. Sergeant York, the iconic World War I hero, was awarded the Medal of Honor when he led an October 8, 1918, attack on a German machine-gun nest during the Meuse-Argonne Offensive, taking thirty-two machine guns, killing twenty-eight German soldiers, and capturing one hundred and thirty-two others.

58. For further information on Tokutaro Nishimura Slocum, especially in connection with his World War I military experience and the campaign he spearheaded for gaining citizenship for Oriental veterans of that war, see Lucy E. Salyer, "Baptism by Fire: Military Service and U.S. Citizenship Policy, 1918–1935,"

Journal of American History 91 (December 2004): 847–76, esp. 847–48 and 868–73. For an interesting and revealing correspondence between Tokie Slocum and Jimmie Omura transacted in the 1935–44 period (but mostly in 1935), see OP.

59. Founded in 1892, the Seattle Yacht Club merged with the Elliott Bay Yacht Club in 1909.

60. Opened in 1923, the Los Angeles Biltmore was at the time the largest hotel in the United States west of Chicago. The ballroom was the most elaborate of the hotel's public rooms. See "Biltmore Hotel: Interior Decorations," www .publicartinla.com/Downtown/figueroa/Pershing_Square_History/biltmore _decor_history.html (accessed on September 7, 2010).

61. Launched with a grand banquet in 1907, the Fairmont Hotel in San Francisco's exclusive Nob Hill neighborhood was under construction at the time of the city's Great Earthquake of 1906. Designed by Bay Area architect Julia Morgan, it quickly became a venue for elegant balls and a parade of presidential visits.

62. The ship *Chichibu Maru* was built in 1930 for the Yokohama-San Francisco run and used as a Japanese Navy transport/hospital ship during World War II.

63. Bill Hosokawa, in *JACL in Quest of Justice* (New York: William Morrow, 1982), 75–76, notes that the term "Sayonara Ball" was first used to describe the JACL's closing banquet at its 1934 National Biennial Convention held in San Francisco, when the event, originally slated for the plush Fairmont Hotel atop Nob Hill, was switched to the spacious Palace Hotel ballroom owing to an ill-starred reservation conflict, which "helped to confirm Issei charges that JACL was indeed overly concerned with the social side of life."

64. The New York 400 is associated with Caroline Webster Shermerhorn Astor (1830–1908), a prominent American socialite of the last quarter of the nineteenth century. A social arbiter, she determined that among the very rich people in New York City there were only four hundred people who could be counted as members of the city's fashionable society.

65. For the Anti-Axis Committee's official wartime position, which was articulated one week following Japan's attack on Pearl Harbor, see the article "Little Tokyo Lid Clamped: Anti-Axis Committee of Japanese-Americans Pledges Its Loyalty" in the *Los Angeles Times* for December 14, 1941. According to this article, archived in OP,

> Chairman Fred Tayama of the anti-Axis committee issued a statement which read, in part: "The United States is at war with the Axis. We shall do all in our power to wipe out vicious totalitarian enemies. Every man is either friend or foe. We shall investigate and turn over to authorities all who by word or act consort with the enemies. We must and will mobilize our maximum energies to facilitate America's war program. We must not play into enemy hands."

This statement, which included a pledge to support the U.S. government and unequivocally repudiate Japan, was announced to five hundred attendees of a public meeting held on December 13, 1942, at the committee's headquarters at 118 North San Pedro Street in Los Angeles' Little Tokyo.

66. Organized in 1921, the Seattle Progressive Citizens League became the Seattle chapter of the national Japanese American Citizens League after its 1930 founding in Seattle. The Tolan Committee, officially named the House Select Committee Investigating National Defense Migration, conducted hearings in four major West Coast cities (San Francisco, Los Angeles, Portland, and Seattle) between February 21 and March 12, 1942, to assess the need for the wartime exclusion of Japanese Americans from the West Coast.

67. No information was found for a group by this name.

68. Started in 1931 by twelve young men, the Seattle Junior Chamber, better known as the Seattle Jaycees, restricted its aim to making Seattle a better place to live.

69. Although born in Moloka'i, Hawai'i, Walter Takeo Tsukamoto (1904–61) was largely raised and schooled in Sacramento, California. After graduating from UC Berkeley's Boalt Law School, he launched a very successful law practice in Sacramento. According to one source, after marriage in 1930 Tsukamoto "began in earnest his commitment to make America a better place for Americans of Japanese ancestry by becoming a super zealot of the JACL and leading the organization in all of its causes." In 1931 Walter Tsukamoto became the first president of the Sacramento JACL and was reelected to that office five more times, until 1936. In 1936, too, he was elected to the then-nonpaying post of executive director of the national JACL. In 1938 he was elected as the president of the national JACL. At its 1940 biennial convention, Tsukamoto stated "in no uncertain terms that the Nisei are prepared to protect, defend and perpetuate the American way of life and are fully committed to conscription into the armed services." During World War II, Tsukamoto and his family were incarcerated at the Tule Lake Relocation Center. However, "after several threats were made against him, for the sake of the safety for his family and himself from possible attacks by certain Tule Lake inhabitants who despised him for his pro-American stance, it became necessary for the Tsukamoto family to leave Tule Lake." See Doris Tsukamoto Kobayashi, Charles Kobayashi, and Laura Kobayashi Ashizawa, "Colonel Walter Takeo Tsukamoto: September 15, 1904–January 20, 1961," June 15, 2002, www.javadc.org/tsukamoto.htm.

70. Located in central Washington, this highly productive agricultural valley is named after the Yakima tribe of Native Americans. For the pre–World War II history of people of Japanese ancestry in this area, see Thomas Heuterman, *The Burning Horse: The Japanese-American Experience in the Yakima Valley 1920–1942* (Cheney: Eastern Washington University Press, 1996).

71. Omura is likely referring here to his April 2, 1935, "Drift Times" column in the *New World Daily* titled "Citizens League." However, its content does not quite match Omura's description of the editorial in question.

72. For a comprehensive assessment of this campaign, see Salyer, "Baptism by Fire."

73. For information on the nature and significance of this case, see Dennis Yamamoto, "*Takahashi v. Fish and Game Commission*," in Niiya, *Encyclopedia of Japanese American History*, 381.

74. Enacted in 1922, the Cable Act effectively revoked the U.S. citizenship of any woman who married an Asian alien. In 1931 the Cable Act was amended so that females, even after marrying aliens ineligible for U.S. citizenship, were permitted to retain their citizenship. The Cable Act was repealed in 1936.

75. The *Hokubei Asahi* was a short-lived newspaper, lasting for only four years. According to Omura, in Omura/Hansen interview, "it was formed [in 1931] by strikers at the *Nichibei* [*Shimbun*] who were locked out over a dispute on wages" (204). Its staff included Howard Imazeki and Tamotsu Murayama (1906–68), about whom Omura writes: "[He was] a gung-ho newspaperman. Most of his work was with the Japanese section, but he shared some of his reports with the English section." Both Imazeki and Murayama were rabidly pro-JACL. According to Bill Hosokawa, in *JACL in Quest of Justice*, "Tamotsu Murayama [was] born in the United States [in Seattle, Washington] but educated in Japan, with aspirations for a newspaper career. He spoke a fractured brand of English but was a spellbinder in Japanese, and invaluable [to the fledgling JACL] in contacts with the Issei, many of whom regard the Nisei as potential rivals for community leadership" (25). When in 1935 the *New World Daily* merged with the *Hokubei Asahi* to create the *New World Sun* (under the coeditorship of Imazeki and Omura), Murayama regularly contributed featured articles to its pages in English. According to Bill Hosokawa, in *Colorado's Japanese Americans: From 1886 to the Present* (Boulder: University Press of Colorado, 2005), 171, Murayama spent the World War II years in Japan. However, see also Michael Jin, "Beyond Two Homelands: Migration and Transnationalism of Japanese Americans in the Pacific, 1930–1955" (PhD diss., University of California, Santa Cruz, 2013), 225–33, in which he elaborates, "Murayama's extensive experience working for both American and Japanese media outlets made him both stand out among Nisei journalists in Japan and become an ideal collaborator to . . . [Japan's] wartime intelligence work."

76. Established in 1850, the settlement of Walnut Grove, California, located south of Sacramento, claimed a large Japanese American community as early as 1914. It was racially segregated up to the start of World War II. For a historical description of the town, illustrated by photographic images and a cartographical representation of its Nikkei businesses in 1940, see Japantown Atlas Project,

"Northern California—Walnut Grove," http://japantownatlas.com/map
-walnutgrove.html (accessed on September 11, 2010).

77. Bill Hosokawa, in *Nisei: The Quiet Americans* (New York: William Mor-
row, 1969), 204, observes that Mike Masaoka established the Intermountain
District Council in 1939 and duly became its first chair. The only JACL district
council extant during World War II, it encompassed chapters in Utah (Salt Lake
City and Ogden); Idaho (Boise Valley, Idaho Falls, Pocatello, and Rexburg); and
Oregon (Snake River Valley).

78. Testimony of Mike M. Masaoka, National Secretary and Field Executive
of the Japanese American Citizens League, Hearing before the Select Committee
Investigating National Defense Migration, House of Representatives, 77th Cong.,
2d sess., San Francisco, California, part 29, 11142. See Shiho Imai entry for Mike
Masaoka (1915–91), in the *Densho Encyclopedia*, http://encyclopedia.densho.org/
(accessed on December 23, 2014).

79. Presumably this comment was communicated orally by Kido to Omura.

80. In 1935 the Nye-Lea Act, granting American citizenship to World War I
veterans of Asian ancestry, was passed. In the words of Lucy Salyer, in "Baptism
by Fire," "for the JACL, the lesson of Nye-Lea was that in the end only military
service and blood sacrifice had succeeded in eroding the racial barriers to political
membership [for Americans of Japanese ancestry]" (875).

81. The Okei Memorial, in Coloma, California, honored Okei Ito, the first
known Japanese woman to be buried on American soil. She was part of the
Wakamatsu Tea and Silk Farm colony, consisting of twenty-two samurai and one
woman, believed to be the first permanent Japanese settlement in North America.
Okei's tombstone was placed on this site with this inscription: "In Memory
of Okei, Died 1871, Aged 19 years. A Japanese Girl" (rendered in English on the
front and in Japanese on the back). By the mid-1930s the gravesite had fallen into
disrepair, and hence the Japanese American community initiated a fund-raising
campaign to beautify both the gravestone and the site.

82. One of the sixteen founders and the first president of the Placer Nisei Citizens Association in 1926, Tom Yego, along with Kay Takemoto and Louis Oki,
served as official Placer County delegates to the 1930 national Nisei convention
in Seattle that founded the Japanese American Citizens League (JACL). In 1934
Yego was elected president of the Placer County chapter of the JACL. See Placer
County Japanese American Citizens League, "Chronological History of the Placer
County JACL," www.placerjacl.org/about.htm (accessed on September 11, 2010).

83. See "Okay . . . Okei!," *New World Daily*, February 18, 1935.

84. For a biographical snapshot of Michi Oka, see her obituary by Katia
Hetter, "Michi Oka Onuma, Community Activist and Journalist/S.F. Resident
Edited English Section of 2 Japanese Papers," in the May 26, 2004, issue of the

San Francisco Chronicle. It notes that she died of natural causes at age ninety-six. According to this death notice, she was a UC Berkeley graduate who was incarcerated during World War II at the Heart Mountain concentration camp in Wyoming, where she worked on the camp paper (the *Heart Mountain Sentinel*). After the war, she edited the English section of a San Francisco Japantown-based newspaper started by her father Shigeki Oka, the *Progressive News and Press* (which later became the *Hokubei Mainichi*). In the mid-1970s she became the English editor for the *Nichi Bei Times* and remained in this capacity until 1997. Omura, in his August 22–25, 1984, interview with me for the Japanese American Project of Cal State Fullerton's Oral History Program, commented on his relationship with Oka:

> [When] I . . . took over the job as editor for the *New World Daily*, Yasuo [Sasaki] had an assistant . . . , a girl named Michi Oka. It seemed like we didn't hit it off, for some reason. One thing, I guess, was that her father was known as an *aka* [Communist] in the [Japanese American] community. That might have bothered me. The second one was that she had no personality. So we didn't particularly get along, although we didn't have any conflicts. Besides, my policy didn't suit her anyway. So she quit after . . . a couple of months or so.

85. For an overview of this league, see Samuel O. Regalado, "'Play Ball!' Baseball and Seattle's Japanese-American Courier League, 1928–1941," *Pacific Northwest Quarterly* 87 (Winter 1995/96): 29–37. For a comprehensive and detailed discussion of the *Japanese-American Courier* and its editor and publisher, James Y. Sakamoto, and the connection of both with the Japanese American Citizens League, see Mark Morzol, "*Japanese-American Courier* (1937–1940): A Seattle Ethnic Press Report," in Seattle Civil Rights and Labor History Project, http://depts.washington.edu/civilr/news_Courier.htm (accessed on September 13, 2010).

86. Hito Okada (1907–84) was born in Salt Lake City, Utah. In 1935–36 he served as president of the Portland, Oregon, JACL chapter. He later became the national JACL treasurer. At the 1942 Tolan Committee hearings in Portland, Okada was one of those who testified. During World War II, he was the only national JACL officer to move from the organization's San Francisco office to its relocated one in Salt Lake City. In 1946 Okada was elected national JACL president and was reelected to that office in 1948. See Hosokawa, *JACL in Quest of Justice*, passim.

87. The eldest child of Tatsuya and Kan Arai, Clarence Takeyo Arai (1901–64) was a Seattle lawyer who organized the Seattle Progressive Citizens League in 1921 and was one of the key figures in the founding of the Japanese American Citizens League in 1930 when eight charter affiliates, including the Seattle Progressive Citi-

zens League, met in Seattle at a convention held at the Seattle Chamber of Commerce Building. For an oral history interview that encompasses Arai's life and activities, from his courtship and marriage to the time of his death, see the May 1988 interview by Tracy Lai with his widow, Yone Bartholome, for Densho.

88. During our August 22–25, 1984, interview, Omura registered this recollection about Hosokawa in response to my question as to whether he knew Hosokawa in Seattle prior to World War II:

> Yes, I knew Bill Hosokawa before the war. I used to play in a YMCA Nisei basketball league and, not always, but sometimes, he played center for the [?] Nippons, and I played for the rival Baptist High Stars. . . . I always remembered him as sort of a sourpuss. He didn't have any personality, and you couldn't get close to him. Or you didn't want to get close to him. He was a tall fellow [six feet], taller than the ordinary Nisei, and he was well built; he wasn't spindly.

See Omura to Hansen, in Hansen, *Japanese American World War II Evacuation Oral History Project, Part 4: Resisters*, 296.

89. See April 26, 1935, letter from Saburo Kido to Jimmie Sakamoto.

90. Before becoming affiliated with the International Institute in San Francisco, Annie Clo Watson (1891–1960) had experienced a career that began in the early 1920s at the YMCA of Flint, Michigan (during which time she was associated with the New York School of Social Work). She moved in 1928 to the American Federation of International Institutes when she became the executive director for the International Institute of San Antonio, Texas. In 1956 she received a scroll of appreciation from the Japanese American Citizens League for her work in World War II in visiting many of the Japanese American detention camps and in securing homes for resettling Nikkei during and after the war. See "Annie Clo Watson Papers, 1934–1960," Immigration History Research Center, University of Minnesota, www.ihrc.umn.edu/research/vitrage/all/wa/GENwatson.htm (accessed on September 15, 2010).

91. Born in the unincorporated mining community of Volcano, located in California's Amador County, Angelo Joseph Rossi (1878–1948), a successful florist and Republican, served from 1931 to 1944 as the mayor of San Francisco. Relentlessly anti-Communist and fiercely opposed to labor organizing and strikes, Rossi moved resolutely to thwart the San Francisco general strike of 1934, after which he issued this fiery pronouncement: "I pledge to you that as Chief Executive in San Francisco I will, to the full extent of my authority, run out of San Francisco every Communist agitator, and this is going to be a continuing policy in San Francisco." In the late 1930s he attacked Harry Bridges, the suspicioned Communist leader of the West Coast CIO from Australia, on the grounds of his ideology

and his alien status. During World War II, Rossi took a strong stand against people of Japanese ancestry, while at the same time requesting an exemption for those
like himself (who was accused of making fascist salutes at prewar right-wing rallies) of Italian ancestry. See the Wikipedia entry for "Angelo Joseph Rossi," http://
en.wikipedia.org/wiki/Angelo_Joseph_Rossi (accessed on September 15, 2010).

92. Iwao Kawakami (1907–76) was born in the San Francisco Bay Area. In
1929 he became the editor for the *Nikkei Shimin,* a semimonthly publication
for the New American Citizens League. When that organization soon afterward
evolved into the Japanese American Citizens League, the publication assumed
the new name of *Pacific Citizen.* During the 1930s Kawakami was a poet and
journalist affiliated with a number of Japanese American community newspapers,
including the *New World Sun,* coedited by Jimmie Omura and based in San Francisco. Before World War II, he was married twice; the second time, in 1941, to the
poet Toyo Suyemoto. Together they had a son, Kay, before getting separated later
that same year (and ultimately divorced in 1951). During the war Kawakami was
imprisoned at the Tanforan Assembly Center in California and the Topaz Relocation Center in Utah, where he was a staff member on the camp newspaper, the
Topaz Times.

93. Born in Fukui, Japan, Curtis Wayo Otani (1908–99), the retired owner
and proprietor of Otani Advertising Agency, died in Honolulu, Hawai'i.

94. For information on the subcommittee of the House on Un-American
Activities Committee (aka Dies Committee) chaired by John M. Costello
(1903–76) to investigate Japanese Americans, see Brian Niiya's "Dies Committee"
entry in the *Densho Encyclopedia,* http://encyclopedia.densho.org/ (accessed on
November 12. 2014). A California congressional representative, Costello was born
in Los Angeles and graduated in 1924 from Loyola Law School. He later served as
a Democrat in the U.S. Congress from 1935 to 1945.

95. For this quoted remark and related aspects of Masaoka's testimony to the
Dies Committee, see posting on "Conscience and the Constitution" website:
"House Un-American Activities Committee, Dies Committee, Costello Sub-
Committee," *Research Report Prepared for Presidential Committee on JACL Resolu-
tion #7* [aka *The Lim Report*], submitted to the JACL in 1990 by Deborah K. Lim,
www.resisters.com/study/LimPartIIB.htm#IIB6 (accessed on November 12, 2014).

96. See "'Personality' Needed," *New World Sun,* January 1, 1936, 7 (OP).

97. Following Omura's *New World Sun* resignation, two items appeared in
that newspaper about this action. The first briefly noted the resignation and
added that Omura was relocating to the Pacific Northwest after being feted by
friends at several farewell parties. The second was a commentary that appeared in
Curt Otani's "Uncle Curt Says" column:

Jimmie Omura was criticized by some readers because he printed his frank opinions; others who wanted to see the truth come to light supported him. Being human, we all make mistakes now and then, and Jimmie likewise might have made a few mistakes; but whatever he wrote he had good intentions—to give FACTS to the public. If the public can't face the facts, it isn't his fault. Now, Jimmie plans to go north because he has found a more suitable job. Let's hope that he keeps up his principle.

For these items, dated simply January 1936, see OP.

98. For an in-depth biographical overview on Kazumaro "Buddy" Uno (1913–54), see Yuji Ichioka, "The Meaning of Loyalty: The Case of Kazumaro Buddy Uno," chap. 7 in Ichioka, *After Internment*, 153–79.

99. I was unable to locate information for this individual. However, later in this chapter Omura indicates that she came from Reno, Nevada, and was selected over him by publisher Ted Ogasawara to edit a new 1939 monthly magazine called *Pacific Affairs*.

100. Initiated in late 1935 as a national news agency to compete with (and if necessary counter) powerful international news agencies like Reuters, the Domei News Agency (Dōmei Tsūshinsha) served as Japan's news agency through World War II. For further information on the Domei News Agency, see K. M. Shrivastava, *News Agencies: From Pigeon to Internet* (Elgin, IL: New Dawn Press, 2007), 17.

101. A native of Scotland, James Gordon Bennett Sr. achieved eminence as the founder, editor, and publisher of the *New York Herald*, with which he was affiliated from 1835 to 1866 and which he steered into becoming the American newspaper with the largest circulation. Under Bennett's leadership, the *Herald* was officially independent in its politics.

102. Born in Japan, Yamato Ichihashi (1878–1963) came as a high school student to San Francisco and then matriculated at Stanford University, where he completed both his bachelor's and master's degrees in economics, before earning his doctorate degree at Harvard. In 1913 he returned to Stanford to become professor of Japanese history and government, and in 1932 his classic account of the early history of the Japanese in the United States, *Japanese in the United States: A Critical Study of the Problems of the Japanese Immigrants and Their Children*, was published by Stanford University Press. During World War II, Ichihashi was incarcerated at four different governmental detention facilities, and at war's end he returned to his post at Stanford. See the following sources: Yuji Ichioka, "Attorney for the Defense: Yamato Ichihashi and Japanese Immigration," in *Before Internment*, 227–57; Gordon H. Chang, *Morning Glory, Evening Shadow: Yamato Ichihashi and His Internment Writings, 1942–1945* (Stanford, CA: Stanford University Press, 1997); and Online Archives of California, "Guide to the Yamato

Ichihashi Papers, 1918–1963," Stanford University Archives, www.oac.cdlib.org/findaid/ark:/13030/tf7z09n9k7/ (accessed on September 25, 2010).

103. The letter from Omura appeared in the *Great Northern Daily News* in the column titled "Deadline Conductor," with him being represented as "guest conductor" and identified as being "formerly of New World-Sun, S.F." For an undated copy of this document, see OP.

104. Founded in 1900, the Japanese Association of North America (JANA) was a Seattle association, but it included small, scattered local organizations. In 1931 JANA merged with the Seattle Japanese Chamber of Commerce, which had been founded in 1928, to form the Japanese Chamber of Commerce and Japanese Association of North America. Many of the functions of these organizations were ceremonial or commemorative, but their main purpose was to perpetuate Japanese traditions. In addition, they acted as intermediaries between the Japanese government and the Issei who were denied U.S. citizenship by law. See Special Collections, University of Washington Libraries, Manuscript Collection No. 1235, "Preliminary Guide to the Japanese Association of North America Records 1916–1941," www.lib.washington.edu/specialcoll/findaids/docs/papersrecords/JapaneseAssociationofNorthAmerica1235.xml (accessed on September 28, 2010).

105. Seattle Nisei, including James Sakamoto and Clarence Arai, founded the Seattle Progressive Citizens League on September 27, 1921, to assist Issei gain U.S. citizenship rights and to challenge the escalating anti-Japanese sentiments and actions then sweeping the West Coast. The league met three times between 1921 and 1928, but it served as a model community organization that would later inspire Seattle's Nisei community leaders to revive its activities. This revival, in concert with other Nisei organizations in the West Coast, precipitated the founding convention in Seattle of the Japanese American Citizens League in 1930. See "Seattle's Civil Rights Organizations: Seattle Progressive Citizens League (forerunner to JACL), 1921–29," Seattle Civil Rights and Labor History Project, http://depts.washington.edu/civilr/organizations.htm#progressive%20citizens (accessed on September 28, 2010).

106. Whereas Washington's 1889 constitution had banned the sale of land to "aliens ineligible in citizenship," the only aliens then ineligible for citizenship were Asians. The Alien Land Law of 1921 extended the ban to cover leasing or renting land and renewing old leases. Issei circumvented this law by arranging to have white farmers, the technical owners of land, employ Japanese farmers as managers. Also, Issei farmers purchased land in the names of their Nisei children, U.S. citizens, or in the name of other, older Nisei, although that loophole was closed in 1923 by an amendment to the Alien Land Law of 1921.

107. To appreciate the force of Omura's assessment here, see Nicole Grant, "White Supremacy and the Alien Land Laws of Washington State," Seattle Civil

Rights and Labor History Project, http://depts.washington.edu/civilr/alien_land_laws.htm (accessed on September 28, 2010).

108. See Ichioka, "*Dai nisei mondai*," 10–52.

109. The 1921 yearbook, *Tolo*, for Seattle's Franklin High School described graduating senior Jimmie Sakamoto, who had played varsity football, as the "best line player ever seen in Seattle high school football." See Joseph R. Svinth, "'I Heard the Bell': James Y. Sakamoto, Japanese American Boxer and Journalist," *Journal of Combative Sport* 5 (January 2004): 2.

110. In its entry for James Sakamoto, HistoryLink.org's *Online Encyclopedia of Washington State History*, www.historylink.org/index.cfm?DisplayPage=output. cfm&file_id=2050 (accessed on September 28, 2010), expresses this point somewhat differently: "On the one hand, Sakamoto promoted the philosophy of good citizenship and opportunity and the desirability for Nisei . . . to become 'one hundred percent Americans.' On the other hand, the *Courier* was known for promoting understanding and better ties with Japan, and initially supported Japanese imperialist forays into China and Asia."

111. Sited near current-day Dillingham, Alaska, Nushagak is situated in northern Bristol Bay near the confluence of the Wood and Nushagak rivers. After the United States purchased Alaska from Russia in 1867, the government built a weather station at Nushagak. Thereafter, two canneries were built there. For historical photographs of the salmon canning industry in Nushagak, see University of Washington Libraries, Digital Collections, http://content.lib.washington.edu/cdm4/item_viewer.php?CISOROOT=/cobb&CISOPTR=356 (accessed on October 2, 2010).

112. For an array of early-twentieth-century photographs of Squaw Harbor and other Kodiak Island sites, see University of Washington Libraries, Digital Collections, http://vilda.alaska.edu/cdm4/results.php?CISOOP1=exact&CISOFI ELD1=CISOSEARCHALL&CISOROOT=all&CISOBOX1=Fishing&CISOST ART=11,301 (accessed on October 2, 2010).

113. Flat-bottom boats with blunt bows, and notable for their ability to navigate shallow waters, scows are commonly used to haul garbage and similar bulk freight.

114. A noncommunicable condition affecting humans, whose cause is unknown and for which no fully effective treatments are available, alopecia areata occasions round patches of hair loss. It is sometimes called spot baldness. Although full recovery of hair is common, permanent hair loss is a possible complication of alopecia areata.

115. Biographical information has not been uncovered for Deeks Chin.

116. According to one glossary of railroad lingo derived from Freeman H. Hubbard, *Railroad Avenue: Great Stories and Legends of American Railroading*

(New York: McGraw-Hill, 1945), "bulls" were also called "flatfoots" or "gum-shoes," but in distinctive railroad terms they were designated as "cinder dicks" and "'bo chasers." See "Catskill Archive," www.catskillarchive.com/rrextra/glossry1.html (accessed on October 3, 2010).

117. Opened in 1928, the Hay-Adams House is located on Lafayette Square, across from the White House. For years a gathering place for some of America's leading artists, writers, and politicians, it quickly attracted prominent Washingtonians and elite travelers.

118. Held on January 20, 1937, President Franklin Roosevelt's second inauguration, acting upon the Twentieth Amendment to the U.S. Constitution, was the initial inauguration to be staged on January 20 rather than March 4. In this address, Roosevelt spoke for and to the "forgotten man" and confidently outlined his New Deal programs. For the written text of the address, accompanied by an audiotape of the original radio broadcast, see "One Third of a Nation," *History Matters: The U.S. Survey Course on the Web*, http://historymatters.gmu.edu/d/5105/ (accessed on October 4, 2010).

119. Probably what Omura meant to indicate here was not Union Station, which is in Washington, DC, but Grand Central Terminal (sometimes incorrectly called Grand Central Station, its name prior to 1913). Located in Manhattan at Forty-Second Street and Park Avenue, it opened to the public in 1871 as the world's largest train station.

120. In 1982 U.S. president Ronald Reagan (1911–2004) appointed American businessman Lee Iacocca (1924–), the son of Italian immigrants, to undertake a private-sector fundraising effort to restore both the Statue of Liberty and Ellis Island. See Iacocca Foundation, "Lee Iacocca," www.iacoccafoundation.org/about/lee.html (accessed on October 4, 2010).

121. According to Roger M. Grace in "Old Menus Tell the History of Hamburgers in L.A.," *Metropolitan News-Enterprise*, January 15, 2004, "During World War I, just as sauerkraut had been re-dubbed 'Liberty Cabbage' to reflect anti-German sentiment, some restaurants referred to hamburger as 'Liberty Steak.' Although the war had ended in 1918, the name apparently stuck, for awhile." See www.metnews.com/articles/2004/reminiscing011504.htm (accessed on October 4, 2010).

122. In the late 1930s Stockton had an approximate population of fifty thousand. It is located in northern California south of Sacramento amid the farmland of the California Central Valley. An inland seaport, Stockton is connected westward with San Francisco Bay by the San Joaquin River. In and around Stockton are thousands of miles of rivers and manmade channels that make up the legendary California Delta. Throughout its history, Stockton's rich peat soil and a

temperate climate have combined with its diverse racial and ethnic labor force to permit the cultivation of virtually every major fruit, nut, and field crop.

123. When in 1904 Ransom E. Olds was forced out of the automobile company he had started, Oldsmobile, he immediately formed a new company, using his initials in its name: REO Motor Car Company. It prospered through the 1920s but floundered during the Great Depression.

124. According to cartographer Ben Pease's map of Japanese American businesses of 1940 in Stockton's Japantown, Chinatown, and Little Manila, the building housing the Nishomoto Transfer/Nippon Hotel was located on the corner of South Center and West Sonora streets. Stockton's Japantown included many hotels, or boardinghouses, where agricultural workers would stay during the winters. According to Pease, "Stockton was one of California's largest and most complex [pre–World War II] Japanese American communities." See Preserving California's Japantowns Project, "Overview Map: Stockton's Japanese American Businesses of 1940," http://japantownatlas.com/map-stockton.html (accessed on October 5, 2010).

125. A census-designated Sacramento County place, the community of Florin, California, was home to a flourishing agricultural economy during the early twentieth century, with strawberries being the principal crop and Japanese Americans being the predominant farming group as well as the target of severe prejudicial animus. For very useful information about the Japanese American experience in Florin, see the article by Marion Kanemoto on the Florin Oral History Project sponsored by the Florin Chapter of the Japanese American Citizens League, www.florinjacl.com/oral_history.htm (accessed on October 5, 2010).

126. A San Joaquin County, California, town located between Sacramento and San Francisco in the northern portion of California's fertile Central Valley agricultural area, Lodi was settled in the middle of the nineteenth century and incorporated in 1906. The town is especially well known for the production of grapes and wine. Pre–World War II Lodi was home to a thriving Japantown, which included, according to Preserving California's Japantowns project director Donna Graves, "boarding houses, stores, restaurants, a tofu maker, and a pharmacy [and] was centered on Main Street between the Buddhist Church and railroad tracks and packing sheds that shipped local produce across the U.S." See National Trust for History Preservation, "Preserving California's Japantowns," www.preservationnation.org/issues/diversity/asian-pacific-american-heritage/preservation-stories/preserving-californias.html (accessed on October 5, 2010); see also Ben Pease's map, "Lodi Japanese American Businesses of 1940," for the Preserving California's Japantowns Project, http://japantownatlas.com/map-lodi.html (accessed on October 5, 2010).

127. According to journalist Barry Yeoman in "Delta Blues," blog entry for September 21, 2008, Rindge Tract is "one of the low-slung rural islands [near the landlocked Port of Stockton] that form the nucleus of California's Sacramento-San Joaquin Delta . . . which was once mostly tidal marsh . . . [that was] tamed in the 19th century into isles of farmland laced with waterways." See http://barryyeoman.com/2008/09/delta-blues/ (accessed on November 11, 2014).

128. Located near Puget Sound on the northern edge of King County some twelve miles from the Seattle border, Richmond Highlands, Washington, was the setting for the Firland Sanatorium, Seattle's municipal tuberculosis hospital from 1911 to 1947, at which time the institution was relocated to a downtown Seattle site (where it continued to operate until its 1973 dissolution). See note 63 in Chapter 1 of this book for an overview of the Firland facility.

129. Having opened its doors in 1930, the Washington Athletic Club has attracted ever since an elite membership of Seattleites in business, political, and social circles. See Washington Athletic Club, "A Cornerstone of Seattle Since 1930," www.wac.net/History.aspx (accessed on October 7, 2010).

130. For an unpublished 2006 editorial and published letter to the editor written from a Quaker perspective by David Chandler on the persisting racism in Visalia, see Visalia Friends Meeting Home Page, "Reflecting on MLK Day in Visalia, 2006," www.quaker.org/visalia/subpages/RacismInVisalia.htm (accessed on October 8, 2010).

131. Although the term "drayage" in recent times has denoted various logistical services in the shipping industry, its original meaning was to transport something a short distance by a truck or some other vehicle.

132. In 1940 Western Wholesale Florists was located on 361 Tehama in San Francisco and managed by Kunihara Furuya.

133. William Scott, in *The Florists' Manual: A Reference Book for Commercial Florists* (Whitefish, MT: Kessinger, 2010), reprint of original 1906 edition by the Florists' Publishing Company, www.amazon.com/Florists-Manual-Reference-Book-Commercial/dp/1162260793/ref=sr_1_1?ie=UTF8&s=books&qid=1286569600&sr=1-1 (accessed on October 8, 2010), provides useful information about packing cut flowers.

134. Information on Ioki Greenhouse was undiscovered. Cartographer Ben Pease, in Japantown Atlas, "Oakland and Alameda Japanese American Businesses of 1940," http://japantownatlas.com/map-oakland.html (accessed on October 8, 2010), notes that "Oakland was the center of the Japanese American flower nursery industry in the East Bay, which extended from Richmond and El Cerrito to San Leandro and Hayward (and also on the San Francisco Peninsula)."

135. Information about Economy Shippers was not ascertained.

136. Harold Raymond Amling (1899–1951) was born in Illinois and died in San Francisco. There, in 1936, he was one of the owners and general manager of Coast Wholesale Florist, Inc. In 1940 his firm at 911 Howard Street was named Amling Wholesale Florist Quality Flowers; its motto was "A Name as Old as the Flower Business." On April 8, 1942, Harold Amling sent two letters to Jim Omura, who had just arrived as a resettler in Denver. The first expressed contentment at Omura's safe arrival and indicated that after he had gotten settled, "maybe we can work something out." Amling's other letter was a recommendation for Omura. It said: "Jim Omura worked for us for about three years and we have found him very reliable in every way, and an exceptionally fine packer who knows good flowers. . . . Although his birth is of Japanese origin, we have found him very Americanized, and to the best of our knowledge, an A-No. 1 American citizen." See OP.

137. It may be that a 1939 California Employment Service-sponsored survey of, presumably, Japanese American employment in the San Francisco Bay Area was conducted, but likely what Omura is referring to here is a 1941 survey compiled by a Nisei associate of his, Charles Kikuchi, for the National Youth Administration's Junior Counseling Service, and is entitled *Japanese American Youth in San Francisco: Their Background, Characteristics, and Problems*. A copy of this survey is included in OP. For a virtual copy of it, see *Japanese American Evacuation and Resettlement Study* [hereafter JERS], Bancroft Library [hereafter BANC], University of California [UCB], Manuscript [MSS] 67/14 c, Folder W 2.41, http://digitalassets.lib.berkeley.edu/jarda/ucb/text/cubanc6714_b316w2_0041.pdf (accessed on December 25, 2014). See page 32 of this survey, where appear both the "wages are low" comment by Omura with respect to San Francisco Flower Market employment, and his belief of it being based upon information from the Japanese Flower Growers Association's secretary.

138. One of the oldest streets in San Francisco's Chinatown, Grant Street during the 1930s included numerous tourist-oriented stores with Japanese American proprietors and employees. For a photo of one such store, taken at the time of the exclusion of people of Japanese ancestry in 1942, see www.bookmice.net/darkchilde/japan/fran.html (accessed on December 25, 2014).

139. For copies of the thirteen "Passing Show" columns by James Omura, dated from December 11, 1939, through July 22, 1940, see OP.

140. On the eve of World War II the Japanese American business district in San Francisco's Japantown was at the intersection of Post and Buchanan streets, where it still remains. For a 1940 map of this Japantown indicating the business establishments on Buchanan Street, see cartographer Ben Pease's rendering for Japantown Atlas, plus explanatory text, http://japantownatlas.com/map-sanfrancisco1.html (accessed on December 25, 1914).

141. Theodore Kenzo "Ken" Ogasawara (1896–1979), who was born in Japan's Shikoku Islands, immigrated to San Francisco in 1924. During World War II, he was incarcerated at Arizona's Gila River Relocation Center, where he edited the Japanese section of the camp's *Gila News-Courier* newspaper. See Arthur A. Hansen, "Cultural Politics in the Gila River Relocation Center 1942–1943," *Arizona and the West* 27 (Winter 1985): 327–62. After the war, Ogasawara lived in Denver, Colorado, and there was the assistant editor for the publication *To'u*. According to a research note within OP, Ogasawara purchased the *Colorado Times* in July 1955 from Fred Kaihara, who died the following month.

CHAPTER 4

1. Keith Maslin, in *An Introduction to the Philosophy of the Mind*, 2nd ed. (Cambridge, UK: Polity Press, 2007), provides an explanation for the philosophical origins of this commonplace expression: "For Descartes, and for Locke and Hume who were strongly influenced by him, experience comprises a series of mental images, secured within the fastness of the private realm of the mind. This is a very thin conception of experience. Private images are presented to the person, who is essentially an inert spectator passively viewing the passing show" (228). Contrast this notion with what Omura, in a galley proof of "The Passing Show" intended for publication within *Current Life* 2 (February 1942), wrote:

> Every Nisei should be unalterably opposed to mass evacuation. Some Nisei Americans publicly encourage voluntary evacuation as a symbol of loyalty. Voluntary evacuation by the Nisei is a false idea of loyalty and is a betrayal of their inherited rights. We should not be so eager to give ground at the first threat to our civil liberties but should struggle to hold on to those inalienable privileges to which we are entitled. In trying periods, such as the crisis we are now experiencing, false gods will appear to advise us. They will attempt to weaken us and then destroy us by subtle preachments and soothing promises for our submission. Whatever promises are made for us beyond the Sierras should not undermine our stern resolve to fight the good fight here where destiny has placed us. We ought not to barter our birthright for gold. (2)

According to an undated note by Omura, the February 1942 issue of *Current Life* "was halted by confiscation by Argonaut Press. This copy [in OP] was obtained by Freedom of Information appeal and claim, Doc. No. 100-2887-1A, Denver FBI file." See also Jean Miyake Downey, review of Satsuki Ina's *From a Silk Cocoon, Japanese-American Incarceration Resistance Narratives, and the Post 9/11 Era*, www .japanfocus.org/-Jean_Miyake-Downey/2234 (accessed on October 14, 2010).

2. First opened in 1914, Shonien, or the Japanese Children's Home, evolved from the social work started in 1912 by the executive secretary of the Rafu Jin-

doka, or Japanese Humane Society of Los Angeles, Rokuichi Kusmoto. For more information on the Shonien, see Ford H. Kuramoto, *A History of the Shonien, 1914–1972: An Account of a Program of Institutional Care of Japanese Children in Los Angeles* (San Francisco: R and E Research Associates, 1976); and Japanese American Community Services, "History: About Shonien," www.jacsfund.org/jax-history.html (accessed on October 14, 2010).

3. For information bearing on the *Japanese American News* (*Nichibei Shimbun*) and the Abiko family, including Yasuo Abiko (1910–88), who published it, see these sources: Online Archive of California, "Finding Aid for the Abiko Family Papers, ca. 1890–1944"; Scott Kurashige, "Abiko, Yasuo (1910–1988)," in Niiya, *Encyclopedia of Japanese American History*, 109–10, www.oac.cdlib.org/findaid/ark:/13030/ft296n98dc/ (accessed on October 14, 2010); and *Nichi Bei Times Weekly*, "History," September 10–16, 2009.

4. For pertinent information on selected aspects of *Current Life*, see James Omura, interview by Frank Abe, December 9, 1990, Frank Abe Collection, Densho, Segments 4–5, http://archive.densho.org/main.aspx (accessed on January 11, 2015); and James Omura, interview by Chizuko Omori and Emiko Omori, Emiko and Chizuko Omori Collection, Densho, Segment 17, http://archive.densho.org/main.aspx (accessed on January 11, 2015). See also OP, for copies of *Current Life* issues and information bearing on its creation, philosophical outlook, contents, contributors, historical development, commercial concerns, and intellectual, social, and cultural consequences.

5. Of the three mainstream papers mentioned by Omura that publicized *Current Life*, only the item in the *San Francisco Chronicle* on October 20, 1941, celebrating its first anniversary, is documented within OP.

6. According to Omura's notes on "Japanese American Journalism" in OP, the Coast Nisei Press was formed on January 3, 1935, aboard the *Chichibu Maru* in the port of San Francisco during the Third Biennial Convention of the Japanese American Citizens League. However, since that convention was held between August 31 and September 3, 1934, this dating is clearly incorrect.

7. Founded in 1902, the *North American Times* (*Hokubei JiJi*) was forced into closure by the World War II Japanese American exclusion and detention experience. It was last published on March 12, 1942. See HistoryLink essay, "Seattle's First Japanese Newspaper, *The Report*, Is Issued in 1899," www.historylink.org/index.cfm?DisplayPage=pf_output.cfm&file_id=3352 (accessed on November 1, 2010).

8. Founded in 1837 as the Railway Express Agency, this firm changed its name to the American Railway Express Agency in 1927.

9. Fortunately, a commercial street map of "Soko-town," accompanied by a walking tour of the district, was developed in 1934–35 under the supervision and

editorial direction of Paul Radin (1883–1959), a renowned University of California, Berkeley, anthropologist. It was part of the Survey of Ethnic Minorities in the San Francisco Bay Area. In an afterword to "A Walk through Japantown—1935," *Hoku-bei Mainichi*, January 1, 1989, Lane Hirabayashi explains that the project's purpose was "to document the cultural adjustment of no less than twelve different Third World and Caucasian minority groups to the city of San Francisco."

10. The map and accompanying text provided in Hirabayashi's piece shows that the Eagle Café was a sukiyaki restaurant located on the west side of Buchanan Street, between Sutter Street and Post Street, and was flanked by a grocery store (Tani Store) and a dry goods establishment (Nakagawa Shohin Kan).

11. For a superb biographical study of Charles Tatsuro Kikuchi (1916–88), see Matthew M. Briones, *Jim and Jap Crow: A Cultural History of 1940s Interracial America* (Princeton, NJ: Princeton University Press, 2012). See also Briones's entry on Kikuchi in the *Densho Encyclopedia*, http://encyclopedia.densho.org/ (accessed on April 13, 2015); and Charles Kikuchi, *The Kikuchi Diary: Chronicle from an American Concentration Camp*, John Modell, ed. (Urbana: University of Illinois Press, 1973, 1993).

12. The first address for *Current Life*'s editorial office was at 1737 Sutter Street. It remained so only through the magazine's October and November 1940 issues. Then it changed to 1956 Bush Street for the monthly issues extending through May 1941. Beginning in June 1941 the editorial office became 1611 Broderick Street, and it continued so until *Current Life*'s last issue in January 1942. Located near San Francisco's Golden Gate Park and Pacific Heights, the Western Addition district, an addition to the city west of Van Ness Avenue (which accounts for its designation), was developed at the turn of the twentieth century.

13. Fumiko "Caryl" (Okuma) Omura/Gertler (1920–2000) was the fourth of five Nisei daughters of her Fukuoka, Japan-born Issei parents Yojiro Okuma (1879–1960) and Kise (Gohara) Okuma (1886–1945). Born and raised in San Francisco, Fumiko obtained her education there at Hearst School, Everett Junior High School, and Mission High School. When she was a young girl, her family lived on Duboce Avenue in the Castro District. In the mid-1930s the Okuma family moved a mile away to 544 Divisadero Street, where according to the 1940 U.S. federal census, the Okumas were the sole family with an Asian surname in their immediate neighborhood. Similarly, Mission High School's mid-to-late 1930s student body was seemingly almost all of Euro-American ancestry. In high school, Fumiko adopted the "English" name of Caryl. On October 4, 1940, she secretly married Utaka Matsumoto [who for the previous ten to fifteen years had used the name James Matsumoto Omura] in Carson City, Nevada. With Omura as publisher and editor and Okuma as business manager, they together managed the *Current Life* magazine, whose first issue appeared in the same month as their marriage. Because Okuma did not desire her parents to know of her marriage, she

continued to use her birth name for business purposes. Both Omura and Okuma were reputed to be "very Americanized," while their magazine was declared to pursue a "pro-American" editorial policy. See FBI File No. 100-2887, San Francisco, Report of Special Agent (Excised-b7c), April 8, 1943, at Denver, Colorado (OP); and FBI File No. 100-18492, San Francisco, Report of Special Agent (Excised-b7c), October 2, 1943, at Denver, Colorado (OP). In an early draft of his memoir, then titled "Shattered Lives," Omura wrote:

> In October of 1940, I married the Managing Editor of Current Life Publication, Caryl Fumiko Okuma. The marriage was kept secret for business purposes. I had not been told at the time that the mother-in-law [Kise Okuma] strongly opposed it. I had never met the father-in-law who was a shoemaker. I, myself, was not overly enthusiastic but was aware that her [Fumiko's] services were needed. The marriage was sealed in Crescent City [Carson City], Nevada.

See OP. After divorcing Jimmie Omura in 1947, Fumiko Okuma got remarried in 1952 to Martin Morton Gertler (1919–87).

14. According to the November 22, 1941, *Kashu Mainichi*, Caryl Fumiko Okuma arrived in Los Angeles by train from San Francisco on November 21, 1941, for a scheduled two-week business trip (which got extended an additional week). During her sojourn in Los Angeles, she garnered several public relations coups. On December 2, 1941, an impressive two-column photo of her displaying the newest issue of *Current Life* appeared in connection with a feature story on it within the mainstream *Los Angeles Daily News*. Almost as imposing was a *Kashu Mainichi* article, published two days later, which branded Okuma as the "original career girl of San Francisco" and portrayed her as "the first nisei woman to enter into a business field, advertising and managing editor, on a national scale."

15. Presumably this message from Okuma to Omura was conveyed by telephone.

16. The San Francisco Flower Market traces its history back to the late 1800s. By 1909 Japanese, Chinese, and Italian flower-growers got together and opened the first flower-growers market. The premises for this market became too small, so in 1924 the growers created the California Flower Market at Fifth and Howard streets. This is the market referenced by Omura. For a comprehensive history of the evolution of the flower market in San Francisco, see Gary Kawaguchi, *Living with Flowers: History of the California Flower Market* (San Francisco: California Flower Market Inc., 1993).

17. Omura is quite possibly referring here to the celebrated Flower Market Café, located at Sixth and Bryant and known "for over 100 years" for its home-style breakfasts. A short walk away from the San Francisco Flower Market, its current address is 597 Sixth Street.

18. Prior to World War II the Sutter Printing Company was located in San Francisco at 1737 Sutter Street, where it was operated by M. Hosaka. Shortly after the declaration of war, the shop was reportedly closed and Hosaka was detained in Utah at the Topaz Relocation Center. See FBI File No. 100-18492, San Francisco, Report of Special Agent (Excised-b7c), June 23, 1943, at Denver, Colorado (OP).

19. In 1942 the Argonaut Publishing Company, located at 544 Market Street in San Francisco, was in its sixty-fifth year of operation, having been launched by its founding editor, Frank Pixley, in 1877.

20. See Greg Robinson, "War Relocation Authority," in the *Densho Encyclopedia*, http://encyclopedia.densho.org/ (accessed on January 10, 2015).

21. Established on March 17, 1941, the Western Defense Command (WDC) was charged with the primary responsibility of coordinating the defense of the Pacific Coast region (Washington, Oregon, California, Idaho, Montana, Nevada, Utah, and Arizona) of the United States and, secondarily, training the soldiers prior to their overseas deployment. The WDC headquarters were located at the Presidio of San Francisco. The WDC's first commanding general was Lieutenant General John L. DeWitt, who concurrently commanded the Fourth U.S. Army. The WDC was disbanded on March 6, 1946. For additional information, see "Western Defense Command" entry in the *Densho Encyclopedia*, http://encyclopedia.densho.org/ (accessed on January 10, 2015).

22. Born in Paris, France, to American parents living abroad, Francis Beverly Biddle (1886–1968) earned both a BA and a law degree from Harvard. President Franklin Roosevelt nominated him in 1935 to chair the National Labor Relations Board, and in 1939 he became a judge on the U.S. Court of Appeals for the Third Circuit. The following year he left this position to become the U.S. Solicitor General. Two years later President Roosevelt named him as the U.S. Attorney General, a post he held throughout most of World War II, resigning in 1945 following Roosevelt's death and at the request of President Harry Truman, who shortly thereafter appointed Biddle as a judge for the International Military Tribunal at Nuremburg, Germany. Biddle is most remembered for his actions as attorney general in directing the FBI arrest of "enemy aliens" on December 7, 1941, which was the precursor to Executive Order 9066 authorizing the U.S. detention camps for the wartime incarceration of Americans of Japanese ancestry. For further information, see Brian Niiya, "Francis Biddle," in the *Densho Encyclopedia*, http://encyclopedia.densho.org/ (accessed on January 10, 2015).

23. The San Francisco address in question was 1623 Webster Street, though by early 1942 the listing for the national JACL headquarters was 2031 Bush Street.

24. An American journalist, columnist, biographer, and novelist, John Franklin Carter (1897–1967) was born in Fall River, Massachusetts, and attended Yale

University. Between 1936 and 1948, under the pen name of Jay Franklin, Carter wrote a syndicated column, "We, The People," that chronicled the presidential administrations of Franklin Roosevelt and Harry Truman.

25. For information on Curtis Burton Munson (1892–1980), a World War I veteran and a midwestern businessman, and the secret report he authored at the request of President Franklin Roosevelt, see Brian Niiya, "Munson Report," in the *Densho Encyclopedia*, http://encyclopedia.densho.org/ (accessed on January 10, 2015).

26. See Bill Hosokawa, *JACL in Quest of Justice: The History of the Japanese American Citizens League* (New York: William Morrow, 1982), 128.

27. Omura does not specify any pages in *Years of Infamy* to support Weglyn's purported achievement, so he quite possibly had in mind all of chap. 1, "The Secret Munson Report," 33–53. However, based on the context of this statement, it seems more likely that his intent was to spotlight pages 39–47.

28. As cited in ibid., 51.

29. Ibid.

30. As quoted by Weglyn in ibid.

31. Testimony of James Y. Sakamoto, General Chairman Emergency Defense Council, Japanese American Citizens League, and Editor, *Japanese-American Courier*, Hearing before the Select Committee Investigating National Defense Migration, House of Representatives, 77th Cong., 2d sess. [hereafter Tolan Committee Hearings], Seattle, Washington, February 28 and March 2, 1942, Part 30, 11472. Asserted Sakamoto:

> Now if it will help to curb public opinion why not put all of us [Nikkei] under protective custody? Or, better still, if you care to, why not place the alien Japanese parents of ours under our [the Japanese American Citizens League] custody? For instance, I can give you one concrete plan. We can have a registration system where every alien must report, let us say, twice a week, to our Japanese American Citizens League headquarters, and if they do not come in to register twice a week, we will report those persons to the Federal Bureau of Investigation, and a check-up will be made. They can be investigated.

32. See "Mike Masaoka's Rebuttal to Critics," Twenty-Seventh Biennial JACL National Convention, Airport Hyatt Hotel, Los Angeles [CA], August 10, 1983, Resisters.com, http://resisters.com/learn-more/jacl/mike-masaokas-rebuttal-to-critics/ (accessed on March 27, 2015).

33. For information on Mike Masaoka's proposal for a "suicide battalion" and the particular context in which he was alleged to have advanced it, see Shiho Imai's entry on Masaoka in the *Densho Encyclopedia*, encyclopedia.densho.org/ (accessed on February 6, 2018).

34. See Audrie Girdner and Anne Loftis, *The Great Betrayal: The Evacuation of the Japanese-Americans during World War II* (London: Macmillan, 1969), 275. The reference in this volume closely corresponds with but does not precisely match Omura's claim.

35. See C. B. Munson, "Japanese on the West Coast," attached to John Franklin Carter memorandum, November 7, 1941, http://home.comcast.net/~eo9066 /1941/41-11/Munson.html (accessed on March 27, 2015). Omura's assessment of Munson's perspective, though somewhat overstated, is a fair one.

36. A U.S. Navy intelligence officer and an expert on the people of Japanese ancestry who lived along the West Coast, Lieutenant Commander Kenneth D. Ringle (1900–1963) was asked in January 1942 by the chief of Naval Operations to prepare a report to determine if it was necessary to evict the Japanese American West Coast community for security reasons. Ringle's conclusion in his February 1942 report was that the mass exclusion of individuals of Japanese ancestry, whether citizens or aliens, was not justifiable, and that as far as security matters were concerned, they should be handled as individual problems instead of a mass population problem. See also Brian Niiya, "Kenneth Ringle," in the *Densho Encyclopedia*, http://encyclopedia.densho.org/ (accessed on January 10, 2015).

37. Ohio-born Stetson Conn (1908–92) was awarded the PhD in history at Yale University in 1938. Following a stint as an Amherst College history professor, he joined the staff of the Office of Military History as a senior editor, a position he held until 1949. He next served as chief of the Western Hemisphere Section, 1949–53, and as deputy chief historian, 1953–58, before taking over in 1958 as chief historian of the Department of the Army.

38. Although practically a self-made man, John Jay McCloy (1895–1989) became one of the most versatile and accomplished men of his time. A graduate of Amherst College, he went on to Harvard Law School, from which, after a two-year interruption as a field artillery army captain in World War I, he earned his law degree in 1921. Thereupon, his basic profession was the law, including service as a Wall Street lawyer, until 1941. In that year, Secretary of War Henry L. Stimson brought him to Washington, DC, as a consultant and then persuaded President Franklin Roosevelt to appoint him as his assistant secretary of war. After the United States entered World War II, McCloy was a key official charged with the program to exclude and incarcerate Americans of Japanese ancestry, which he believed to be "reasonably undertaken" and "humanely conducted." See also Brian Niiya's entry on John J. McCloy in the *Densho Encyclopedia*, http://encyclopedia.densho.org/ (accessed August 10, 2015).

39. At present the onetime Southern District Council of JACL carries the name of Pacific Southwest District. It now encompasses chapters in all counties of California south of Kern and Monterey, plus Arizona, New Mexico, and

the southwestern portion of Nevada. In 1942 it likely was restricted to chapters in the southern California region.

40. This Santa Ana meeting was held on January 11, 1942. See Naval History and Heritage Command, "Ringle Report on Japanese Internment," www.history. navy.mil/research/library/online-reading-room/title-list-alphabetically/r/ringle -report-on-japanese-internment.html (accessed on February 16, 2015). Santa Ana, the seat of Orange County, California, and its most populous city, was founded in 1869; in 1940, as the commercial and cultural hub of Orange County (then a predominantly agricultural area), Santa Ana claimed a population of approximately 32,000 residents and also served as the urban center for the county's decentralized and loosely confederated "Japantown." See Preserving California's Japantown Project, "Japantown Atlas—Southern California—Orange County," http://japantownatlas.com/map-orange.html (accessed on December 2, 2010).

41. Located in northeast Colorado's Weld County, Fort Lupton is a statutory city. In 1940 its population was 1,692. Its basic industry then was agriculture. For a short history of Fort Lupton with relevant information about its Japanese-ancestry population, see Adam Thomas, SWCA Inc. Environmental Consultants, *Crossroads in Eden: Development of Fort Lupton, 1835–2000* (Fort Lupton: Historic Preservation Board, City of Fort Lupton, Weld County, Colorado, 2003), www .fortlupton.org/DocumentCenter/View/398 (accessed on April 7, 2015).

42. Based on indirect evidence, it would appear that this meeting was held on the night of Friday, December 5, at the Japanese Association Hall in Fort Lupton, though the source for this conjecture, Bill Hosokawa, in *Colorado's Japanese Americans*, 85, neither mentions Fort Lupton nor indicates a specific location for the Japanese Association Hall.

43. As explained by Martha Nakagawa in "Analysis: A Look at JACL's Role during WWII, Stance on Resisters," *Pacific Citizen*, July 16–22, 1999, "Resolution 7 [which was directed at "no-nos," not "draft resisters"] never passed, but a motion was approved to form a Presidential Select Committee to research JACL's wartime role so that delegates may make an informed decision on Resolution 7 at the 31st [JACL] Biennial Convention in San Diego in 1990." See posting of Nakagawa's article by Resisters.com, www.resisters.com/news/PC_7-6-99.htm (accessed on March 27, 2015).

44. Assistant to U.S. Attorney General Francis Biddle, James H. Rowe Jr. (1909–84), a lawyer and New Dealer, was the most ardent critic of the proposal for mass exclusion and detention of Americans of Japanese ancestry. It was his belief that this proposal, which he believed was being forced on the Roosevelt administration by public opinion, was unconstitutional. See February 2, 1942, memorandum from Rowe to Grace Tully, President Roosevelt's private secretary (wherein Rowe warns the president of the public pressure and the constitutional

issues involved), which is included in the "FDR and Japanese American Internment" website, www.fdrlibrary.marist.edu/archives/pdfs/internment.pdf (accessed
on December 4, 2010).

45. A graduate of Indiana University, Paul Vories McNutt (1891–1955) went
to Harvard Law School, after which he was a professor at the Indiana University
School of Law. Although McNutt served in World War I, upon leaving the military he returned to his law school job and there became the youngest dean in the
school's history. In 1933 he was elected governor of Indiana and then served one
four-year term in this office. In 1942 Roosevelt appointed McNutt to chair the
War Manpower Commission. This commission, without being accorded much
power, was charged with planning the labor needs of agriculture, industry, and
the armed forces.

46. For the historical context pertinent to the 1990 release by JACL Presidential Select Committee chair Cressey Nakagawa of the official twenty-six-page
digest of the original ninety-five-page Lim Report, see Kenji Taguma, "Study Saying Wartime JACL Leaders Collaborated Can Be Found on Two Websites," *Nichi
Bei Times*, July 1, 2001, www.resisters.com/news/NB_Lim_Online.htm (accessed
on April 15, 2015); and Brian Niiya, "Lim Report," in the *Densho Encyclopedia*,
http://encyclopedia.densho.org/ (accessed on April 15, 2015). See also Bill Hosokawa, "Exhuming the Lim Report," *Pacific Citizen*, July 1–7, 1994, in which he
writes: "I have read both the 26-page digest and a 96-page version. Readers will
find whatever they want in these documents. Those who believe JACL was a craven, unfeeling organization that sold out its people will find evidence that seems
to support their views."

47. See entry for June 4, 1992, within Omura's Redress Diary (OP), where
he details that his attempt to gain access to the JACL's institutional files at the
national JACL office in San Francisco was effectively "brushed-off" by two officials of the organization, Director Dennis Hayashi and Associate Director Carole
Hayashino.

48. One of California's original counties, Monterey County is located on the
Pacific Coast of central California. For information about the historical experi-
ence of Japanese Americans in the Monterey area, see the following sources:
Sandy Lydon, *The Japanese in the Monterey Bay Region: A Brief History* (Capitola,
CA: Capitola Book, 1997); David Yamada, *The Japanese of the Monterey Peninsula:
Their History and Legacy 1895–1995* (Monterey, CA: Monterey Peninsula Japanese
American Citizens League, 1995); and Preserving California's Japantowns, "Mon-
terey," www.californiajapantowns.org/monterey.html (accessed on December 7,
2010).

49. A Nevada native, Leland M. Ford (1893–1965) moved to Santa Monica,
California, in 1919, where he served on its planning commission before being

elected a Los Angeles County supervisor in 1936. In 1939 he was elected to the U.S. House of Representatives. After serving in Congress for two terms, he was an unsuccessful candidate for reelection in 1942 and resumed his prepolitical career in real estate.

50. Omura does not provide a citation for this purported statement made by Masaoka in the mid-1950s. However, on August 10, 1982, in a talk by Masaoka at the twenty-seventh biennial convention of the JACL held at the Airport Hyatt Hotel in Los Angeles, Masaoka uttered a very similar message: "Those people who ask . . . why didn't we [the JACL leadership] do something about all this? Frankly, I think we were misled and we were lulled into a false sense of security." See the text of this Masaoka presentation, http://resisters.com/learn-more/jacl/mike-masaokas-rebuttal-to-critics/ (accessed on April 17, 2015).

51. Although as an actor he was cast as a stereotypical Latin in *The Cisco Kid* television series, Leo Carrillo (1915–57) came from an old and renowned Californio family. In addition to appearing in more than ninety motion pictures, he was a notable preservationist and conservationist in his native California.

52. Born in Macon, Georgia, Henry McLemore (1906–68) was a United Press Internationalist sports columnist before his affiliation with the Hearst newspaper chain.

53. The son of second-generation German Jewish parents, Walter Lippmann (1889–1974) was a graduate of Harvard, where he studied under William James, Graham Wallis, and George Santayana, cofounded the Socialist Club, and edited the *Harvard Monthly*. The youthful author of a series of books about politics, Lippmann cofounded the politically liberal and highly influential *New Republic* magazine. Beginning in 1931, he wrote a nationally syndicated column, "Today and Tomorrow," that ran for thirty years and featured a pragmatic approach to politics that permitted Lippmann to support six Republican and seven Democratic presidential candidates.

54. Born in Minneapolis, Minnesota, Francis James Westbrook Pegler (1894–1965) was an American writer and journalist. As a columnist for the Scripps Howard syndicate at the peak of his career, he was an avid anti–New Dealer, one who lashed out on every seeming opportunity at President Franklin Roosevelt, First Lady Eleanor Roosevelt, and Vice President Henry Wallace. For Pegler, the New Deal was a Communist plot. For a vigorous critical rebuttal to conservative William Buckley's "loving appreciation" of Pegler in the March 1, 2004, issue of *The New Yorker* magazine, see Diane McWhorter, "Dangerous Minds: William F. Buckley Soft-Pedals the Legacy of Journalist Westbrook Pegler in *The New Yorker*," *Slate*, March 4, 2004, www.slate.com/id/2096673/ (accessed on December 7, 2010).

55. A native of Manhattan, Kansas, Damon Runyan (1884–1946) was raised in Pueblo, Colorado. In 1910 he exchanged his *Denver Post* sportswriter job for

employment with the *New York American*, a Hearst daily newspaper. At the peak
of his career in the 1930s, Runyan claimed a daily readership in excess of ten million and was widely regarded as America's premier journalist.

56. The franchise commentator for Mutual Network in the 1930s, Nebraska-
born John Broughton Hughes (1902–82) was known for freely speaking his mind.
He gained notoriety following Pearl Harbor for being one of the earliest and most
strident advocates of mass eviction and detention of Japanese Americans. See
"Correspondence Regarding January 1942 Broadcast [of John B. Hughes]," JERS,
BANC, UCB, MSS, 67/14c, Folder A 16.252 (1/9), http://digitalassets.lib.berkeley.
edu/jarda/ucb/text/cubanc6714_b014a16_0252_7.pdf (accessed on April 7, 2015).
See also JERS researcher Morton Grodzins's report on his July 19, 1943, interview with Hughes in "Letters, Interview, and Broadcast," ibid., Folder A 16.251,
http://digitalassets.lib.berkeley.edu/jarda/ucb/text/cubanc6714_b013a16_0251.pdf
(accessed on April 7, 2015).

57. See Esther Newman's entry for Culbert Olson (1876–1962) in the *Densho
Encyclopedia*, http://encyclopedia.densho.org/ (accessed on February 3, 2015).

58. For information on Togo W. Tanaka (1916–2009), see Brian Niiya's entry
on him in the *Densho Encyclopedia*, http://encyclopedia.densho.org/ (accessed on
March 2, 2015).

59. For relevant information on this event, see "Meeting with Governor Olson"
portion of "Part I: Pre-Evacuation" in Deborah K. Lim, "The Lim Report," www
.resisters.com/study/LimTOC.htm (accessed on December 22, 2010).

60. *Coram nobis*, an ancient writ of the common law, is the designation of a
remedy for setting aside an erroneous judgment in a civil or criminal action that
resulted from an error of fact in the proceeding. For the application of this writ
by Peter Irons and others in the context of the Japanese American post–World
War II redress and reparations movement, see Kenji Murase, "Coram Nobis:
The Error Before Us," *Nikkei Heritage* 11 (Spring 1999): 4–9, in the special issue,
"Coram Nobis and the Continuum of Activism," www.nikkeiheritage.org/nh/
fvx1n2.html (accessed on December 22, 2010). For the signature work on this
subject by Peter Irons (1940–), an emeritus professor of political science at the
University of California, San Diego, and a renowned civil rights/civil liberties
activist, see *Justice Delayed: The Record of the Japanese American Internment Cases*
(Middletown, CT: Wesleyan University Press, 1989).

61. The gist of this policy declaration, according to Paul R. Spickard in "The
Japanese [American] Citizens League, 1941–1942," *Pacific Historical Review* 52
(May 1983): 156, was "Justice, Americanism, Citizenship, Leadership." For an
explanation and discussion of the JACL's "Declaration of Policy" (authored by
Mike Masaoka), see Togo Tanaka, "Period of Recurring Crises, Sept. 1941–April
1942," chap. 4 in "History of the JACL" (1945?), JERS, BANC, UCB, Reel

084.0340, Folder T 6.25, 13-15. Unfortunately, Tanaka's JACL history is not available on the digitized version of the JERS material.

62. For a biographical overview of Isamu Noguchi (1904–88), see Greg Robinson's entry for him in the *Densho Encyclopedia*, http://encyclopedia.densho.org/ (accessed on March 3, 2015). A recent Noguchi biography of note is Hayden Herrera, *Listening to Stone: The Art and Life of Isamu Noguchi* (New York: Farrar, Straus and Giroux, 2015), esp. chap. 19, "California," 169–76, and chap. 20, "Poston," 177–85.

63. Organized with Noguchi's assistance in January 1942, the Nisei Writers and Artists Mobilization for Democracy stemmed in part from Noguchi's feeling that he, an American citizen who was half-Japanese, was being viewed after Japan's December 7, 1941, attack on Pearl Harbor as an alien threat. It was at this point, maintains Noguchi, that he experienced racial prejudice more personally, being made aware that he was not just an American but a Nisei, a Japanese American, and as such had to take action.

64. Born and raised in Illinois and educated at Yale College and Harvard Law School, Archibald MacLeish (1892–1982) was a writer who would eventually be a Harvard professor, a Pulitzer Prize winner for both poetry and drama, and a target of conservative Cold War anti-Communist groups and spokespeople. His critics characterized him caustically as a propagandist and felt it appropriate that during World War II he should serve in such capacities as the director of the War Department's Office of Facts and Figures and as the assistant director of the Office of Information.

65. Formed as a club in Hollywood as early as 1920, the Screen Writers Guild did not become a union until 1933 when a cadre of progressive writers sought a strong protective organization for screenwriters. Having been granted as the exclusive bargaining agency for screenwriters by the National Labor Relations Board, the guild came under attack by the House Committee on Un-American Activities because of its members' alleged far-left leanings.

66. Apart from Omura, three other prominent participants in this organization's meetings were Mike Masaoka, Karl Yoneda, and Larry Tajiri. However, the Bay Region Council for Unity is not mentioned in the memoirs by Yoneda and Masaoka or the only book-length biographical study centered on Larry Tajiri. See, respectively, the following volumes: Karl G. Yoneda, *Ganbatte: Sixty-Year Struggle of a Kibei Worker* (Los Angeles: Asian American Studies Center, University of California, Los Angeles, 1983); Mike Masaoka with Bill Hosokawa, *They Call Me Moses Masaoka: An American Saga* (New York: William Morrow, 1987); and Robinson, *Pacific Citizens*. In Omura's Redress Diary (OP), there is an entry for Sunday, April 9, 1989, which alludes to the Bay Region Council for Unity: "Had long phone interview with Karl Yoneda but he simply avoided any specifics

on the Bay Region Council for Unity." In the notes Omura took on that phone interview (OP), he writes: "Yoneda credits LARRY TAJIRI for formation of Bay Region Council for Unity (as opposed to Isamu Noguchi). He stated: 'Larry approached us to join league' (but Noguchi was the inspiration)."

67. Regarded as San Francisco's "Little Italy" because of it once having a majority Italian-ancestry population, North Beach is a northeastern San Francisco district located close to both Chinatown and Fisherman's Wharf. Information on the precise location of Isamu Noguchi's studio in North Beach in early 1942 could not be unearthed. However, in *Listening to Stone*, 173, Hayden Herrera indicates that it was at the Montgomery Street apartment of the art patron and Abstract Expression mosaicist Jeanne Reynal (1903–83) where "Noguchi organized a group called Nisei Writers and Artists." Since Noguchi was then living in Los Angeles, it seems logical to surmise that his "studio" in San Francisco was in fact Reynal's apartment.

68. Born in Oakland, California, Ernest Satoshi Iiyama (1912–2011) accompanied his parents when in 1920 they returned to live in Japan, where he attended school until 1930. Now considered a Kibei, he came back to California to complete high school and matriculate at the University of California, Berkeley. From members of the progressive Young Democrats of California, he acquired knowledge about civil rights and social justice. In the 1930s he helped to organize both the Oakland chapter of the Japanese American Citizens League and the Nisei Democrats of the East Bay. During World War II, Iiyama was incarcerated at the Tanforan Assembly Center and the Topaz Relocation Center, after which he resettled in Chicago. Along with his wife, Chizu, he later moved to New York, where the Iiyamas were active in the Japanese American Committee for Democracy. Ultimately they moved to the San Francisco Bay Area, where they became moving spirits in the National Japanese American Historical Society and the Japanese American redress and reparations movement. For an obituary of Ernest Iiyama, see *San Francisco Chronicle*, June 26, 2011, www.legacy.com/obituaries/sfgate/obituary.aspx?n=ernest-s-iiyama&pid=152187476#fbLoggedOut (accessed on September 13, 2013).

69. For a cogent overview of the constellation of Nisei Democrats groups (their membership, ideological outlook, and principal aims) that formed in the late 1930s in California (Los Angeles, San Francisco, and Oakland), see Jere Takahashi, *Nisei/Sansei: Shifting Japanese American Identities and Politics* (Philadelphia: Temple University Press, 1997), 68–71.

70. For an in-depth portrait of Karl Yoneda (1906–99), a Kibei activist, union organizer, political aspirant, longshoreman, and author, see the stunning entry on him by Glenn Omatsu in the *Densho Encyclopedia*, http://encyclopedia.densho .org/ (accessed on April 11, 2015). For a short yet substantial, if quite partisan,

biographical account, see Tom Price, "Karl Yoneda, Working Class Hero," http://
recollectionbooks.com/bleed/Encyclopedia/EroshenkoVasily/people_0599.htm
(accessed on January 17, 2011). See also "Finding Aid for the Karl G. Yoneda
Papers, 1928–1989," *Online Archive of California*, www.oac.cdlib.org/findaid/
ark:/13030/tf0c6002wh/ (accessed on January 17, 2011).

71. To supplement the information about Lincoln Seiichi Kanai provided in
the text of this chapter by Omura, see Greg Robinson, "The Great Unknown
and the Unknown Great: Buchanan YMCA Secretary Lincoln Kanai's 'Courage against Injustice' of World War II," *Nichi Bei Weekly*, May 27, 2010; and
the World War II correspondence between Kanai and James Omura (OP), particularly the December 31, 1943, letter from James Omura to Lincoln Kanai, in
which Omura informs Kanai of his future plans: "I am planning to initiate a new
national organization, which would be more democratic in character and more
sincere in advocacy of the cause of the U.S. Japanese. I would think an appropriate title for such an organization would be the American Loyalty League." Omura
then goes on to encourage Kanai to join with him in building this projected
organization.

72. For a recent historical overview of the Acadians, see John Mack Farragher,
*A Great and Noble Scheme: The Tragic Story of the Expulsion of the French Acadians
from Their American Homeland* (New York: Norton, 2005).

73. Omura does not cite a source for this undated statement by Levenson,
who was one of the interviewers involved in the production of the two-volume
1976 *Japanese-American Relocation Reviewed* interview series done under the aegis
of the Earl Warren Oral History Project of the Regional Oral History Office
(ROHO) at the University of California, Berkeley. Levenson, who grew up in
England, was educated at Cambridge University, Radcliffe, and the University of
California, Berkeley. She joined the ROHO staff in 1970.

74. On the temper of this meeting sponsored by the United Citizens Federation, see Togo Tanaka's letter to Morton Grodzins, January 1, 1943, and its
accompanying report-style response to Grodzins's request for information about
the JACL's opposition groups, of which the United Citizens Federation, spearheaded by Tanaka, was notable in mid-February of 1942, in http://digitalassets.lib.
berkeley.edu/jarda/ucb/text/cubanc6714_b211010_0014.pdf (accessed on April 19,
2015). See also Omura's taped and transcribed Denver interview of August 16, 1985,
with George Matsumonji, a JACL member and longtime friend of Omura's who
attended the February 18, 1942, meeting at the Maryknoll Auditorium in Los Angeles (OP). See as well Omura's August 16, 1985, entry in his Redress Diary (OP).

75. In drafting his memoir, Omura consistently misidentified the venue for
the Tolan Committee hearings in San Francisco, placing them at the War Memorial Building instead of the Post Office Building, the actual site for the sessions

held on February 21 and 23, 1942. Since both structures reflect the Beaux Arts style, Omura's confusion is perhaps understandable. Hereafter in this memoir all references by Omura to the War Memorial Building in connection with the Tolan Committee hearings will be rendered as the Post Office Building.

76. Born and raised in Alabama, John J. Sparkman (1899–1985) represented his state in Congress for forty-two years, first in the House of Representatives (1937–46) and then in the Senate (1946–79). Notwithstanding his consistent opposition to civil rights legislation, Sparkman was perceived to be a pro–New Deal liberal throughout his House tenure and even during his first three Senate terms, owing to his being an ardent supporter of unions, public housing, aid to education, hospital and health-care funding, increased public works spending, higher minimum wages, veterans programs, and small businesses. However, after the war Sparkman was among the nineteen southern senators who were a signatory to the Southern Manifesto opposing the 1954 U.S. Supreme Court decision *Brown v. Board of Education of Topeka, Kansas,* and racial integration. After 1962, Sparkman moved sharply to the right, increasingly casting his votes with the conservative coalition of southern Democrats and Republicans. See Samuel L. Webb, "John J. Sparkman," *Encyclopedia of Alabama,* www.encyclopediaofalabama.org/face/Article.jsp?id=h-1441 (accessed on February 25, 2011).

77. Evelyn Teiko (Kirimura) Okamoto (1917–2005) was born and died in Cheyenne, Wyoming, but spent her youth and got her schooling in Denver, Colorado, before leaving that city at age twenty to work as a journalist in San Francisco. There in the late 1930s she was employed by the English-language section of the *Shin Sekai Asahi* (*New World Sun*) under the editorship of Howard Imazeki. In 1939, according to Bill Hosokawa, in *JACL in Quest of Justice,* 69, Kirimura took over the editorship of the *Pacific Citizen* from Jimmie Sakamoto when that JACL paper was returned from Seattle to San Francisco. During World War II, Kirimura was incarcerated at the Tanforan Assembly Center and the Topaz Relocation Center. For further information on Kirimura, see Barbara Hiura, "Ex-journalist Recalls Days at Prewar Newspaper," *Hokubei Mainichi,* October 20, 1993 (OP).

78. As Togo Tanaka, in chap. 5, "Period of Disorganization and Reorganization," of his 1945 *History of the Japanese American Citizens League,* observed:

> The Pacific Citizen has had five editors: Iwao Kawakami, Earl Tanbara, James Sakamoto, Evelyn Kirimura, Larry Tajiri. Curiously enough, the single personality whose influence and views give the publication continuity and consistency of purpose, remains submerged in the background—Saburo Kido. Despite shifts in editors, the Pacific Citizen remains almost unchanged throughout all its history with respect to: (1) Its ceaseless cam-

paigning against discriminatory practices as they affect resident Japanese, especially Nisei, and (2) Its similarly ceaseless campaigning to build up the J.A.C.L. organization as the all-embracing, all-powerful organization among all Japanese in the United States.

79. Unfortunately, Omura does not identify the name of the university chancellor who provided this comment about his testimony at the Tolan Committee hearings; nor does he indicate the date and the occasion of this comment. It is quite likely, however, that the unamed person Omura had in mind was Dr. Ray Lyman Wilbur (1879–1949), who served as the president of Stanford University from 1916 to 1943 and subsequently filled the role of that university's chancellor until his 1949 death. When in October 1941 the Northern California Committee on Fair Play for Citizens and Aliens of Japanese Ancestry was formed, Wilbur was a charter member. Then, on March 21, 1942, on the first of the two days of the Tolan Committee hearings in San Francisco, Wilbur sent a letter to Lieutenant General John L. De Witt, head of the Western Defense Command, with this message: "Whenever and wherever the constitutional guarantees are violated in the treatment of a minority, no matter how unpopular or helpless, the whole fabric of American government is weakened. . . . The test of America is the security of its minority groups." This information on Wilbur is found in Audrie Girdner and Anne Loftis, *The Great Betrayal: The Evacuation of the Japanese-Americans during World War II* (London: Macmillan, 1969), 25, 126.

80. Omura does not provide sufficient information in his textual reference to the reputed letter from the Auburn Nisei girl protesting the violation of her constitutional rights to properly document it here. Since Omura's June 20, 1994, death occurred while his memoir manuscript was still in progress, this situation and others akin to it are not surprising. In the month prior to his death, a series of entries in his Redress Diary highlights the nature of his notes problem: (5/18/94) "Past few days been going back on lost computer items"; (5/21/94) "Continued posting notes in computer"; (5/28/94) "Finished Notes around 6:30 [p.m.] and the next step is coordination. Failed to find several items that stick in my mind but feel it necessary to proceed with the text and hopefully they might show up"; and (6/7/94) "Finally coordinating the 'Notes' by six o'clock this evening. . . . Few items in my mind have yet to be found but expect to go and write plus revisions for publication. Important that framework is completed with filling in later."

81. For Louise Suski's purported "For the Children's Sake" editorial, see *Rafu Shimpo*, March 22, 1942. Suski's actual title for this editorial was "What's the Use?" though Omura assuredly captures its gist. "For the first time," wrote Suski,

we are confronted with the questions: If we are rightly American citizens, why can't we be treated as such? Why should all of us suffer for the crime of the few, if any? What are we going to tell our children? How can we explain to them why we cannot stand up for our rights as American citizens? How can we convince them that this is a democratic country, the melting pot of the world, a country comprised of all peoples in the world? As nisei, are we going to be trampled down without a fight? George Washington and his tired men met many hardships in the cold winter nights but won in the end. Why shouldn't nisei fight for our rights, even if it is a losing battle? At least we nisei can say that we lost but only after a hard battle.

For additional information about Louise Suski (1905–2003), see the two biographical essays on her by Patricia Wakida in the *Densho Encyclopedia*, http://encyclopedia .densho.org/ (accessed on April 9, 2015), and "Through the Fire: Louise Suski," on the Japanese American National Museum's Discover Nikkei website, www.discover nikkei.org/en/journal/2013/4/23/louise-suski/ (accessed on April 9, 2015).

82. Paul Jacobs and Saul Landau, eds., *To Serve the Devil: A Documentary Analysis of America's Racial History*, vol. 2: *Colonials and Sojourners* (New York: Vintage Books, 1971), 166–67. The portion of Omura's Tolan Committee testimony cited in this source was not voiced by him during his February 23, 1942, appearance in San Francisco at the Post Office Building but was included in the addendum that he mailed the committee from Denver the following month.

83. The oldest son of immigrant Issei farm peasants from a village near Okayama, Henry Nobuo Tani (1914–65) took over his late father's San Francisco insurance business on graduating in 1938 from Stanford University. After testifying in his leadership capacity with the San Francisco JACL chapter before the Tolan Committee (Statement of Henry Tani, Executive Secretary, Japanese American Citizens League, Tolan Committee Hearings, San Francisco, California, February 21 and 23, 1942, Part 29, 11148–52), Tani was incarcerated during World War II (with his wife and child) at the Tanforan Assembly Center in California and the Topaz Relocation Center in Utah.

84. In 1935 University of California School of Dentistry graduate Carl T. Hirota (1910–75) married Uta Ogawa Hirota (1910–2010), the daughter of an Issei pharmacist. During World War II, the Hirotas were detained in the Topaz Relocation Center in Utah, where Carl was a camp dentist and chaired the Temporary Community Council charged with establishing a system of "self-government" for the imprisoned population. He departed the camp to participate with the 442nd Regimental Combat Team and served the U.S. Army Dental Corps as a captain. See obituary for Uta Hirota in the *San Francisco Chronicle*, January 2, 2010.

85. The son of a physician father and a schoolteacher mother, Frank Herron Smith (1879–1965) received his BA degree from the University of Kansas in 1902 and then completed a course of study in theology at Northwestern University, after which he began work as an overseas Methodist missionary by establishing

churches in Japan and Korea. In 1926 he and his wife, Gertrude Barnford Smith (1880–1957), returned to the United States and resided in Berkeley, California. There he assumed the position of the Pacific Japanese Mission's superintendent and oversaw twenty-two Methodist churches in the western states. In 1935 the Smiths returned to Japan, where Dr. Smith spoke and wrote against Japanese military leadership and Japan's decision to join the Axis Powers with Germany and Italy. In the wake of Pearl Harbor, he gave broadcasts in an effort to stop mass hysteria, acted on behalf of Issei as an interpreter for parole boards in alien enemy internment camps, and provided assistance during the Tolan Committee hearings in San Francisco. During the war, too, he ministered to congregations in all ten of the War Relocation Authority-run concentration camps for Americans of Japanese ancestry. In addition, he advocated for the fair treatment of those in the incarcerated population, both during and after their camp detention, and looked after their business and real property interests. Fluent in the Japanese language, Dr. Smith was utilized by the Office of War Information during the war years to prepare scripts and make radio broadcasts to Japan. His death, in Palo Alto, California, occurred on August 6, 1965, the twentieth anniversary of the day the United States dropped an atomic bomb on the Japanese industrial city of Hiroshima. See "Smith Family Papers on World War II, MS 065," Library Services, Robert E. Kennedy Library, California Polytechnic State University, San Luis Obispo, http://lib.calpoly.edu/specialcollections/findingaids/ms065/ (accessed on March 2, 2011); and "Closely Related Pastorates: Frank Herron Smith," chap. 3 in Mary Patterson Clark, ed. and comp., *The History of the First Methodist Church of Lawrence, Kansas 1915–1954* (Lawrence: First Methodist Church of Lawrence, Kansas, Sesquicentennial Committee, 2004), http://fumcweb.com/history/Clarke History/AllPages.pdf (accessed on March 2, 2011).

86. See Hosokawa, *JACL in Quest of Justice*, 148–49; and Masaoka, with Hosokawa, *They Call Me Moses* Masaoka, 85–89, esp. 87–88.

87. See Charles Kikuchi, *The Kikuchi Diary: Chronicle from an American Concentration Camp*, ed. John Modell (Urbana: University of Illinois Press, 1973, 1993), entry for June 6, 1942, 111. See also, in OP, Omura's notes on Katayama, which he bases on an untitled August 21, 1942, document written by Kikuchi. Here it states that Katayama's brother was the financial secretary for the JACL and that Taro Katayama had worked on the *Pacific Citizen* and, in addition to writing "most of the speeches for the JACL leaders appearing before the (Tolan) Committee, . . . [was a member of] the Artist and Writers group organized by Isamu Noguchi."

88. For an informed description of Public Law 503, see Brian Niiya's entry in the *Densho Encyclopedia*, http://encyclopedia.densho.org/ (accessed on February 8, 2018).

CHAPTER 5

1. Presumably Omura is here referring to U.S. Supreme Court associate justice Owen J. Roberts. See Muller, *Free to Die for Their Country*, 122, 181, for an explanation of Roberts's roles in a June 1945 plurality ruling by the Supreme Court holding "that a desire to create a legal test case could amount to an innocent motive for not complying with the Selective Training and Service Act," and in a presidential review board in March 1947 that recommended amnesty for Nisei draft resisters on the grounds that "they felt they had been unlawfully imprisoned and unjustly treated and did not believe that they were required to honor their obligations as American citizens while America was breaching its obligations to them."

2. Roger Daniels, *Concentration Camps USA: Japanese Americans and World War II* (New York: Holt, Rinehart and Winston, 1971), 123–29; and Douglas W. Nelson, *Heart Mountain: The History of an American Concentration Camp* (Madison: State Historical Society of Wisconsin, for the Department of History, University of Wisconsin, 1976).

3. Richard Drinnon, *Keeper of Concentration Camps: Dillon S. Myer and American Racism* (Berkeley: University of California Press, 1987), 127, 300–301.

4. William Minoru Hohri, *Repairing America: An Account of the Movement for Japanese-American Redress* (Pullman: Washington State University Press, 1984), 13–33.

5. Andrew Sakaye Nakahata, "A Lost Chapter of World War II" (senior honors thesis in history, Wesleyan University, 1989).

6. Gretel Ehrlich, *Heart Mountain* (New York: Viking Press, 1988), chaps. 29–33, 263–305.

7. See Frank Chin, "Come All Ye Asian American Writers of the Real and the Fake," in Jeffrey Paul Chan, Frank Chin, Lawson Fusao Inada, and Shawn Hsu Wong, eds., *The Big Aiiieeeee!: An Anthology of Chinese American and Japanese American Literature* (New York: Penguin Books, 1991), 1–92, esp. 52–82 with respect to the Heart Mountain Fair Play Committee. Chin's plays, *Chickencoop Chinaman*, first produced in 1972, and *The Year of the Dragon*, first produced in 1974, were published together by the University of Washington Press in 1981. Prior to Omura's death in 1994, Chin had published one novel, *Donald Duk* (Minneapolis: Coffee House Press, 1991), as well as a single volume of short stories, *The Chinaman Pacific & Frisco R.R. Co* (Minneapolis: Coffee House Press, 1988).

8. See Frank Chin, "The Last Organized Resistance," *Rafu Shimpo*, December 19, 1981.

9. According to Martha Nakagawa, in "Analysis: A Look at JACL's Role during WWII, Stance on Resisters," *Pacific Citizen*, July 16–22, 1999, what the JACL

passed at the 1990 convention was Resolution 13, which "recognized but did not apologize to the resisters."

10. Omura's reference here is to the more than thirty thousand Americans who avoided the draft by taking up residence in Canada. In September 1974, President Gerald R. Ford established an amnesty program for these draft evaders mandating them to work in alternative service occupations from six to twenty-four months. In 1977, Ford's successor, Jimmy Carter, offered a pardon to any draft evaders who requested one.

11. Whereas "draft evaders" refers to those individuals attempting to flee the draft, "draft resisters" denotes persons explicitly refusing military service.

12. In the absence of reference information by Omura, the content of this sentence defies precise documentation. This is particularly true with respect to the alleged commentary attributed to Nisei soldiers. As for the trial testimony of an FBI investigating agent, this can be confirmed in a general sense by reference to data found in Eric Muller's *Free to Die for Their Country*, 108. According to Muller, the defense attorney for the sixty-three Heart Mountain draft resisters being tried in Cheyenne, Wyoming, in June 1944, "was able to elicit testimony from the FBI agents . . . that each and every one of the . . . defendants had . . . neither said nor done anything 'against the United States [n]or indicate[d] any disloyal attitude,' had expressed no desire to go to Japan, and had 'indicated a desire to fight for this country if he were restored to his rights as a citizen.'"

13. For information on the Heart Mountain Relocation Center, see the entry on it by Mieko Matsumoto in the *Densho Encyclopedia*, http://encyclopedia .densho.org/ (accessed on April 29, 2015).

14. In addition to the Heart Mountain camp in Wyoming, the War Relocation Authority administered nine other camps: Manzanar and Tule Lake in California; Poston and Gila River in Arizona; Minidoka in Idaho; Topaz in Utah; Amache in Colorado; and Rohwer and Jerome in Arkansas. For additional information on these WRA centers, see, respectively, the entries in the *Densho Encyclopedia*, http://encyclopedia.densho.org/contents/ (accessed on April 29, 2015) by Glen Kitayama (Manzanar), Barbara Takei (Tule Lake), Thomas Y. Fujita-Rony (Poston), Karen J. Leong (Gila River), Hanako Wakatsuki (Minidoka), Michael Huefner (Topaz), Bonnie J. Clark (Amache), and Brian Niiya (Rohwer and Jerome).

15. On July 1, 1944, President Franklin Roosevelt signed Public Law 78-405, called the Denaturalization Act of 1944. It created a procedure whereby American citizens could lose their citizenship in time of war by renouncing it in writing. In late 1944 and early 1945, about 5,500 inmates at the Tule Lake Segregation Center made application to renounce their U.S. citizenship under the provisions of Public Law 78-405. For in-depth information on the Denaturalization Act of 1944,

see the superb entry on it by Cherstin Lyon in the *Densho Encyclopedia*, http://
encyclopedia.densho.org/ (accessed on August 6, 2015).

16. Caryl's Malt & Sandwich Shop held its grand opening on September 4,
1942, at 2008 Larimer Street, "in the heart of Denver's Japanese colony." See "Caryl
Opens a Malt and Sandwich Shop" article and companion advertisement in the
September 11, 1942, issue of the *Rocky Nippon*. The address for the Osumi business
was 2010 Larimer Street. For information about the Japanese American community
in World War II Denver, see Gil Asakawa, "Resettlement in Denver" in the *Densho
Encyclopedia*, http://encyclopedia.densho.org/ (accessed on August 24, 2015).

17. Jimmie Omura moved the Pacific Coast Evacuee Placement Bureau from
its original site in Denver on 1023 Nineteenth Street to the Larimer Street location in September 1942. He discontinued the placement bureau's operation on
April 1, 1943, after exactly one full year of operation.

18. The date of sale for Caryl's Malt & Sandwich Shop was August 2, 1943.
See "Caryl's Is Sold to Virginia Couple," *Rocky Shimpo*, August 9, 1943.

19. A World War I veteran, Thomas Phillip Stroupe was born in Aberdeen,
South Dakota, in 1894 and died in San Francisco, California, in 1946. In 1942
Stroupe's San Francisco photography studio was located on 690 Market Street. For
the allegation about Stroupe's link to Naval Intelligence, see the January 16, 1946,
entry in the diary that Omura maintained in the wake of World War II (OP).

20. The Japanese American National Museum researchers mentioned by
Omura were Nancy Araki and Brian Niiya.

21. See note 23 below for more information on Harry Matsunaka. According
to the diary maintained by Fumiko Caryl (Okuma) Omura in February–March
1942, when she preceded her husband, Jimmie Omura, to Denver for the purpose
of finding a place that could be used as both a family residence and an office for
the transplanted *Current Life* magazine, she made the acquaintance on March 19
of Harry Matsunaka, "a radio man." In Caryl Omura's words, Matsunaka was "a
journalist at heart, [and] he fell for Current Life since he had just resigned as the
(English section) editor of the Rocky Shimpo." Through Matsunaka, apparently,
Caryl Omura met Tetsuko Toda, "the daughter of the [then] editor [and publisher, Shiro Toda] of Rocky Shimpo." For Caryl Omura's 1942 diary, see OP.

22. Joe Grant Masaoka (1909–70) was incarcerated in 1942 at the Manzanar
Relocation Center in eastern California, where he was employed by the War
Relocation Authority as a documentary historian. From 1942 to 1951 he was the
regional director of the Japanese American Citizens League in Denver, Colorado,
and he also established the JACL regional office in San Francisco.

23. Tetsuko Mary (Toda) Matsunaka (1924–66) was the second of seven Nisei
children (and the eldest daughter) of their Issei parents, Shiro Toda (1881–1957)
and Yoshiko Toda (1897–1982). After her father, the publisher and editor of the

Denver-based *Rocky Nippon* Japanese vernacular newspaper, was arrested by the U.S. government on March 2, 1943, and charged with printing seditious material in his paper, Tetsuko Toda assumed the ownership, on April 23, 1943, of the *Rocky Nippon*, which then became the *Rocky Shimpo*. As for Tetsuko Toda, on October 15, 1951, she married Harry Hiroshi Matsunaka, a Denver Nisei who had served as the English-language editor of the *Rocky Shimpo* prior to the appointment of Jimmie Omura in January 1944. For additional information on the Toda family, see the Densho interview done with Tetsuko Toda Matsunaka's younger sister, Shyoko Toda Hiraga, by Art Hansen and Frank Abe on September 28, 2012, in Seattle, Washington, http://archive.densho.org/main.aspx (accessed on August 16, 2015). In 1946 Shyoko Toda married Noboru Hiraga (1922–84), a Kibei-Nisei who had worked during World War II as the editor of the Japanese section of the *Rocky Shimpo* until April 1944, when along with Jimmie Omura he also was pressured by the U.S. government to resign his position.

24. The *Colorado Times* [*Kakushu jiji*] commenced publication as a Japanese vernacular newspaper in Denver in 1908 as the *Denver Shimpo*. In 1918, following a merger with another paper, it assumed the name of the *Colorado Times*. According to James Omura (OP), "it was published by John Nakagawa's [Issei] father and continued under him until 1932 . . . [when] it was sold to [Issei] Fred I. Kaihara." As the paper's publisher-editor, Kaihara (1887–1955) introduced an English-language section in August 1942. He sold the paper in July 1955 to Ted Ogasawara. The newspaper ceased publication in 1969. See Brian Niiya's entry on the "Colorado Times" in the *Densho Encyclopedia*, http://encyclopedia.densho.org/ (accessed on August 17, 2015).

25. See "Colorado's First Post War Bussei Rally Successful," *Colorado Times*, February 9, 1943, a follow-up story to the promotion of the rally that appeared in that newspaper five days earlier announcing that the subject for Joe Masaoka's keynote talk would be "What We Are Up Against." On the other hand, in Omura's "Nisei Life" column for the February 10, 1943, *Rocky Nippon*, he took Joe Grant Masaoka to task for providing "vague, evasive and indirect" replies to questions from the floor. "This sort of evasion, misrepresentation and indirection of reply is characteristic of ranking J.A.C.L. officials," charged Omura. "It is regrettable that in these times we cannot face the issues squarely, judge them soberly on their merits and expose the lies which hamper our future course in America."

26. Born in Denver, Thomas J. Morrissey (1899–1967) attended St. Regis College and in 1923 graduated from the University of Denver Law School. In 1933 Morrissey was appointed, at age thirty-three, to be the country's youngest federal district attorney, a position held by him until 1947. See "Thomas J. Morrissey, 68, Prominent Denverite Dies," *Rocky Mountain News*, December 21, 1967, http://files.usgwarchives.net/co/denver/obits/m/morrissey_thomas_1967.txt (accessed on May 28, 2012).

27. The law office for Robert L. McDougal (1903–88) in 1945 was within the historic Majestic Building, located at 209 Sixteenth Street in downtown Denver. See *Denver, Colorado, City Directory, 1945*.

28. A federal freedom of information law permitting full or partial disclosure of previously unreleased U.S. government-controlled information and documents, the Freedom of Information Act (FOIA) was signed into law by President Lyndon B. Johnson on July 4, 1966, and has thereafter been periodically amended.

29. See FBI File No. 100-18492, San Francisco, Report of Special Agent (Excised – b7c), dated June 23, 1943, at Denver, Colorado (OP).

30. Nathaniel ("Nat") J. L. Pieper (1908–75) was born in St. Louis, Missouri, and died in Tampa, Florida. Unfortunately, no information bearing on his FBI service as a special agent and head of the San Francisco FBI office is included in the two most likely sources treating the lives and careers of former FBI special agents: *Society of Former Special Agents of the FBI* (Paducah, KY: Turner Publishing, 1998); and National Law Enforcement Museum, *FBI Oral Histories* [of former special agents], www.nleomf.org/museum/the-collection/oral-histories/index-2.html (accessed on August 9, 2015).

31. A Missouri-born recipient of both an AB and a JD from Washington University in St. Louis, Sterling F. Tremayne (1917–2008) served as a special agent for the FBI in Seattle, Washington, as well as several other U.S. cities. According to the entry on him in *Society of Former Special Agents of the FBI*, 220, Tremayne entered FBI service as a special agent in October 1940 and thereafter served in the agency offices in San Diego, Seattle, and Chicago as a street agent and field supervisor.

32. See letter from Kazushi Matsumoto to James Omura, October 2, 1944 (OP). See also reply letter from James Omura to Kazushi Matsumoto, October 17, 1944, ibid., for a full background explanation of the purported usage by Omura of the "James Iwasa" name in early 1943 at Fort Lupton ("which is and has been," writes Omura, "the stronghold of the JACL in Colorado").

33. No information has been disclosed as to the so-called Denver Japanese Hall.

34. For the announcement of this event, see "Public Meeting," *Colorado Times*, March 11, 1943, and the bulletins within the *Rocky Nippon* on March 10 and 12, 1943. On the day before this gathering, the *Colorado Times* printed an article by K. O. [Kaz Oka] of the *Poston Chronicle*, in which he charged that "the most vehement critics of the JACL . . . the most persistent carpers are those who are either pro-Axis or egotistic and unfitted to assume their dutiful responsibilities or are grossly ignorant of the League's true aims and background." Oka, an ardent JACL supporter, allowed that the League had made some small mistakes

in judgment, but it was striving to counterbalance these and deserved "the whole-hearted support of every freedom-loving Japanese American because it is the only Nisei organization dedicated to their cause of justice and liberty." In closing his jeremiad, Oka turned to scripture: "And before censuring the JACL . . . thoroughly digest (if you dare!) this bit of pertinent advice which Jesus gave unto his disciples [in the Gospel of Matthew] . . . : Thou hypocrite, first cast out the beam out of thine own eye; and then shalt thou see clearly to cast out the mote out of thy brother's eye." Very likely Oka had been fired up by Omura's open letter in the February 20, 1943, *Rocky Nippon* issue delineating ten reasons for his differences with the JACL (e.g., "The J.A.C.L. is ostensibly dedicated to the promotion of Americanism, but during the period leading up to the Evacuation, it refused to stand upon its constitutional grounds. For 'future considerations,' we were virtually sold down the river"), and closing with his challenging the JACL to "a public examination of any and all points . . . covered."

35. Hirota, a member of the Berkeley, California, chapter of the JACL, became president of the Western Young Buddhist League in 1948.

36. For the *Colorado Times* treatment of this event, see "JACL Draws Capacity Audiences" in the March 18, 1943, issue. The penetration of the JACL in Colorado—particularly Denver—and its platform, especially with regard to the military role of Japanese Americans, was dramatically noticeable in the pages of the *Colorado Times* during the days of 1943 prior to the March 14 public meeting at the Japanese Methodist Church.

37. See "Young Buddhists Hail Talk by National Secretary," *Colorado Times*, March 18, 1943.

38. Omura did not avail himself of this opportunity until March 28, 1943. For an assessment of his presentation, see Gene Gohara, "Omura Addresses Public Meeting," *Rocky Nippon*, March 29, 1943. See also the full text of Omura's talk, "Why I Oppose the J.A.C.L.," *Rocky Nippon*, March 31, 1943, and his appraisal of the event in which it was featured in his April 2, 1943, *Rocky Nippon* "Nisei Life" column. In addition, see "Mr. Omura Replies to His Critics," *Rocky Shimpo*, April 14, 1943.

39. Pando, located in the White River National Forest between Leadville and Minturn, Colorado, was a small camp for construction workers who built Camp Hale. Opened in 1942, this huge facility comprised over one thousand temporary structures and housed roughly 2,500 men. See Metropolitan State College of Denver, "Camp Hale History," www.mscd.edu/history/camphale/chh_001.html (accessed on December 22, 2011).

Fitzsimons Army Hospital was named in 1920 after William T. Fitzsimons, the first American medical officer fatality in World War I. Located on a 577-acre site in Aurora, Colorado, the facility was one of the army's major World War II medical training centers, and it saw heavy use treating military casualties from overseas battlefields. See Wikipedia entry for "Fitzsimons Army Medical Center," http://en.wikipedia.org/wiki/Fitzsimons_Army_Medical_Center (accessed on December 22, 2011).

During World War II, Robbins Incubator Company of Denver, Colorado, was a global provider of incubation equipment notable for producing rugged machines providing superb hatchability and chick quality.

For a discussion of the World War II role played by Omura and the Pacific Coast Evacuee Placement Bureau in resolving Nisei employment discrimination through the War Manpower Commission in relation to the Pando, Fitzsimons, and Robbins sites, see Omura's interview with Hansen, 277, as cited in Chapter 1, note 26.

40. Evidence suggests that this Denver event was held on March 15, 1943, involved JACL representatives (Mike and Joe Grant Masaoka and Larry Tajiri) and War Manpower Committee regional officials, and revolved around the problems attendant on using Japanese Americans to meet the intermountain region's manpower crisis. See "War Manpower Commission and the Nisei," *Colorado Times*, March 20, 1943. There is no mention in this article of interaction between any of the three JACL representatives and James Omura.

41. Omura offered no citation for the quotation by McCloy, but its content is consistent with the context of the January 1943 decision for the United States to utilize Japanese Americans as combat troops.

42. Following graduation from the U.S. Naval Academy, Ellis Mark Zacharias Sr. (1890–1961) was commissioned, and by 1939 he had progressed to the rank of captain. From June 1942 until August 1943, he was the Office of Naval Intelligence's deputy director. For a life history of Zacharias based upon information supplied by his son, Jerrold M. Zacharias, see U.S. Navy–Office of Information Biographies Branch, "Bio of Ellis M. Zacharias, Sr.," June 29, 1961, http://ussslcca25.com/zach04.htm (accessed on December 23, 2011).

43. Although the Office of Naval Intelligence was established in 1882 "for the purpose of collecting and recording such naval information as may be useful to the Department [of the Navy] in time of war, as well as peace," it did not earnestly tackle its role as the naval intelligence arm until 1898, when the United States declared war on Spain in response to the U.S. battleship *Maine*'s sinking in the Spanish-controlled harbor of Havana, Cuba. During World War II, the ONI's responsibilities as well as budget and staff grew significantly.

44. Missouri-born Cecil H. Coggins (1902–87) was a medical officer with the Office of Naval Intelligence during World War II. In 1935, while working for

ONI, he set the stage for a new generation of counterintelligence experts when he uncovered an Axis spy ring that confirmed an intelligence threat to the United States.

45. See transcript of General Strong's April 14, 1943, telephone conversation with General John DeWitt, commander of the Western Defense Command and Fourth Army, http://blogs.archives.gov/TextMessage/2013/11/22/a-slaps-a-slap -general-john-l-dewitt-and-four-little-words/ (accessed on May 31, 2015), for an insight into their shared view of Americans of Japanese ancestry. This document, which appears on the guest blog of Alan Walker, a processing archivist at Archives II in College Park, Maryland, is drawn from the "Gen. John L. DeWitt Personal Papers—Records Relating to Military Service, 1921–1926," National Archives Identifier 7432140 (Online Public Access posting pending).

46. For a useful biographical overview on Henry L. Stimson (1857–1950), see Brian Niiya's entry on him in the *Densho Encyclopedia*, http://encyclopedia.den-sho.org/ (accessed on August 6, 2015).

47. See Cherstin Lyon's entry on "Loyalty Questionnaire" in the *Densho Encyclopedia*, http://encyclopedia.densho.org/ (accessed on August 17, 2016).

48. According to Eric L. Muller in *American Inquisition: The Hunt for Japanese American Loyalty in World War II* (Chapel Hill: University of North Carolina Press, 2007), upon the creation of the Japanese American Joint Board (JAJB) on January 20, 1943, it was directed to play two roles:

> (1) to transmit the investigation report and copies of the [loyalty] questionnaires to the War Relocation Authority, together with its recommendation concerning the release of subject individuals from relocation centers on indefinite leave; and (2) . . . [to] state whether the Joint Board has any objection to the employment in plants and facilities important to the war effort of any of those American citizens of Japanese ancestry who are released by the War Relocation Authority pursuant to its recommendation. (39)

Put briefly, writes Muller, "the JAJB was to advise the WRA about granting leave to internees, and was to pass judgment on whether released internees could take jobs in war industries." For the government's coding of the 1943 loyalty questionnaire responses, see Chizu Omori, "The Loyalty Questionnaire," in Mike Mackey, ed., *Guilt by Association: Essays on Japanese Settlement, Internment, and Relocation in the Rocky Mountain West* (Powell, WY: Western History Publications, 2001).

49. Established on March 17, 1941, as the command formation of the U.S. Army, the Eastern Defense Command (EDC) was responsible for coordinating the defense of the Atlantic Coast region of the United States. The EDC was disbanded in 1946.

50. For the Tule Lake Relocation/Segregation Center, see the entry by Barbara Takei in the *Densho Encyclopedia*, http://encyclopedia.densho.org/.

51. See Emmett J. Scott, *The American Negro in the World War* (self-published, 1919), http://net.lib.byu.edu/estu/wwi/comment/scott/ScottTC.htm (accessed on August 10, 2015). See also Chad L. Williams, *Torchbearers of Democracy: African American Soldiers in the World War I Era* (Chapel Hill: University of North Carolina Press, 2013).

52. See Ulysses Lee, *The Employment of Negro Troops* (Washington, DC: Center of Military History United States Army, 1966), www.history.army.mil/books/wwii/11-4/index.htm (accessed on August 10, 2015). See also Christopher Paul Moore, *Fighting for America: Black Soldiers—The Unsung Heroes of World War II* (New York: One World, 2005); and Charles Knauer, *Let Us Fight as Free Men: Black Soldiers and Civil Rights* (Philadelphia: University of Pennsylvania Press, 2014).

53. See James M. Omura, Executive Director Pacific Coast Evacuee Placement Bureau, letter to Hon. Henry L. Stimson, Secretary of War, February 5, 1943; and Henry L. Stimson, Secretary of War, letter to Mr. James M. Omura, Executive Director Pacific Coast Evacuee Placement Bureau, February 9, 1943 (OP).

54. The precise date of the *Rocky Shimpo*'s joint publication of Stimson's February 9, 1943, letter to Omura and Omura's February 15, 1943, rejoinder to Stimson is unclear, but indications suggest that they appeared in print on February 19, 1943. Both letters are available in OP.

55. The source from which Omura derived the decorated Nisei veteran's 1980s public address could not be determined.

56. See the richly detailed entries by Franklin Oda on the 100th Infantry Battalion, and on the 442nd Regimental Combat Team, in the *Densho Encyclopedia*, http://encyclopedia.densho.org/ (both accessed on August 17, 2016).

57. Created in 1909 in Wisconsin's Monroe County, Camp McCoy was utilized during World War II as a training facility for units from across the United States preparing to enter combat. The all-Nisei 100th Infantry Battalion was the first unit to train at this camp after its 45,000-acre 1938–42 expansion.

58. See two other letters sent by Omura to Stimson, dated February 21, 1943, and February 23, 1943, along with a February 28, 1943, reply to Omura from Stimson transmitted through his assistant secretary of war, Colonel William P. Scobey (OP).

59. Paul Vories McNutt (1891–1955) was born, bred, and educated in Indiana. In 1942, President Franklin Roosevelt named McNutt the chair of the newly created War Manpower Commission. Although carrying little real power, this agency was charged with planning to balance the labor needs of agriculture, industry, and the armed forces. While in this leadership capacity, McNutt publicly urged "the extermination of the Japanese in toto." When asked for clarification, McNutt

indicated that he was referring to the Japanese people as a whole—not just the military—"for I know the Japanese people."

60. Likely Omura's contacts with McNutt were by telephone, as OP contains correspondence neither between Omura and McNutt nor between Omura and the McNutt-chaired War Manpower Commission.

61. For information on the Heart Mountain Congress of American Citizens, see the entry on this organization by Glen Kitayama in Niiya, *Encyclopedia of Japanese American History*, 191–92. See also the overview of its activities by its leader Frank Inouye, "Immediate Origins of the Heart Mountain Draft Resistance Movement," *Peace and Change* 23 (April 1998): 148–66.

62. Frank Tadao Inouye (1920–95) was born in Los Angeles, California, and died in Honolulu, Hawai'i. The best biographical overview of Inouye is supplied by his physician son, Allan A. Inouye, as a front-matter essay, "My Father, Frank T. Inouye," in a book coauthored by Frank T. Inouye and Edward J. Kormondy, *The University of Hawai'i-Hilo: A College in the Making* (Hilo: University of Hawai'i-Hilo, 2001), xv–xvii. See also Frank Inouye's unpublished memoir, "Odyssey of a Nisei: A Voyage of Self-Discovery." This manuscript is available in the Special Collections Department of the University of Cincinnati Library.

63. See Daniels, *Concentration Camps USA*, 120; and Nelson, *Heart Mountain*, 104.

64. See Nelson, *Heart Mountain*, 106.

65. See Daniels, *Concentration Camps USA*, 120–21.

66. Born in the Republic of Hawai'i, Robert Kiyoshi Okamoto (1889–1974) was a student of chemistry and engineering at the University of Hawai'i, where he completed two years in the mid-1920s. He later volunteered for service during World War I but was deferred for undisclosed reasons. Thereafter, he worked in Hawai'i as a sugar mill superintendent, a construction engineer, and a soil test engineer. In 1933 he migrated to San Pedro, California. Going broke in the Depression, he cobbled together an income in southern California through journalism, business promotional activities, extra jobs for Hollywood films, and adult-education teaching of soil chemistry in the Los Angeles high school districts of Torrance and Glendale. Okamoto was likely the first Nisei educator to serve in the continental United States public schools. He was in his early fifties when he was incarcerated in Wyoming at the Heart Mountain concentration camp. On March 27, 1944, he was forcibly transferred to the Tule Lake Segregation Center for attempting to have Heart Mountain's project director, Guy Robertson, removed from his post for incompetence. He was later returned to Wyoming to stand trial in October–November 1944 with the other six Heart Mountain Fair Play Committee leaders, plus James Omura, for conspiracy to counsel draft evasion. Convicted of this charge, Okamoto and his fellow FPC leaders—Omura

was exonerated—were meted out a four-year imprisonment sentence at the Leavenworth Federal Correctional Institute, though it was cut short in December 1945 when the U.S. Tenth Circuit Court of Appeals overturned their convictions. Credited as one of the first Nisei to call for redress while imprisoned in a World War II Japanese American concentration camp, Okamoto renewed his efforts on behalf of redress in California during the postwar years. Never married and without children, on his death Okamoto was consigned to a pauper's grave within East Los Angeles' Evergreen Cemetery. During a ceremony held on August 21, 2009, through the initiative of Marie Masumoto and her husband, Earnie Masumoto, Okamato's grandnephew, Okamoto was given a proper memorial to his life. See the following sources: Martha Nakagawa, "From Pauper to Patriot: Rediscovering Fair Play Committee Leader Kiyoshi Okamoto," *Nichi Bei Times*, September 3–9, 2009; Yosh Kuromiya, "Brutal Irony in Discovery of Fair Play Committee Leader's Gravesite," letter to the editor, ibid.; Chizu Omori, "Rabbit Ramblings: Kiyoshi Okamoto, An Unsung Hero of the Camp Resistance Movement," *Nichi Bei Weekly*, January 20, 2011; and Earnest Masumoto, "Remarks for Kiyoshi Okamoto," www.resisters.com/news/okamoto_masumoto.htm (accessed on April 30, 2012). For Omura's post–World War II assessment of Okamoto, see Jimmie Omura, "Father of the Fair Play Committee," *Rocky Shimpo*, July 3, 1947, which concludes with these words:

> But when we consider the various facets of the Evacuation, we find a mere handful of Nisei out of more than 80,000 of them who did not quake at government ire and firmly stood their ground against the government injustices. To these and to Kiyoshi Okamoto we pay our respects. They at least defended their liberty and the constitutional rights of an individual in a democracy in no uncertain fashion. They are not traitors to their heritage.

67. See Sharon Yamato's entry on Paul Takeo Nakadate (1914–64) in the *Densho Encyclopedia*, http://encyclopedia.densho.org/ (accessed on August 11, 2015); and also Yamato's article on him posted on the Japanese American National Museum's Discover Nikkei website, www.discovernikkei.org/en/journal/2015/1/13/unraveling-family-mysteries/ (accessed on August 11, 2015).

68. In scouring the copies of the *Gila News-Courier* during the interval of late January to early March 1943, this quoted passage attributed to project director Leroy Bennett avoided my detection.

69. See "Army Means Business: Intimidation, Coercion Not to Be Tolerated," *Colorado Times*, February 18, 1942. This article, citing the *Gila News-Courier*, quotes this statement from Captain Norman Thompson being made following a visit to the Gila site by Colonel William Scobey, aide to Under-Secretary of War John J. McCloy.

70. According to Eric Muller, in his "Draft Resistance" entry in the *Densho Encyclopedia*, http://encyclopedia.densho.org/ (accessed on June 2, 2015), "there is no record of criminal prosecutions for draft resistance at Manzanar or Gila River."

71. The term "cannon fodder" per se does not appear in any of the four February 1943 Omura-to-Stimson letters archived in OP.

72. The reference here is to the Espionage Act of 1917, which was enacted on June 15, 1917, shortly after the U.S. entry into World War I. It provided penalties of twenty years imprisonment and fines up to ten thousand dollars for those convicted of interfering with military recruitment.

73. Elmer Shirrell was replaced as project director of the Tule Lake Relocation Center by Harvey M. Coverley (1903–94) in December 1942. Coverley functioned in this capacity during the registration crisis and then was supplanted just prior to the outset of the segregation program by Raymond Best, who then remained as director throughout the history of the Tule Lake Segregation Center. For a detailed portrait of Harvey Coverley, see Gordon H. Chang, *Morning Glory, Evening Shadow: Yamato Ichihashi and His Internment Writings, 1942–1945* (Stanford, CA: Stanford University Press, 1997), 500–501, n51.

74. After military service during World War I, Tennessee-born Clarence C. Ward (1894–1955) moved to California, where he later became Santa Barbara County's district attorney, serving between 1923 and 1931. In 1940 he was elected as a Republican to the California State Senate. In 1941–42 he was a member of the California State Legislature's Joint Fact-Finding Committee on Un-American Activities. According to Carey McWilliams, *Prejudice; Japanese-Americans: Symbol of Racial Intolerance* (Boston: Little, Brown, 1944): "Shortly after January 1, 1943, Senator Ward . . . representing the anti-Japanese forces in the state, toured California outlining the tactics and strategy of the campaign [to prevent the excluded Japanese American population from resettling in California]. This tour represented the first attempt to *organize* a state-wide agitation against the return of the Japanese" (233, emphasis in original).

75. Raymond Rawson Best (1895–1976) was born in Vicksburg, Michigan, and died in Sacramento, California. There is very little readily available biographical information on Raymond Best, although an obituary for him appeared in the September 1, 1976, *Sacramento Bee*. Prior to being named the director of the WRA's Tule Lake Segregation Center in 1943, Best filled administrative jobs at two other WRA "relocation centers" and served as the director of WRA "isolation centers" at Moab, Utah, and Leupp, Arizona.

76. On the loyalty registration in the WRA camps, see "Japanese Americans," chap. 3, on Densho's homepage, http://nikkeijin.densho.org/legacy/reference_ch3_04_loyalty_registration_en.html (accessed on September 4, 2015). See also entry for "Loyalty Questionnaire" by Cherstin M. Lyon in the *Densho Encyclopedia*, http://encyclopedia.densho.org/ (accessed on September 4, 2015).

77. See entry on "A More Perfect Union: Japanese Americans and the U.S. Constitution (exhibition)," by Abbie Salyers Grubb in the *Densho Encyclopedia*, http://encyclopedia.densho.org/ (accessed on September 3, 2015).

78. For information on Japanese American military resisters during World War II, see Shirley Castelnuovo, *Soldiers of Conscience: Japanese American Military Resisters in World War II* (Westport, CT: Praeger, 2008); and Brian Niiya's entry "Military Resisters" in the *Densho Encyclopedia*, http://encyclopedia.densho.org/ (accessed on September 3, 2015).

79. Located next to Hattiesburg, Mississippi, Camp Shelby was established in 1917 and served during World War II as the training center for both the Japanese American 442nd Regimental Combat Team and the 100th Battalion.

80. In 1946 the Committee on Naval Affairs and the Committee on Military Affairs of the U.S. House of Representatives were consolidated into the House Armed Services Committee.

81. For the context of this oft-quoted statement by DeWitt, see Alan Walker, "A Slap's a Slap: General John L. DeWitt and Four Little Words," https://text -message.blogs.archives.gov/2013/11/22/a-slaps-a-slap-general-john-l-dewitt-and -four-little-words/ (accessed on May 18, 2016). Walker, a processing archivist at Archives II in College Park, Maryland, posted this internet item on November 22, 2013.

82. Omura's reference here is clearly to the Japanese American Citizens League.

83. See Niiya, *Encyclopedia of Japanese American History*, 285–86, for a profile of the Poston center and suggestions for further reading as to its history and demography. See also Thomas Fujita-Rony's entry for Poston (Colorado River) in the *Densho Encyclopedia*, http://encyclopedia.densho.org/.

84. For information on the causes, conditions, and consequence of this seven-day general strike in the Poston 1 camp, see the following sources: Alexander Leighton, *The Governing of Men: General Principles and Recommendations Based on Experience at a Japanese Relocation Camp* (Princeton, NJ: Princeton University Press, 1945); Gary Y. Okihiro, "Japanese Resistance in America's Concentration Camps: A Re-evaluation," *Amerasia Journal* 2 (1973): 20–34; and Niiya, *Encyclopedia of Japanese American History*, 388.

85. Kazuo Kay Nishimura (1911–88) lived in the bachelor barracks in the Poston 1 camp, where he served on the Temporary Community Council. Born in Seattle, Washington, he lived in Japan for fifteen years before returning to Seattle in 1927. After working as a business manager and interpreter-translator for two Japanese American vernacular newspapers in Seattle and Los Angeles, in 1940 Nishimura became a rice grower in California's Imperial County. In the period between the Japanese attack on Pearl Harbor and Nishimura's incarceration at

Poston in May 1942, he served as executive secretary for the Imperial County Citizens Welfare Committee and as an interpreter and translator for the Federal Bureau of Investigation, Immigration and Naturalization Service, in El Centro, California. At 10:30 p.m. on November 14, 1942, Nishimura, while asleep in his Block 14 quarters, "was assaulted by a gang of eight men dressed in Samurai hoods and armed with pieces of pipe."

86. Leighton, *Governing of Men*, 164, provides a useful portrait of George Sadayoshi Fujii (1915–95).

87. For information on Heber, California-born Isamu Uchida (1915–?), see Leighton, *Governing of Men*. Uchida departed Poston in October 1943 and then entered Tule Lake Segregation Center. In December 1944 he left the Tule Lake camp after renouncing his U.S. citizenship and was imprisoned at the Santa Fe Internment Center where on March 12, 1945, he was one of four men badly injured in the so-called Santa Fe Riot. For information on that event, see the Wikipedia entry, http://en.wikipedia.org/wiki/Santa_Fe_Riot (accessed on June 5, 2015).

88. In fact, Saburo Kido, who lived in Poston 1, was beaten twice by camp inmates. The first assault, by five unidentified assailants, occurred on the evening of September 25, 1942. The second, and far worse, attack on Kido happened on January 31, 1943, when eight assailants, in view of his wife and child, beat him with wooden clubs so severely that he required three weeks of hospitalization. See Matthew T. Estes and Donald H. Estes, "Hot Enough to Melt Iron: The San Diego Nikkei Experience 1942–1946," *Journal of San Diego History* 42 (Summer 1996): 126–73, esp. 143–47. A digitized copy of this article is available at www.sandiegohistory.org/journal/96summer/nikkei.htm (accessed on February 2,2012).

89. In his entry on Saburo Kido (1902–77) in the *Densho Encyclopedia*, http://encyclopedia.densho.org/ (accessed on August 11, 2015), Brian Niiya writes: "The Kidos [left Poston and] resettled in Salt Lake City, where he [Sabura Kido] taught Japanese for the military at Fort Douglas, Utah and worked for the JACL. He continued to write for the *Pacific Citizen*."

90. For information on the Manzanar confinement facility, see the entry written by Glen Kitayama in the *Densho Encyclopedia*, http://encyclopedia.densho.org/. See also Harlan D. Unrau, *Manzanar National Historic Site, California: The Evacuation and Relocation of Persons of Japanese Ancestry during World War II: A Historical Study of the Manzanar War Relocation Center* (Denver: U.S. Department of the Interior, National Park Service, 1996).

91. *Inu* is a Japanese term denoting "dog" and connoting "informer." See Brian Masaru Hayashi's entry "Informants/'inu,'" in the *Densho Encyclopedia*, http://encyclopedia.densho.org/ (accessed on August 30, 2015).

92. See the entry "Fred Tayama" by Brian Niiya in the *Densho Encyclopedia*, http://encyclopedia.densho.org/ (accessed on August 30, 2015).

93. See Ralph P. Merritt, with supervision by Robert L. Brown, *Final Report, Manzanar Relocation Center* (Independence, CA: War Relocation Authority, 1946). One short portion of the five-volume report deals with "Gangs at Manzanar," which is available online through Calisphere, University of California, http://content.cdlib.org/view?docId=ktob69n45v&doc.view=frames&chunk. id=doe3516&toc.id=doe3406&brand=calisphere (accessed on August 31, 2015).

94. On the Cow Creek CCC camp in Death Valley and the experience of its Japanese American contingent detained there for a short stay in the wake of the Manzanar Riot of December 5–6, 1942, see Tad Uyeno, "Point of No Return," *Rafu Shimpo*, August 22–October 20, 1973; and Ralph P. "Pete" Merritt Jr., *Death Valley—Its Impounded Americans: The Contributions by Americans of Japanese Ancestry during World War II* (Death Valley, CA: Death Valley 49ers Inc., 1987). See also Tetsuden Kashima, *Judgment without Trial: Japanese American Imprisonment during World War II* (Seattle: University of Washington Press, 2003), 143–44.

95. In support of his contention about Togo Tanaka being a government informer, Omura supplies in his research notes (OP) two documentary items that doubtless convinced him of Tanaka's culpability. The first of these items, titled "Informer[s] for Navy Intelligence," is a June 11, 1942, letter from Commander K. D. Ringle of the Office of Navy Intelligence to M. S. Eisenhower, director of the War Relocation Center, listing thirty-three individuals (mostly JACL leaders, including Togo Tanaka) for whom Ringle certifies his "confidence." See NA, Records of the War Relocation Authority, WRA Administration, Washington, DC, central files, Folder 92.040-Commander Ringle. The second item, titled "Togo Tanaka," is an excerpt from a June 21, 1943, memorandum from D. M. Ladd (presumably an FBI agent) to J. Edgar Hoover, FBI director, in which Ladd writes: "And of the sixty-six persons who were removed [from the Manzanar Relocation Center following the December 5–6, 1942, "riot" at Manzanar and remanded to protective security at the Cow Creek Civilian Conservation Corps located at Death Valley National Monument in eastern California] only two could be considered as having given information of value to the Bureau. These are Fred Tayama . . . and Togo Tanaka." See NA, FBI File No. 43-20447-50. On the other hand, Tanaka could deny this accusation of his alleged perfidy by claiming that any information he provided that the FBI found of value was offered not surreptitiously as a spy but expressed publicly, consistent with his prewar role as a journalist and his wartime function at Manzanar as a documentary historian. See in particular Tanaka's April 23, 1943, letter to Morton Grodzins, staff member of the University of California, Berkeley-sponsored Japanese [American] Evacuation and Resettlement Study [JERS], BANC, Folder W 1.05, http://digitalassets.lib. berkeley.edu/jarda/ucb/text/cubanc6714_b211010_0014.pdf (accessed on September 2, 2015), esp. 109–11.

96. See Arthur A. Hansen entry on Harry Ueno (1907–2004) in the *Densho Encyclopedia*, http://encyclopedia.densho.org/ (accessed on August 24, 2015).

97. See Arthur A. Hansen and David A. Hacker, "The Manzanar Riot: An Ethnic Perspective," *Amerasia Journal* 2 (Fall 1974): 112–57. See also Brian Hayashi's entry, "Manzanar Riot/Uprising" in the *Densho Encyclopedia*, http://encyclopedia.densho.org/ (accessed August 24, 2015).

98. See the entry on "Jerome" by Brian Niiya in the *Densho Encyclopedia*, http://encyclopedia.densho.org/.

99. Nisei Thomas T. Yatabe (1897–1977) grew up in San Francisco and there worked to establish the San Francisco chapter of the American Loyalty League (ALL) in 1919. Moving to Fresno in 1922 to launch his dental practice, Yatabe was instrumental in founding the Fresno ALL chapter, a precursor of the Japanese American Citizens League. The fourth national JACL president, Yatabe served from 1934 to 1936. During World War II he was confined at the Fresno Assembly Center in central California and the Jerome Relocation Center in southeastern Arkansas. Two secondary sources discuss Yatabe's Jerome beating and subsequent removal from that camp: Diane C. Fujino, *Heartbeat of Struggle: The Revolutionary Life of Yuri Kochiyama* (Minneapolis: University of Minnesota Press, 2005), 63; and John Howard, *Concentration Camps on the Home Front: Japanese Americans in the House of Jim Crow* (Chicago: University of Chicago Press, 2008), 208.

100. John Misao Yamazaki (1885–1995) was born in Japan but came as a young man to Los Angeles. One of the few Japanese Christians in that city, Yamazaki attended services at St. Mary's Episcopal Mission, where he served as a lay minister. Encouraged by the diocesan leadership to join the ministry, Yamazaki moved to Connecticut and there enrolled at Trinity University and Berkeley Divinity School. Upon his 1913 ordination, the Reverend Yamazaki returned to Los Angeles.

101. See the comprehensive entry on "Topaz" by Michael Huefner in the *Densho Encyclopedia*, http://encyclopedia.densho.org/.

102. For information on Issei artist Chiura Obata (1885–1975), see the entry on him by Greg Robinson in the *Densho Encyclopedia*, http://encyclopedia.densho.org/ (accessed on September 4, 2015). At Topaz, Obata was also beaten by fellow inmates for being cooperative with the camp administration. See Sandra C. Taylor, *Jewel of the Desert: Japanese American Internment at Topaz* (Berkeley: University of California Press, 1993), 136; and Sumiko Kobayashi's October 2008 entry "Imprisoned without Trial" on the Medford Leas Residents Association website, http://mlra.org/imprisonedwithouttrial.htm (accessed on September 4, 2015).

103. For information on south-central Idaho's Minidoka Relocation Center, see the "Minidoka" entry by Hanako Wakatsuki in the *Densho Encyclopedia*,

http://encyclopedia.densho.org/. On the draft resistance movement at Minidoka, see Muller, *Free to Die for Their Country*, esp. 70–76, wherein Muller depicts the movement as being one of "hushed protest." See also Eric L. Muller, "The Minidoka Draft Resisters in a Federal Kangaroo Court," chap. 8 in Fiset and Nomura, *Nikkei in the Pacific Northwest*, 171–89.

104. See Art Hansen interview with James Omura, 295–96; and the Louis Fiset interview with Kenji Okuda, August 9, 1995, Seattle, Washington, transcript on file at the University of Washington Libraries, Manuscripts, Special Collection, University Archives. See also Louis Fiset, *Camp Harmony: Seattle's Japanese Americans and the Puyallup Assembly Center* (Urbana: University of Illinois Press, 2009), passim and, particularly with respect to Sakamoto's dramatically downsized role at Minidoka, 166; and Frank Miyamoto, "The Seattle JACL and Its Role in the Evacuation," JERS, BANC, UCB, MSS 67/14c, Folder T6.24.

105. For a very substantial and authoritative overview of the Gila camp, see the entry on "Gila River" by Karen J. Leong in the *Densho Encyclopedia*, http://encyclopedia.densho.org/.

106. See Charles Kikuchi, "Development and Analytical Summary of JACL in Gila," JERS, BANC, UCB, MSS 67/14c, Folder K8.22, http://digitalassets.lib.berkeley.edu/jarda/ucb/text/cubanc6714_b164k08_0022_2.pdf (accessed August 24, 2015).

107. On the support from the JACL Intermountain District Council that kept the national JACL afloat, see Joel Tadao Miyasaki, "Claiming a Place in the Intermountain West: Japanese American Ethnic Identity in Utah and Idaho" (master's thesis, Utah State University, 2006).

108. For an overview of Milton Stover Eisenhower (1899–1985), see the entry by Brian Niiya in the *Densho Encyclopedia*, http://encyclopedia.densho.org/ (accessed on August 31, 2015). With respect to Eisenhower's complicity with the propagandistic representation of the World War II eviction and detention of Americans of Japanese ancestry, see the 1942 documentary film, *Japanese Relocation*, produced by the Office of War Information, www.youtube.com/watch?v=6201QuAEoIw (accessed August 31, 2015).

109. In 1939 Indiana-born and Oxford-educated journalist Elmer Davis (1890–1958) was asked to fill in on CBS Radio for news analyst H. V. Kaltenborn and he became an instant success (by 1941 the nightly audience for his brief newscast and comment reached 12.5 million listeners). That same year, President Franklin Roosevelt appointed Davis to assume direction of the newly created U.S. Office of War Information, which (with some three thousand employees) was designed to consolidate government services. In this capacity, Davis not only recommended to Roosevelt that Japanese Americans be permitted to enlist for army and navy service, but also urged the president to oppose congressional bills depriving them of citizenship and mandating wartime incarceration.

110. As quoted by Eric Muller in *Free to Die for Their Country*, Mike Masaoka addressed the convention delegates at the Special Emergency National Conference of the JACL held November 17–24, 1942, at the Japanese Christian Church in Salt Lake City, Utah, saying these words:

> We believe that we are entitled to share in the good things of democracy just as much as we should share in the sacrifices and the heartaches of our country. . . . Being deprived of the right to serve our country in the armed forces today [meant that the Nisei are] being deprived of our biggest chance to prove to those who are skeptical that our loyalty is as great as that of any other group. . . . Somewhere, on the field of battle, in a baptism of blood, we and our comrades must prove to all who question that we are ready and willing to die for the one country we know and pledge allegiance to.

111. For the text and context of this note, see Muller, *Free to Die for Their Country*, 46.

112. Ibid.

113. The only readily available knowledge about Captain John M. Hall (n.d.) is that during World War II he was attached to the office of Assistant Secretary of War John J. McCloy as an assistant executive.

114. Massachusetts-born William Franklin ("Frank") Knox (1874–1944), a Spanish-American War veteran and later a newspaper reporter and publisher, was nominated in the 1936 election as the Republican Party's vice presidential candidate. Four years later, Democratic president Franklin Roosevelt named Knox as the forty-sixth secretary of the navy. Knox's principal legacy relative to the World War II Japanese American exclusion and detention experience was his December 15, 1941, declaration that Nikkei sabotage on Hawaiʻi was responsible for the success of the December 7 Japanese attack on Pearl Harbor, which fueled the momentum leading to President Roosevelt issuing Executive Order 9066 on national security grounds.

115. A Nisei born in Los Angeles, California, the Reverend Donald Kaoru Toriumi (1914–80) graduated from the Princeton Theological Seminary. Slightly more than a month prior to the World War II eviction of Nikkei from Los Angeles in 1942, the Reverend Toriumi was installed as pastor of the Japanese Union Church (Congregational and Presbyterian) of Los Angeles. On May 3, 1942, just a week before he, his wife (neé Sophie Tajima, the daughter of the Reverend Kengo Tajima), and his congregation were incarcerated at the Santa Anita Assembly Center in Arcadia, California, the Reverend Toriumi delivered a sermon based on Romans 8:35–39 entitled "The Tie That Binds," which was later included with counterpart sermons by Nikkei clerics in a self-published mimeographed booklet. See Allan A. Hunter and Gurney Binford, eds., *The Sunday Before: Sermons by*

Pacific Coast Pastors of the Japanese Race on the Sunday before Evacuation to Assembly Centers in the Late Spring of 1942 (Los Angeles, 1945), 18–22, www.gtuarchives .org/documents/sundaybefore-small.pdf (accessed on May 1, 2012).

116. For a life history of Los Angeles-born Frank Seishi Emi (1916–2010) with specific attention to his wartime and postwar role as a spokesman for the Heart Mountain Fair Play Committee, see the entry on him by Esther Newman in the *Densho Encyclopedia,* http://encyclopedia.densho.org/ (accessed on September 3, 2015).

117. For a portrait of Isamu ("Sam") Horino (1914–2002), see Frank Abe, Resisters.com, archives, 2007, http://resisters.com/2007/06/27/sam-horino-in -time-magazine-1942/, and esp. http://resisters.com/conscience/the_story/ characters/horino_sam.html (accessed on May 26, 2016).

118. Born in Nagano, Japan, Guntaro Kubota (1903–67) studied Japanese law and graduated from Tokyo's Meiji University before coming to the United States on the last boat prior to the United States' halting of Japanese immigration. With his Nisei wife, Gloria, and their daughter Grace, Guntaro Kubota was imprisoned first at the Santa Anita Assembly Center and then at the Heart Mountain Relocation Center. The only Issei immigrant on the Heart Mountain Fair Play Committee (FPC), he translated the FPC's English-language bulletins into Japanese to assist the organization in financing a court case with financial aid from the camp's Issei population. An enemy alien ineligible for the U.S. military draft, Kubota risked the possibility of being charged with espionage or sabotage and given a death penalty for his involvement with FPC activities. Nonetheless, determined to fight for the rights of his citizen children (his son Gordon was born at Heart Mountain), he openly championed the FPC cause. With the other six Nisei leaders of the FPC, he was charged, arrested, and convicted for conspiracy to counsel draft resistance in November 1944 in a federal trial held in Cheyenne, Wyoming, and then imprisoned for a four-year sentence at Kansas's Leavenworth Federal Correctional Institute. Along with his fellow FPC steering committee members, his time at Leavenworth ended when in December 1944 the U.S. Tenth Circuit Court of Appeals overturned their common conviction.

119. A Denver, Colorado-based lawyer, Samuel David Menin (1906–95) was known as a courtroom battler, in both a figurative and literal sense. In March 1940 he physically tangled with another lawyer, O. Otto Moore, in a Denver courtroom, during a case pitting the two men as legal representatives for rival old-age pension organizations. See "O. Otto Moore, Samuel Menin Trade Punches," *Greeley Daily Tribune* (Greeley, Colorado), March 8, 1940. Moreover, Menin was not a stranger to wartime draft evasion cases. In June 1942 he unsuccessfully defended in Denver a member of a religious sect who sought an exemp-

tion both from the army and noncombatant service. For additional information on Menin's background and role in the July 1944 Cheyenne federal-court mass trial for the sixty-three Heart Mountain draft resisters, see Muller, *Free to Die for Their Country*, 103 and 108–10.

120. See Jimmie Omura, "Let Us Not Be Rash," *Rocky Shimpo*, February 28, 1944, in Appendix 3.

121. For biographical information on Mitsuye Endo (1920–2006), see Brian Niiya's entry in *Densho Encyclopedia*, https://encyclopedia.densho.org/ (accessed on August 18, 2016); and City University of New York, Women's Leadership in American History, "Mitsuye Endo Persevering for Justice," www1.cuny.edu/portal_ur/content/womens_leadership/mitsuye_endo.html (accessed on August 29, 2015).

122. On the ex parte *Mitsuye Endo* case, see the entry by Brian Niiya in the *Densho Encyclopedia*, http://encyclopedia.densho.org/ (accessed on August 29, 2015). See also Roger Daniels, *The Japanese American Cases: The Rule of Law in Time of War* (Lawrence: University of Kansas Press, 2013), 37–38, 60–64, 70–72, and 76–79.

123. For an overview of *United States v. Masaaki Kuwabara et al.*, see Leagle, www.leagle.com/decision/194477256FSupp716_1598/UNITED%20STATES%20v.%20MASAAKI%20KUWABARA (accessed on August 29, 2015).

124. Born in Lemoore, California, Louis Earl Goodman (1892–1961), the son of immigrant European Jews, grew up in San Francisco, where he attended Lowell High School before matriculating at the University of California, Berkeley. There he received his BA in 1913 and, two year later, his law degree from that institution's Hastings College of Law. In private practice in San Francisco from 1915 to 1942, Goodman was a Selective Service Local Board member from 1940 to 1942. In November 1942, President Franklin D. Roosevelt nominated Goodman for a seat on the U.S. District Court for the Northern District of California, and during the next month he was confirmed for this seat by the U.S. Senate and received his commission for it. During the last three years of Goodman's life, from 1958 to 1961, he served as a chief judge in Palo Alto, California. For additional and still more consequential biographical information on Goodman, see Muller, *Free to Die for Their Country*, 132–35.

125. See ibid., 143, for Judge Goodman's pronouncement and chap. 7, "A Shock to the Conscience," 131–60 passim, for the larger context informing it.

CHAPTER 6

1. The Japanese Publishing Company in Denver, Colorado, published the *Rocky Nippon* (*Rokki Nippon*) from 1933 to 1943, when its name changed to the *Rocky Shimpo* (*Rokki Shimpo*), which then lasted as a newspaper until 1951.

2. This foundry was apparently removed just before the end of the war. Omura's job as a ladle operator consisted of operating hand-controlled mechanisms to pour and regulate the flow of molten metal into molds to produce castings or ingots.

3. See Brian Niiya's entry on the "Rocky Shimpo (newspaper)," in the *Densho Encyclopedia*, http://encyclopedia.densho.org/ (accessed on August 23, 2015).

4. The oldest private university in the Rocky Mountain region of the United States, the University of Denver (DU) was founded in 1864. During World War II, DU Chancellor Caleb F. Gates Jr. actively recruited students from the War Relocation Authority detention camps, where they were joined by students from the substantial population in the Denver area of so-called voluntary evacuees.

5. A northeast Denver neighborhood, Park Hill was platted in 1887. Although African Americans were among Park Hill's first settlers, the community was declared by its developer to be a "whites only" area. In the early 1900s, when Park Hill's new homes were first offered for sale, its schools were integrated even though socialization by ethnic minority students with white students was proscribed.

6. An office within the U.S. government during both World War I and World War II, the Alien Property Custodian served as the custodian of property belonging to U.S. enemies. See Paul V. Myron, "The Work of the Alien Property Custodian," *Law and Contemporary Problems* 11 (Winter–Spring 1945): 76–91; and James L. Duncanson, "The Representational Function of the Alien Property Custodian," *Fordham Law Review* 82 (1946), http://ir.lawnet.fordham.edu/cgi/ (accessed on July 24, 2012).

7. As director of the U.S. Justice Department's Alien Enemy Control Unit during World War II, Columbia University Law School graduate Edward J. Ennis (1908–90) strongly opposed in early wartime the incarceration of some seventy thousand U.S. citizens of Japanese ancestry. Moreover, after the war he testified on behalf of some of those who had been detained. Nonetheless, in his wartime post he discharged his assigned charges with respect to internment, parole, repatriation, and other internal practices involving enemy aliens. See the following obituary for Ennis: "Edward J. Ennis, 82; ACLU Official Fought Interning Japanese-Americans," *Los Angeles Times*, January 12, 1990, http://articles.latimes.com/1990-01-12/news/mn-17_1_internal-security (accessed on May 28, 2012). On the Alien Enemy Control Unit's program during World War II, see U.S. National Archives and Record Administration, "Brief Overview of the World War II Enemy Alien Control Program," www.archives.gov/research/immigration/enemy-aliens-overview.html (accessed on May 31, 2012).

8. On the Old Raton Ranch, see P. S. Herrick, "Old Raton Ranch/Fort Stanton, New Mexico," www.bookmice.net/darkchilde/japan/raton.html (accessed on

May 31, 2012); see also John J. Culley, "World War II and a Western Town: The Internment of the Japanese Railroad Workers of Clovis, New Mexico," *Western Historical Quarterly* 13 (January 1982): 43–61.

9. For information on the role of repatriation within the operation of the Justice Department's Alien Enemy Control Unit during World War II, see U.S. National Archives and Record Administration, "Brief Overview," as cited in note 7 above.

10. Tom Campbell Clark (1899–1977) was born in Dallas, Texas, and died in New York City. For an overview of Clark's life and career, see Alexander Wohl, *Father, Son, and Constitution: How Justice Tom Clark and Attorney General Ramsay Clark Shaped Democracy* (Lawrence: University Press of Kansas, 2013), www .nebookfair.com/book/9780700619160 (accessed on September 9, 2015). The most important government positions held by Tom Clark were U.S. attorney general (1945–49) and associate justice of the U.S. Supreme Court (1949–67). However, following Japan's attack on Pearl Harbor and the entry of the United States into World War II, Clark was appointed by then U.S. attorney general Francis Biddle as the civilian coordinator of the Enemy Alien Control Program. This led to his taking a prominent role in shaping the policies that led to the World War II West Coast exclusion of Americans of Japanese ancestry and their detention in interior concentration camps.

11. For an overview of the life and career of Francis Beverley Biddle (1886–1968), see the entry on him by Brian Niiya in the *Densho Encyclopedia*, http:// encyclopedia.densho.org/ (accessed on November 20, 2012).

12. Established on December 19, 1941, the Office of Censorship was an emergency wartime agency charged with aiding in the censorship of all ingoing and outgoing U.S. communications. See Michael Sweeney, *Secrets of Victory: The Office of Censorship and the American Press and Radio in World War II* (Chapel Hill: University of North Carolina Press, 2001).

13. See Haruo Higashimoto, "The Utah *Nippo* and World War II: A Sociological Review," revised version of a paper read at the Nineteenth Annual Conference of the Association for Asian American Studies, Salt Lake City, April 26, 2002, www.cs.kyoto-wu.ac.jp/bulletin/6/higasimoto.pdf (accessed on June 2, 2012). See also Takeya Mizuno, "The *Utah Nippo*: A Guardian Torn between Two Nations," chap. 7 in "The Civil Libertarian Press, Japanese American Press, and Japanese American Mass Evacuation" (PhD diss., University of Missouri, 2000), 284–331.

14. For information on the Civil Affairs Division of the WDC, see Brian Niiya's entry on the WDC's commanding general, General John DeWitt, in the *Densho Encyclopedia*, http://encyclopedia.densho.org/ (accessed on November 20, 2015), where he writes: "Dewitt appointed [Karl] Bendetsen to head the newly formed Civil Affairs Division and the Wartime Civil Control Administration on

March 12 [1942], putting him [in] charge of the logistics of removing 110,000 people [Japanese Americans] from their homes and communities."

15. No information could be found for "Taro Azuma" in connection with the *Utah Nippo.*

16. As stated in the finding aid for the *Civilian Agency Records of the Department of Justice,* www.archives.gov/research/holocaust/finding-aid/civilian/rg-60 .html (accessed on November 20, 2015): "For some 15 months after the establishment [on May 19, 1942] of the [Justice Department's] War Division[,] the Special War Policies Unit was responsible for directing and coordinating the activities of the Department of Justice relating to espionage, sabotage, sedition, subversive activities, and the registration of foreign agents. This Unit was abolished when the War Division was reorganized on August 28, 1943."

17. For Fred Kaihara and the contract for Togo Tanaka to be a *Colorado Times* columnist, see James Gatewood's interview with Togo Tanaka, December 13, 1997, in Darcie C. Iki, project director, *REgenerations Oral History Project: Rebuilding Japanese American Families, Communities, and Civil Rights in the Resettlement Era,* vol. 2: *Los Angeles Region* (Los Angeles: Japanese American National Museum, 2000), 455. For the online version of this interview's transcript, see University of California, Calisphere, http://content.cdlib.org/view?docId=ft358003z1&&doc .view=entire_text (accessed on September 23, 2015).

18. In his notes on this interview (OP), Omura writes: "Office of War information subsidized the newspaper (*Colorado Times*) on a $3000 to $4000 monthly stipulation. (Koide) acknowledges hav[ing] no hard evidence but believe[s] this is correct. He says it can be checked." In the finding aid Gary Y. Okihiro prepared for JARP, June 13, 1974, *The Oral History Tapes of the Japanese American Research Project,* "Tape Numbers 1-112: A Survey," the date assigned this interview is April 25, 1967, instead of the April 19, 1967, date provided by Omura.

19. The recipient in his lifetime of three Pulitzer Prizes for his creative work, Illinois-born Archibald MacLeish (1892–1982) was a Yale- and Harvard-educated lawyer, poet, progressive writer, and Librarian of Congress, who served during World War II as assistant director of the U.S. Office of War Information and director of the Department of War's Office of Facts and Figures. The latter of these two propagandistic governmental units was established on October 24, 1941, to disseminate in the United States information about defense efforts and policies. For a recent assessment of Archibald MacLeish's role in relation to the function of the Office of Facts and Figures, see Ramon Girona and Jordi Xifra, "The Office of Facts and Figures: Archibald MacLeish and the 'Strategy of Truth,'" *Public Relations Review* 35 (September 2009): 287–90.

20. Born into an affluent northern California family and well educated, Alan Cranston (1914–2000) prior to World War II worked as a journalist for the Inter-

national News Service, edited the first unexpurgated translation of Adolf Hitler's *Mein Kampf* to be published in the United States, acted as a lobbyist for the Common Council for American unity (an organization opposing discrimination against the foreign-born), and even coauthored a play based on his newspaper experiences. After military service in World War II, Cranston, a perfervid believer in world government, wrote a book, *The Killing of the Peace* (1945), which synopsized the failed post–World War I bid to get the United States to join the League of Nations.

21. For information on the Japanese American Committee for Democracy, see Greg Robinson's sterling entry on that organization in the *Densho Encyclopedia*, http://encyclopedia.densho.org/ (accessed on July 31, 2015).

22. For a contemporary overview of *Doho*, see Togo Tanaka's wartime report "Doho," in JERS, BANC, UCB, Folder A 1.104. For a historical analysis, see Takeya Mizuno, "The Japanese-Language Press and the Government's Decision of the Japanese Mass Evacuation during World War II: Three Japanese Newspapers' Reception of the War, the Japanese Americans' Wartime Status, and the Evacuation," paper presented in 1997 at the annual convention of the Association for Education in Journalism and Mass Communication held in Chicago, available online at http://list.msu.edu/cgi-bin/wa?A3=ind9709e&L=AEJMC&E=7BIT& P=176828&B=—&T=TEXT%2FPLAIN;%20charset=US-ASCII (accessed on June 4, 2012); see esp. 4–7, and nn49–104. For two retrospective accounts, see Karl Yoneda, *Ganbatta: Sixty-Year Struggle of a Kibei Worker* (Los Angeles: Asian American Studies Center, University of California, Los Angeles, 1983), 98–99; and James Oda, *Heroic Struggles of Japanese American Partisan Fighters from America's Concentration Camps* (Los Angeles: privately printed, 1980), 258–66.

23. A Massachusetts native son, Bradford Smith (1909–64) served with the U.S. Office of War Information (OWI) as chief of its Central Pacific Operations from 1942 to 1945. The Bradford Smith Papers, covering Smith's career from 1942 to 1948, are archived at UCLARL; see the finding aid for these papers, www.oac .cdlib.org/findaid/ark:/13030/tf4w1006f7/ (accessed on June 4, 2012). On June 13, 1942, President Franklin Roosevelt established the OWI, whose first director was Elmer Smith. It was charged with conveying information to the world and empowered to conduct propaganda to foreign nations to contribute to an Allied victory.

24. For information on the Suitland facility, see its homepage, www.archives. gov/dc-metro/suitland/agencies/index.html (accessed on September 2, 2015).

25. For information on the life and career of Illinois-born and Colorado-raised Eugene Sisto Cervi (1906–70), see "Gene Cervi," www.newsbios.com/newslum/ cervi.htm (accessed on June 4, 2012); and "Eugene Cervi Award," www.iswne.org/ highlights/eugene-cervi-award-nominations-due-march/article_cfccfbae-51d9-11e1 -be74-0019bb2963f4.html (accessed on June 4, 2012).

26. An Augusta, Georgia, native, Cranston Williams (1895–1989) managed successively the Southern Newspaper Publishers Association and the American Newspaper Publishers Association.

27. The Inland Press Association, a nonprofit organization owned by its member newspapers and operated by a volunteer board, was founded in 1885 by a group of U.S. newspapers seeking solutions to common problems. Its chief role is providing business research, training, networking, and idea-sharing services to member companies. Founded in 1903, the Southern Newspaper Publishers Association's animating purpose is to serve newspapers in southern states as a clearinghouse for relevant information.

28. See Kaz Oka, "Why I Disagree with Mr. Omura," *Colorado Times*, April 10, 1943.

29. See Deborah K. Lim, "Research Report Prepared for Presidential Select Committee on JACL Resolution #7" (aka "Lim Report"), submitted in 1990, in Japanese American Voice: Making Our Voices Heard, www.javoice.com/limreport/limPartIA.htm#IA6 (accessed on June 8, 2012), in which the following statement drawn from an undated letter from Kazuo Oka to President Franklin Roosevelt is quoted: "I have cooperated both before and after Pearl Harbor with the Federal Bureau of Investigation." For biographical information on Kazuo Oka, see the obituary for his wife, Sachi Oka (1916–2011), in the *Monterey Herald*, March 1, 2011, www.legacy.com/obituaries/montereyherald/obituary.aspx?n=sachi-oka&pid=149030054 (accessed on June 8, 2012). For an edited and annotated version of the Lim Report, see "Counterpoint: The Lim Report," chap. 9 in William Minoru Hohri, with Mits Koshiyama, Yosh Kuromiya, Takashi Hoshizaki, and Frank Seishi Emi, *Resistance: Challenging America's Wartime Internment of Japanese-Americans* (Lomita, CA: The Espistolarian, 2001), 129–56.

30. For historical information on the failed 1944 legislative measure seeking to bar "Japanese aliens ineligible to citizenship" from owning land in Colorado, see Kara Miyagishima, "Colorado's *Nikkei* Pioneers: Japanese Americans in Twentieth Century Colorado" (master's thesis, University of Colorado, Denver, 2007), 175–78.

31. The General Assembly is bicameral, composed of the Colorado House of Representatives and the Colorado Senate. It operates in a manner quite similar to the U.S. Congress. The tenure of the thirtieth governor of Colorado, John Charles Vivian (1889–1964), extended from 1943 to 1947. For more information on Vivian and his political career, see the guide prepared by George Orlowski and Erin McDanal for "The Governor John Charles Vivian Collection at the Colorado State Archives," www.colorado.gov/dpa/doit/archives/govs/vivian.html (accessed on June 9, 2012).

32. In addition to serving three times as House Speaker for Colorado, Homer L. Pearson (1900–1985) was the state's lieutenant governor from 1946 to 1948.

33. A daily newspaper published in Denver from 1859 to 2009, the *Rocky Mountain News* almost died during the 1940s but was revived when it was changed from a broadside format to a tabloid design.

34. Founded in 1923 by conservative Frank Gannett in Rochester, New York, as an outgrowth of a business he had begun in Elmira, New York, the Gannett Company, Inc., became famous as a consequence of purchasing small independent newspapers and developing them into a large chain. By 1942 the company was notable for having its wire service provide its local papers with national stories from Washington, DC, and thirteen bureaus. See "Gannett Company," www.answers.com/topic/gannett-company (accessed on June 9, 2012).

35. A star reporter and longtime columnist for the *Rocky Mountain News*, Lee Taylor Casey (1889–1951) served for a short time as that newspaper's editor. Possessing a clear sense of right and wrong and capable of writing with frank penetration, his World War II columns defended the rights of American citizens of Japanese ancestry.

36. Begun in 1868 when Colorado was still a territory, the Colorado State Penitentiary is sited in Cañon City, which is Fremont County's most populous city and seat. For a useful historical portrait of this prison, see Gerald E. Sherard, "A Short History of the Colorado State Penitentiary," www.colorado.gov/dpa/doit/archives/pen/history.htm (accessed on June 9, 2012).

37. Whereas the national office of the JACL during World War II was located in the Beason Building in Salt Lake City, Utah, the JACL's regional office in Denver was in the Midland Savings Building.

38. A search of 1944 issues of *Pacific Citizen* did not turn up the date of this forum noted by Omura. However, during this period numerous articles appeared in the *Pacific Citizen* on the forum's topic. One of them, "Colorado Petitioners Demand Two Classes of Citizens, Says Denver Editor on Protests," from January 15, 1944, is focused on a Lee Casey *Rocky Mountain News* column published four days earlier.

39. For more information on Matsumonji and his relationship with Omura as a family friend and supporter, see the interview Omura transacted with Matsumonji on August 16, 1985 (OP).

40. The thirty-second governor of Arkansas, Homer Martin Adkins (1880–1964), a onetime Ku Klux Klan member, served in this capacity from 1941 to 1945.

41. Robert Harvey, in *Amache: The Story of Japanese Internment in Colorado during World War II* (Dallas: Taylor Trade, 2004), 69, has provided this verbal

biographical snapshot of James Gary Lindley (1888–1967): "A native of Moberly, Missouri, Lindley had earned an undergraduate degree from the University of Arizona. Before coming to Granada, Lindley had also served as the chief engineer for the southwestern division of the Soil Conservation at Albuquerque [New Mexico]."

42. According to the February 26, 1944, issue of the *Granada Pioneer*, the "Amache Five" consisted of Mitsuye Oshita, Susumu Yenokida, George Satoshi Marumoto, Chikara Kunisaki, and Kazuo Kunitake. On the draft resistance activity at the Amache camp, see Cherstin M. Lyon, "The Obligations of Citizenship," chap. 5 in *Prisons and Patriots: Japanese American Wartime Citizenship, Civil Disobedience, and Historical Memory* (Philadelphia: Temple University Press, 2012), 120–54, esp. 120–44.

43. On the draft resistance movement at the Minidoka detention center and its consequences, see Eric L. Muller, "The Minidoka Draft Resisters in a Federal Kangaroo Court," chap. 8 in Fiset and Nomura, *Nikkei in the Pacific Northwest*, 171–89.

44. See the March 28, 1944, "Timely Topics" column by Saburo Kido in the *Pacific Citizen*. Writes Kido: "This type of news reporting of draft dodging by the Rocky Shimpo is a reprehensible thing. Undoubtedly it is going to influence many in the centers. . . . The editor evidently seems to believe that his weak editorial, 'Let Us Not Be Rash,' clears him of any implications."

45. Headed by a U.S. assistant attorney general appointed by the president of the United States, the Criminal Division of the U.S. Department of Justice develops, enforces, and supervises the application of all federal criminal laws in the United States.

46. A Caucasian woman, Genevieve Sylvia (King) Toshiyuki (1913/15?–2002?) lived in 1944 with her husband, Frank Toshiyuki, on Eighteenth Street in Denver, Colorado. According to data unearthed from diverse sources and resourcefully collated by Frank Abe, she was born in North Dakota and raised in Oroville, California, north of Sacramento. During the World War II confinement of the Toshiyuki family at Wyoming's Heart Mountain Relocation Center in 1942–43, Sylvia met and befriended Kiyoshi Okamoto, whose resistance writings she brought to Jimmie Omura's attention in 1944 at a time when she and her husband were operating a Chinese restaurant in Denver. This action precipitated Omura championing the Okamoto-led Heart Mountain Fair Play Committee draft resistance in the *Rocky Shimpo*. Toshiyuki also put Okamoto in touch with a Denver attorney, Samuel David Menin (1906–95), who defended Heart Mountain's first sixty-three draft resisters in their June 1944 mass trial at the federal district court in Cheyenne, Wyoming.

47. Frank Kenji Toshiyuki (1915–95) was born in California to Issei parents (Tomiji and Nao Toshiyuki) and died in Hawai'i. At some point just prior to World War II, he married Genevieve Sylvia King, and they had a son in 1939. Together they were detained in the Santa Anita Assembly Center before being incarcerated in the Heart Mountain Relocation Center from September 1942 to September 1943.

48. Unfortunately, a copy of this letter from Okamoto to Biddle is not included within OP. However, this collection does include numerous letters between Kiyoshi Okamoto and James Omura, plus many more of Okamoto's letters with a variety of correspondents. These letters reveal his salient concerns and unique style of representing them.

49. Anthropologist Asael Tanner Hansen (1903–91) received his PhD at the University of Wisconsin in 1930. In 1944 he left his professorship at Miami University in Oxford, Ohio, to become a community analyst for the War Relocation Authority at its Heart Mountain detention center in Wyoming. See also Brian Niiya's entry on "Asael T. Hansen" in the *Densho Encyclopedia*, http://encyclopedia .densho.org/ (accessed on August 28, 2015).

50. This quoted remark attributed to Asael Hansen, Heart Mountain's community analyst, is not found in the documentation within OP. Likely it appeared in the weekly trend report Hansen prepared on March 11, 1944, for submission to both Heart Mountain Relocation Center director Guy Robertson, and E. H. Spicer, head of the Community Analysis Section of the War Relocation Authority. For an overview of Hansen's work at Heart Mountain from 1942 to 1945, see Asael T. Hansen, "Community Analysis at Heart Mountain Relocation Center, *Applied Anthropology* 5 (Summer 1946): 15–25. See also Asael T. Hansen, "My Two Years at Heart Mountain: The Difficult Role of an Applied Anthropologist," in Roger Daniels, Sandra C. Taylor, and Harry H. L. Kitano, *Japanese Americans: From Relocation to Redress* (Salt Lake City: University of Utah Press, 1986), 33–37.

51. Harvard-educated Roger Nash Baldwin (1884–1981) was a pacifist who was imprisoned for his refusal to comply with the World War I military draft. A founder of the American Civil Liberties Union in 1920, Baldwin became the ACLU's first executive director and continued in this position until his 1950 retirement. See also Brian Niiya's entry for the "American Civil Liberties Union," in the *Densho Encyclopedia*, http://encyclopedia.densho.org/ (accessed on September 26, 2015).

52. This reply letter from Roger Baldwin (precise date unknown) to Kiyoshi Okamoto's March 28, 1944, letter was printed on April 15, 1944, as the *Heart Mountain Sentinel*'s lead article. Its key points were these: (1) that the Heart Mountain Fair Play Committee draft resistance group had "a strong moral case"

but "no legal case at all"; and (2) that "men who counsel others to resist military service are not within their rights and must expect severe treatment."

53. See Richard Drinnon, *Keeper of Concentration Camps: Dillon Myer and American Racism* (Berkeley: University of California Press, 1987), 127, 300–301.

54. For an overview of the *Heart Mountain Sentinel*, see the entry by Patricia Wakida on this camp newspaper in the *Densho Encyclopedia*, http://encyclopedia .densho.org/ (accessed on September 10, 2015).

55. For the "Janus-faced" accusation, see the editorial in the March 18, 1944, *Heart Mountain Sentinel*; for the denigration of the *Rocky Shimpo*, see the *Heart Mountain Sentinel* editorial for April 8, 1944.

56. See testimony of Robert G. Lawrence, Special Agent, FBI, in the appeal of *Kiyoshi Okamoto, et al. v. United States of America* at the U.S. Circuit Court of Appeals, Tenth Circuit, District of Wyoming, Cheyenne, Wyoming, May Term, 1945, 80 (OP). According to Lawrence, Paul Nakadate told him in an April 26, 1944, interview (witnessed by FBI special agent Harry W. McMillen) that he on one occasion had contacted Jim Omura, editor of the *Rocky Shimpo*, with reference to the untrue story "that a camp wide strike was pending among the evacuees at Heart Mountain Center because he wanted to focus attention on the conditions in the Center."

57. See letter from Frank Emi to James M. Omura, April 13, 1944 (OP).

58. For the frequency of the Fair Play Committee's meetings during February and March 1944, see Muller, *Free to Die for Their Country*, 78.

59. Michigan-born Thomas Blake Kennedy (1874–1957), a 1897 graduate of Syracuse University College of Law, was named in 1921 as a federal judge in the U.S. District Court for the District of Wyoming, whose appeals are heard by the U.S. Court of Appeals for the Tenth Circuit.

60. Hito Okada (1907–84), born and educated in the state of Washington, held the office of treasurer for the national Japanese American Citizens League in the immediate pre–World War II and wartime period. On February 28, 1942, Okada testified at the Tolan Committee hearing in Portland, Oregon, and declared that aliens should be evacuated and, if necessary, even Japanese who are American citizens; see www.santacruzpl.org/history/articles/159/ (accessed on June 15, 2012). After World War II, Hito Okada served as the national JACL president from 1946 to 1950.

61. For information on the mass trial of sixty-three Heart Mountain Relocation Center draft resisters in June 1944, see the following two *Densho Encyclopedia* entries by Eric Muller: "Heart Mountain Fair Play Committee," and "Draft Resistance," http://encyclopedia.densho.org/ (both accessed on February 4, 2016).

62. No readily available information exists of Henry L. McMillen's FBI tenure of service. As for McMillen's testimony at the June 1944 federal trial in Cheyenne,

Wyoming, for the sixty-three Heart Mountain draft resisters, it is seemingly unavailable to researchers.

63. On the *Pacific Citizen*, see Greg Robinson's entry in the Densho *Encyclopedia*, http://encyclopedia.densho.org/ (accessed on February 4, 2016).

64. It is unclear as to precisely what publication Omura is referencing here. The *JACL Reporter*, first launched in January 1945, was a monthly circulated exclusively to JACL members. The apparent year under consideration by Omura in this connection is ostensibly 1944, not 1945, so perhaps he was thinking of another publication. Or possibly during Saburo Kido's JACL presidency in 1944 he distributed an unofficial JACL publication bearing the same (or similar) title.

65. Spain, a neutral country during World War II, represented Japanese interests in the United States; similarly, Switzerland, also a neutral nation, represented U.S. interests in Japan.

66. When founded as a weekly in 1926, the Cheyenne-based *Wyoming Eagle* was the only newspaper in the state with a Democratic editorial policy. It later became a daily paper.

67. In 1930 President Herbert Hoover named Philadelphia-born Owen Josephus Roberts (1875–1955), a University of Pennsylvania Law School graduate, to the Supreme Court. During Franklin Roosevelt's presidency, after Japan's Pearl Harbor attack, Roberts was appointed to head the commission investigating that action. His committee's 1942 report on Pearl Harbor was highly critical of the U.S. military. Arguably, Roberts's experience on this committee led him to dissent from the Supreme Court's 1944 decision in *Korematsu v. the United States of America* upholding incarceration of excluded West Coast Americans of Japanese ancestry. For a biographical survey of Roberts, see Montgomery McCracken, "Owen J. Roberts—A Short Biography," www.mmwr.com/home/the-firm/our-history/owen-j.-roberts—-a-short-biography—-/default.aspx (accessed on July 13, 2012).

68. The source for the precise quoted description of the Nisei draft resisters by Justice Owen Roberts, chair of President Harry Truman's Amnesty Board, eludes confirmation, but according to Cherstin M. Lyon, in *Prisons and Patriots: Japanese American Wartime Citizenship, Civil Disobedience, and Historical Memory*, chap. 7, 222n1, the board's report is available in the Tom C. Clark Papers, Box 66, Truman Presidential Library, Independence, Missouri. As noted by Lyon: "The board members sympathized with the Nisei. They believed that they were loyal citizens who had refused the draft as a means of protesting their wartime treatment. Full presidential pardons were recommended" (176).

69. It is unclear here as to which Fair Play Committee leader retroactively claimed that the draft resisters erred in refusing to submit to preinduction physicals in 1944. Since Omura's principal contact with a former FPC leader while

writing his memoir was Frank Emi, it possibly was he who voiced this opinion to Omura.

70. See the correspondence of May 1942 between James M. Omura and Calladay, Calladay & Wallace, Counselors at Law, Washington, DC (OP).

71. See Frank Chin, "The Last Organized Resistance," *Rafu Shimpo*, December 19, 1981.

72. Robert Gordon Lawrence (1913–99?), according to the *Society of Former Special Agents of the FBI*, served as an FBI agent from 1939 to 1963.

73. There is no written documentation in OP, for this alleged communication by Lawrence to Omura, so Omura's terminology as to being "personally informed" by Lawrence presumably refers to oral communication.

74. For biographical information about Edward Vaughn Dunklee (1888?–1963) in the context of the Dunklee family, see the finding aid for the Dunklee Family Papers at the Denver Public Library, http://eadsrv.denverlibrary.org/sdx/pl/toc .xsp?id=WH1282&qid=sdx_q5&fmt=tab&idtoc=WH1282-pleadetoc&base=fa&n =15&ss=true&as=true&ai=Advanced (accessed on July 13, 2012).

75. Michigan-born and -educated Charles Jeremias Hedetniemi Sr. (1914–2006) was employed between 1942 and 1951 in the U.S. Department of Justice's Office of Alien Property. For an obituary for Hedetniemi, see "Charles J. Hedetniemi, Falls Church Councilman," *Washington Post*, July 11, 2006, www.washington post.com/wp-dyn/content/article/2006/07/10/AR2006071001180_pf.html (accessed on July 14, 2012).

76. For a ten-page content analysis of selected *Rocky Shimpo* issues by Charles J. Hedetniemi, dated April 17, 1944, see OP.

77. For a biographical snapshot of Carl L. Sackett (1876–1972), see Muller, *Free to Die for Their Country*, 96–97.

78. See "Center Council Asks Paper to Retract Article," *Pacific Citizen*, April 15, 1944. See also in this same connection, "Report Omura Discharged by Denver Paper," *Pacific Citizen*, April 22, 1944.

79. See letter from James M. Omura, English Editor, *Rocky Shimpo*, to Mr. S. Nakashima, Chairman, Community Council, Heart Mountain Relocation Center, April 18, 1944 (OP).

80. The search to locate the source of this claim by Omura as to the War Department's opinion about the *Rocky Shimpo*'s influence upon camp resistance activity proved futile.

81. The apology by President Reagan was extended during the signing ceremony for the Civil Liberties Act of 1988. For the content of that act, see www .civics-online.org/library/formatted/texts/civilact1988.html (accessed July 16, 2012); for President Reagan's remarks at the August 10, 1988, ceremonial event, see www .youtube.com/watch?v=MooPi2Ycuxo (accessed on July 16, 2012).

82. For a finding aid relative to the Office of Alien Property Custodian, see www.archives.gov/research/holocaust/finding-aid/civilian/rg-131.html (accessed on July 16, 2012); for President Harry Truman's October 14, 1946, letter to James Markham at the termination of his duties as Alien Property Custodian, see www.trumanlibrary.org/publicpapers/index.php?pid=1767&st=&st1= (accessed on July 16, 2012).

83. Only one page, the third and last of the April 3, 1944, letter James M. Omura, Authorized Agent, The Rocky Shimpo, sent to Hon. James E. Markham, Alien Property Custodian, is included in OP. Omura concludes this letter as follows: "We fully realize the delicate position in which we find ourselves as a result of this global war and have no intention of endangering our position under the Trading with the Enemy Act unduly. However, I do not wish you to consider us enemies. We, too, are American citizens in the main."

84. A review of the *Rocky Nippon* for 1942 and 1943, documents that Omura never published his "Know the Facts" column for this named publication. However, after the *Rocky Nippon* changed its name in April 1943 to the *Rocky Shimpo*, Omura initiated his "Know the Facts" column in the May 28, 1943, issue. As a preface, Omura explains the column's nature:

> KNOW THE FACTS is dedicated to the highest ideals of Man. It is basically founded on truth and is specifically aimed to expose the lies that are being foisted daily upon the uninformed and undiscriminating public. . . . I shall attempt to give to the best of my abilities a truthful account of the vital issues revolving around the life of the Nisei and other U.S. Japanese. . . . It is too much to expect everyone to like this column, for in presenting the truth I am likely to step upon more than a few tender toes. The truth will hurt; but my object here is to let you KNOW THE FACTS.

85. See "The Rocky Shimpo Affirms Its Stand," April 7, 1944 (OP). The policy statement contained within this editorial reiterated the core of Omura's February 28, 1944, "Let Us Not Be Rash" editorial: "We further agree that the government should restore a large part of those rights BEFORE asking us to contribute our lives in the welfare of the nation—to sacrifice our lives on the field of battle."

86. In closing his four-page reply letter, April 17, 1944, to Elmer Smith (OP), Omura wrote: "There are always at least two sides to all questions, Mr. Smith, and I doubt that you have explored even to a small degree the other side of this issue. . . . I am of the impression that I am speaking to a closed mind." For more information about Elmer Richard Smith (1909–60), see the entry by Brian Niiya in the *Densho Encyclopedia*, http://encyclopedia.densho.org/ (accessed on February 5, 2016).

87. Denver was founded in 1858 by land developer General William H. Larimer Jr. (1809–75). He lent his own name to the city's main street. By the 1880s, Larimer Street was Denver's central shopping and entertainment area. Following the 1893 silver crash, however, it underwent a sharp decline, with the district degenerating into a Skid Row. About this same time, immigrant-generation Issei first arrived in Colorado as visitors and students, followed by a large eastward wave of Pacific Coast Nikkei to work on the railroad and in the mines, and somewhat later in farming. By about 1900, some of these Japanese nationals began congregating in the Nineteenth Street and Larimer Street location, but the bulk of this new, mostly male, laboring population to populate this Denver neighborhood were those Issei who had been drawn to Colorado to work on sugar beet farms. Their infusion into what had been previously settlement space for Chinese immigrants, known as "Hop Alley," transformed the Larimer Street district into a Japantown, a place filling the social and economic needs of Nikkei. Initially, this meant that Larimer Street consisted of a seedy strip of gambling dens, flophouses, saloons, noodle shops, and brothels for its Issei denizens. In time, especially with the increase in its Issei women and American-born Nisei-generation populations, the Denver Japantown became notable for its Japanese-language schools, Japanese-language newspapers (which later included English-language supplements), and Buddhist temples and Christian churches. By 1940, when Denver boasted a Japanese-ancestry population of over eight hundred, the overwhelming number of them lived in the Larimer Street section of the city's downtown. The coming of World War II swelled Denver's Japanese American population to approximately five thousand. Once West Coast restrictions on Japanese American lessened with the closing of World War II, the Nikkei population in Denver and the elaborated Japantown declined quite precipitously. See Daryl Maeda, "Japanese Americans in Colorado," Enduring Communities Project, Japanese American National Museum, http://media.janm.org/projects/ec/pdf/EC-CO-Essay-Timeline.pdf (accessed on July 25, 2012); and Historic Larimer Square Denver Colorado, "The History of Larimer Square," www.larimersquare.com/history/ (accessed on July 25, 2012).

88. For information on this report by Minoru Yasui and Joe Grant Masaoka, see Martha Nakagawa, "Analysis: A Look at JACL's Role during WWII, Stance on Resisters," *Pacific Citizen*, July 16–22, 1999, www.resisters.com/news/PC_7-6-99.htm (accessed on February 5, 2016). For a copy of the report "Visit to Cheyenne County Jail with Japanese American Draft Delinquents," by Min Yasui, Attorney, and Joe Grant Masaoka, JACL Regional Representative, based on interviews conducted on April 28, 1944, 6:30 to 10:00 p.m., see OP. This report is also included within Hohri et al., *Resistance*, 71–81.

89. See Min Yasui letter to James Omura, April 21, 1944 (OP).

90. Born in Denver, Thomas G. Currigan (1920–75) served as Denver's city auditor from 1955 to 1963, after which he spent the next five years as Denver's mayor. Another native son, William Henry McNichols (1910?–97)—his father, William Henry McNichols, was Denver's auditor (1931–55) and his brother Stephen was Colorado's governor (1957–63)—succeeded Currigan as mayor (1968–83). McNichols's successor, Texas-born and -educated Federico Fabian Peña (1947–), followed his stint as Denver mayor (1983–91) with service in the presidential administration of Bill Clinton as U.S. secretary of transportation (1993–97) and U.S. secretary of energy (1997–98).

91. Presumably, Omura is here referring to the Justice Department's Community Relations Service honoring Yasui with its Award for Public Service in 1964.

92. For a cogent and concise discussion of the interesting test case involving Seattle's Mary Asaba Ventura, who was married to the Filipino labor activist Mamerto Ventura, see Rick Baldoz, *The Third Asiatic Invasion: Empire and Migration in Filipino America, 1898–1946* (New York: New York University Press, 2011), 216–17.

93. For an overview of Minoru Yasui's trial on June 12, 1942, before district court judge Alger Fee, see Brian Niiya's "Yasui v. United States" entry in the *Densho Encyclopedia*, http://encyclopedia.densho.org/ (accessed on February 5, 2016). James Alger Fee (1888–1959) was born in Pendleton, Oregon, and earned a law degree from Columbia University. After serving a four-year stint on the Oregon Circuit Court, he was appointed in 1931 by President Herbert Hoover to Oregon's federal district court.

94. For confirmation of this contention by Omura, see Barbara Annette Bellus Upp, "Minoru Yasui: You Can See the Mountain from Here" (PhD diss., University of Oregon, 1997), 50–51. However, after explaining that Yasui had offered this view in the context of a hypothetical conversation with FBI agent Ray Mize on March 30, 1942, immediately following the curfew violation, Upp provides this qualification: "The conversation, as reported, indicates use of speculation to implicate, unfairly, out of context. It is in the nature of speculative conversations that they are highly susceptible to misinterpretation if taken out of context."

95. The subject of Minoru Yasui only surfaces in one exchange of letters between James Omura and Dale Minami. In a postscript to his letter of March 29, 1983, to Minami, Omura writes: "Do you have Min Yasui's transcript of his original trial in Portland before Judge Fee? Ran across an administrative communication relative to Yasui stating that in order to secure the Pacific Coast all Japanese Americans must be evacuated. Interesting!" In his reply letter to Omura, April 12, 1983, Minami states:

> In response to your question about Min Yasui's transcript, I do not have a copy although I could obtain one. I believe Min did respond in answer

to a hypothetical that evacuation might be desirable although I do not believe those echoed his true sentiments and that he was, in essence, "trapped" into making such a statement. Which brings up another issue: since I am now in effect representing Min Yasui in the attempt to vacate his conviction, I have established an attorney-client relationship with him. Thus, I cannot offer any advice nor assistance in relationship to information on Min. My work for you should thus be restricted only to helping you obtain your FOIA files or interpreting legal issues and memoranda which may require my assistance. My ethics require me to segregate your case completely from Min's representation.

See OP for this Omura-Minami postal exchange.

96. See Upp, "Minoru Yasui," 51–52. FBI agent Ray Mize also reported that Yasui said that "he regretted what he did." Still, qualifies Upp, Mize's report was "somewhat out of context." Upp's depiction merits full disclosure here because of the delicacy of Mize's conversation with Yasui: "Mize's version was, 'I [Mize] asked him [Yasui] if he felt that during these particular times his action would reflect very favorably on the Japanese colony, and Mr. Yasui stated that when thinking it over he did not think that it would be a very good reflection and that he in a certain sense was sorry that he had taken the action that he had.'" "When later addressed with, 'I believe Mr. Mize also said that you were sorry that you had taken the action that you had,' Yasui replied, 'The question was whether I believed any repercussions would happen from my testing the constitutionality of the curfew act, and I believed that possibly there would be repercussions that would be harmful to the Japanese colony.'"

97. Michi Yasui Ando (1920–2006) completed her University of Oregon undergraduate studies in 1942, but owing to the U.S. government-imposed curfew on West Coast Americans of Japanese ancestry, she was unable to attend the graduation ceremonies. Chagrined at the government's unwillingness to grant her a dispensation from the curfew policy, she clandestinely boarded a bus that evening and traveled from Eugene, Oregon, to join her brother Robert in Denver, Colorado. There, she attended Denver University and received her master's degree in Education. Michi's husband, Toshio John Ando (1920–?), was a young law student whom she met on first coming to Denver in 1942. When Minoru Yasui came to live in Denver in 1944, he established his law practice in Denver's Nihon-machi with Toshio Ando.

98. Although the published version of Minoru Yasui's lead article in the April 19, 1944, issue of the *Rocky Shimpo* is not included in OP, a typescript of it is available therein as the exclusive content of the four-page April 18, 1944, letter Min Yasui mailed to the *Rocky Shimpo*. In Yasui's letter of April 21, 1944, cited above in note 89, he states: "I have noted the leading article which you had given

my opinions in the April 19th issue of the Rocky Shimpo. This, I believe, was done fairly and in good faith of your commitments to me, and I sincerely thank you for your presentation. In my personal relationships with you, I have no reason to question your good faith towards me."

99. The Doberman Pinscher, Rex, owned by Jimmie and Caryl Omura was frequently entered into American Kennel Club-sanctioned dog shows in 1944, held primarily in Denver, and was accorded numerous first-prize ribbons in variable categories.

100. The U.S. District Court for the District of Wyoming is the federal district court whose jurisdiction comprises the state of Wyoming and those portions of Yellowstone National Park situated in Montana and Idaho. It has locations in Cheyenne and Casper, the former utilized for the 1944 court conspiracy case involving the leaders of the Heart Mountain Fair Play Committee and James Omura.

101. For a discussion of "yellow journalism" relating to William Randolph Hearst and pertinent to both the Spanish American War and World War II, see Jessica L. Szalay, "World War II Newsreels: The Legacy of Yellow Journalism," www.fresnostate.edu/socialsciences/historydept/documents/organizations/hindsight/Szalay%20Vol.%204.pdf (accessed on February 6, 2016).

102. There is very little readily available information on Sidney S. Jacobs (1907–74) apart from his longtime legal practice in Denver and the name of his spouse, Mary.

103. The correspondence of Caryl Omura in the summer and fall months of 1944 vividly documents her husband's Laramie County Jail mistreatment and her efforts to mitigate it. Back-to-back letters written by her on September 11 and 12, 1944 (OP) merit special attention.

104. Lloyd Carson Sampson (1890–1950) was the 1947 president of the Wyoming State Bar.

105. Although specific documentation relating to Jacobs's insensitive treatment of Omura eluded detection within OP, this alleged deportment is consistent with the impersonal and sometimes antagonistic attorney-client relationship that prevailed between the two men before, during, and (most especially) after the November–December 1944 conspiracy trial in Cheyenne.

106. For a life portrait of Abraham Lincoln Wirin (1901–78), see Donald Collins's luminous entry on Wirin in Niiya, *Encyclopedia of Japanese American History*, 412–13.

107. See Caryl Omura's letter to James Omura, August 24, 1944 (OP), in which she writes: "Art [Emi] wrote to me asking if we would like Wirin to handle your case. . . . I thought it over and I wrote back that since I had managed to raise the initial fee . . . I did not feel that it was proper to do so."

108. See Paul Nakadate letter, March 7, 1944, to Mr. Omura (OP). In a post-script, Nakadate characterizes Okamoto with these words: "I would safely and gladly say to you he [Okamoto] was simple but he didn't give a damn for money, recognition nor his life. He was working for the people."

109. A short bilingual (Japanese/English) oral history interview with Katsusa-buro Kawahara (1899–?) in Steven Misawa, ed., *Beginnings: Japanese Americans in San Jose* (San Jose, CA: Japanese American Community Senior Service, 1981), 33–44, details his lucrative pre–World War II agricultural operation.

110. This information most likely was communicated orally by Nakadate to Omura, as there is no evidence of it within the Omura-Nakadate correspondence file in OP.

111. Letters of appeal from Caryl Omura to assist in funding Jimmie Omura's defense fund were legion, especially for the months of August and September 1944. See the correspondence file for Caryl Omura in OP. A typical one is that dated August 31, 1944, sent to Mr. Ted Segawa, then detained at the Poston Relo-cation Center in Arizona. It closed with these words:

> It is with this in mind that I appeal to you for whatever generous contri-bution you, your friends, and their friends will be able to contribute to the "Omura Defense Fund." . . . This "Defense Fund" is being raised at present to release Mr. Omura on bond to prepare his case. Knowing that you know of him and his sentiments, I have taken the liberty of asking your support. I sincerely hope your better judgment will not fail him.

112. Not surprisingly, Omura's autobiographical oral evidence for this state-ment is unsupported by written documentation within OP.

113. See letter from Caryl [Omura] to Jimmie [Omura], August 11, 1944 (OP). See also letter from Jimmie Omura to Caryl Omura, August 16, 1944, ibid., in which he details their desperate financial situation owing to having to raise his bail. In this same letter, Omura sounds a prophetic note, declaring that "I am going to write a book with Paul [Nakadate] when this is over. It will make inter-esting and illuminating reading."

114. A U.S. Army Air Corps veteran and a graduate of the George Washing-ton University School of Law, James V. Bennett (1894–1978) served from 1937 to 1964 as the director of the Federal Bureau of Prisons. While working as an inves-tigator for the U.S. Bureau of Efficiency from 1924 to 1930, Bennett authored the report, *The Federal Penal and Correctional Problem*, which paved the way for the Federal Bureau of Prison's creation. For a concise summary of Bennett's achieve-ments as the director of the Federal Bureau of Prisons, see Federal Bureau of Pris-ons, "Former Bureau of Prisons Directors," www.bop.gov/about/history/directors .jsp (accessed on August 3, 2012).

115. See letter from James V. Bennett, Director, Bureau of Prisons, Department of Justice, Washington, DC, to Mrs. Caryl F. Omura, Denver, Colorado, September 18, 1944 (OP). See also Caryl Omura to Federal Bureau of Prisons, Washington DC, August 28, 1944; and James V. Bennett, Director, Department of Justice, Bureau of Prisons, Washington, DC, September 4, 1944, to Caryl Omura; both in ibid.

116. Norbert E. Tuck (1899–1961) served as Laramie County's sheriff from 1943 to 1961. See Laramie County, "Sheriff Department History," http://webgate.co.laramie.wy.us/_departments/_sheriff/sheriffs/tuck.asp (accessed on August 3, 2012).

117. Although the correspondence file in OP, is quite extensive with respect to the postal interaction of James Omura and Frank C. Cooper, there is virtually no biographical information on Cooper contained within it.

118. See Eric L. Muller, "A Penny for Their Thoughts: Draft Resistance at the Poston Relocation Center," *Law and Contemporary Problems* 68 (Spring 2005): 119–58.

119. There is no information either on the Reverend Clark P. Garman or the Colorado Council of Churches in Denver within OP. Moreover, no such information of any sort, historical or contemporary, could be found on ancestry.com and other likely data sites.

120. See Eric L. Muller, "Betrayal on Trial: Japanese American 'Treason' in World War II," *North Carolina Law Review* 82 (June 2004): 1759–98. For an online version of this article, see the Japanese American National Museum's Discover Nikkei website, www.discovernikkei.org/en/journal/2008/5/6/enduring -communities/ (accessed on October 2, 2015). In Caryl Omura's letter of August 11, 1944, to Jimmie Omura, as cited above in note 113, she writes: "I met her [Mrs. Sylvia Toshiyuki] at the Sedition trial of the three Nisei sisters on Monday and at her request made arrangements with appointment with Mr. Jacobs. He has been attending the trial to study the leading criminal lawyer, [?] Robertson, defend the girls."

121. Apparently Omura first heard about the possibility of a declaratory judgment from the *Rocky Shimpo*'s lawyer, Edward Dunklee. In a reply letter to Omura on May 1, 1944, Dunklee responded to his request for an opinion as to "the position of the Fair Play Committee in advising a resistance to the draft in order to bring about a test case involving the validity of WRA leave regulations and the detention of citizens in relocation centers." After setting forth some alternative advice, Dunklee concluded his letter with this information:

> There is one other method, and that is by asking the Court for a declaratory judgment upon the subject matter asked for without having an actual

case to go up on. In my own experience as Chairman of the State Recovery Act I asked the Supreme Court of Colorado for a declaratory judgment upon the question of the constitutionality of the Act without the delay of an actual case and they gave me such a decision. See OP.

122. Evidence suggests that it might have been an obscure Nebraska law as against an obscure Oklahoma law that Sampson indicated as a precedent for a declaratory judgment; see www.nebraskalegislature.gov/laws/statutes.php?statute =25-21,149 (accessed on February 7, 2016).

123. Information, including a first name, could not be found for this Issei lawyer at the Heart Mountain Relocation Center who assisted the Fair Play Committee's draft resistance cases.

124. Tsutomu Tom Kawahara (1925–96), the Nisei son of Katsusaburo Kawahara and Nobu Kamichika Kawabara, was a Heart Mountain Fair Play Committee member during World War II. His Issei father helped fund the court costs for the draft resisters and their Fair Play Committee leaders.

125. For more information on Alice Nakadate (1915–99), see the World War II and post–World War II correspondence between her and both James Omura and Caryl Omura within OP.

126. See Brian Niiya's entry for background information on Isamu ("Sam") Horino (1914–2002) in the *Densho Encyclopedia*, http://encyclopedia.densho.org/. His younger brother, Minoru Horino, was among the sixty-three Heart Mountain draft resisters in the June 1944 trial held in Cheyenne's federal courthouse.

127. For useful biographical information on Guntaro Kubota (1915–99), see Brian Niiya's entry on him in the *Densho Encyclopedia*, http://encyclopedia.densho.org/ (accessed on February 7, 2016).

128. Nebraska-born John Coleman Pickett (1896–1983), a U.S. Army veteran of World War I, carved out his legal career in Wyoming. Although he maintained his private practice in Cheyenne from 1922 to 1949, during this interval he consecutively served as an assistant state attorney general of Wyoming from 1923 to 1925, as a county and prosecuting attorney of Laramie County, Wyoming, from 1928 to 1934, and as the assistant U.S. attorney for the District of Wyoming from 1935 to 1939. See entry for "John Coleman Pickett," *Biographical Directory of Federal Judges*, www.fjc.gov/servlet/nGetInfo?jid=1885&cid=999&ctype=na& instate=na (accessed on August 7, 2012). For Pickett's personal background and professional legal career, see United States Court of Appeals for the Tenth Circuit, "Special Memorial Service for the Honorable John C. Pickett, April 18, 1985," www.10thcircuithistory.org/pdfs/updated_history/memorials/Pickett_memorial. pdf (accessed on August 7, 2012).

129. On the Heart Mountain Fair Play Committee, see Eric L. Muller's entry in the *Densho Encyclopedia*, http://encyclopedia.densho.org/ (accessed on February 8, 2016). For the perspective of one of this committee's leaders on the FPC and the 1944 trial of its leaders, Frank Emi, see "Fair Play Committee: Frank Seishi Emi," chap. 7 in Hohri et al., *Resistance*, 95–117.

130. At the time of World War II, the *Wyoming Eagle* was Wyoming's only Democratic newspaper. Vern Lechliter (1912–91) is buried in Lakeview Cemetery in Cheyenne.

131. Back in Denver, Omura sent letters of gratitude to each jury member for their fair and just treatment and verdict in his trial. See, for example, Omura's letter to Mr. C. A. Black, November 29, 1944 (OP), in which he closed with these sentiments: "I have been a very forceful champion of a living democracy. I am not among those Nisei who profess loyalty to the United States simply for convenience but I believe enough in the principles of democracy to be willing to defend those principles at all cost. In this connection, I have been very much disappointed in my own racial generation."

132. On Ben Kuroki (1917–2015), see entry stub for him in the *Densho Encyclopedia*, http://encyclopedia.densho.org/ (accessed on February 7, 2016); see also Richard Goldstein, "Ben Kuroki Dies at 98; Japanese-American Overcame Bias to Fight for U.S.," *New York Times*, September 5, 2015, www.nytimes.com/2015/09/06/us/ben -kuroki-dies-at-98-fought-bias-to-fight-for-us.html (accessed on February 7, 2015).

133. For information on the Supreme Court's *Keegan v. United States* 325 U.S. 478 (1945) ruling, see Justia.com U.S. Supreme Court Center, http://supreme. justia.com/cases/federal/us/325/478/ (accessed on November 28, 2012). For the historical context of the Keegan ruling pertinent to the Heart Mountain Fair Play Committee leaders' exoneration, see, Muller, *Free to Die for Their Country*, 121–23.

134. Muller, *Free to Die for Their Country*, 123–24.

135. Although Jimmie Omura did communicate with Alice Nakadate, there is no mention that he was confident of a reversal of her husband Paul Nakadate's conviction, along with the other six Fair Play Committee leaders, by the Tenth Circuit Court of Appeals. Likely, Omura conveyed this message through his and his wife Caryl Omura's periodic telephone calls to Alice Nakadate. On the other hand, he sent her a very uplifting letter on January 1, 1946 (OP), immediately after he had been apprised of the conviction's reversal by the appellate court, which he characterized as "a vindication for Paul and for all those who associated themselves in whatever manner with the program of the Fair Play Committee." He went on to say:

> Those who have any appreciation of their constitutional rights will honor the memory of these courageous FPC leaders. They had the courage and

intestinal fortitude to defend a lost cause when others feared when the test came to even stand up and be counted. Those who will chronicle the events of the evacuation cannot honestly ignore the truly noble attempt the FPC made in its militant fight in the name of justice, democracy and freedom.

136. Omura stayed in touch with Lechliter after the trial. In a prophetic letter from James Omura to Vern Lechliter, January 1, 1945 (OP), Omura divulged this future intention: "I have been thinking of writing a detailed account of the events which eventually led to my indictment and the efforts of the authorities expended on its attempt to either throttle my editorials or to railroad me into oblivion. I do not think the last chapter has been written yet."

137. In the wartime diary Charles Kikuchi maintained for the UC Berkeley-based Evacuation and Resettlement Study, he noted on April 19, 1944:

> The trouble with Jimmy is that (he) has had a deep hatred for the JACL for years now and he takes every opportunity to discredit that organization. . . . Jimmy has always been an outspoken individual but sometimes he is not diplomatic or tactful enough. I know that he has the courage of his convictions and he has always been quite definite in taking a strong pro-American stand. He is honest in his opinions and I give him credit for taking a vigorous position.

AFTERWORD

Epigraph: Sharon Noguchi, "A Wartime Hero Wins His Due," *San Jose Mercury News*, April 19, 1989, 7B.

1. Bill Hosokawa, *Nisei: The Quiet Americans* (New York: William Morrow, 1969).

2. Dillon S. Myer, *Uprooted Americans: The Japanese Americans and the War Relocation Authority during World War II* (Tucson: University of Arizona Press, 1971).

3. Roger Daniels, in Frank Abe, dir., *Conscience and the Constitution* (Seattle: Resisters.com Productions); first aired on PBS on November 30, 2000. See also the extended interview with James Omura in the two-disc collector's edition DVD of the film, released in 2011 and available through Resisters.com.

4. Nelson, *Heart Mountain*. Nelson completed his thesis in 1970 and was praised for it in the acknowledgments of Daniels's book, but it was not readily available to the public until its publication in book form in 1976, after the appearance of his mentor Daniels's book.

5. Roger Daniels, *Concentration Camps, USA: Japanese Americans and World War II* (New York: Holt, Rinehart and Winston, 1971). An expanded version,

retitled, is *Concentration Camps, North America: Japanese in the United States and Canada during World War II* (Malabar, FL: Krieger, 1981; 2nd ed., Krieger, 1993).

6. Michi Weglyn, *Years of Infamy: The Untold Story of America's Concentration Camps* (New York: William Morrow, 1976), 67.

7. April 15, 1991, entry in Omura's Redress Diary, OP.

Selected Bibliography

The references below are restricted to books, articles, and documentary films that directly illuminate the life and journalistic career of James Matsumoto Omura. Pertinent chapters within books are not individually denoted as references, only the titles of the books in which these items appear. An expanded bibliography is available on the Stanford University Press website at www.sup.org/nisei.

BOOKS

Chan, Sucheng, ed. *Remapping Asian American History*. Walnut Creek, CA: AltaMira Press, 2003.

Chin, Frank. *Born in the USA: A Story of Japanese America, 1889–1947*. Lanham, MD: Rowman & Littlefield, 2002.

———. "Come All Ye Asian American Writers of the Real and the Fake." In *The Big Aiiieeeee! An Anthology of Chinese American and Japanese American Literature*, edited by Jeffrey Paul Chan, Frank Chin, Lawson Fusao Inada, and Shawn Hsu Wong. New York: Penguin Books, 1991.

Fiset, Louis, and Gail M. Nomura, eds. *Nikkei in the Pacific Northwest: Japanese Americans and Japanese Canadians in the Twentieth Century*. Seattle: University of Washington Press, 2005.

Hansen, Arthur A. *Barbed Voices: Oral History, Resistance, and the World War II Japanese American Social Disaster*. Louisville: University Press of Colorado, 2018.

———, ed. *Japanese American World War II Evacuation Oral History Project, Part 4: Resisters*. Munich: K. G. Saur, 1995.

Hohri, William Minoru. *Repairing America: An Account of the Movement for Japanese-American Redress*. Pullman: Washington State University Press, 1984.

———, ed., with Mits Koshiyama, Yosh Kuromiya, Takashi Hoshizaki, and Frank Seishi Emi. *Resistance: Challenging America's Wartime Internment of Japanese-Americans*. Lomita, CA: The Epistolarian, 2001.

Hosokawa, Bill. *Colorado's Japanese Americans: From 1886 to the Present*. Boulder: University Press of Colorado, 2005.

Jacobs, Paul, and Saul Landau, eds. *To Serve the Devil: A Documentary Analysis of America's Racial History*, vol. 2: *Colonials and Sojourners*. New York: Vintage Books, 1971.

Mackey, Mike, ed. *A Matter of Conscience: Essays on the World War II Heart Mountain Draft Resistance Movement*. Powell, WY: Western History Publications, 2002.

————, ed. *Remembering Heart Mountain: Essays on Japanese American Internment in Wyoming*. Powell, WY: Western History Publications, 1998.

Muller, Eric L. *Free to Die for Their Country: The Story of the Japanese American Resisters in World War II*. Chicago: University of Chicago Press, 2001.

Murray, Alice Yang. *Historical Memories of the Japanese American Internment and the Struggle for Redress*. Stanford, CA: Stanford University Press, 2008.

Nelson, Douglas W. *Heart Mountain: The History of an American Concentration Camp*. Madison: State Historical Society of Wisconsin, for the Department of History, University of Wisconsin, 1976.

Nomura, Gail M., Russell Endo, Stephen H. Sumida, and Russell C. Leong, eds. *Frontiers of Asian American Studies: Writing, Research, and Commentary*. Pullman: Washington State University Press, 1989.

Robinson, Greg, ed. *Pacific Citizens: Larry and Guyo Tajiri and Japanese American Journalism in the World War II Era*. Urbana: University of Illinois Press, 2012.

Yoo, David. *Growing Up Nisei: Race, Generation, and Culture among Japanese Americans of California, 1924–49*. Urbana: University of Illinois Press, 2000.

ARTICLES

Emi, Frank. "Resistance: The Heart Mountain Fair Play Committee's Fight for Justice." *Amerasia Journal* 17 (1991): 47–51.

Hansen, Arthur A. "James Matsumoto Omura: An Interview." *Amerasia Journal* 13 (Fall 1986): 99–113.

————. "The 1944 Nisei Draft at Heart Mountain, Wyoming: Its Relationship to the Historical Representation of the World War II Japanese American Evacuation." *OAH Magazine of History* 10 (Summer 1996): 48–60.

FILMS

Abe, Frank, dir. *Conscience and the Constitution*. Documentary. Seattle: Resisters.com Productions, 2000.

Omori, Emiko, dir. *Rabbit in the Moon*. Documentary. Hohokus, NJ: New Day Films, 1999.

Yashima, Momo, dir. *A Divided Community: 3 Personal Stories of Resistance*. Documentary. Self-marketed, 2012.

Index

Page numbers followed by "f" refer to photographs. Page numbers followed by roman numerals refer to footnotes. Page numbers followed by "n" refer to endnotes.